Management for Professionals

More information about this series at http://www.springer.com/series/10101

Nils Urbach • Maximilian Röglinger
Editors

Digitalization Cases

How Organizations Rethink Their Business for the Digital Age

 Springer

Editors
Nils Urbach
Project Group BISE of Fraunhofer FIT
University of Bayreuth
Bayreuth, Germany

Maximilian Röglinger
Project Group BISE of Fraunhofer FIT
University of Bayreuth
Bayreuth, Germany

ISSN 2192-8096   ISSN 2192-810X   (electronic)
Management for Professionals
ISBN 978-3-030-07005-2   ISBN 978-3-319-95273-4   (eBook)
https://doi.org/10.1007/978-3-319-95273-4

Testimonials

Teaching on digitalization needs real-life cases. In this book you can find them—21 interesting cases on different industries and important emerging technologies!

Thomas Hess
Professor of Information Systems and New Media, LMU Munich

Digitalization is reshaping business on a global scale, and it is evident that organizations must transform to thrive in the digital economy. *Digitalization Cases* provides firsthand insights into the efforts of renowned companies. The presented actions, results, and lessons learned are a great inspiration for managers, students, and academics.

Anna Kopp
Head of IT Germany, Microsoft

Understanding digitalization in all its facets requires knowledge about its opportunities and challenges in different contexts. Providing 21 cases from different companies all around the world, *Digitalization Cases* makes an important contribution toward the comprehensibility of digitalization—from a practical and a scientific point of view.

Dorothy Leidner
Ferguson Professor of Information Systems, Baylor University

For the corporate world, digitalization is a challenge and an opportunity at the same time. Companies that want to succeed in the digital age need to realize the benefits of emerging technologies, develop new business models, and transform themselves internally as well as in their interaction with customers, partners, and suppliers. This publication stands out by providing well-structured cases that are academically sound and highly business relevant with tangible results. Recommended reading for everyone who is responsible for digitalization in companies.

Helmuth Ludwig
Global Head of Information Technology, Siemens

This is a must-read volume for anyone with an interest in how opportunities shaped by digital technologies are being embraced by organizations from different industries. By structuring each case study into situation faced, actions taken, results achieved, and lessons learned, the compendium provides an accessible and valuable resource for executives looking to take their organizations on a digital transformation journey.

Joe Peppard

Principal Research Scientist, Center for Information Systems Research, MIT Sloan School of Management

This book is a great source of inspiration and insight on how to drive digitalization. It shows easy to understand good practice examples which illustrate opportunities and at the same time helps to learn what needs to be done to realize them. I consider this book a must-read for every practitioner who cares about digitalization.

Martin Petry

Chief Information Officer and Head of Business Excellence, Hilti

In the fast-paced digital economy, we need to reflect, consolidate, and collectively learn for meaningful progression. This outstanding book provides 21 carefully selected cross-sector cases to offer not only these much-needed learning experiences, but also the evidence that makes these insights credible.

Michael Rosemann

Professor for Information Systems, Queensland University of Technology

This book shows in an outstanding clarity the already ongoing changes due to digitalization. It becomes clear that disruption is manageable through actively driven digitalization. In practice, however, disruption will primarily affect those who show themselves to be passive. The cases presented in this book underline that courage to change is the requirement of practice.

Markus Richter

Chief Information Officer, German Federal Office for Migration and Refugees

Practically all organizations today recognize the need to respond to digital opportunities and threats. Yet, they struggle to know how to react. Part of the problem is that there are so few good examples for them to learn from. *Digitalization Cases* provides a wealth of detailed and rigorous case studies presented in a consistent format across different countries and industries. The book is a great resource for anyone who wishes to understand the deep mechanics of digital transformation.

Michael Wade

Professor of Innovation and Strategy, IMD Lausanne

Today, digitalization entails significant challenges for companies across all industries. To succeed in a fast-changing environment, they must transform existing work routines, processes, and structures. Including a number of detailed case studies, *Digitalization Cases* provides insights in real-world projects that handle digitalization in different ways. Considering various countries and industries, the book serves as an excellent compilation for understanding the complexity and diversity of digitalization.

Thomas Wölker
Chief Information Officer, REHAU

Foreword

For 50 years, the mantra for information technology was to enable business strategy: understand a company's people, products, services, customer relationships, and processes and then implement technology to make them more efficient, scalable, and reliable. IT continues to play that role, but that is not why technology is disrupting businesses. The new role of information (digital) technologies is to *inspire* business strategy.

Digital technologies (social, mobile, analytics, cloud, Internet of things, blockchain, artificial intelligence, and many more) provide three important capabilities: (1) unlimited connectivity, (2) ubiquitous data, and (3) massive automation. Being inspired by technologies means recognizing the customer value propositions that these capabilities make possible. Those value propositions depend on enriching traditional products and services with data and software.

Digital technologies are readily accessible. In other words, employees, competitors, customers, and partners can all access the technologies and make demands as to how a company deploys them. As a result, digital technologies cannot be a source of competitive advantage. Anything great a company does with digital technologies and related data will be replicated. Thus, digital mostly raises the bar in terms of baseline expectations for information-rich products and services and for seamless customer experiences.

But while identifying creative applications of digital technologies and data cannot create competitive advantage, executing a value proposition better than anyone else can be a huge source of competitive advantage. Of course, strategy execution with digital technologies is harder than an enthusiastic iPhone user might imagine. To deliver offerings consistent with new value propositions, companies need to introduce new processes, platforms, skills, and roles. The necessary changes are massive.

Suddenly, every company must excel at both operational excellence (core business operations) and rapid innovation (developing new value propositions for customers). And those two requirements are nearly opposite in nature! Operational excellence depends on disciplined enterprise processes usually supported by large enterprise systems. Rapid innovation depends on agile teams usually supported by reusable business and technology components. The former is about process optimization; the latter is about test and learn processes.

Established companies are in the midst of transforming to become digital, but the transformation journey is proving to be long and winding. I have been studying digital transformations for 4 years, and, as far as I know, no company has yet completed that journey. Nonetheless, researchers are discovering how companies progress on their journeys.

The case studies in this book start to capture best principles and practices for digital transformations. They provide some in-depth insights into what is and isn't working. It's a good start. The journey may be long, but it's exciting. The best companies will fulfill extraordinary visions that improve their customers' lives. As you review these cases, we hope you find some hints as to how you might help a company become more digital.

Cambridge, MA   Jeanne W. Ross

Preface

In the digital age, emerging technologies significantly influence processes, products, services, and business models, e.g., by connecting individuals, organizations, machines, and other "things," by enabling novel working, collaboration, and auto- mation models, as well as by providing access to untapped data sources. The resulting digital economy is highly volatile, uncertain, complex, and ambiguous. This raises a wide range of challenges for organizations. Hyperconnected customers with individual needs, opaque regulatory requirements, as well as continuously increasing competitive pressure from start-ups and digital giants are just a few examples. However, today's business environment also offers untapped potential. Among many others, these include the further development and disruption of existing business models, the identification of previously unknown customer needs, the exploration of new markets, and the collaboration with other market players. To thrive in such an environment, organizations must unfold the potential of digital technologies in their business strategies and business models, reimagine their work routines, processes, and structures, as well as manage and govern IT infrastructures that are central to their value propositions.

Our idea behind editing this book is to present a rich compilation of real-world cases on digitalization. With all economic and societal sectors being challenged by digital technologies, we aim at illustrating how organizations leverage their capabilities to create disruptive innovation, to develop digital business models, and to transform themselves. For this book, we have gathered 21 cases on how companies and public organizations rethink their business for the digital age. The case descriptions report on best practices and lessons learned from different organizations that succeeded in tackling the challenges and seizing the opportunities of the digital world. The cases provide insightful examples for practitioners as well as interesting cases for researchers, teachers, and students. All cases follow a unified schema, making them easily accessible to readers.

The cases of this book are grouped into three major blocks, representing the major action fields of digitalization. Part I contains cases of *digital disruption*, a field that refers to the monitoring and analysis of emerging technologies. It also includes the development of competencies for leveraging these technologies. The cases of this part stem from Deutsche Telekom, Lufthansa Systems, Baur Group, and Porsche. Part II represents cases related to *digital business*, a field covering the realization of new business models that are enabled by digital technologies and disrupt the traditional business. It often results from the smart fusion of the physical and digital world. The cases report about Kaeser Compressors Danske Bank, GKN, and the Presbyterian Church of Ghana, among others. Finally, Part III covers cases on *digital transformation* which refers to technology-induced organizational change. It embraces the organizational, processual, and technological efforts necessary for organizations to succeed in the digital age. This part includes cases from ABB, Engel, the US Federal Communications Commission, Volkswagen, Deutsche Bahn, the Super Hospital Aarhus, and AXA.

We want to thank several people for supporting the compilation of this book. Most importantly, we thank Marie-Sophie Denner for continuously supporting us in managing the overall book project. We are also very grateful to Christian Rauscher from Springer who supported the project from the publisher's side. Finally, we thank all colleagues who served on the editorial board of this book and who dedicated much time and effort in providing reviews to further develop the cases presented in this book.

We hope you will enjoy reading the book and working with the cases, and we invite you to contact us for questions, feedback, and discussions.

Bayreuth, Germany   Nils Urbach
Bayreuth, Germany   Maximilian Röglinger
April 2018

Editorial Board

We are grateful for the support of colleagues and friends who supported this book project by serving on its editorial board.

Contents

About the Editors

Nils Urbach is Professor of Information Systems and Strategic IT Management at the University of Bayreuth, Germany, as well as Deputy Director of the FIM Research Center and the Project Group Business and Information Systems Engineering of Fraunhofer FIT. Nils has been working in the fields of strategic information management and collaborative information systems for several years. In his current research, he focuses on digital transformation, smart devices, and blockchain, among others. His work has been published in renowned academic journals such as the *Journal of Strategic Information Systems (JSIS), Journal of Information Technology (JIT), IEEE Transactions on Engineering Management (IEEE TEM), Information and Management (I&M)*, and *Business and Information Systems Engineering (BISE)* as well as in the proceedings of key international conferences such as the International Conference on Information Systems (ICIS) and European Conference on Information Systems (ECIS). Nils can be contacted via nils.urbach@uni-bayreuth.de.

Maximilian Röglinger is Professor of Information Systems and Value-based Business Process Management at the University of Bayreuth, Germany, as well as Deputy Director of the FIM Research Center and the Project Group Business and Information Systems Engineering of Fraunhofer FIT. Maximilian has been working in the fields of business process management and customer relationship management for many years. His current research centers around digitalization, digital technologies, and setups for agile and ambidextrous organizations. Maximilian's work has been published in leading academic journals including the *Journal of Strategic Information Systems (JSIS), Journal of the Association for Information Systems (JAIS), Decision Support Systems (DSS)*, and *Business and Information Systems Engineering (BISE)* as well as in the proceedings of key international conferences such as the International Conference on Information Systems (ICIS), European Conference on Information Systems (ECIS), and the International Conference on Business Process Management (BPM). Maximilian can be contacted via maximilian.roeglinger@uni-bayreuth.de.

Introduction to Digitalization Cases: How Organizations Rethink Their Business for the Digital Age

Nils Urbach and Maximilian Röglinger

Abstract

Digitalization confronts organizations with huge challenges and opportunities. With all economic and societal sectors being affected by emerging technologies, the digital economy is highly volatile, uncertain, complex, and ambiguous. Against this backdrop, this book reports on best practices and lessons learned from organizations that succeeded in tackling the challenges and seizing the opportunities of the digital economy. It illustrates how 21 organizations leveraged their capabilities to create disruptive innovation, to develop digital business models, and to digitally transform themselves. These cases stem from various industries and countries, covering the many facets that digitalization may have.

1 The Impact of Digitalization—and Motivation for This Book

Digitalization reflects the adoption of digital technologies in business and society as well as the associated changes in the connectivity of individuals, organizations, and objects (Gartner 2016; Gimpel et al. 2018). While digitization covers the technical process of converting analog signals into a digital form, the manifold sociotechnical phenomena and processes of adopting and using digital technologies in broader individual, organizational, and societal contexts are commonly referred to as digitalization (Legner et al. 2017).

The key driver of digitalization are digital technologies. Due to considerable investments in technological progress, various digital technologies are on the mar-

N. Urbach (✉) · M. Röglinger
University of Bayreuth, Bayreuth, Germany
e-mail: nils.urbach@uni-bayreuth.de; maximilian.roeglinger@uni-bayreuth.de

© Springer International Publishing AG, part of Springer Nature 2019
N. Urbach, M. Röglinger (eds.), *Digitalization Cases*, Management for
Professionals, https://doi.org/10.1007/978-3-319-95273-4_1

ket. Thereby, an ever-faster commoditization and time-to-market can be observed. For example, early hardware-heavy information and communication technologies such as the telephone required 75 years to reach 100 million users, whereas lightweight applications such as Instagram achieved the same coverage in little more than 2 years (Statista 2017). Digital technologies include both emerging technologies such as the Internet of Things (IoT) or blockchain and more established technologies such as social media, mobile computing, advanced analytics, and cloud computing (SMAC) (Fitzgerald et al. 2014; Gartner 2017). Loebbecke (2006) refers to digital technologies as all technologies for the creation, processing, transmission, and use of digital goods. Further, Yoo et al. (2010) argue that digital technologies differ from earlier technologies in three characteristics: re-programmability, which separates the functional logic of a device from its physical embodiment, homogenization of data, which allows for storing, transmitting, and processing digital content using the same devices and networks, and a self-referential nature yielding positive network externalities. Digital technologies can be further classified with respect to whether they involve humans actively or passively, how they treat data, whether their input and output is purely digital or can also be physical, or whether they serve infrastructural or application-oriented purposes (Berger et al. 2018). In sum, digital technologies enable platforms, autonomous products, sensor-based data collection, analytical insight generation, as well as analytical and augmented interaction.

Based on advances in digital technologies, digitalization impacts business and society. Digital technologies enable innovative business models such as the platform-based models of well-known companies including AirBnB, Uber, or Facebook, or decentral models enabled by blockchain and 3D printing (Fridgen et al. 2018; Goodwin 2015). Digitalization also changes industry structures (Gimpel et al. 2018): reduced entry barriers make technology-savvy start-ups flourish and digital giants such as Google or Apple push forward to manifold sectors. Regarding the IoT, for example, 50 billion smart devices are expected to be connected to the Internet by 2020, having an economic impact of $7 trillion (Macaulay et al. 2015; Wortmann and Flüchter 2015). Further, the volume of available data is known to double every 3 years (Henke et al. 2016), and insights-driven businesses are predicted to take away $1.2 trillion per year from less-informed competitors by 2020 (McCormick et al. 2016). Digitalization also empowers customers and impacts our private lives. Today, more people have access to cellphones than to toilets, and one in five people has an active Facebook account (Halleck 2015; UN International Telecommunication 2014). In the digital age, wowing customers is more critical—and more challenging—than before, independent from an organization's position in the value network, as customers decide themselves how to interact organizations (Hosseini et al. 2018). Likewise, employee behavior and thought patterns evolve towards a new future of work, calling for new work and collaboration models (Brynjolfsson and McAfee 2014).

Digitalization, however, is neither a new phenomenon nor will it be the final evolutionary stage of information and communication technology (Porter and Heppelmann 2014). Data has been processed and exchanged digitally for more than half a century. An early example is electronic data interchange. Further, the Internet has been used for civil purposes since the 1990s, and e-commerce was first promoted around the year 2000. With smart devices and mobile applications, digitalization experienced an additional boost. While, in former times, digitalization only concerned data managers of corporate IT departments, it now affects all business departments as well as product and service offerings (Urbach and Ahlemann 2018; Urbach et al. 2017). Consequently, discussions moved (again) from support to core processes, from efficiency to excitement, from hygiene factors to opportunity factors, as well as from cost reduction to revenue generation.

In our opinion, the most significant characteristics of digitalization are not the usage of data or adoption of technology, but the unprecedented speed of change and level of connectedness, which also facilitates the customers' dominant role as well as the convergence of the physical and the digital world (Gimpel et al. 2018). As such, digitalization shapes a world that is at once the cause and effect of its own characteristics: volatility (i.e., constant and massive changes), uncertainty (i.e., lack of predictability), complexity (i.e., multitude of interrelated and self-organizing actors), and ambiguity (i.e., confounding cause and effect relationships) (Bennett and Lemoine 2014).

As our discussions with senior managers (e.g., Chief Executive Officers, Chief Information Officers, Chief Digital Officers, and Digital Transformation Officers) in the last years showed, nobody doubts that digitalization "came to stay", continuing to impact on all facets of organizations, i.e. customer relationships, value propositions, data analytics, operations, organizational setups, collaboration, and transformation management itself (Gimpel et al. 2018). Rather, the key questions relate to the "what" and the "how", i.e. what organizations should look like in the future and how the to-be state can be reached both in an agile and adaptive manner as well as without jeopardizing existing assets and capabilities (A.T. Kearney and Project Group BISE of Fraunhofer FIT 2017). Many organizations already defined accountabilities for digitalization and set up transformation initiatives. Nevertheless, digitalization remains a vague concept. What is missing are success stories, good practices, and lessons learned that make the benefits of digitization tangible, help prioritize investments, choose among action possibilities, reveal "internal home-work" that needs to be done before customer-facing initiatives make sense, and provide a platform for exchanging thoughts on challenges and opportunities ahead. However, in our research and project work, we also came across many successful companies—be it incumbents or start-ups—that successfully leveraged their capabilities to create digital innovation, develop digital business models, and transform themselves. These organizations have valuable first-hand insights to share.

Against this background, we initiated the *Digitalization Cases* book project to match the supply and demand for ideas, experiences, benefits, and lessons learned related to digitalization. Together with an editorial board of forward-thinking digitalization experts, we compiled 21 identically structured case descriptions that provide rich insights into the digitalization activities of renowned organizations from diverse countries and industries.

Below, we first structure the field of digitalization into digital disruption, digital business, and digital transformation as a first step to make it more tangible (Sect. 2). After that, we overview the cases included in this book structured around these three fields of action (Sect. 3). We conclude with hints on the unified structure of the included cases and on how to read this book (Sect. 4).

2   Structuring the Field of Digitalization

To structure the field of digitalization, we use an enterprise architecture model that consists of five layers (Fig. 1). These layers include: business model, business processes, people and application systems, data and information, and technological infrastructure. To tackle the challenges and to seize the opportunities of the digital age, it is essential for organizations to align these layers.

Considering the turbulence of business environments and the rich set of opportunity available, a key challenge for organizations in the digital age is to distinguish sustainable opportunities promising in the long run from short-term hypes. Against this backdrop, an organization's *business model* is of utmost importance, as it enables exploiting existing market potentials and seizing new opportunities. Business models specify on target markets, operating models as well as cost and revenue streams. This also involves the organization's value propositions, describing which customer needs are satisfied by which product and service offerings. In the digital age, digital technologies allow for entirely new business models such as platform-based business models or innovative decentral models.

To turn their business model into reality, organizations require cross-functional work routines structured around *business processes*. In the digital age, process thinking must not only span across departmental but also organizational boundaries, covering entire value networks and ecosystems. Thereby, business processes define the tasks to be performed to achieve specific goals. Beyond established business process management (BPM) concepts that support efficient and stable execution of routine operations, organizations also require agile BPM concepts that support non-standard operations, the management of emerging and proactive organizational behavior as well as fast reactions to changing customer needs.

The tasks included in business processes can be performed manually by employees, automatically by machines or application systems, or collaboratively. Thus, *people* are part of an organization's structure that systemizes roles, responsibilities, and reporting lines. In line with the shift towards agile BPM concepts, organizations must also foster people agility by moving from hierarchical to networked-like structures as well as by fostering employees' digital mindset and related skills. Further, organizations must account for new roles involved in business processes such as crowd workers, freelancers, robots, and autonomous things. Particularly, the collaborative execution of tasks is strongly advanced by technologies related to human–machine interaction, artificial intelligence, smart devices, and robotics. Many of these technologies also push the frontier of automation, because not only well-structured, but also unstructured tasks can be automated. Consequently, organizations need not only adopt traditional enterprise systems (e.g., enterprise resource planning or customer relationship management systems), but also novel system types such as mobile apps or digital assistants.

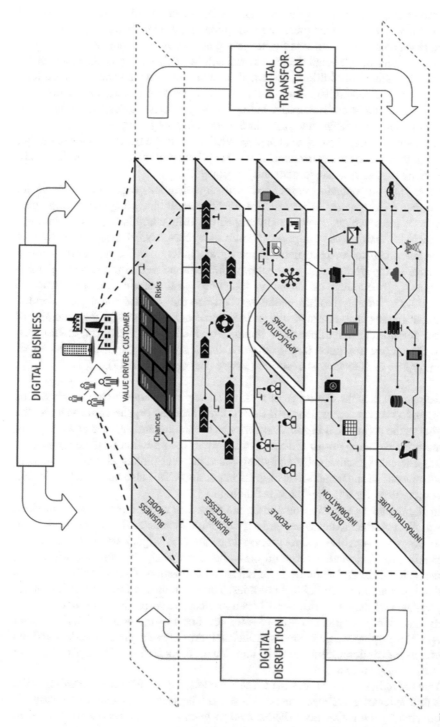

Fig. 1 Structuring the field of digitalization along the enterprise architecture

Employees, application systems, and machines create and process *data and information*. In line with the increasing adoption of digital technologies, the volume of data available is growing rapidly, revealing new knowledge potential. Structured data (e.g., tables or relational databases) can still be analyzed by means of statistical analytical methods. In addition, modern algorithms, leveraging advances in artificial intelligence (e.g., cognitive computing or deep learning), allow for an increasingly precise processing of unstructured data (e.g., texts, graphics, videos, and audio files). Big data analyses enable analyzing and combining large amounts of data from different sources, and thereby enable organizations to make better decisions, predict trends in their business environments, reveal optimization potential, and, above all, understand the needs of customers and employees.

To exploit the potential associated with digitalization, organizations need an appropriate *technological infrastructure*. Besides traditional components (e.g., personal computers, tablets, servers, network, and security components), the infrastructure includes also novel components such as cyber-physical systems as well as shared resources such smart meters, smart grids, autonomous cars, or cloud infrastructure. In the digital age, conventional information and communication infrastructure is becoming increasingly integrated with production infrastructure (operations technology) to bridge the gap between the physical and digital world.

Organizations that aim to thrive in the digital age must unfold the potential of digital technologies, rethink their business models, and transform themselves. Accordingly, we see three major fields of action spanning the different layers of the enterprise architecture as described above (Legner et al. 2017):

- Companies face the challenge of making strategic decisions on the timely use of disruptive technologies. Due to the extensive impact on organizations at large, the goal of the action field *digital disruption* is to monitor and analyze emerging and maturing technologies to reduce uncertainty in the selection of technologies. In this context, systematically analyzing potentials and threats as well as deriving recommendations for action is of great importance. This also includes developing competences for utilizing these technologies.
- In the digital age, many companies are forced to adapt their business models, e.g. from product to customer and service orientation as well as from stand-alone to ecosystem-enabled value propositions. In fact, digitalization is not about making existing models more efficient, but about designing new models. Thus, the action field *digital business* refers to the realization of new business models that are enabled by digital technologies. This often results from the fusion of the physical and digital world. Data-driven services, smart products, product-service hybrids, and platforms are examples for new business opportunities in the digital age. Developing viable business models requires organizations to understand the effects of digitalization on the individual, organizational, competitive, and increasingly societal level.
- Due to fundamental changes in business models, a thorough transformation of the entire enterprise architecture is necessary. The technology-induced change is covered by the action field *digital transformation*. This embraces the necessary

goal-oriented organizational, processual, and technological transformation necessary for organizations to succeed in the digital age. Digital transformation requires organizations to understand how business models can be implemented and how digitalization itself changes how organizations must be managed. Existing business processes and organizational structures, application systems and data as well as the underlying infrastructure need to be aligned with the requirements of new customer needs and business models in an integrated manner.

3 Introducing Cases of Digitalization

We classified the digitalization cases included in this book in line with whether they relate to digital disruption, digital business, and digital transformation. Below, we briefly overview all cases structured around these three fields of action.

3.1 Digital Disruption

First, the case of Schmitz et al. reports on *Deutsche Telekom*, which aimed to implement a digital strategy and identified Robotic Process Automation (RPA) as an enabling technology to digitalize and automate transactional processes. In addition to the setup and execution of the RPA initiative, the case outlines the most important results, such as an increasing number of automated transactions per month.

In their case with *Lufthansa Systems*, Ripolles et al. tackle the challenge of creating software applications while accounting for desired security levels. By applying the so-called Multi-cloud Secure Application (MUSA) approach to create a new prototype, the case not only demonstrates the use of this approach, but also analyzes the impact it has on development, deployment, and operations.

Confronted with novel customer interaction forms such as attended shopping or virtual fitting, the fashion retailer *Baur* aims at systematically accounting for the customer perspective in its site engineering process. By conducting an extensive survey among different customer segments, Baier et al. provide valuable insights into the use of digital technologies not only for product selection, but also in ordering, packaging, and delivery processes.

Auf der Mauer et al. report on the case of the automobile manufacturer *Porsche*, aiming to leverage predictive maintenance. With predictive maintenance requiring a deep integration with the machines to be monitored, *Porsche* developed a solution concept called 'Sound Detective', an approach based on deep learning algorithms that monitors sound sequences from microphone. The case demonstrates the feasibility of the Sound Detective's reference architecture and discusses challenges as well as learnings during its implementation.

3.2   Digital Business

As *KAESER COMPRESSORS*, a manufacturer of compressed air systems and services, started to transform and expand its traditional business model, a service-based operator model was introduced where customers no longer purchase customized air compressors, but pay a monthly rate for the air they used. Besides the introduction of the service-based operator model, the case of Bock et al. highlights related benefits for both *KAESER* and its customers.

In their case with *Danske Bank*, Staykova and Damsgaard report on the challenges of an established bank regarding the new technologies and changing customer preferences. The case demonstrates how *Danske Bank* ventured into disruptive digital initiatives and launched 'MobilePay', a digital payment platform used by more than 90% of the Danes today.

Further, Wildhirt et al. describe the case of *GKN*, a leading manufacturer of high precision parts for the automotive industry, that faces the question of how to deliver the technology of metal additive manufacturing to its customers. Together with a 3D printing start-up, *GKN* realized a new business model and succeeded in digitalizing related back-end processes.

The case of Blaschke presents the recently lunched digital platform *Helix Nebula—The Science Cloud*, which aims to deliver easy and large-scale access to a broad range of commercial cloud computing services, competing with leading digital platforms. The case shows how the organization implemented different consecutive and interrelated actions to cope with complexity.

As *Sitecore*, market leader in the web content management industry, was forced to include an integrated commerce and content platform in its product portfolio, they required a commerce engine. Henningsson and Nishu show how *Sitecore* established the strategic rationale for the acquisition of a company named SMITH. In the end, *Sitecore* investigated the feasibility of achieving its strategic aspirations, and is about to integrate both the technology and the development team of the e-commerce engine into a coherent platform.

Asiedu and Boateng contributed the case of the *Presbyterian Church of Ghana*, which struggled to reach out to larger and younger communities, and therefore developed an interactive online presence as well as launched social media activities. Besides the development of an online community and a better promotion of worship services, mobile money and a point of sale device were used to facilitate cashless payment of voluntary contributions.

Nissen et al. report on the consulting provider *Dr. Kuhl Unternehmensberatung*, which decided to develop a flexible architecture for virtually assessing the project management situation in the form of a digital assessment tool available to its clients. The case describes the design and development of a prototype process model and suggests other consultancies to build up experience and knowledge in virtualizing own services as soon as possible.

Using an anonymous *insurance company* as example, Weingarth et al. present a strategic digital transformation initiative driven by the top management to build up digital capabilities and to meet the state-of-the-art agility/innovation requirements.

The case demonstrates that actively managing cultural change is paramount across all business and functional areas right from the beginning.

3.3 Digital Transformation

As for digital transformation, Sandberg et al. discuss how *ABB* became a global leader in the process automation industry by successfully transforming their operations. Facing the infusion of digital technology into *ABB*'s physical production environment, the case describes a substantial adjustment that led to an ambitious transformation of the organization's business model.

As the strongly customer-oriented company *ENGEL Austria GmbH* aimed to decrease the lead time of one of its machines by at least 30%, Value Stream Mapping was used to document the production process and identify weak as well as opportunity points. After that, subject-oriented Business Process Management served as foundation for specifying new and improved processes. In sum, the case of Moser and Říha describes the optimization of cross-company processes as well as the digitalization formerly manual processes.

Deelmann and Müller present the case of *BruderhausDiakonie*, a social services organization, willing to engage in digital transformation under the slogan "standardization before digitalization". By identifying routine tasks, implementing an easy-to-use technology platform and mobile devices, as well as giving data security a number one priority, the organization already achieved the first digitalization successes.

At *Aarhus Denmark*, the case of Meister et al. captures the initiative of the Danish Government to build five super hospitals in different regions that implement vertically and horizontally digitalized processes by having a common information architecture. The preliminary results deduced from the case are used to define a basic framework and to define a method called "maturity index for hospital 4.0" to measure the digital maturity of hospitals.

Also located in the healthcare sector, the case of Vogt et al. focuses on the digital transformation of care processes by presenting the innovation project Bea@Home at *Charité*. Introducing this new care model, the development and implementation of coordinated processes across all relevant healthcare sectors has been identified as an important foundation for inter-sectoral change processes before technological aspects can be addressed.

The case of Scheffler and Wirths shows how the insurance company *AXA* plans to unlock the potential of its data. Focusing on this challenge, they founded a Data Innovation Lab to build up an interdisciplinary work environment between the Data Analytics and the Data Management Office. The target operating model shows how *AXA* simultaneously increased data and customer centricity.

Operating in a challenging business environment, *Volkswagen* was required to build up skills through new corporate education and training solutions. In their case, Wildgrube et al. elaborate on the establishment of the *Volkswagen* Education Lab, an independent unit for target group centered problem-solving.

The case of Fortmann et al. demonstrates how *Deutsche Bahn Vertrieb* reorganized its IT division in the passenger transportation industry. After restructuring the IT division into a single digital IT unit, channel-spanning strategies were enabled, and the organization experienced a boost in motivation and employee engagement, although bringing different modes of operation together took longer than expected.

The last case of our book examines how the *U.S. Federal Communications Commission (FCC)* executed its IT modernization effort. Desouza et al. outline how *FCC* analyzed the current status of IT and human resources and conceived several initiatives for diverse employees and other stakeholders in the process of IT modernization.

4   How to Read the Cases

The case descriptions compiled in this book aim to provide insightful examples for practitioners and interesting cases for researchers, teachers, and students. Each case illustrates how a specific company or public organization leveraged its capabilities to create disruptive innovation, to develop digital business models, and to digitally transform itself.

To make the case descriptions easily accessible and comparable for readers, they follow a unified structure, which has been initially proposed by vom Brocke and Mendling (2017). Each case elaborates on the situation faced in the focal organization, the actions taken, the results achieved as well as lessons learned. The situation faced highlights the initial problem situation and specifies the needs, constraints, incidents, opportunities, and objectives that induced action. The actions taken reflect what the organization did to tackle challenges and opportunities. The results achieved reflects on realized and expected outcomes of the actions taken and how they changed the organization. Finally, the lessons learned reflect the overall case and propose learnings empirically grounded transferrable to other contexts.

Due to the unified structure, each case can be read independently from all other cases. Readers may read the cases in line with their preferences regarding digital disruption, digital business, or digital transformation. Further, many cases reveal the organization where the case was conducted such that readers can select cases by the most similar organization or industry, or just focus on the cases that interest them most.

References

A.T. Kearney, Project Group BISE of Fraunhofer FIT (2017) Designing IT setups in the digital age. https://www.fim-rc.de/wp-content/uploads/Designing-IT-Setups-in-the-Digital-Age.pdf. Accessed 24 April 2018
Bennett N, Lemoine J (2014) What VUCA really means for you. Harv Bus Rev 92(1/2):27
Berger S, Denner M-S, Röglinger M (2018) The nature of digital technologies: development of a multi-layer taxonomy. Paper presented at the 26th European Conference on Information Systems (ECIS 2018), Portsmouth
Brynjolfsson E, McAfee A (2014) The second machine age: work, progress, and prosperity in a time of brilliant technologies. Norton, London

Fitzgerald M, Kruschwitz N, Bonnet D, Welch M (2014) Embracing digital technology: a new strategic imperative. MIT Sloan Manag Rev 55(2):1–12

Fridgen G, Lockl J, Radszuwill S, Rieger A, Schweizer A, Urbach N (2018) A solution in search of a problem: a method for the development of blockchain use cases. Paper presented at the 24th Americas Conference on Information Systems (AMCIS 2018), New Orleans, LA

Gartner (2016) Hype cycle for emerging technologies 2016. https://www.gartner.com/document/3383817?ref=ddrec. Accessed 24 April 2018

Gartner (2017) IT glossary: digitalization. https://www.gartner.com/it-glossary/digitalization. Accessed 24 April 2018

Gimpel H, Hosseini S, Huber R, Probst L, Röglinger M, Faisst U (2018) Structuring digital transformation: a framework of action fields and its application at ZEISS. J Inf Technol Theory Appl 19(1):Art. 3

Goodwin T (2015) The battle is for the customer interface. TechCrunch. http://techcrunch.com/2015/03/03/in-the-age-of-disintermediation-the-battle-is-all-for-the-customerinterface/. Accessed 25 April 2018

Halleck T (2015) Facebook: one out of every five people on earth have an active account. International Business Times. http://www.ibtimes.com/facebook-one-out-every-five-peopleearth-have-active-account-1801240. Accessed 25 April 2018

Henke N, Bughin J, Chui M, Manyika J, Saleh T, Wiseman B, Sethupathy G (2016) The age of analytics: competing in a data-driven world. https://www.mckinsey.com/business-functions/mckinsey-analytics/our-insights/the-age-of-analytics-competing-in-a-data-driven-world. Accessed 24 April 2018

Hosseini S, Merz M, Röglinger M, Wenninger A (2018) Mindfully going omni-channel: an economic decision model for evaluating omni-channel strategies. Decis Support Syst 109(2018): 74–88

Legner C, Eymann T, Hess T, Matt C, Böhmann T, Drews P, Maedche A, Urbach N, Ahlemann F (2017) Digitalization: opportunity and challenge for the business and information systems engineering community. Bus Inf Syst Eng 59(4):301–308

Loebbecke C (2006) Digitalisierung: Technologien und Unternehmensstrategien. In: Scholz C (ed) Handbuch Medienmanagement. Springer, Berlin, pp 357–373

Macaulay J, Buckalew L, Chung G (2015) Internet of things in logistics: a collaborative report by DHL and Cisco on implications and use cases for the logistics industry. http://www.dhl.com/content/dam/Local_Images/g0/New_aboutus/innovation/DHLTrendReport_Internet_of_things.pdf. Accessed 24 April 2018

McCormick J, Doty C A, Sridharan S, Curran R, Evelson B, Hopkins B, Little C, Leganza G, Purcell B, Miller E (2016) Predictions 2017: artificial intelligence will drive the insights revolution

Porter ME, Heppelmann JE (2014) Spotlight on managing the internet of things – how smart, connected products are transforming competition. Harv Bus Rev 3. http://www.gospi.fr/IMG/pdf/porter-2014-hbr_howsmart-connected-products-are-transforming-competitionhbr-2014.pdf. Accessed 7 July 2018

Statista (2017) Internet of things – number of connected devices worldwide 2015–2025. https://www.statista.com/statistics/471264/iot-number-of-connected-devices-worldwide/. Accessed 25 April 2018

UN International Telecommunication Union (2014) http://www.un.org/apps/news/story.asp?NewsID=47629#. Accessed 24 April 2018

Urbach N, Ahlemann F (2018) IT management in the digital age – a roadmap for the IT organization of the future. Springer, Heidelberg

Urbach N, Drews P, Ross J (2017) Digital business transformation and the changing role of the IT function. MIS Q Exec 16(2):ii–iv

vom Brocke J, Mendling J (2017) Frameworks for business process management: a taxonomy for business process management cases. In: vom Brocke J, Mendling J (eds) Business process management cases: digital innovation and business transformation in practice. Springer, Heidelberg, pp 1–17

Wortmann F, Flüchter K (2015) Internet of Things. Bus Inf Syst Eng 57(3):221–224
Yoo Y, Henfridsson O, Lyytinen K (2010) Research commentary – the new organizing logic of
    digital innovation: an agenda for information systems research. Inf Syst Res 21(4):724–735

Nils Urbach is Professor of Information Systems and Strategic IT Management at the University of Bayreuth, Germany, as well as Deputy Director of the FIM Research Center and the Project Group Business and Information Systems Engineering of Fraunhofer FIT. Nils has been working in the fields of strategic information management and collaborative information systems for several years. In his current research, he focuses on digital transformation, smart devices, and blockchain, among others. His work has been published in renowned academic journals such as the Journal of Strategic Information Systems (JSIS), Journal of Information Technology (JIT), IEEE Transactions on Engineering Management (IEEE TEM), Information and Management (I&M), and Business & Information Systems Engineering (BISE) as well as in the proceedings of key international conferences such as the International Conference on Information Systems (ICIS) and European Conference on Information Systems (ECIS).

Maximilian Röglinger is Professor of Information Systems and Value-based Business Process Management at the University of Bayreuth, Germany, as well as Deputy Director of the FIM Research Center and the Project Group Business and Information Systems Engineering of Fraunhofer FIT. Maximilian has been working in the fields of business process management and customer relationship management for many years. His current research centers around digitalization, digital technologies, and setups for agile and ambidextrous organizations. Maximilian's work has been published in leading academic journals including the Journal of Strategic Information Systems (JSIS), Journal of the Association for Information Systems (JAIS), Decision Support Systems (DSS), and Business & Information Systems Engineering (BISE) as well as in the proceedings of key international conferences such as the International Conference on Information Systems (ICIS), European Conference on Information Systems (ECIS), and the International Conference on Business Process Management (BPM).

Part I
Digital Disruption

Enabling Digital Transformation Through Robotic Process Automation at Deutsche Telekom

Manfred Schmitz, Christian Dietze, and Christian Czarnecki

Abstract

(a) **Situation faced**: Due to the high number of customer contacts, fault clearances, installations, and product provisioning per year, the automation level of operational processes has a significant impact on financial results, quality, and customer experience. Therefore, the telecommunications operator *Deutsche Telekom* (DT) has defined a digital strategy with the objectives of zero complexity and zero complaint, one touch, agility in service, and disruptive thinking. In this context, *Robotic Process Automation* (RPA) was identified as an enabling technology to formulate and realize DT's digital strategy through automation of rule-based, routine, and predictable tasks in combination with structured and stable data.

(b) **Action taken**: Starting point of the project was the aim to implement DT's digital strategy. In an early stage of the project, it was decided to utilize RPA as enabler, in particular to drive digitization and automation of transactional activities. From a methodical perspective, the set-up and conduction of the RPA project was structured into (1) organization and governance, (2) processes, and (3) technology and operations. From the content perspective, the

M. Schmitz (✉)
Detecon Consulting FZ-LLC, Dubai, United Arab Emirates
e-mail: Manfred.Schmitz@detecon.com

C. Dietze
Detecon Consulting FZ-LLC, Dubai, United Arab Emirates
e-mail: christian.dietze@detecon.com

C. Czarnecki
Hochschule für Telekommunikation Leipzig, Leipzig, Germany

© Springer International Publishing AG, part of Springer Nature 2019
N. Urbach, M. Röglinger (eds.), *Digitalization Cases*, Management for Professionals, https://doi.org/10.1007/978-3-319-95273-4_2

RPA project defined and implemented a multitude of detailed RPA use cases, whereof two concrete use cases are described.

(c) **Results achieved**: Within less than 6 months from the project start, the first transactions were performed automatically through RPA. In March 2016, approx. 229 thousand automatic transactions were successfully realized. Since then, the number of automatic transactions through RPA per month has been increasing significantly. The increase of automatic transactions per month was realized through a growing amount of usage of RPA in different process areas of DT. Within 1 year, the number of automatic transactions per month has been increased to more than 1 million.

(d) **Lessons learned**: The case provides an example for a concrete technology-induced change as part of a digital transformation. The concept of RPA provides an opportunity to automate human activities through software robots. The lessons learned utilizable for future RPA projects are: (1) Agile design and implementation are important for a successful digital transformation. (2) Understand technical innovations as enabler of the digital transformation. (3) Investigate technical and organizational interrelations from the beginning. (4) RPA is more than a pure cost cutting instrument. (5) The impact of RPA on the people dimension should be managed carefully from the beginning.

1   Introduction

Recently, digital technologies are seen as an important driver for technology-induced changes of organizations and business models, referred to as *digital transformation* (e.g., Matt et al. 2015; Legner et al. 2017). In this context, *Robotic Process Automation* (RPA) is an innovative approach to transform the process execution without changing the underlying application systems. The general idea of RPA is that software robots perform formerly human work (Allweyer 2016). In contrast to robotics in production processes (Groover 2008), RPA does not use tangible robots but autonomous acting software systems—so-called software robots. They learn and adopt human activities, and handle application systems through user interfaces. From a technical perspective, the realization of RPA ranges from simple rule-based tools to complex tools based on machine learning and artificial intelligence (Willcocks et al. 2015; Czarnecki 2018). Compared to traditional process automation through process-aware systems (Rosemann and vom Brocke 2010; Dumas et al. 2013), RPA does not require changes of the existing application landscape, but replaces the human interaction through a software system (Willcocks et al. 2017) (cf. Fig. 1). There are vendors offering RPA solutions that range from rule-based emulation of simple activities to self-learning of complex activities through artificial intelligence (Schmitz 2017). The benefit of RPA is seen in the fast implementation

Fig. 1 General RPA architecture (Czarnecki 2018)

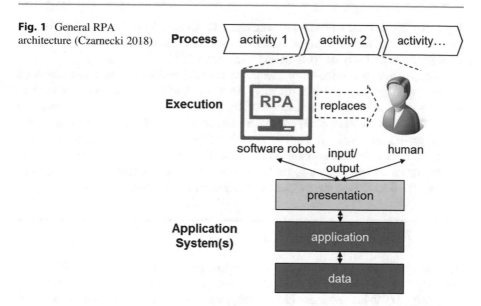

results combined with high increases in efficiency. In summary, RPA is a new technical approach to process automation that has the potential to enable a technology-induced digital transformation (Lacity et al. 2015; Willcocks et al. 2017). Different cases of RPA usage are documented, such as the automation of core processes at Telefonica O2 (Lacity et al. 2015), the RPA usage at the University Hospitals Birmingham as well as at Gazprom Energy (Willcocks et al. 2015). Scheer (2017) has collected eight RPA use cases ranging from a bank in Great Britain to a car dealership chain in the United States. Furthermore, an analysis of different standard software systems for RPA shows that the general systems are applicable in different industries, however, some suppliers offer specific pre-defined processes (Schmitz 2017). Hence, the general concept of RPA can be seen as industry agnostic. In this case its application is illustrated based on a concrete project in the telecommunications industry. Consequentially, the application presented in this case contains industry-specific requirements.

Subject of this case is the integrated telecommunications operator *Deutsche Telekom AG* (DT) which is one of the largest operators worldwide with approximately 200 million customers in 50 countries (Plunkett 2016). Headquartered in Germany, DT offers fixed-line, mobile, application, and business services based on extensive own network infrastructures. As most traditional telecommunications operators, DT faces the challenge of new competitors offering services via DT's network—so-called Over-the-Top (OTT) provider (Czarnecki and Dietze 2017a). In combination with overall stagnating revenues of the telecommunications market (Telecommunications Industry Association 2015), DT has to invest in innovations while reducing costs through increased efficiency. Hence, virtualization and automation are major pillars of DT's strategy. These strategic challenges are typical for the current transformational needs of the telecommunications industry (Peppard and

Rylander 2006; Pousttchi and Hufenbach 2011; Czarnecki and Dietze 2017b) that can be summarized in changed market conditions, restructured value chains, and new products and services (Czarnecki and Dietze 2017a).

Focus of this case is the work stream *Process Digitalization* which is understood as an important part of DT's strategy. As a concrete realization, RPA is used to achieve the goal of highly efficient workflows. This chapter describes the concrete implementation of RPA at DT. The first author of this chapter has worked on the entire project as a consultant. The situation faced (cf. Sect. 2), the action taken (cf. Sect. 3), and the results achieved (cf. Sect. 4) are a summarized description based on the author's observations as well as official project documentations. The lessons learned (cf. Sect. 5) are a retrospective discussion of the case.

2 Situation Faced

As one of the world's leading and fastest growing integrated operators, DT continuously faces challenges in terms of competition, cost pressure, and operational efficiency. DT is headquartered in Germany and has *National Companies* (NatCos) in several European countries and in the USA. DT provides fixed, mobile, as well as broadband products and services to its customers.

In 2016, DT has reported more than 200 million fixed, mobile, and broadband customers globally. *Telekom Deutschland GmbH* (TDG)—the organizational unit that is in charge of consumers as well as small and medium enterprises within Germany—has a customer base of around 75 million fixed, mobile, and broadband customers. This requires efficient and effective processes to meet the demands of existing customers and new subscribers.

According to the industry-specific reference *model enhanced Telecom Operations Map* (eTOM), processes in the telecommunications industry can be categorized into customer-facing processes and technical processes (Czarnecki and Dietze 2017b). Customer-facing processes comprise activities that are related to customer order handling, customer (change) requests, and customer complaint management. For the management and execution of customer-facing processes, TDG has established several call centers and back offices. Technical processes comprise activities including technical provisioning, dispatching, performance measurement, maintenance, and fault management. For the technical processes, a dedicated business unit within TDG was established that is responsible for the technical field service in Germany. The unit is called *Deutsche Telekom Technical Services GmbH (DTTS)*.

Across Germany, DTTS has to handle a significant amount of customer contacts, fault clearances, installations, and product provisioning per year that are depicted in Table 1.

The given number of customer contacts, fault clearances, installations and product provisions requires efficient and effective processes, a high degree of process automation, and a large workforce supported by appropriate capabilities and tools to successfully perform their daily work. Especially in those areas, DTTS has identified

Table 1 Number of activities performed by DTTS per year

Customer contacts	Fault clearances	Installations	Product provisioning
12 million	5 million	2.1 million	5 million

a couple of shortcomings that directly affect customer experience and customer satisfaction.

As an important part of DT's customer-facing processes, DTTS has the overall objective to provide customers with a highly efficient and effective technical field service. In general, DTTS considers latest technologies as an important enabler to provide state-of-the-art services to customers. Through technology penetration, DTTS has the ambition to be ahead of its competitors and to play at the forefront in international comparison.

However, through reviews and surveys, DTTS has identified several challenges in their existing field service operations that included:

- Incomplete technical provisioning of new products and services;
- Inefficiencies in dispatching;
- Ineffective fault management processes;
- Waiting times of customers not in line with set targets; and
- Dissatisfied customers while dealing with technical field service staff.

The overall situation persuaded DTTS to consider RPA as an enabling technology to address several of the challenges listed above. At the same time, DTTS has seen RPA as an enabler to formulate and realize its digital strategy. The cornerstones of the digital strategy developed by DTTS and the key actions taken by DTTS to deploy RPA are described in Sect. 3.

Increased process automation through the usage of software robots, and reduced time-to-market for new products and services were expected. Furthermore, a higher degree of process automation should lead to a lower number of technical field service employees required for process execution. These objectives were in line with the overall target of DTTS to reduce personnel cost by decreasing the number of full time employees (FTE) in the technical field service organization.

Besides the argument of FTE and cost reduction, several other factors including customer experience, process transparency, technology disruption, and innovative strength have also motivated DTTS to consider RPA as a major technological enabler for its digital strategy realization.

3   Action Taken

In this section a summarized description of the actions taken based on observations during the project and documented deliverables is provided. The explained actions and artifacts are related to design decisions based on specific practical requirements, and consensus of the involved executives and team members. Therefore, the

Table 2 Cornerstones, core elements, and enablers of DTTS digital strategy

Cornerstones—DTTS digital strategy

Digital journeys	Process digitization	Predictive services	Digital assistant
• Omni channel journeys • Self service • Live contact	• Digital and AI workflows • Digitization and automation of transactional activities • Remote and no touch installation	• Predictive maintenance • Predictive care and sales • Advanced analytics	• Digital service bots • AI capabilities support agent

Technology Enabler: Robotic Process Automation (RPA) (focus of this case)

structure and terminology might differ from general references. The case is reflected in the lessons learned (cf. Sect. 5).

As described in the previous section, DTTS faced various challenges related to efficiency and effectiveness. In order to address those challenges, DTTS has developed a digital strategy for the domains quality, growth, and efficiency (cf. Table 2). Selected principles of this digital strategy are summarized in the objectives of *zero complexity* and *zero complaint*, *one touch*, *agility in service*, and *disruptive thinking*. As part of the digital strategy, enabling technologies that facilitate the transformation were taken into consideration. As part of the implementation, DTTS has defined four cornerstones that are namely *digital journeys*, *process digitization*, *predictive services*, and *digital assistants*. Each cornerstone includes a selection of core elements to be considered for successful realization of the digital strategy. Table 2 provides an overview of the four strategic cornerstones with their respective core elements.

In an early stage of the project, DTTS took the decision to utilize RPA—which is the focus of this case—as technology enabler of its strategy implementation, in particular to drive digitization and automation of transactional activities. Therefore, an RPA project was set up in order to facilitate technology-induced organizational changes with the overall target of a process automation level that allows a reduction of 200 FTEs (cf. Sect. 2). This overall objective was used as starting point for the actions taken in the RPA project. As the project was conducted in an agile manner, the further analysis of the situation and continuous definition of operational targets was part of the project implementation described in this section.

From the methodical perspective, the set-up and conduction of the RPA project were structured into (1) organization and governance, (2) processes, and (3) technology and operations, which are described in the following subsections. From the content perspective, the RPA project defined and implemented a multitude of detailed RPA use cases, of which two concrete use cases are described more in detail in Sects. 3.4 and 3.5.

3.1   Organization and Governance

Due to the strategic importance of the digital strategy, the realization of quick results and savings was a major requirement. Hence, a lean and agile organization was defined to reflect this mindset (cf. Fig. 2). A major challenge was the interrelation between project and line organization. The overall responsibility for the RPA implementation was linked to the *Automation & Development Department*. The design and implementation of RPA in various concrete processes (e.g., field service, proactive problem solving) was structured according to a project organization methodology, while the operations of the automated solutions have been handled by the IT line organization. Overall, the *Automation & Development Department* was accountable and responsible for the entire lifecycle of the RPA solution.

In the design and implementation domain, a team of RPA project leaders was defined to drive multiple smaller automation activities as separate subprojects following a SCRUM-based agile development method (e.g., Maximini 2015; McKenna 2016). The RPA project leaders had a central role in identifying, designing, and implementing concrete RPA use cases that contribute to the overall objective of increased process automation. The project leaders were supported by a project office that was responsible for overall project management activities. Especially with respect to the various separate subprojects, a central project office was important. For each concrete use case, a team responsible for the design and implementation of the individual RPA process automation was formed. Jointly with the RPA project leader, this team worked according to a project-based approach.

After the implementation, the RPA use case was handed over to a dedicated team responsible for testing and operations of all automated processes. They were also responsible for change management to ensure necessary adaptations of the RPA implementations. These changes could be triggered by user requirements, but also by adaptations of underlying systems, such as user interfaces, web pages, or tool templates. Finally, a team responsible for reporting of the RPA automation was defined. They were in charge of calculating the license fees to the external RPA vendors. These fees typically follow a pay-as-you-grow principle and are based on the number of automated process steps or the number of executed transactions.

Furthermore, governance aspects have been considered in order to ensure a successful RPA implementation. As software robots take over work originally performed by humans, social partners and human resources (HR) have been involved as part of the overall governance. Their approval was a mandatory prerequisite to start the implementation of concrete RPA use cases. Whenever the automation led to a headcount reduction in a specific organizational unit, the options to transfer these employees to another position were discussed with the social partners.

3.2   Processes

One of the key tasks of the RPA project leaders was the identification of relevant processes that could be automated by RPA. Furthermore, a prioritization of the

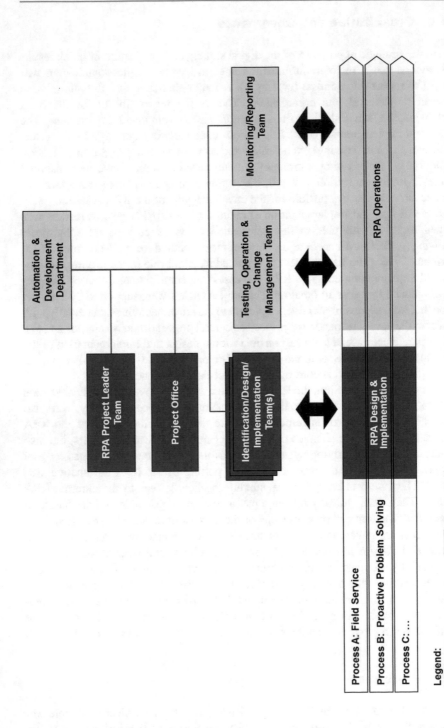

Fig. 2 RPA organizational set-up

processes was required to balance the ease of implementation with related saving potentials. Some processes were identified that could be easily automated by RPA foreshadowing low saving potentials, while others promised substantial savings related to high implementation efforts. Therefore, end users have been involved into the identification and prioritization of use cases. For typical work areas, such as, field technician, back office, or dispatching, end users were selected to support the respective teams. The RPA project leaders visited those users at their workplaces to understand their daily tasks. The detailed operational understanding helped to identify and prioritize ideas for RPA use cases. Furthermore, in later phases of the implementation, the project leaders were also able to directly guide the users to areas where process automation helps to simplify their work. This was an important factor for the acceptance of the RPA implementation.

After the identification and a first prioritization of RPA use cases, a two-week workshop called *CAMPUS* was conducted. Using creative moderation techniques, for each RPA case, about 20 users, 5 software developers, and the dedicated project leader worked together for 2 weeks to further detail the use case. This resulted in a design of multiple concrete RPA concepts, detailed requirements specifications, and the first RPA prototypes. At the end, approx. 1000 RPA ideas were discussed, 50 qualified RPA use case were formulated, and five RPA prototypes were implemented.

The prioritization of RPA use cases was based on the following two dimensions:

1. *Process complexity; and*
2. *Amount of process execution.*

Leveraging these two dimensions allowed the achievement of a prioritization of the processes according to their maximum of impact in an optimal manner. Overall, it was the target to find the optimum between the two dimensions *process complexity* and *number of process execution.* This was a slightly simplified perspective as it focused on the potential benefit side only and neglected the required efforts as well as costs for the automation implementation of the different processes. Therefore, this approach was used as a first prioritization step to derive a 'short-list' of potential automation processes. It was followed by a cost evaluation of the short-listed processes to derive the final decision.

Following this approach, for each qualified RPA use case an individual qualification sheet was created. The qualification sheet included a description of the process, detailed specifications of its automation, and an evaluation of implementation efforts as well as saving potentials (e.g., Becker et al. 1999; Bandara et al. 2015).

Based on an appropriate set of specifications produced during the CAMPUS workshop the concrete implementation of each RPA use case was initiated. Typically the implementation of a specific RPA use case took between 6 and 8 weeks and was based on multiple small implementation tasks—so-called sprints—following a SCRUM-based agile development method. Each sprint involved the project leader, design and implementation experts, operations experts, and external vendors, and resulted in an implementation of one or two concrete process steps following the minimum-viable-product (MVP) approach.

3.3 Technology and Operations

At the beginning of the project the decision was taken to realize the RPA use cases with the external partners *Bluepond* and *Almato*. The key reason referred to the objective of fast results to ensure the acceptance of RPA within DTTS. The functional—not the IT—department was responsible for the vendor selection as well as the operations of the RPA solution. The objective was to get a higher flexibility compared to a standard IT-based approach with long release cycles. Hence, the RPA project had to cover vendor management and operations of the RPA software and hardware.

As the migrated processes should run fully automated, it is of utmost importance that the software robots are available 24/7.Therefore, operational support was organized through the RPA project. Also, the reporting of the migrated processes and their actual operational status had to be available in real time. The vendors offered their own dashboards to report the status for their respective RPA systems. As DTTS decided for a dual-vendor strategy, no vendor agnostic integrated dashboard was available. Consequentially, a proprietary dashboard system was developed in-house. Considering the security, several technical requirements arose. As the software robots emulate end-user inputs, they had to be aligned with the access protection of all relevant application systems. This was a significant effort, as DTTS has more than 1000 RPA software robots running. Each of them, for example, required individual logins that have to be securely stored. In addition, the confidentiality level of all accessed information had to be investigated carefully.

As a result of the RPA project, 50 qualified uses cases were identified and prioritized according to process complexity and number of process execution (cf. Sect. 3.2). The implementation of those use cases has been started at the end of 2015 and was still running in December 2017. It follows an illustration of two exemplary use case which have been yielded substantial results.

3.4 Use Case 1: Field Service App

One of the most complex use cases was the development of a field service app. The objective was to bundle the most important support tools for field service technicians into one app. The implementation was based on RPA combined with further technologies, such as voice recognition and machine learning.

A major problem of the as-is process was that the field service technician had to perform a functional test at the customer's premises to complete an order. For this purpose, a technician had to trigger a mobile service that started an in-house service. After that, it triggered a functional test in the relevant IT systems. The result had to be transported to the field service technician by telephone or chat. In total, this

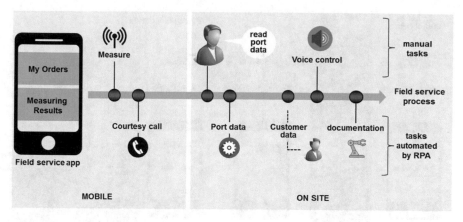

Fig. 3 Use case 1—field service target process

process required at least 10–15 min. of attention for all involved employees. During that time, the field service technician had to guarantee that the customer is reachable at its premises.

The process was streamlined and automated utilizing RPA. Figure 3 shows the target process that has been implemented in the field service app.

Underlying the paradigm of agile development, not all functionalities have been developed at once. The initial development focused on the RPA-based service within the app to measure the quality of the connection line to the customer premise.

Today, the implementation of the complete target process has been finished. Now, the field service technician sends a request via an app to the software robot that passes it directly to the related test systems. Afterwards, the software robot waits for the confirmation and sends the test result back to the field service technician via app. The process duration was reduced to a maximum of 1 min. Furthermore, during that time the field service technician can proceed with his work.

Based on the RPA solution, a rollout of the field service app to approx. 3000 external service employees—including third-party service providers—was realized after 8 weeks.

3.5   Use Case 2: Proactive Problem Solving

Proactive problem solving is another use case that is still under development in 2018, following the approach described earlier. It is based on the main idea to proactively avoid an incident instead of reacting on it. The case combines RPA with big data analytics. The starting point of the case is the likeliness of a thunderstorm predicted by weather forecast. The target process of this RPA use case is shown in Fig. 4.

In this RPA use case, big data and geographical analytics allow the prediction whether a household might be affected by a thunderstorm. In that case, customers are

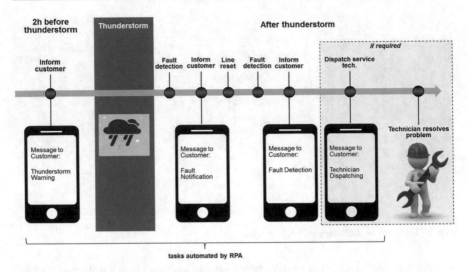

Fig. 4 Use case 2—proactive problem solving target process

informed with the recommendation to disconnect their devices to avoid technical issues. RPA software is used to trigger this message based on the results of the analytics. The software robot automates the initiation of the information message to customers based on the results of the analysis of the analytics part. Thereby, the number of future problems decreases. If still an error occurs, the monitoring systems generate an alarm. Both, another message to the customer as well as standard fault error analysis actions (e.g., measurements and resets) are triggered. Similar to the previous use case, the software robot initiates the procedures of line reset and line measurement for fault detection. After the problem resolution through these standard approaches, an automatic solution message is sent to the customer. Nonstandard issues require technical experts that are also triggered by RPA including the dispatching procedure.

4 Results Achieved

The project with the objective to introduce RPA in DT's technical field service operations (DTTS) started in the fourth quarter of 2015. Section 3 describes the chosen approach and the general approach applied during the execution of the project.

Within less than 6 months from the project start, the first transactions were performed automatically through software robots. In March 2016—the first month in which RPA was successfully implemented—approx. 229,000 automatic transactions were successfully realized. Since then, the number of automatic transactions through RPA per month has been increasing significantly. The increase of monthly automatic transactions was realized through a growing number of RPA

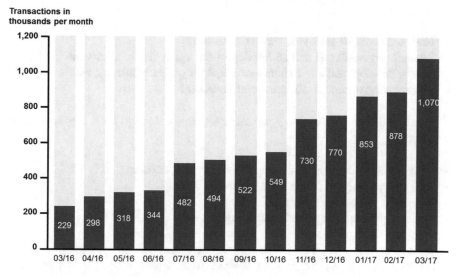

Fig. 5 Number of automatic transactions through RPA per month

usages in different process areas of DTTS. Within 1 year, the number of automatic transactions per month has been increased to more than one million. Figure 5 shows the increasing number of automatic transactions through RPA at DTTS in the time period from March 2016 until March 2017.

DTTS has implemented a multi-solution platform with more than 1000 RPA clients. Through the high number of RPA clients, a saving of 800 FTE was realized. The FTE saving potential at DTTS led to a *Return On Investment* (ROI) for the implemented RPA clients within less than 3 months and allowed 60–80% of cost savings in the areas in which the RPA clients were implemented.

At the same time, the RPA implementation at DTTS is one of the biggest RPA implementations worldwide. Through this, DTTS has underlined its innovation culture and strength. It belongs to one of the first telecommunications operators successfully deploying RPA clients on such a large scale.

Through the deployment of RPA clients, key benefits were observed in the three areas of *customer satisfaction*, *financial performance*, and *process compliance*.

The key drivers of *improved customer experience* through RPA deployment are mainly:

- Easy interaction through the usage of natural language;
- 24-h availability for 7 days per week;
- Instant access and avoidance of waiting queues; and
- Fast resolving of issues, without dispatching and involvement of field service technicians.

The key drivers for *improved financial performance* through RPA deployment are mainly:

- Reduced cost (40–90%) for serving customers;
- Actually no weekends and no holidays—the system is always running;
- Lower development and maintenance cost for online platforms; and
- Increased opportunities for cross and upselling.

The key drivers for *improved process compliance* through RPA deployment are mainly:

- Elimination of human errors—results are always the same;
- Full transparency of actions and decisions;
- Increased processing speed; and
- Agile scaling reacting on changes of demand.

In summary, the project at DTTS that was set up for the deployment of more than 1000 RPA clients has reached the desired goals within a short timeframe. The automation of one single end-to-end process took on average 6–8 weeks. In all use cases, cost saving potentials ranging from 30% to 60% were identified and realized through the implementation and deployment of RPA. Through the significant cost savings realized, a breakeven for the investments was achieved within a timeframe of 3–9 months. These figures indicate the financial benefits validly. Though, the exact financial figures related to the project are subject to confidentiality.

The overall success of the RPA project at DTTS led to the establishment of a continuous pipeline of additional processes to be optimized. RPA works well in environments wherein structured information needs to be processed automatically. By means of simple RPA implementations, automation levels of up to 80% could be achieved. For higher automation levels, additional advanced technologies such as *Artificial Intelligence* (AI) had to be used in combination with RPA. Besides cost reduction, the deployment of RPA led to an improved customer experience that was measured through different key performance indicators before and after project execution. Customer experience particularly improved through the usage of a technical field service application.

5   Lessons Learned

The case provides an example of a technology-induced change of process execution as part of a digital transformation. The concept of RPA provides an opportunity to automate human activities through software robots. The case describes how DT used RPA to achieve its strategic targets of process digitalization. In this section, a post-implementation review summarizing the actions taken and results achieved is served.

In general, the results can be linked to increased automation that is a typical part of Business Process Management (BPM) (Dumas et al. 2013). In this context, process-aware systems, such as Business Process Management Systems (BPMS) as well as extensive business applications (e.g., CRM, ERP), are discussed (Dumas et al. 2013). By means of RPA, a new concept is proposed that does not require changes of applications but automates processes through existing user interfaces (Willcocks et al. 2017). With respect to the core elements of BPM (Rosemann and vom Brocke 2010), the results are related to *the IT-enabled process implementation and execution* that is understood as the transformation of a process model in an automated execution. As described in Sect. 3, RPA adopts formerly human processes through either rule-based definitions or self-learning concepts. Hence, the results contribute new concepts to the field of process automation.

The case described provides a concrete example how RPA is used at DT. First, from a strategic perspective RPA is identified as an enabling technology for DT's digital strategy and linked to the objectives of digital journeys, process digitization, predictive service, and digital assistant. Second, from a methodical perspective an agile project approach is illustrated that resulted in 50 qualified RPA use cases. Third, from an operational perspective two exemplary use cases related to field service and proactive problem solving were discussed in detail. The advantages shown in the case are increased flexibility and fast implementation, as RPA was mainly implemented by the business side without changes to the existing application landscape. While executing the project, it was observed that it is easier to educate open-minded employees in the IT part of RPA, than to explain the business perspective of RPA to employees with a pure technical background.

Significant measurable results in the dimensions customer experience (e.g., 24-h availability), financial performance (e.g., more than 40% reduced costs), and process compliance (e.g., elimination of human errors) were documented (cf. Sect. 4). While some implementation details are specific for DT, most parts of the RPA concept and project approach can be used as a reference for prospective process automation projects:

- The general idea of RPA (i.e., automating manual tasks without changing underlying application systems) can be applied to various industries. Standard systems for RPA are available.
- The cornerstones of the digital strategy combined with RPA as enabling technology can be transferred to other digital transformations.
- The project set-up and agile approach allowed fast implementation results and integration of the business side that can be used as references for similar projects.
- Different benefit dimensions show that process automation goes beyond pure cost cutting.

From the specific perspective of the telecommunications industry, its transformational needs are widely discussed by researchers and practitioner (e.g. Grover and Saeed 2003; Picot 2006; Czarnecki et al. 2010; Bub et al. 2011; Czarnecki and Dietze 2017b). In this context, the case addresses the typical requirements of increased flexibility and efficiency (e.g. Bruce et al. 2008) that are especially important for traditional telecommunications operators to react on new competitors (e.g., OTT players) (Czarnecki and Dietze 2017a). Hence, the case serves as a reference for researchers and practitioners in the telecommunications industry.

From the general perspective of process automation, the case provides insights into the new concept of RPA (Allweyer 2016; Willcocks et al. 2017; Czarnecki 2018). As a contribution to future RPA projects, the following lessons learned were derived from the case:

1. *Agile design and implementation are important for a successful digital transformation.* Fast changing market requirements are an essential driver of digital transformations. In this case, 25 experts developed a first prototype after 2 weeks and launched an initial solution after 6–8 weeks. The concept of RPA supports this agile development process, because of the fast adaptation and integration of RPA systems. It also helped in the acceptance of process automation, as beneficial results were shown quickly and triggered the demand of further automation.
2. *Understand technical innovations as enabler of the digital transformation.* Already during the formulation of the strategy, concrete innovations (such as RPA) were considered. From the beginning of the project, experts were involved to assure the investigation of technical aspects in each project stage. Furthermore, different innovations were combined, for example, RPA, mobile apps, as well as machine learning.
3. *Consider technical and organizational interrelations from the beginning.* The digital transformation described covered various organizational entities and involved various technologies. Therefore, transparency was an important factor to identify and manage interrelations. Furthermore, an organizational set-up was used embracing design and operations, and balances between project and line organization.
4. *RPA is more than a pure cost cutting instrument.* Even though RPA replaces humans with software robots, the innovation potential goes beyond cost cutting. In the case, RPA was used as enabler to reinvent the existing processes. The proactive problem solving, for instance, catalyzed a process innovation. These are additional benefits overpassing the pure monetary benefits that are given as well.
5. *The impact of RPA on the people dimension should be managed carefully from the beginning.* The automation of human interactions is a sensitive topic. Concerns and objections should be addressed from the beginning through a transparent communication, ideally integrated in a comprehensive change management approach (e.g., Carter 2013). Early involvement of the people affected by the process automation was shown as a promising approach. It did not only contribute to the identification of the processes to be automated but also helped to reduce the fear of change due to automation.

As RPA is an innovative topic, the case offers various starting points for future research. From a BPM perspective, the integration between RPA and process-aware systems (Dumas et al. 2013) requires further guidance. Especially, if the software robot learns the process independently, concepts are required governing the compliance between RPA activities and defined business processes. Furthermore the process complexity still limits RPA. Thus, further research on combining RPA with machine learning and artificial intelligence is required. So far, RPA is seen as an independent software system that is added to the user interface layer. This offers the advantage of a fast implementation. Consequently, the integration between RPA and application systems, as well as the standardization of interfaces are topics for future discussions. In this context, the link between RPA and existing reference frameworks (e.g., ITIL, eTOM) should be discussed. From a practical perspective, the current landscape of RPA solutions is complex (Schmitz 2017) and requires further guidance.

References

Allweyer T (2016) Robotic process automation–Neue Perspektiven für die Prozessautomatisierung

Bandara W, Guillemain A, Coogans P (2015) Prioritizing process improvement: an example from the Australian Financial Services Sector. In: vom Brocke J, Rosemann M (eds) Handbook on business process management, vol 2. Springer, Berlin, pp 289–307

Becker J, Uthmann CV, zur Mühlen M, Rosemann M (1999) Identifying the workflow potential of business processes. IEEE Comput Soc:10

Bruce G, Naughton B, Trew D et al (2008) Streamlining the telco production line. J Telecommun Manag 1:15–32

Bub U, Picot A, Krcmar H (2011) The future of telecommunications. Bus Inf Syst Eng 3:265–267. https://doi.org/10.1007/s12599-011-0178-0

Carter L (ed) (2013) The change champion's field guide: strategies and tools for leading change in your organization, 2nd edn, and updated edn. Wiley, San Francisco, CA

Czarnecki C (2018) Robotergesteuerte Prozessautomatisierung. In: Gronau N, Becker J, Kliewer N et al (eds) Enzyklopädie der Wirtschaftsinformatik – Online-Lexikon, 10. Auflage. GITO Verlag, Berlin

Czarnecki C, Dietze C (2017a) Domain-specific reference modeling in the telecommunications industry. In: Maedche A, vom Brocke J, Hevner A (eds) Designing the digital transformation. Springer, Cham, pp 313–329. https://doi.org/10.1007/978-3-319-59144-5_19

Czarnecki C, Dietze C (2017b) Reference architecture for the telecommunications industry: transformation of strategy, organization, processes, data, and applications. Springer, New York

Czarnecki C, Winkelmann A, Spiliopoulou M (2010) Services in electronic telecommunication markets: a framework for planning the virtualization of processes. Electron Mark 20:197–207. https://doi.org/10.1007/s12525-010-0045-8

Dumas M, La Rosa M, Mendling J, Reijers HA (2013) Fundamentals of business process management. Springer, Berlin

Groover MP (2008) Automation, production systems, and computer-integrated manufacturing, 3rd edn. Prentice Hall, Upper Saddle River, NJ

Grover V, Saeed K (2003) The telecommunication industry revisited. Commun ACM 46:119–125. https://doi.org/10.1145/792704.792709

Lacity M, Willcocks LP, Craig A (2015) Robotic process automation at Telefonica O2. The London School of Economics and Political Science, London

Legner C, Eymann T, Hess T et al (2017) Digitalization: opportunity and challenge for the business and information systems engineering community. Bus Inf Syst Eng 59:301–308. https://doi.org/10.1007/s12599-017-0484-2

Matt C, Hess T, Benlian A (2015) Digital transformation strategies. Bus Inf Syst Eng 57:339–343. https://doi.org/10.1007/s12599-015-0401-5

Maximini D (2015) The scrum culture. Springer International Publishing, Cham

McKenna D (2016) The art of scrum. Apress, Berkeley, CA

Peppard J, Rylander A (2006) From value chain to value network. Eur Manag J 24:128–141. https://doi.org/10.1016/j.emj.2006.03.003

Picot A (ed) (2006) The future of telecommunications industries. Springer, Berlin/Heidelberg

Plunkett JW (2016) Plunkett's telecommunications industry almanac 2017: the only comprehensive guide to the telecommunications industry

Pousttchi K, Hufenbach Y (2011) Value creation in the mobile market: a reference model for the role(s) of the future mobile network operator. Bus Inf Syst Eng 3:299–311. https://doi.org/10.1007/s12599-011-0175-3

Rosemann M, vom Brocke J (2010) The six core elements of business process management. In: vom Brocke J, Rosemann M (eds) Handbook on business process management, vol 1. Springer, Berlin, pp 107–122

Scheer A-W (2017) Performancesteigerung durch Automatisierung von Geschäftsprozessen. AWS-Institut für digitale Produkte und Prozesse, Saarbrücken

Schmitz B (2017) Robotic process automation: Leistungsübersicht über am Markt verfügbare Softwarelösungen. Hochschule für Telekommunikation Leipzig, Leipzig

Telecommunications Industry Association (2015) TIA's 2015–2018 ICT market review & forecast

Willcocks L, Lacity M, Craig A (2015) The IT function and robotic process automation. The London School of Economics and Political Science

Willcocks L, Lacity M, Craig A (2017) Robotic process automation: strategic transformation lever for global business services? J Inf Technol Teach Cases 7:17–28. https://doi.org/10.1057/s41266-016-0016-9

Manfred Schmitz is Managing Partner at Detecon Consulting FZ-LLC, Abu Dhabi, UAE. He holds an MSc degree in electrical engineering from University of Applied Science in Cologne as well as an MBA from Henley Management College in the UK. He provides more than 20 years of experience in telecommunication business. He gained severe experience as Software Engineer at Siemens, Technology Manager at VIAG Interkom (now Telefonica O2), Head of Service Management at MobilCom Multimedia and Senior Manager at Vodafone Group Technology. In more than 10 years at Detecon he performed more than 60 projects and developed towards an Managing Partner. He is Detecon's thought leader for CAPEX & technology strategy, as well as automation and operation topics including e.g. Managed Services, automation and RPA.

Christian Dietze is Partner at Detecon Consulting FZ-LLC, Abu Dhabi, UAE. Christian has been working in the international telecommunications industry for more than 15 years. He has held various leading positions in the telecommunications industry and has been responsible for the management and quality assurance of significant re-structuring projects. Christian is a senior advisor in digital transformation and most recently he has been supporting chief executives of leading international telecommunications operators to successfully establish their digital business units. In the TM Forum he has a leading position in the further development of eTOM and the development of the Digital Maturity Model (DMM). He received his Master's in Computer Science from the University of Koblenz-Landau, Germany.

Christian Czarnecki is Professor of Information Systems at the *Hochschule für Telekommunikation Leipzig*, Germany. During his academic career, he received a Doctor of Engineering from the University of Magdeburg. He has worked in different consulting companies for more than 10 years, and has managed numerous transformation projects in Europe, North Africa, and the Middle East. His research includes digital transformation, process management, and enterprise architectures. In the industry organization TM Forum he is involved in the further development of the reference model enhanced Telecom Operations Map (eTOM). His work has been published in leading academic journals, in proceedings of international conferences, and in various books.

Airline Application Security in the Digital Economy: Tackling Security Challenges for Distributed Applications in Lufthansa Systems

Balázs Somoskői, Stefan Spahr, Erkuden Rios, Oscar Ripolles, Jacek Dominiak, Tamás Cserveny, Péter Bálint, Peter Matthews, Eider Iturbe, and Victor Muntés-Mulero

Abstract

(a) **Situation faced**: In the era of pervasive digitalization, the airline IT software industry is facing a number of challenges from the combination of new distribution channels, social media, Big data, Cloud Computing, etc. One of the major challenges in creating smart and scalable software applications is how to tackle security challenges when components are distributed and operated in hybrid and multiple clouds, whose providers may be independent and heterogeneous. The difficulties reside not only in identifying and expressing the desired level of security in the application, but also in how the security guarantees are influenced by the cloud services used.

(b) **Action taken**: We exemplify the case with a flight scheduling application prototype developed by Lufthansa Systems and explain how novel

B. Somoskői · S. Spahr · T. Cserveny · P. Bálint
Lufthansa Systems, Raunheim, Germany
e-mail: Balazs.Somoskoi@lhsystems.com; Stefan.Spahr@lhsystems.com;
Tamas.Cserveny@lhsystems.com

E. Rios · E. Iturbe
Tecnalia Research & Innovation, Bilbao, Spain
e-mail: Erkuden.Rios@tecnalia.com; Eider.Iturbe@tecnalia.com

O. Ripolles (✉) · V. Muntés-Mulero
CA Technologies, Cornellà de Llobregat, Spain
e-mail: Oscar.Ripolles@ca.com; Victor.Muntes@ca.com

J. Dominiak
CA Technologies, Warsaw, Poland
e-mail: Jacek.Dominiak@ca.com

P. Matthews
CA Technologies, Datchet, UK
e-mail: Peter.Matthew@ca.com

© Springer International Publishing AG, part of Springer Nature 2019
N. Urbach, M. Röglinger (eds.), *Digitalization Cases*, Management for Professionals, https://doi.org/10.1007/978-3-319-95273-4_3

approaches are used to address security issues during the development of such a prototype by following the MUSA approach. MUSA stands for Multi-cloud Secure Applications and refers to an EU-funded research project that is developing an integrated solution for the development and operation of secure multi-cloud applications accounting for those security aspects from the beginning. We introduce the MUSA Security DevOps framework and lessons learned from using it.

(c) **Results achieved**: Lufthansa Systems tested MUSA tools in an exercise to create, deploy and control a new secure application prototype. We describe how these tools were used in the context of the case study presented in this paper. We also analyze the impact that they had in the development, deployment, and operation of the multi-cloud prototype. This analysis is done by means of a user-centered evaluation using questionnaires and informal interviews.

(d) **Lessons learned**: The most important lesson is the importance of a sound risk analysis from which the security decisions are taken. MUSA framework supports the automation of the risk analysis in a per component basis, helping to systematize the creation of the application risk profile. Another important aspect is how implementing a SecDevOps approach in a multi-cloud scenario proves that it is highly valuable to include security topics together with the regular DevOps methodology. Finally, we must underline the need for cloud standards which enable homogeneous cloud service descriptions that ease the comparison of the services and the offered security controls.

1   Introduction

The adoption of the cloud computing paradigm has opened new business possibilities thanks to the availability of huge virtual computing resources at a low cost. A combination of different cloud offerings is expected to bring a Capital Expense (CapEx) reduction to cloud adopters, while achieving high availability and scalability ratios. At the same time, many potential users are still reluctant to move critical data and applications to commercial clouds, due to a perceived lack of trust in providers in the security domain. Currently, cloud security is still considered one of the major factors inhibiting the widespread adoption of cloud solutions (North Bridge 2013).

In this work, we describe how to overcome the lack of insight into cloud security controls and decide which cloud offerings are more suitable to an application according to the risk profile adopted by the cloud consumer. Our description uses the case of a multi-cloud application from Lufthansa Systems. The use case application is a flight scheduling application prototype to evaluate new architectures and security technologies to benefit from cloud advantages. The current commercial version serves more than 64 airlines around the globe for their daily business, ranging from small to large carriers and using different business models.

Lufthansa Systems GmbH & Co. KG (lhsystems.com) is one of the world's leading providers of IT services in the airline industry. It draws its unique strengths from an ability to combine profound industry know-how with technological expertise and many years of project experience. The company offers an extensive range of successful and market-leading products to its more than 300 airline customers. Approximately 2100 employees worldwide work in 16 locations on aviation IT but also on further digitizing the airline industry. For years, Lufthansa Systems has been advising and supporting airlines in their digital transformation, demonstrating what sustainable airline processes can look like and helping customers implement concrete projects—with data analytics, personalization, mobility and new developments such as eye tracking and dynamic navigation maps. The spectrum includes solutions and consulting services for improving the efficiency and differentiation of all aspects of an airline as well as for optimizing the entire travel chain for passengers.

Lufthansa Systems as a software application provider is becoming more open to using cloud based web applications. The practice in the past was to provide fat client applications for an airline's internal network, where the complete application system landscape was built up behind the company firewalls in a secure zone. Security controls were mainly reduced to authentication and authorization only. By exposing the system landscape to the Internet, a holistic approach towards security is required. This holistic approach includes identifying the assets of the company, analysing the possible threats on all the identified assets, studying and applying the corresponding control mechanisms, and monitoring runtime behavior. All of these tasks must be applied continuously and following developing trends. Due to the complexity of this approach, companies often dedicate a complete department to these tasks.

The method presented in this document is based on the adoption of MUSA solution[1] for the creation and administration of the Lufthansa Systems prototype application to ensure its security capabilities. Integrating security related best practices and a toolset like MUSA into the development process for (new) applications seems to be a very promising way to reduce the effort and to make the whole development process more agile.

[1]The MUSA solution is the main result of the project MUSA—Multi-cloud Secure Applications project of the European Union's Horizon 2020 research and innovation programme under grant agreement No 644429.

2   Situation Faced

From year to year, the need for the airline industry to work more cost-effectively grows. Strategic alliances of individual airlines (i.e. former competitors) happen in order to use the synergetic effects to establish the necessary market power (vertical integration). Similarly, also "platforms" including different companies along the travel chain arise (horizontal integration), where companies not related to the aviation industry participate. Besides efficiency, airlines aim for commercial and service differentiation to expand their revenue streams and explore new revenue potentials. Both strategic goals were enforced and driven by an increase in the utilization of Data Analytics & Artificial Intelligence, Internet of Things, cloud services, etc. As indicated by the CEO of Lufthansa Systems Olivier Krueger, "Digitalization has a significant influence on working processes, business models and our daily life. This applies to the aviation industry as well. The core of our company strategy is to put airlines in a perfect position for the digital future" (Lufthansa Systems 2017).

The steps taken to move the digitalization further supposed a self-regulating disruption in management from prediction through automated adjustments in the flight operations to real-time information to travelers. Other benefits include flexible commercial offerings, services including individual spot pricing and a management of digital customer touchpoints along the travel chain.

To support such cooperation and platforms, the airline companies need, amongst other things, an IT infrastructure, application software landscape and system operation with high flexibility and usability. The applications must support different kinds of collaboration models, better than today.

Cloud computing, often referred to as "the cloud," has been one of the hottest paradigms in IT in recent years. The popularity is based on the scalability and flexibility, which are key factors in the fast changing business environment. The main idea is that the cloud enables companies to consume an expanding computing resource, such as a virtual machine, storage or an application, as a utility, rather than having to build and maintain on-premise infrastructures.

Multi-cloud applications are the most challenging applications in heterogeneous cloud ecosystems with multiple cloud providers, since they need to be able to maximize the benefits of the combination of the cloud resources in use. A multi-cloud application is a distributed application over heterogeneous cloud resources whose components are deployed in different cloud service providers and still work in an integrated way and transparently for the end-user.

There are many reasons for deploying a multi-cloud architecture, including reducing dependency on a single vendor, increasing flexibility and decreasing the effect of disasters. In these scenarios, data integrity, selective confidentiality and selective data exchange are needed together with a high level of secure communication between different cloud environments (i.e. multi-cloud environment) or between a public cloud and on premise cloud or other application environments.

Lufthansa Systems is always looking for new technologies and solutions to help in meeting new market requirements of its customers. Therefore, Lufthansa Systems started the investigating the usage of cloud based solutions. The migration to multi-cloud based infrastructure could provide significant benefits. For example:

- In development and test cases, there are often periods of high resource demand and periods of low or no demand. The pay-per-use model is an answer to this challenge. By using this model, we could achieve cost savings and more optimal resource usage.
- With the possibility for scalability and provisioning, the adoption of new business requirements can be realized much quicker with less costs.
- Distribution of an application over multiple clouds may give a better response time to the end user (depending on the application architecture).

However, such new technology brought new challenges as well. Primarily, these challenges are related to cloud based service requirements. Within these requirements, one of the main ones is related to the area of security. In any case, Lufthansa Systems and almost all IT companies are looking for opportunities to reduce costs and to have a scalable and secure IT infrastructure. Therefore, these companies must find a solution for security related questions.

In our case study, we focus on how security requirements (data integrity, confidentiality, access control, localization, availability, etc.) can be guaranteed in application components, through MUSA security-by-design and assurance mechanisms.

3   Action Taken

The use case application prototype is used to evaluate and to demonstrate the benefits of moving beyond standalone software functionality towards a design supporting Software as a Service (SaaS) operations in cloud environments. In the SaaS delivery model, application services are cloud-hosted and offered to customers on demand over the Internet with specific pricing and licensing options. In this SaaS model, many customers share the same services and therefore a strict isolation of customer-owned data is essential.

In this Section, we want to describe Lufthansa Systems' experience using novel multi-cloud security tools in the MUSA framework to tackle the challenges related to security while building, deploying, and operating a distributed flight schedule planning application in a multi-cloud environment. Firstly, we describe the underlying architecture created to enable scalability and performance. Then, we describe the tools offered by MUSA and how Lufthansa Systems applied them in their application.

Novel Application Prototype Description and Architecture
Virtualized cloud environments are offering a scale on demand infrastructure. Virtual nodes can incrementally be added or removed to the cluster. Such elasticity addresses the performance issues to create a reactive application. But beside this,

elasticity in a multi-cloud setup can create additional security challenges such as the added need for securing the additional communication channels.

For the prototype application of the use case described in this paper, we developed some primary flight-planning supporting services (e.g. fleet, airport etc.). Common application infrastructure components like the user and configuration manager or the integration-bus are centrally developed and provided in an environment similar to a Platform as a Service (PaaS).

In general, the flight scheduling application prototype is a multi-layered, distributed web-application and provides a scalable platform of loosely coupled component-oriented building blocks. In contrast to monolithic approaches, server-side-applications are decomposed in self-contained, collaborating and independently scalable business-components, where each of them is capable of running in its own process and of interacting by use of lightweight REST style communication protocols and by asynchronous messaging.

The main drivers for the implementation of this application in this use case are:

- Designing the scheduling application prototype by using Domain Driven Design (DDD). DDD is a strategic approach in software design, providing best practices and patterns to facilitate the process of business domain analysis and functional modelling of the domain logic. Successfully applied, the software model closely resembles business domain concepts and enables direct and unambiguous linguistic translations with feature-responsible domain experts.
- Encompassing major software architecture patterns like those represented by REST, Command Query Responsibility Segregation (CQRS) and Event-Sourcing (ES). In combination, these styles of architectural patterns are complementary and they cover non-functional criteria on different architectural levels. In turn, a layered architecture enables us to address various non-functional and conceptual requirements with explicit design decisions on each level.

The application components are build-up using a microservice approach. The application is vertically split in decoupled read and write models, each of them optimized with respect to layering and specific processing requirements. Commands invoke state-changing behavior, whereas queries are used to read information.

In the application that we discuss in this paper, we introduce a prototype which was branched from the actual product development to ensure independence and stability of the prototype. Our focus in this paper is on exploring new ways of developing and delivering applications into a multi-cloud environment using the tools offered by the MUSA project. With this, we aim at reducing the overall complexity introduced by the distributed microservices based architecture. The flight schedule creation performed by the airlines is part of their strategic planning and it considers multiple influencing factors into the schedule, like available and targeted amount of aircrafts (the fleet), revenue gained by ticket sales, airport time constraints for landing, turnaround times on the ground etc. In fact, it is a very complex business process and the described application architecture reflects this complexity in the form of a large number of microservices.

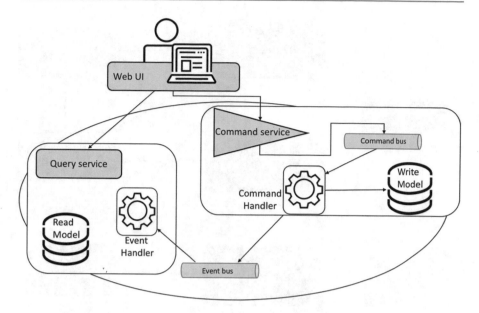

Fig. 1 CQRS Pattern used in the flight scheduling application prototype

Figure 1 illustrates a functional CQRS-Component consisting of a distinct read and write model to segregate command and query processing. Synchronization between read and write models is based on an event propagation mechanism. Commands trigger business logic within the write-model and result in state-changes on data-aggregates. Each state-change is represented by an event and published for updates to all subscribed read models. Services of the scheduling application prototype are designed by standardized component patterns.

In Fig. 2, we depict the simplified component model of the prototype presented. The central gateway provides a single entry-point into the system as a reverse proxy. Some pre-authentication step is also performed here. The security module provides authentication and authorization features, identity management, and administration. The presentation layer of the fleet-maintaining module resides on a webserver, and it is realized as a single webpage. The webpage frontend is communicating with the backend via REST interfaces, the command REST calls are directed to the write submodule, the query REST calls are directed to the read submodule. Both read and write submodules have a persistence layer realized by a MongoDB.[2] The connection between the two modules is realized via messaging. The corresponding message broker is Kafka[3] with a supporting Zookeeper.[4]

---

[2]https://www.mongodb.com
[3]https://kafka.apache.org/
[4]https://zookeeper.apache.org/

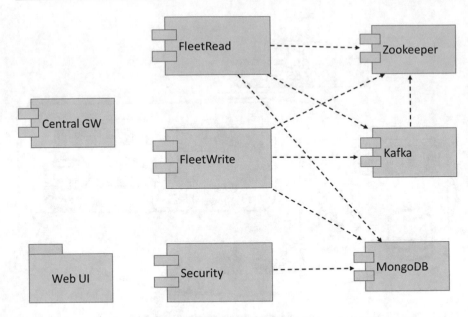

Fig. 2 Diagram of the different components of the Lufthansa Systems' prototype

Innovations for a Secure Multi-Cloud Environment

Actions taken to consider and tackle the security of the multi-cloud application consist in adopting the MUSA solution to support the security-aware design and operation of the application. The MUSA solution promotes the use of the MUSA framework that includes:

- Security-by-design mechanisms to allow application self-protection at runtime.
- Methods and tools for the integrated security assurance in both the engineering and operation of multi-cloud applications.

The MUSA framework was conceived as a DevOps complimentary environment supporting the creation and administration of secure multi-cloud applications. Thus, MUSA supports the integration of security into multi-cloud applications not only during design but also during deployment and operation. The focus is to respond to security related issues of multi-cloud applications, and not to the functional and other performance issues of multi-cloud. Other previous solutions by EU-funded research projects such as MODAClouds (2012) and PaaSage (2012) already focused in QoS and functional aspects of multi-cloud.

The framework is offered as a prototype integrated tool-suite consisting of five tools as shown in Fig. 3. The different tools can be accessed from the MUSA framework front-end, which offers a Kanban style dashboard that supports the multi-disciplinary DevOps team designing, deciding upon and ensuring the security

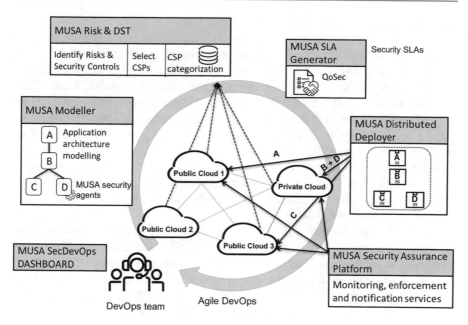

Fig. 3 The MUSA framework tools

aspects of the application components. In the following we describe the objective and use of each of the tools in the supported security engineering process.

MUSA Modeller

The use of the MUSA Modeller is the initial design step. The MUSA Modeller is a web editor that allows the DevOps team creating and maintaining multi-cloud application models written in MUSA extended Cloud Application Modelling and Execution Language (CAMEL) language (Rios et al. 2017). The model specifies the set of components of the application along with their deployment and security requirements specification. The model is a Cloud Provider Independent Model (CPIM), meaning that it does not specify the particular cloud services that the application will use. The DevOps team can optionally specify the use of MUSA security agents that will work at runtime together with the application components in order particular security requirements are ensured. The model will serve as one of the inputs to make the selection of such services later, aided by the Decision Support Tool.

Relationship to Described Use Case We use the MUSA Modeller to define our prototype components using the CAMEL model. By building this model we can have an overview of the complete system containing all the deployment requirements and dependencies as well. Furthermore, this model is the input for all our further activities.

MUSA Risk Analysis and Decision Support Tool

As the second design step, it is necessary to obtain the security requirements of the multi-cloud application in the form of security controls required from cloud service providers. To that aim, the DevOps team is guided through a risk classification process based on the STRIDE risk categorisation methodology (Microsoft 2005), complemented with OCTAVE risk methodology (Alberts and Dorofee 2002) for the calculation of the risk probability of occurrence and impact, and with OWASP Risk Rating Methodology (OWASP 2013) for the risk mitigation process. For each application component, the tool shows the threats corresponding to the type of component (i.e. web service, database, etc.). Then, for each threat, the user has to assign a score (from 0 to 9) to each of the available likelihood factors and impact factors, which are combined to obtain a final risk value where Risk = Likelihood × Impact.

As mentioned previously, the risk values associated with each threat are then grouped according to the categories identified by STRIDE (Spoofing, Tampering, Repudiation, Information disclosure, Denial of service, and Elevation of privilege), obtaining six different risk values, one per category. With this categorization, the user has a summarized but comprehensive view of the risks, making it easier to identify which of the six threat categories has a higher risk.

Once the risk profile of each of the components is defined, the MUSA Decision Support Tool (DST) aids the DevOps team in the selection of the cloud services in which the components will be deployed. The tool computes the service match-making with the security controls specified and ranks the cloud service combinations by requirements fulfilment degree.

Relationship to Described Use Case We plan to use MUSA's Risk Analysis tool to introduce a completely novel approach for risk management. Formerly, risk assessment was not performed using formal methods in our development lifecycle. To the best of their knowledge, architects and developers defined possible threats and manually defined some control mechanisms based on their experience. Later in the operations phase further hardening measurements were applied by the operations team before going into production in our own in-house datacenters. By using MUSA's Risk Analysis tool we plan to implement a structured and systematic process for risk assessment focused in multi-cloud environments.

MUSA SLA Generator

Service Level Agreements (SLAs) are formal contracts documenting the features of delivered services and related performance expectations, the so-called Service Level Objectives (SLOs). In MUSA, the SLA Generator automates the creation of the Security SLA of the multi-cloud application under work, which collects the security SLOs guaranteed by the application to its clients. The process takes as input: (i) the MUSA extended CAMEL model of the application resulting from the Modeller, (ii) the Risk profile and the selection of Cloud Services made in the Risk Analysis and DST tool, (iii) the SLAs of the cloud services selected and (iv) the security metrics defined by the DevOps team as being of interest related to the security SLOs in each component. With all this information, the Composite Security SLA of the multi-cloud application is calculated for the overall application. Note that the application's Security SLA depends on the Security SLAs of its individual components as well as the Security SLAs of the cloud services they use.

Relationship to Described Use Case Once we have analysed risks and established the proper mitigation actions through the definition of the security controls, we plan to use the MUSA SLA Generator to compose an SLA for our end customers, the airline users. Formerly, SLAs against the in-house datacenter operator concentrated mainly on pure operational aspects (uptimes, availability, performance, etc.) Customers growing requirements on privacy and security push airlines to put more emphasis on the security aspects of their tools. In order to answer this demand, we plan to introduce security commitments into the SLAs we offer to our customers and into the expected SLAs we plan to sign with selected cloud service providers as well.

MUSA Distributed Deployer

The MUSA Deployer enables the automated configuration and deployment of the multi-cloud application components in cloud resources from heterogeneous cloud providers, thus allowing their interoperation even if they are running in different cloud settings.

Relationship to Described Use Case We aim at automating our development lifecycle as much as possible, moving further towards continuous delivery. To enable this effort, we are planning to use the framework tools providing automated cloud resource provisioning and automated deployment onto those cloud resources.

MUSA Security Assurance Platform

The MUSA SecAP integrates monitoring, enforcement, and notification services in a SaaS solution that enables the continuous security assurance of the multi-cloud application at operation, once all the components and MUSA agents are deployed and running. The monitoring is done over the security metrics specified in the Composed Security SLA and in case actual or potential violations of the security service level objectives are detected, corresponding alarms are raised and reaction recommendations are given.

Relationship to Described Use Case Widening the scope of the SLA towards security aspects demands the extension of the monitoring capabilities in this direction. We introduce some agents provided by the SecAP into our Security and Fleet modules to provide even more information from the application level into the correlations. We expect having a more precise misuse detection and enable more proactivity within the operations team.

4   Results Achieved

This section presents the results of the development of the Lufthansa Systems application using MUSA tools. We first provide a first description of general improvements provided by the application under development, according to the description in Sect. 3. Then, we analyze each MUSA tool and the impact they had in the development, deployment, and operation of our multi-cloud application. The use case application is developed using the design methods and technologies described in Sect. 3. A key finding is that using Domain Driven Design results in a better communication between domain specialists and software architects and developers. Until now, after the first few cycles of implementing the application, the involved software architects testify to a better solution, compared to previous developments in the same domain.

Regarding the usage of CQRS and event sourcing (ES), results are disputed. Using complex architectural styles for each and every component of the application is not efficient related to the complexity of the resulting systems and the maintainability. Complexity needs to be adjusted to the requirements of each specific problem. As we observed during the development process when handling some basic data, CQRS plus ES seemed to be very computationally intensive and could become a bottleneck. Debski et al. (2018) evaluated the used architecture regarding scalability and performance issues. They showed the successful implementation of their prototype (which was the predecessor of the use case application we describe). They proved the horizontal scalability and observed no change in the response time for the read model and the write model components of the CQRS pattern.

To evaluate the tools developed by MUSA, an evaluation team from Lufthansa Systems performed an analysis on the tools themselves and on their applicability to the needs from Lufthansa Systems. This user-centered evaluation was performed by means of questionnaires and informal interviews. There were several criteria to select the ideal respondents: they should not have significant knowledge about security, they should not be familiar with this project and, in particular, with the MUSA concept, and they should have different levels of experience, from junior to senior employees.

Following these criteria, the evaluation team was very heterogeneous regarding experience in cloud computing, security awareness and differed in their organizational and development roles as well. Furthermore, in the Lufthansa Systems evaluator team we had two special roles: a business decision maker and a user experience expert. Their contribution to the evaluation delivered very valuable thoughts and ideas.

At the beginning of the interview there was the possibility to express their professional opinion on multi-cloud solutions for airline applications. The evaluators see a clear advantage for having a multi-cloud environment in reducing the risk of unavailability of a service or a limitation of a data compromise compared to a single CSP setup. As a potential drawback, the evaluators mention the increased complexity of handling data integrity and managing security on multiple platforms.

```
internal component FleetReadModule {
    order: 6
    IP public: true

    provided communication ReadModelPort{port: 18080 }

    required communication KafkaPortReq{port: 9092 mandatory }
    required communication MongoDbPortReq{port: 27017 mandatory }
    required communication CentralGatewayPortReq{port: 80 mandatory }

    required host BasicUbuntuReqSet

    configuration ReadModelConfiguration{
                CHEF configuration manager ChefReadModelConfiguration {
                        cookbook: 'Containers'
                        recipe: 'nlsched-fleet-read_start'
                }
            }
        }
```

Fig. 4 Fleet read module described using CAMEL

MUSA Modeller The modeler was used to describe the complete application as a whole. The CAMEL model provides the team with an overview of the components and the connections between them. As an example, Fig. 4 presents a snippet of the CAMEL code written to describe the Fleet Read Module component with its connections to other components, the required cloud resource, and even the corresponding CHEF[5] cookbook for supporting its automatic deployment. All these language elements will be very important in subsequent steps of the integrated MUSA approach.

MUSA Modeller Evaluation The CAMEL model was very useful to gain more insight on our prototype, but by increasing the number of components the DevOps team can easily get lost. It would be very interesting to have some graphical interface to support this task, like an overview diagram about the components.

MUSA Risk Analysis and Decision Support Tool Each of the application components went through a detailed risk analysis process using the MUSA Risk Assessment tool and risk scenarios were formed based on a predefined threat catalogue based on data collected in the scope of the SPECS project. This threat catalogue listed 136 possible threats to the application component organized in six STRIDE categories. Each of the threats in the catalogue is mapped in a many-to-many relationship to a set of NIST 800-53 (NIST 2014) certificate based security controls which are suggested to the user as an initial set of controls needed to

---

[5]https://www.chef.io/chef/

Table 1 Example of threats found in a database component

STRIDE category	Threat
Spoofing identity	• Sensitive data exposure
Tampering with data	–
Repudiation	• Overly permissive cross-domain Whitelist
Information disclosure	• Token leakage via log files and HTTP referrers • Data breaches • Weak identity, credential & access management
Denial of service	–
Elevation of privileges	–

Table 2 Threats, security controls and their status in a database component

Threats	Security controls	Risk mitigation status
Token leakage via log files and HTTP referrers	IA-5 authentication management	Mitigated
Sensitive data exposure	SC-23 session authenticity SC-8 transmission confidentiality and integrity	Mitigated
Data breaches		Resolved
Weak identity, credential & access management	IA-5 authentication management	Accepted
Overly permissive cross-domain Whitelist	SA-13 trustworthiness	Mitigated

mitigate the selected threats. A total of 904 NIST security controls were used by the tool.

The process of getting to a final set of controls for the Lufthansa Systems application was iterative. The MUSA Risk Assessment allows the user to choose the appropriate threats and assess their importance in a structured manner guiding the user through series of simple sliders which affect the threat likelihood or its importance. Next, the user is asked to select security controls for each of the chosen threats. Initially, the set of suggested controls for the threat is presented, and it can be extended at will. As an example, Table 1 presents the threats found in a database component of the Lufthansa Systems application. In this table, threats are categorized following the six STRIDE categories mentioned before. Following with the analysis of this database component, Table 2 lists the security controls that have been chosen for each threat. Moreover, the mitigation status is also presented following the ROAM approach (Baah 2017), which considers four possible status: Resolved, Owned, Accepted and Mitigated. It is worth mentioning that the data breach threat need no security control since it has been resolved.

Guiding the user through such predefined process enables shortening the time of the application risk analysis as well as it helps in defining a more complete picture of the threats which are crucial for security of the application and threats which although apparently relevant, do not actually represent significant risk to the overall application requirements.

Once the risk specification was complete, the evaluation team was then asked to evaluate the MUSA Cloud Service Selection tool, where the output of the MUSA Risk Analysis tool was used in order to select the best providers for the selected application components. The selection of cloud service providers is a non-trivial process. It requires that the security controls offered by the providers are appropriately characterized and matched with the controls required by the application. The MUSA Cloud Service Selection uses the CCM Consensus Assessments Initiative Questionnaire (CAIQ)[6] standard and can consume all of the CCM catalogue data. We used a subset of the data for the testing with 36 available Cloud providers and four Infrastructures as a Service (IaaS) providers within the subset. These four cloud providers were presented to the evaluation team.

MUSA Risk Analysis and Decision Support Tool Evaluation The use of Kanban-style user interfaces has proven to be convenient for both the overall process and for the risk analysis itself. This not only allowed for smooth collaboration between the different participants in the DevOps team (application architects, developers, security experts, service administrators, and service business managers) but also helped in process agility. As a minor remark, evaluators requested tooltips and other types of guidance.

Besides, our architects, developers, and evaluators were emphasizing how much they learned only by using this tool. With the evolution of the tool, now we get very useful recommendations for which control mechanism to apply in case of the identified threats. This list of controls is much longer than the intuitive one made during former developments.

The time required to choose the adequate CSP has been considerably reduced since all the information is clearly presented and also linked with the risks detected. This way, it is possible to clearly picture on the level of security requirements fulfilment provided by each CSP. In general, the Cloud Service Selection tool performed as expected. Most non-positive comments from the evaluators were focused on the lack of documentation explaining how the tool ranks cloud service combinations, which is still in production.

In general, MUSA risk management approach was considered very adequate for our goals since it helped use case owners in Lufthansa Systems to manage risks during the development process without overloading or slowing it.

MUSA SLA Generator The SLA Generator was applied on some of the previously mentioned components. The SLA generation receives as input the application model created before, enriched with the detailed risk profile. This detailed risk profile already contains the proposed security controls to apply. In the SLA generator we

---

[6]https://cloudsecurityalliance.org/media/news/consensus-assessments-initiative-questionnaire-caiq-v-3-review/

chose the corresponding metrics, which need to be monitored in order to gain a feedback about the satisfaction of the controls offered by the CSP.

MUSA SLA Generator Evaluation The SLA Generator got a very positive feedback since this tool gives the end user a lot of information on threats, security controls and metrics and therefore it draws attention to unknown security aspects for application design. Nevertheless, this abundance of information can be seen as a drawback for novice users.

Security SLAs are a new approach that we did not follow before, but we have seen their potential to be an instrument to ease the relationships with our clients. The business aspects of applications could be discussed on top of the formalized collection of security guarantees offered by the application and stated in the Security SLA. This will improve the transparency of the controls offered and how they relate to the ones offered by the cloud providers in the chain.

MUSA Distributed Deployer The deployer provided the DevOps team with a deployment script which contains all the information, configurations and instructions needed to execute the deployment of the multi-cloud components. In our case, the MUSA Deployer tool used the CHEF tool in order to orchestrate and automatize the process. According to the Chef architecture, we have developed a Chef Cookbook with many Chef Recipes in order to automate the installation process of the prototype application. In particular, for each component, a couple of recipes has been written: the first recipe allows to copy all the provided software artefact inside the target machine and install the component, while the second one handles the start-up of the component itself. It is also worth mentioning that the prototype uses the Docker software containerization platform, so the first Chef Cookbook necessary to set up the environment, is the one that takes care of installing and starting Docker on the target machine. As an example, Fig. 5 presents part of the deployment script of our prototype.

MUSA Distributed Deployer Evaluation The MUSA deployer seems to fit our initial expectations. The usability of the UI is very high, although the messages, instructions and the resulting deployment implementation plan are not easily understandable by the user. Nevertheless, we believe that using this tool we expect faster and more controlled deployments.

MUSA Security Assurance Platform The MUSA Security Assurance Platform was used for retrieving the information from the agents and showing to the users the information on continuously monitored metrics defined in the components' SLAs. The monitoring annotation library has been integrated into the prototype application components and selection of basic events for security has been done. Nevertheless, the complete list of events is still an ongoing task.

MUSA Security Assurance Platform Evaluation The MUSA SecAP has still a limited functionality by means of monitorable metrics. However, we found the

```
        sla_id : 135798642

        creation_time : 1481472793

        monitoring_core_ip : value

        monitoring_core_port : null

    ▼  csps [1]

        ▼  0  {2}

            ▼  iaas {4}

                    provider : OpenStack

                    zone : RegionOne

                    user : ubuntu

                    network : 38a20d88-71a0-4880-9436-43b025a8b18d

            ▶  pools [1]

        ▶  slos [0]

        ▶  measurements [0]

        ▶  annotations [0]
```

Fig. 5 General view of the Implementation plan of Lufthansa Systems prototype

capabilities of this tool very promising and we expect even more new correlations to be identified in between observing events from different layers and recognised misuse of the system. The integration with common monitoring tools might be an issue though: the willingness of using multiple different tools for monitoring is still questionable. During discussions with research partners in the MUSA project we got some new ideas about observable activities and the corresponding mitigation actions. We introduced new capabilities into our application which can be activated by the enforcement mechanisms of the Security Assurance Platform.

The MUSA Security Assurance Platform also brings the opportunity to continuously monitor the Security SLA of the application to demonstrate its fulfilment to the clients and reduce discrepancies. Another interesting feature of the MUSA Security Assurance Platform is the integrated management of enforcement agents such as identity manager, access control policies enforcement mechanisms and vulnerability scanners. The integration of enforcement agents in the prototype is a path that is being explored to ensure the dynamicity of the reaction measures when a SLO in the Security SLA is not fulfilled.

MUSA Tools Evaluation Summary

The evaluation allowed us to gather relevant information, in particular for the different MUSA tools and framework. Our application consists of multiple components communicating with each other. With this complexity, the capabilities supported by the chosen cloud approach were essential. Some example of key requirements in this direction were cloud services and providers offering component lifecycle management, load balancing, service lookup, central logging, etc. Multiple

PaaS solutions were analysed and all those platforms seemed to fit our expectations. It is worth mentioning that this evaluation study was performed using an initial version of the MUSA tools. Thus, some new functionalities were still not available.

5   Lessons Learned

As we have seen in the Sections above, in our use case the MUSA framework was successfully used for (a) identifying the cloud providers that best fulfilled application security requirements based on a new mechanism for assessing risk using agile approaches, (b) creating SLAs based on the detected security requirements, (c) automatically deploying the prototype application components using the identified providers and (d) monitoring the application aspects related to security and to control compliance with agreed SLAs. From the development of this use case we can extract the following lessons learned.

Impact of Using a Multi-Cloud Architecture
Cloud computing has passed the point where its adoption was in question. It is a widely used strategy providing infrastructure and applications as a service. It is so ubiquitous that many users do not even realize that their applications are cloud-based. Cloud architectures have also evolved from a single public or private cloud into a hybrid cloud that consists of private and public cloud infrastructures. The next stage of evolution of the cloud is the multi-cloud application. Although multi-cloud architectures can support agility and speed, there are two main challenges or barriers to adoption: interoperability between services in a multi-cloud architecture and security. Both of them suffer from the lack of standardization.

Correct Adoption of New Technologies
The introduction of new technologies like event sourcing, CQRS or the adoption of cloud computing-based infrastructure solutions demand training. It is important not to underestimate this necessary training. Also, an effective communication within the teams and between management and development teams is crucial, accompanied by a profound change management practice.

The introduction of new technologies like the MUSA framework requires the development team taking a risk to fail during the first steps. The effort in solving these startup-problems can be compensated for by a wealth of new possibilities that these tools provide to the developer or, in our case, to the security experts designing these aspects for our application. The direct support by the researchers of the MUSA team and the opportunity to share experience and know-how with other multi-cloud developers were very helpful.

Application Architectural Decisions
For the development of the use case prototype, the setup of the evaluation scenarios and the deployment of the application artifacts, the general rule of thumb to start with a simple setup and evolve it to a more complex setup was (as usual) very valuable.

We started with plain Java archives first, then we used Docker containers and step by step we enriched with additional infrastructure components to manage the containers, to collect metrics, etc. It is very important not to reinvent the wheel and, for example, use proven technology stacks such as Docker, Kubernetes,[7] Marathon[8] or the ELK stack.[9]

Choosing the Correct Providers

The selection of cloud service providers is a non-trivial process. It requires that the security controls offered by the providers are appropriately characterized. Consequently, there is a clear need for standards for cloud services description including offered security features, in order to be able to compare heterogeneous and independent cloud services.

MUSA framework helped in this task by offering tools for analyzing the risks and specifying the security requirements of our components. In fact, the risk driven security specification is one of the unique selling propositions of MUSA compared to other solutions. The tool can also compute the service match-making with the security controls specified and ranks the cloud service combinations by requirements fulfilment degree. As indicated above, having a clear characterization of the providers is also very enriching form the team's perspective since it can offer details and insights on the services that had not been considered before.

SecDevOps: Security Embedded in DevOps Is Worth It

Another innovation brought by the MUSA framework is the integrated SecDevOps (Security Development Operation) approach, which addresses the needs of multi-cloud applications by considering security and privacy as primary design tenets, thus, including security and privacy requirements and by-design practices since the very beginning of the development.

Implementing such a SecDevOps approach is of course a cultural change in organizing the teams, the work and the responsibilities. It needs to be accompanied by a thorough change management process to reorganize the existing organization of developing, delivering and operating an application and the necessary infrastructure.

The used architecture, built up on microservice-based components, supports this approach in a perfect manner. Specific teams are responsible for development and operation of a (range) of component(s). This approach reduces communication overhead between different organization units (i.e. Development, Operations) which is mostly accompanied by pushing responsibilities for mistakes back and forth between them.

Also, with SecDevOps, the responsibility for handling the security considerations of these components is within the scope of the team. This is an advantage, because the development team itself knows best of the requirements, the architecture and the

---

[7]https://kubernetes.io/

[8]https://mesosphere.github.io/marathon/

[9]https://www.elastic.co/products

technologies used for a specific application component (i.e. a microservice). SecDevOps is no longer a marketing buzzword of tool developers (Mohan and Othmane 2016).

The lessons learned will be used to accompany the further implementation of the SecDevOps approach for more and more products in the near future. It shows that it is even more valuable to include security topics together with the regular DevOps methodology.

In conclusion, multi-cloud computing is an opportunity for organizations to free themselves from vendor lock-in and develop a reusable and flexible approach for business process support. It increases complexity and exposes new cumulative vulnerabilities that provide more opportunity for software companies to partner with their customers to manage and secure an emerging new architecture.

Acknowledgements This work is supported by the European Commission through the MUlti-cloud Secure Applications (MUSA) project under Project ID: 644429.

References

Alberts CJ, Dorofee A (2002) Managing information security risks: the Octave approach. Addison-Wesley Longman Publishing Co., Boston, MA

Baah A (2017) Agile quality assurance. Bookbaby, Cork

Debski A, Szczepanik B, Malawski M, Spahr S, Muthig D (2018) A scalable, reactive architecture for cloud applications. IEEE Softw 35(2):62–71

Lufthansa Systems (2017) Airline forum 2017: Lufthansa Systems takes airline customers into the digital world. Available via https://www.lhsystems.com/article/airline-forum-2017-lufthansa-systems-takes-airline-customers-digital-world. Accessed Dec 2017

Microsoft (2005) The STRIDE threat model. Available via https://msdn.microsoft.com/en-us/library/ee823878(v=cs.20).aspx. Accessed Aug 2017

MODAClouds Project (2012) MOdel-Driven Approach for design and execution of applications on multiple Clouds. FP7-ICT-2011.1.2. 2012–2015. Available via http://www.modaclouds.eu/project/. Accessed Aug 2017

Mohan V, Othmane L (2016) SecDevOps: is it a marketing buzzword? Department of Computer Science, Technische Universität Darmstadt, Darmstadt

NIST (2014) NIST Special Publication 800-53 Revision 4. Available via https://nvd.nist.gov/800-53. Accessed Aug 2017

North Bridge (2013) The future of cloud computing 3rd annual survey, Available via http://www.northbridge.com/2013-cloud-computing-survey. Accessed Apr 2017

OWASP Foundation (2013) OWASP top 10 – 2013. Technical Report. OWASP Foundation. Available via https://www.owasp.org/index.php/Main_Page. Accessed Aug 2017

PaaSage Project (2012) Model based cloud platform upperware. FP7-ICT-2011.1.2. 2012–2016. Available via http://www.paasage.eu/. Accessed Aug 2017

Rios E, Iturbe E, Palacios MC (2017) Self-healing multi-cloud application modelling. In: Proceedings of the 12th international conference on availability, reliability and security, p 93. ACM

Balázs Somoskői works as a Software Architect at Lufthansa Systems. After obtaining his masters in Electrical engineering and applied informatics in year 2000, he worked as a software developer mostly in telecommunication and airline industry area. He later worked as lead developer and software architect. His main focus is on middleware solutions for application integration and software security solutions for standalone and cloud applications within the company. He has been involved in EU funded research and development project and now also acting as technology advisor of the CTO.

Stefan Spahr works as a senior software architect for airline applications and as a CTO advisor for Cloud solutions and research projects at Lufthansa Systems GmbH & Co. KG in Berlin, Germany. Before his current job he worked as a software engineer, a development- and implementation-project manager and as a database expert in different departments of the company. He participated in different EU FP7 and H2020 projects on Cloud computing. His main professional interests are Cloud computing architectures and related (emerging) technologies, domain driven design, distributed systems and big data. Stefan has been with Lufthansa Systems over 20 years and holds a Graduate Degree in Computer Science (Dipl.-Inform. FH).

Erkuden Rios is R&D project manager of Cybersecurity and Safety team within the ICT Division of Tecnalia. She is specialized in trust and security engineering technologies and has worked in a number of large European and Spanish national projects on the subject such as ANIKETOS, SWEPT, TACIT, RISC, CIPHER and SHIELDS. Erkuden collaborates with technology platforms and forums such as ECSO and the Spanish Technology Platform on Trust & Security—eSEC. After obtaining her MSc in Telecommunication Engineering at the University of Basque Country (Spain), she worked for Ericsson Spain for 6 years before joining Tecnalia in 2003.

Oscar Ripollés received his degree in Computer Engineering in 2004 and his Ph.D. in 2009 at the Universitat Jaume I in Castellon (Spain). He has also been a researcher at the Université de Limoges (France) and at the Universidad Politécnica de Valencia (Spain). Dr. Ripollés has more than 60 publications in the computer science field, which cover different topics but are mainly focused on computer graphics and computer vision. Prior to joining CA Technologies, he was the software manager of Neuroelectrics in Barcelona (Spain), where he was also researching in neuroimaging.

Jacek Dominiak is a perpetually knowledge-hungry Principal Researcher at CA Strategic Research team on a quest without destination, to suffice his inner desire to know the all the "nuts and bolts" of ever changing technology. His research interests include data analytics, IoT, model based decision systems, visualization, critical system based IT infrastructure management and UI interactions and question asking. Jacek has close to 15 years of industry experience across mission critical Unix-based clusters operating in aviation, state and banking industries as well as enterprise and financial programing. Jacek enjoys innovation across all the industry axis from the initial design time until the final delivery. Jacek career began as a Network Analyst for the UK National Health Service, from where he moved on to be a Unix Engineer and Delivery Lead at HP RMC, working with state level and industry leading corporations across the range of industries. Jacek has been involved in number of projects across treating about multi-clouds and security, IoT, co-authored several patents and publications.

Tamas Cserveny is CTO-Advisor at Lufthansa Systems. During his professional career he spent most of the time with the Netline product line of Lufthansa Systems. During the last years he was working on creating the new Netline/ ProfitLine product-line architecture using DDD, Event Sourcing and CQRS.

Peter Balint is an Architect at Nokia R&D. Peter has more than 10 years' experience in Infrastructure security and infrastructure design in different industries (airline, financial and telecommunication). Earlier he worked as a CTO Advisor at Lufthansa, during this time Peter was involved in cloud migration project and in infrastructure security activities. Peter obtained Bachelor Degree and Master Degree in Széchenyi István University, MBA degree in University of Pannonia. In September of 2016 Peter got enrolled for Széchenyi István University PhD program, for a period of 4 years. Peter's research areas are cloud, SDN and IPV6.

Peter Matthews is a Research Scientist in the Office of the CTO at CA Technologies. Peter is based in the UK working both as a contributing researcher and coordinator of research, collaborating with CA Technologies R&D departments, European Research Institutes and Academia. Peter has more than 40 years of IT experience ranging from mainframe programming, Unix development and relational databases to secure cloud computing, DevOps and management of information systems. Peter's research work has been concerned with leading edge technology for a major proportion of that time. Projects have included machine learning algorithms for soccer clubs, multi-level secure database systems and object oriented application infrastructures. Peter has leveraged his experience by participating in the CA Technologies corporate strategy team. He has led groups investigating the influence of macro social, political and economic trends on future technology. As part of the strategy team and a topic leader Peter's work has influenced the technical direction of CA Technologies in several areas.

Eider Iturbe is R&D engineer of Cybersecurity and Safety team within Tecnalia. She is specialized in trust and security engineering technologies and has broadened its expertise through her participation in different European and Spanish national projects such as MUSA, ANIKETOS, SWEPT, TACIT and CIPHER. Eider graduated in Telecommunication Engineering from the University of the Basque Country (Spain) and in the European Master in project management at the same university. Before joining Tecnalia in 2009, she worked for software consultancy firms where she acquired management skills and a great technical expertise in the security field.

Victor Muntés-Mulero is VP, Strategic Research and member of CA Strategic Research. He is responsible for leading research projects and coordinate the corporate research strategy to impact the strategic direction of CA Technologies products and services. His duties include identifying opportunities within the company that can be transformed into research relationships performed in collaboration with university faculty and students. He has more than 65 peer-reviewed research publications, as well as several granted patents. He is also the author of a book titled "Genetic Query Optimization for Large Databases", as well as several book chapters. Prior to joining CA Technologies, he was a professor at the Universitat Politècnica de Catalunya (UPC), where he performed research related to managing very large data volumes. His PhD studies were funded by IBM through its Centre for Advanced Studies (Toronto, Canada), and were focused on very large join query optimization for relational databases.

Digital Technologies for Ordering and Delivering Fashion: How Baur Integrates the Customer's Point of View

Daniel Baier, Alexandra Rese, Nikita Nonenmacher, Steve Treybig, and Benjamin Bressem

Abstract

(a) **Situation faced**: Digital technologies such as augmented/virtual reality, chatbots, image processing, messaging services, or speech recognition have the potential to fundamentally change ordering and delivery in online-fashion shops: Disrupting customer interaction formats like attended shopping, curated shopping, scanned shopping, or virtual fitting may increase customer experience, satisfaction, and sales. However, when smaller amounts of money are available, the question arises as to in which of them to invest. Baur, a major German online fashion retailer, is faced with this question and wants to integrate the customer's point of view in the site engineering process explicitly.

(b) **Action taken**: Secondary research as well as workshops with experts and customers were applied to generate lists of aspects to be improved and potential improvements by digital technologies in the company's ordering and delivery process. A representative sample of 15,865 customers was confronted with these aspects and potential improvements and asked to evaluate them. 9722 customers returned completed questionnaires. Many of them additionally included detailed comments. The survey data were analyzed and the improvements were prioritized for implementation. The

D. Baier (✉) · A. Rese
University of Bayreuth, Bayreuth, Germany
e-mail: daniel.baier@uni-bayreuth.de; alexandra.rese@uni-bayreuth.de

N. Nonenmacher
empiriecom GmbH & Co KG and Baur Group, Burgkunstadt, Germany
e-mail: nikita.nonenmacher@empiriecom.com

S. Treybig · B. Bressem
Baur Versand GmbH & Co KG and Baur Group, Burgkunstadt, Germany
e-mail: steve.treybig@baur.de; benjamin.bressem@baur.de

© Springer International Publishing AG, part of Springer Nature 2019
N. Urbach, M. Röglinger (eds.), *Digitalization Cases*, Management for Professionals, https://doi.org/10.1007/978-3-319-95273-4_4

survey methodology yielded recommendations for action to such an extent that it is now integrated in the company's site engineering process.

(c) **Results achieved**: Overall, the survey showed that the customers are satisfied with the company's current ordering and delivery process. However, with regard to selection, packaging, and delivery several changes are necessary. Many customers rated potential improvements like virtual fitting and curated shopping as attractive whereas most of them were indifferent with regard to scanned shopping, personalized areas, attended shopping, or C2C inspiration. The survey research resulted in valuable input for the company what actions should be taken in terms of digital technologies to implement. In addition, the company received valuable information on how to improve the ongoing site engineering process.

(d) **Lessons learned**: Improvements aimed at integrating digital technologies—in particular virtual fitting by relying on virtual reality as well as curated shopping by making use of chatbots and messaging services—were rated by many customers as attractive and should also be implemented by other online fashion retailers. Other digital technology-based improvements are of lower priority. From a methodological point of view, customer surveys—if developed carefully and integrated in the company's site engineering process—provide valuable support when selecting digital technologies for implementing improvements.

1   Introduction

Baur, the company under study in this paper, is the core company of Baur Group, an essential part of Otto Group, Hamburg. In the business year 2016/2017 (March to February), Otto Group's sales accounted for €12.5 bill. worldwide with 56% ordered online (see Otto Group 2017). Products with a focus on fashion and furniture are available via more than 100 online-shops in more than 30 countries. The Baur Group, Burgkunstadt, has more than 3900 employees and generated €667 mill. in sales in the business year 2016/2017. The company's history goes back to 1925, when Baur was founded as one of Germany's first mail order companies. Today, 80% of Baur's sales are ordered online, placing the online shop baur.de (see Fig. 1) among the Top-10 in Germany when it comes to sales figures. The target customers are women between the ages of 40 and 55, and accordingly products are offered with a focus on fashion and furniture. baur.de has received numerous awards as one of the "best" online shops in Germany from a customer's and expert's point of view (e.g. Computerbild, Focus, IFH Köln). empiriecom GmbH & Co KG, also a Baur Group member, is responsible for site engineering at baur.de and more than 40 other online shops within the Otto Group.

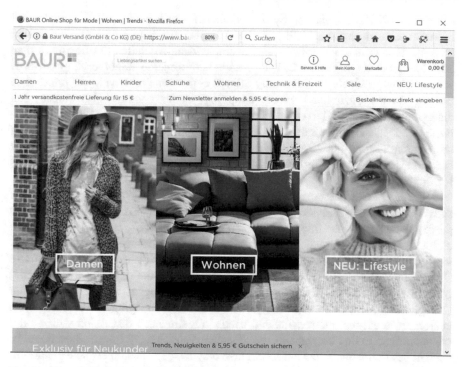

Fig. 1 Landing page of baur.de (October 10, 2017)

Baur offers its products in a constantly growing, but highly competitive market: Online selling of goods to consumers in Germany had an estimated sales volume of €52.7 bill. in 2016 and a 12.5% growth compared to 2015 (BEVH 2017). The relevance of the online channel becomes obvious when looking at fashion as it is the commodity group with the highest online sales volume in Germany (€11.2 bill. in 2016, BEVH 2017). In this overall (offline and online together) stagnating market with 0.7% growth from 2015 to 2016, the larger online players (especially the Top-3 Amazon, Otto Group, Zalando) have expanded their market shares to the detriment of smaller retailers who are struggling to survive (IFH Köln 2017). So, e.g., in 2016, Zalando's fashion sales in Germany, Austria, and Switzerland accounted for €1.8 bill. with 14.8% growth compared to 2015 (Zalando 2017) whereas offline retailers such as Laurèl, SinnLeffers, Wöhrl, and Zero dramatically lost sales volume and were threatened with insolvency proceedings. In total, the online sales volume shares in 2016 are estimated at 21% for men's fashion and 29% for women's fashion and they are still expected to increase (IFH Köln 2017).

The reasons for this ongoing success of the online channel are manifold (see, e.g. Baier and Stüber 2010; Stüber 2013; BEVH 2017; IFH Köln 2017): Online fashion shopping saves time and takes comfort a step further. The customer can order products at home or in the office, even at friends or when travelling. The shops are always open, guidance and advice on the ordering and delivery process are offered 24 h/7 days supported by self-explanatory websites/apps, call-centers, and recommendation engines. Online (fashion) shops have huge ranges (e.g. compared to the offerings in small towns). For example Zalando claims to offer more than 200,000 products (Zalando 2017). Detailed information about each product is available and products are frequently offered at the same or even lower prices than offline. On the other hand, online shopping—at least today—also comes with disadvantages compared to offline shopping. Fit, combinability, and haptic perception are difficult to check online. Products have to be sent to the customer's home. If the customer does not like them he/she sends them back, a frequent practice accompanied by extra effort and disappointment for the customer and high costs for the retailer.

All online fashion retailers are aware of these problems. To preserve customer satisfaction, loyalty, and consistently ensure the company's enduring success, they permanently seek to improve the customer interface. Here, (new) digital technologies such as virtual/augmented reality, chatbots, image analysis, or messaging services are welcome enablers for improvements (see, e.g. Pantano 2015): Virtual/augmented reality can help customers to check the fit or the combinability of clothing by seeing them worn by a video-recording of oneself or an avatar ("magical mirror", "virtual fitting"). Chatbots and messaging services can help customers to express their wants and needs in a simulated discussion with a sales consultant and to find the right apparel ("attended shopping"). Image analysis can be used to determine one's size or to recognize products: The customers take pictures of people wearing clothes they like, send them to the retailer, and receive shopping recommendations ("scanned shopping", "curated shopping"). With this background of vast digital technological options, the question arises as to which digital technologies and potential improvements an online fashion retailer should invest.

In this paper we describe how Baur solved this problem. A project team, consisting of members of the chair of innovation and dialog marketing at the University of Bayreuth together with a research group of students as well as employees from Baur and empiriecom was formed. They examined how Baur could disclose the customer's point of view with regard to potentially disrupting digital technological options in the ordering and delivery process and developed an instrument for this purpose. The new instrument—a customer survey—was prototypically applied and proved to be so successful in deciding on potential improvements that it is now an essential part of Baur's site engineering process. We present below how the instrument was developed, implemented, and utilized.

2   Situation Faced

At Amazon, the number 1 global online retailer, it is believed "that advances in technology ... will increase customer experience on the internet" (Amazon 2017, p. 2). Consequently, Amazon invests large amounts of their sales volume (2016 worldwide sales: $ 136.0 bill.) in developing, implementing, and testing potential digital technology-based improvements (2016: $ 16.1 bill., Amazon 2017, p. 28).

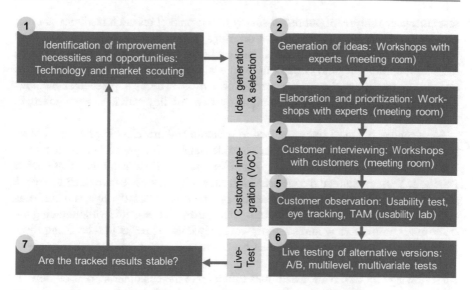

Fig. 2 (Idealized) site engineering process at Baur with seven stages (adapted from Lauber 2013, p. 117)

For example in 2013, Amazon checked for 1976 potential improvements to its website using web labs (Amazon 2014 p. 5). Web labs are "live" A/B-tests exposing large parts of the audience to alternative versions of websites (e.g. the original and a modified version). As a result, various performance measures can be obtained (e.g. average visit length, conversion rate). The aim is to support the decision on whether a modified version should go "live" or not (see, e.g., Baier et al. 2015 or Baier and Rese 2017 for testing improved navigation menus and presentation formats of a major German online fashion shop).

Smaller online retailers, such as Baur, are more limited in their usage of web labs. Due to considerably smaller sales volumes (2016/2017: €667 mill.) and more traditional (not capital market value oriented) principles, Baur is only able to invest a comparatively small amount of money into developing, implementing, and testing improvements. According to Lauber (2013, p.117), the former CEO of empiriecom, only 4–6 web labs are feasible per year for a typical German online fashion retailer like Baur due to the costs for designing and prototypically implementing improvements as well as restricted time slots for testing. As a consequence, Baur—like many other online retailers—has implemented a funnel- or stage-gate-like site engineering process that permanently helps to generate huge numbers of improvement ideas but is also able to reduce them stage-by-stage to a small number of candidates that have to be implemented and tested "live".

Figure 2 describes this site engineering process for baur.de in an idealized form with seven stages (adapted from Lauber 2013): In a first stage, improvement necessities and opportunities are identified (and defined). The use of technology and market scouting is one way of achieving this objective. Baur applies secondary research (e.g. analysis of published surveys from market research institutes or other companies, overviews of competitor offerings, technological forecasts, complaint overviews concerning own offerings) and knowledge transfer from other companies (inside or outside the Otto Group), universities, research institutes, and start-ups. In addition, from time to time, primary research is used. Overall, sophisticated methods including process mining, data mining, or web mining activities are applied to available data.

A second and a third stage are used to generate and preselect improvement ideas based on this input. Experts inside and outside Baur are integrated in these activities which aim at develop ideas and prioritize them. It should be mentioned that Lauber (2013, p. 120) has studied the prioritization capability of these experts at Baur over a 2-year period: He documented the expert predictions of "best" improvement ideas and later compared them to results from "live" tests. The experts (without taking the customer's point of view into account) were only able to predict the "best" improvement ideas in 20–40% of the documented cases.

In the fourth and fifth stage, small samples of customers are engaged in interviewing and observation activities to integrate the customer's point of view. A main advantage of performing customer interviewing is that the improvements under study do not have to be implemented so far and it is possible to test several of them within one interview. However, in order to receive reliable and valid results, the improvements have to be presented in the "voice of the customer (VoC)". That means that they must be explained to the customer precisely in her/his words, using (if possible) visualizations and animations. After finishing the customer interviewing stage, the "best" improvements so far are implemented for customer observation in the usability lab. Small samples of customers are tracked when visiting modified websites in a laboratory setting (using e.g. eye tracking, mouse tracking, and TAM interviewing, see also Baier et al. 2015; Schreiber and Baier 2015; Baier and Rese 2017). The process of implementing and observing should be repeated until the respondents say they are highly satisfied. Again, the customer's reactions help to reduce the number of potential improvements in the funnel. Finally, in the sixth and seventh stage, the potential improvements go "live", i.e. larger parts of the audience are confronted with the modified websites. In the sixth stage, A/B-tests are used to choose "best" improvements which then have to demonstrate their performance across all customers in the seventh stage.

As with other stage-gate approaches for generating and selecting "best" candidates, the above process helps to find the "best" improvements in an efficient manner: The number of candidates decreases by eliminating potentially ineffective ones whereas the potentially effectiveness of and the testing costs for the remaining ones increase. Lauber (2013, p. 110) reports that 5 years after introducing such a process at Baur, the conversion rate increased by +191% and the contribution to earnings by +699%. However, the quality of the instruments used in the seven stages is crucial for the overall performance. Faced with the huge number of potential improvements enabled by digital technologies, the restricted amount of money that Baur can use for its site engineering process, and the prioritization inaccuracies that had been documented, the project team decided to rethink the instruments and to consider a representative large-scale customer survey (in addition to the common practice of customer interviewing and observation in the usability lab) to better integrate the customer's point of view.

The project team was well aware of the fact that consumer surveys are in the center of a fierce debate by practitioners and scientists: On one side, some authors declare that "consumer surveys are dead" (see e.g. Ganeshan 2016). They argue that nowadays—with efficient tools to develop and spread questionnaires electronically (e.g. Qualtrics)—the consumer is plagued by and annoyed with too many badly composed and irrelevant surveys. Consequently, it is nearly impossible to receive response rates higher than 1% without substantial incentives. However, if substantial incentives are granted, the focus of the respondents is on "earning money", resulting in ill-considered, sometimes random answers. In both cases uncontrollable errors and misleading results are to be expected. On the other side, some authors e.g. Swinscoe (2016), totally disagree. They argue that many consumers and in particular customers are willing to give valuable feedback when the respondents are motivated and the questionnaires are carefully designed. Swinscoe (2016, p. 3)—similar to many other authors—summarizes these requirements with the motto "...let them speak. But, do it simply, do it promptly, do it freely and make sure that you act on it quickly!"

3   Action Taken

The project's schedule consisted of four phases: First, the ordering and delivery process at Baur was analyzed from a customer's perspective against the background of the following questions: Which are the main steps, which aspects may increase or decrease customer satisfaction, which improvements could be enabled by digital technologies? Second, interviewing techniques were evaluated and adapted for collecting the customer's point of view. Third, questionnaires following Swiscoe's (2016) recommendations were designed and distributed among Baur's customers. Fourth, the responses were aggregated and checked for being representative, reliable, and valid. The final results are discussed in the next section.

In the first phase (preselection of improvement aspects and potential improvements based on digital technologies throughout the ordering and delivery process) secondary research as well as expert and customer workshops were employed. The project team analyzed the website of Baur and their competitors, published comparisons of the quality of German online fashion retailers' ordering and delivery processes (e.g. UPS 2015; DHL 2016; hmmh 2016), published customer satisfaction surveys dealing with online fashion retailing (e.g. IFH Köln 2017), technological forecasts, customer studies, and complaint overviews from Baur's customer database. As a result, two lists of aspects to be improved and potential improvements were developed. Two small workshops with experts ($n = 3$, $n = 4$) and two with customers ($n = 12$, $n = 10$) were used for completing the lists (see Fig. 3).

Steps	A. Display	B. Selection	C. Payment	D. Delivery	E. Wrapping	F. Return delivery	G. After sales service
Improvement aspects	Availability info (A1), Catwalk (A2), Mobile app (A3)	Curated shop. (B1), Size recommend. (B2), Product recom. (B3), 1-click (B4), Mail confirmation (B5), Order swiftness (B6)	Payment options swiftness (C1-C8)	Delivery costs (D1), Delivery flatrate (D2), Delivery status information (D3), Delivery swiftness (D4)	Wrapping funct. (E1), Wrapping material (E2), Wrapping design (E3), Wrapping recyclability (E4)	Return form simpl. (F1), Home-based return (F2), Return info by mail (F3), Refund swiftn. (F4), Return swiftn. (F5), Ext. return deadline (F6)	Careful personal data usage (G1), Service channel accessibility (G2-G6), Newsletter design (G7)
Potential improvements	Story telling, Style recommendations, Creative filtering option, 3D product presentation, Selectable presenter, Catwalks, Availability information	Virtual fitting (B1), Attended shop. (B2), Curated shop. (B3), Scanned shop. (B4), Personalized area (B5), C2C inspiration (B6)	Amazon payment (C1), Abonnement commerce, High number of payment opt., Innovative payment options	Free shipping (D1), Same-day-deliver. (D2), Fixed-time-deliver. (D3), Car-trunk-delivery, Automated delivery, Extended tracking	Gift wrapping (E1), Advert. brochures (E2), Recyclable wrapping, Wrap. ret., High quality wrap.design, High quality wrap. mat.	Home-based-return delivery (F1), Car trunk return delivery, Shop-based-return delivery, Extended return deadline	High number of service channels, Fast service channels, Bonus system (G1), Personalized newsletter

Fig. 3 Steps, improvement aspects, and potential improvements based on digital technologies for Baur's ordering and delivery process

Both lists follow the steps in an online fashion company's ordering and delivery process from a customer's perspective as similarly discussed in published studies (e.g. UPS 2015; DHL 2016; hmmh 2016): A customer visits a shop and is informed about the shop and available products (A. Display). He/she selects some of them (B. Selection). Then, he/she chooses a payment option (C. Payment). Later on, the products are delivered (D. Delivery), the customer comes into contact with the package and its content (E. Packaging). If he/she does not like some of the ordered products he/she has the option to return them (F. Return delivery). If questions arise, customer service is contacted (G. After sales service).

For the list of improvement aspects hmmh's (2016) benchmarking study of 30 online fashion retailers with respect to fulfillment offered major inputs: Aspects such as speed (process time from ordering to delivery), customer friendliness, number of payment options, delivery costs, packaging material, service, and return delivery costs were investigated and compared. Objective measures were used in this benchmarking study. So, the number of days needed for product delivery and payment options were counted and experts were asked to rate the customer friendliness of the shop. It should be mentioned that Baur was not included in the hmmh (2016) benchmarking study. In addition, the focus was not on improved customer interaction formats based on new digital technologies, and the customer's viewpoint was not integrated. For example, the question whether "good" packaging is equally important compared to many payment options cannot be answered credibly by the results of this study.

The list of potential improvements based on digital technologies was determined by investigating innovative online shops, press releases of planned activities by retailers, scientific publications, as well as studies (e.g. IFH Köln 2017). In addition, the results of former research projects at the chair in Bayreuth were included. Table 1 displays a sample of potential improvements for the Selection step and how these improvements could be explained to a customer. As the potential numbers of steps, aspects, and potential improvements are (much) higher than the results presented in Fig. 3, together with Baur a further reduction was performed to only provide realistic and expected important ones. Figure 3 presents the final list—after diverse condensing and diminishing rounds within the team and together with the experts. Later, for the questionnaire, again a reduction was necessary. Therefore, only the improvements with numbers (e.g. B1, B2) were used in the customer surveys.

In the second phase (design of interviewing techniques) it became apparent that the instrument had to serve two different objectives: On the one hand (as needed in the first stage of the site engineering process) the instrument should be able to prioritize improvement aspects throughout Baur's ordering and delivery process. The standard method for this purpose is the Importance-Performance-Analysis (abbreviated to: IPA, originally proposed by Martilla and James 1977, reexamined and extended under a service quality perspective by Cronin and Taylor 1992 and Löffler and Baier 2013). The IPA approach consists of determining which aspects (also: attributes, components, dimensions, factors, steps within a process) may influence the customer's satisfaction with a company's offering and then asking a sample of customers to rate these aspects. Usually, the ratings are collected using

Table 1 Potential improvements based on digital technologies for the selection step in Baur's ordering and delivery process

Potential improvement	Explanation to the customer	Enabling digital technologies
Virtual fitting	You can try on apparel on a computer-generated model to determine the right size and compare outfits. The model can be edited and adapted according to your wishes.	Virtual/augmented reality
Attended shopping	You can chat with a consultant individually when making an order (e.g., style, size, color advice).	Chat bots, messenger services
Curated shopping	After an individual style consultation (via an online questionnaire and/or telephone call) or by sending photos with desired apparel to us, you receive proposals according to your wishes.	Chat bots, messenger services, image analysis
Scanned shopping	Your body measurements could be determined via a webcam to suggest suitable apparel.	Image analysis
Personalized area	You have an individually configured area on the website with personalized purchase recommendations. This is done on the basis of stored data, previous orders, your preferences and style.	Chat bots, messenger services
C2C inspiration	You have the option of presenting newly acquired outfits in the form of photos on the website of baur. de. Other customers can let themselves be inspired and buy these outfits.	Image analysis

so-called Likert scales. So e.g. the respondents are asked to rate the importance on a 7-point-scale ranging from 1 = "not at all important" to 7 = "very important" and the performance on a 7-point-scale ranging from 1 = "not at all satisfied with this aspect at the company" to 7 = "very satisfied with this aspect at the company". Averaging the answers across the respondents then results in mean importance and mean performance ratings of the sample. A two-dimensional grid where the aspects are plotted according to their performance and importance helps to derive norm strategies for the aspects: "Keep up good work" (if performance and importance ratings are high), "Concentrate here" (if performance ratings are low but importance ratings are high), "Low priority" (if performance and importance ratings are low), "Possible overkill" (if performance ratings are high but importance ratings are low). The IPA approach is widely used in practice (see Löffler and Baier 2013) due to its simplicity. Löffler and Baier (2013) proposed combining this approach with collecting comments from the respondents in a similar fashion to the so-called Critical Incident Technique (abbreviated to: CIT, Flanagan 1954). There, the respondents are asked to remember positive and negative experiences regarding these aspects. The additional collection of comments is done for two reasons: First, the free text brings about more insight: Which issues were discussed most frequently? Second, these comments can be used to validate the IPA results: The number of positive and negative comments together reflects the importance of an aspect, the difference between the number of positive and the number of negative comments reflects the company's performance. When examining the technology acceptance of augmented reality improvements for online fashion and furniture shopping (see e.g. Rese et al. 2014, 2017; Baier et al. 2015; Pantano et al. 2017), this cross-validation approach already proved to be successful.

In addition, the instrument should be able to prioritize specific improvements (as needed in the fourth stage of the site engineering process): Many improvements are possible (e.g. virtual fitting, same-day-delivery) but the instrument should help to decide which improvements really have the potential to increase customer satisfaction. The standard method for this purpose is the Kano approach (originally proposed by Kano et al. 1984, extended e.g. by Berger et al. 1993). The basic assumption of these approaches is that the satisfaction generated by an improvement (low to high) depends on the implemented functionality of this improvement (low to high or not realized to fully realized), whereas this dependency may follow different forms. So e.g. the relation could be linear (i.e. proportional increase of satisfaction with functionality, abbreviated to: one-dimensional), progressively increasing (abbreviated to: attractive), degressively increasing (must-be), or independent (indifferent). The measurement approach mainly consists of posing two questions for each improvement: "How would you feel if the improvement were realized?" "How would you feel if the improvement were NOT realized?" Usually, the ratings are collected on a 5-point ordinal scale ranging from 1 = "I like it that way" to 5 = "I dislike it that way". The answers are then used to categorize the improvement from a single respondent's point of view: Improvements that the respondent likes if realized and dislikes if not realized, are categorized as one-dimensional. Improvements that the respondent likes if realized but where he/she is indifferent if they are not realized, are categorized as attractive. Improvements, where the respondent is more or less indifferent if realized but dislikes if they are not realized, are categorized as must-be. Improvements with other answers are categorized as indifferent, questionable, or reverse. Berger et al. (1993) proposed two indices to aggregate the single respondent's point of view across a sample of respondents: For each improvement, the satisfaction index (SI) measures the share of respondents that categorize the improvement as attractive or one-dimensional. The dissatisfaction index (DI) measures—with a negative sign—the share of respondents that categorize the improvement as attractive or one-dimensional.

In the third phase (questionnaire design and distribution) the list of improvement aspects was integrated into a so-called IPA questionnaire and the list of potential improvements into a so-called Kano questionnaire (see Fig. 4). The questionnaires were planned to be distributed among Baur customers through an (optional) newsletter link. Respondents alternatively were linked to either one of the two questionnaires. For the analysis, the results from both questionnaires were combined. The IPA and Kano questionnaires were developed as discussed: The improvements were explained using (pre-tested) understandable, precise language, and (if possible) visualizations (see e.g. in Fig. 4 the explanation of the potential improvement "virtual fitting"). The questionnaires were implemented electronically (using the tool Qualtrics) and distributed among subsamples of Baur's customers in December 2016 and with a reminder in January 2017 using the company's electronic newsletter. The response rate was surprisingly high: The IPA questionnaire was

Fig. 4 Kano questionnaire excerpt presenting the potential improvement "virtual fitting" and the asking respondents to answer the functional and dysfunctional questions on 5-point-scales

opened by 6680 customers and completed by 4472 respondents. The Kano questionnaire was opened by 7185 customers and completed by 5250 respondents. Nearly half (43.8–47.9% across the eight steps) of the respondents provided comments on positive experiences, the share of respondents describing negative experiences was much smaller (13.8–18.4%).

In the fourth phase (check on being representative, reliable, valid, analysis) the received answers were investigated. Concerning socio-demographics and shopping the IPA (in brackets: Kano) sample consisted of 83.1% (81.0%) female respondents. 19.7% (19.2%) of the sample was 60 years and older, 62.6% (61.5%) between 40 and 59 years old. 28.1% (30.0%) order once a month from Baur, 26.4% (21.0%) at least two times a month. According to the Baur management, the two sample profiles reflect Baur's customer base quite well. Various split-half techniques were performed to check reliability: The answers of the respondents from the first week were compared to all others and other random splits were used. Across most comparisons no significant differences appeared. Cross-validation between importance and performance assessment of the eight steps derived from scales and comments (see above) also showed converging results. Overall, the collected data were positively checked for being representative, reliable, and valid.

4   Results Achieved

Initial results (see Figs. 5, 6, and 7) were presented to Baur's responsible managers in January 2017, final presentations followed in March and April 2017. The results received high interest: Fig. 5 reflects Baur's performance across the different steps of the ordering and delivery process and the importance of these steps from a customer's point of view.

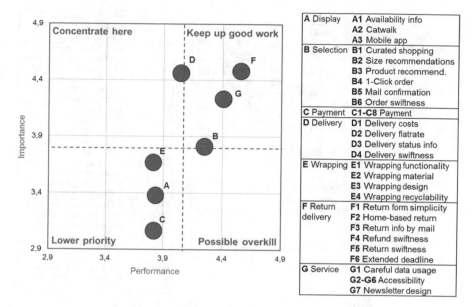

A Display	A1 Availability info
	A2 Catwalk
	A3 Mobile app
B Selection	B1 Curated shopping
	B2 Size recommendations
	B3 Product recommend.
	B4 1-Click order
	B5 Mail confirmation
	B6 Order swiftness
C Payment	C1-C8 Payment
D Delivery	D1 Delivery costs
	D2 Delivery flatrate
	D3 Delivery status info
	D4 Delivery swiftness
E Wrapping	E1 Wrapping functionality
	E2 Wrapping material
	E3 Wrapping design
	E4 Wrapping recyclability
F Return delivery	F1 Return form simplicity
	F2 Home-based return
	F3 Return info by mail
	F4 Refund swiftness
	F5 Return swiftness
	F6 Extended deadline
G Service	G1 Careful data usage
	G2-G6 Accessibility
	G7 Newsletter design

Fig. 5 Results from the IPA analysis for the process steps (A to G); scales range from 1 = "not at all important" to 7 = "very important" (Importance) resp. 1 = "not at all satisfied with this aspect at Baur" to 7 = "very satisfied" (Performance)

As can be seen from this IPA analysis (see Figs. 5 and 6), Baur performs quite well, in particular in the important steps "F. Return delivery", "G. Service", "B. Selection", and "D. Delivery". However, improvements are possible in the less important steps "E. Wrapping", "A. Display", and "C. Payment". The more in-depth Fig. 6 reflects the ratings for the different aspects in each step and allows insights into the priority of digital technology-based improvements. In addition to the more conventional aspects "D1. Delivery costs", "E4. Wrapping recyclability", "E1. Wrapping functionally", "D2. Delivery flatrate", and "E2. Wrapping material", "B2. Size recommendations", "B3. Product recommendations", and "B1. Curated shopping" with clear connections to digital technologies are also located in or near the critical quadrant "Concentrate here". While the responsible managers were not taken by surprise by the overall positive evaluation of their ordering and delivery process by their customers, for the first time they could see the different evaluation aspects in direct comparisons.

The results from the Kano analysis (see Fig. 7) showed—in accordance with the high level of satisfaction with the current ordering and delivery process resulting from the IPA analysis in Figs. 5 and 6—that most of the potential improvements based on digital technologies fall into the "indifferent" category. The majority of the interviewed customers—at least currently—do not mind whether Baur improves its ordering and delivery process by digital technology-based innovations such as "B6. C2C inspiration", "B2. Attended shopping", "B5. Personalized area", or "B4. Scanned shopping". These potential improvements would neither increase

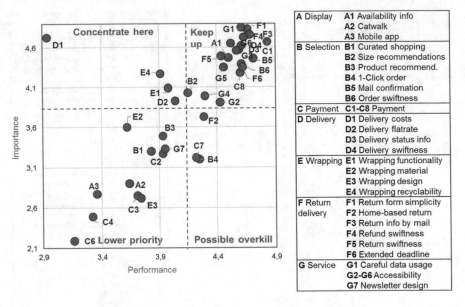

Fig. 6 Results from the IPA analysis for the improvement aspects (A1 to G7)

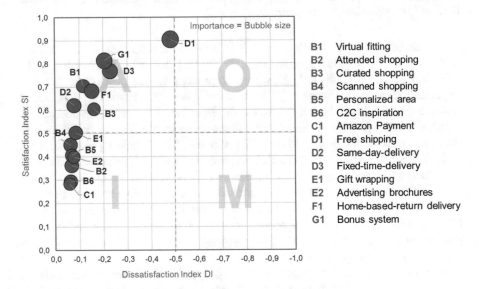

Fig. 7 Results from the Kano analysis for the potential improvements

satisfaction when offered nor dissatisfaction when not offered. However, the improvements "B1. Virtual fitting" and "B3. Curated shopping" were categorized as attractive: Many interviewed customers (57% for virtual fitting, 39% for curated shopping) would like them to be offered. These new customer interaction formats compete with more conventional improvements such as "G1. Bonus system" (62%), "D3. Fixed-time-delivery" (57%), "F1. Home-based-return delivery" and "D2. Same-day-delivery" (54%), and "E1. Gift wrapping" (42%). A typical must-be improvement did not show up in the survey. Here, again the high satisfaction level of the customers is revealed.

To conclude: The high satisfaction of Baur's customers with the current ordering and delivery process was expected, but the confirmation through the surveys reassured this assessment. In addition, the specific strengths and weaknesses of the customer interface and the underlying internal processes could now be evaluated in much more detail and starting points for improving by digital technologies were given. Currently, the two potential improvements that were prioritized by the customers—virtual fitting based on virtual/augmented reality as well as curated shopping based on chatbots, messaging services, and image analysis—are further developed and implemented by Baur and members of the project team. The Baur and Otto Group have established a so-called "Wissenschaftscampus E-Commerce" [Ecommerce science campus] in Burgkunstadt (see Otto Group 2017 p. 43), where companies, research institutes, and universities intensify their cooperation. Baur, the University of Bayreuth, and the Fraunhofer-Society (in particular the Fraunhofer-Project Group Business & Information Systems Engineering) are major partners. Five innovation labs have started to work in Burgkunstadt, one of which focuses on virtual/augmented reality, and another on customer interaction.

Overall, the high response rates of the surveys and the high willingness to give detailed comments on aspects and specific improvements took the responsible managers by surprise. The project was a clear vote for more integration of the customer's voice into the site engineering process. In particular, the project showed that Baur's approach to site engineering—technology-driven and customer-oriented in combination—can be supported by such surveys.

5 Lessons Learned

The case discusses the customer's point of view on digital technologies for ordering and delivering fashion and how Baur integrates this point of view in its site engineering process. In the following, we discuss five lessons learned:

First, ordering and delivery processes of online fashion retailers have to be improved permanently. Other players are "one click away" and compete on convenience, price, and service. The case demonstrated how active even small retailers like Baur are in this field.

Second, online fashion retailers with a similar customer and product profile to Baur can increase customer satisfaction and sales by customer interaction formats based on digital technologies. The surveys show that in particular virtual fitting using virtual/augmented reality and curated shopping using chatbots, messaging services, and image analysis, were rated as attractive improvements by many customers. On the other hand, most customers were indifferent concerning customer interaction formats like C2C inspiration, attended shopping, personalized area, or scanned shopping.

Third, the case shows that "customer surveys are not dead". They are an adequate instrument to understand the customer's point of view concerning potential improvements based on digital technologies. If questionnaires are carefully designed, customers are willing to give valuable feedback. The high response rates, the high numbers of comments, the positive checks for being representative, reliable, and valid as well as the—to some extent—the surprising results support these findings.

Fourth, the stage-by-stage site engineering process that Baur uses together with the discussed extension can be an inspiring example for other companies that also rely on a close digital customer interaction: The basic process has proven its effectiveness over years (with impressive performance values in comparison with the years before its introduction) and can also be used nowadays to decide on improvements based on (new) digital technologies. The extension convinces in this case.

Fifth, from a more general point of view, the case discusses how a small retailer (Baur) can compete with large capital market value-oriented online players (Amazon): The customer's point of view must be respected, attractive improvements have to be implemented. In order to restrict expenses, stage-by-stage (site engineering) processes can be used. They generate numerous improvement ideas and afterwards reduce them to a small number of promising ones.

References

Amazon (2014) Annual report 2013. Amazon.com, Inc., Seattle, WA. www.amazon.com

Amazon (2017) Annual report 2016. Amazon.com, Inc., Seattle, WA. www.amazon.com

Baier D, Rese A (2017) Online-shop site engineering using eye tracking, TAM, and A/B-tests: an empirical application. Paper presented at the 4th German-Polish Symposium on Data Analysis and its Applications (GPSDAA-2017), Wroclaw, September 25

Baier D, Stüber E (2010) Acceptance of recommendations to buy in online retailing. J Retail Cust Serv 17(3):173–180

Baier D, Rese A, Schreiber S (2015) Analyzing online reviews to measure technology acceptance at the point of scale: the case of IKEA. In: Pantano E (ed) Successful technological integration for competitive advantage in retail settings. IGI Global, Hershey, PA, pp 168–189

Berger C, Blauth R, Boger D et al (1993) Kano's methods for understanding customer-defined quality. Cent Qual Manag J 2(4):3–36

BEVH (2017) Interaktiver Handel in Deutschland 2016. Studie des Bundesverbands E-Commerce und Versandhandel e.V. (BEVH), Berlin. www.bevh.org

Cronin JJ Jr, Taylor SA (1992) Measuring service quality: a reexamination and extension. J Mark 56(3):55–68

DHL (2016) DHL Customer Journey Studie 2016: Vom Klick bis zur Klingel – Von der Online-Bestellung bis zum Paketempfang. DHL Express Germany GmbH, Bonn. www.dhl.de

Flanagan JC (1954) The critical incident technique. Psychol Bull 51(4):327–359

Ganeshan S (2016) The dead-zone: why customer surveys are dead. MyCustomer.com. www.mycustomer.com

hmmh (2016) hmmh Studie: Fulfillment Benchmarking – im Fokus: Fashion. hmmh multimediahaus AG, Bremen. www.hmmh.de

Kano N, Seraku N, Takahashi F, Tsuji S (1984) Attractive quality and must-be quality. J Jpn Soc Qual Control 14(2)

IFH Köln (2017) Branchenfokus Damen- und Herrenbekleidung 2017. IFH Köln and BBE Handelsberatung GmbH, Köln. www.ifhkoeln.de

Lauber D (2013) E-Commerce an der Schwelle zur Sättigungsphase – Produktivität von E-Commerce-Aktivitäten wird erfolgskritisch. In: Heinemann G, Haug K, Gehrckens M (eds) Digitalisierung des Handels mit ePace. Springer Gabler, Wiesbaden, pp 105–122

Löffler S, Baier D (2013) Using critical incidents to validate the direct measurement of attribute importance and performance when analyzing services. J Serv Sci Manag 6(5a):1–11

Martilla JA, James JC (1977) Importance-performance analysis. J Mark 41(1):77–79

Otto Group (2017): Geschäftsbericht 2016/17. Otto GmbH & Co KG, Hamburg. www.ottogroup.com.

Pantano E (ed) (2015) Successful technological integration for competitive advantage in retail settings. IGI Global, Hershey, PA

Pantano E, Rese A, Baier D (2017) Enhancing the online decision-making process by using augmented reality: a two country comparison of youth markets. J Retail Cust Serv 38:81–95

Rese A, Schreiber S, Baier D (2014) Technology acceptance modeling of augmented reality at the point of sale: can surveys be replaced by an analysis of online reviews? J Retail Cust Serv 21(5):869–876

Rese A, Baier D, Geyer-Schulz A, Schreiber S (2017) How augmented reality apps are accepted by customers: a comparative analysis using scales and opinions. Technol Forecast Soc Change 127 (November):306–319

Schreiber S, Baier D (2015) Multivariate landing page optimization using hierarchical bayes cbc analysis. Stud Classif Data Anal Knowl Organ 50:465–474

Stüber E (2013) Personalisierung im Internethandel: Die Akzeptanz von Kaufempfehlungen in der Bekleidungsbranche, 2nd edn. Springer Gabler, Wiesbaden

Swinscoe A (2016) Some people say that customer surveys are dead, they're wrong and here's why. Forbes. www.forbes.com

UPS (2015) 2015 UPS pulse of the online shopper. A customer experience study. UPS of America, Inc., Atlanta, GA. www.ups.com

Zalando (2017) Geschäftsbericht Zalando 2016. Zalando SE, Berlin. www.zalando.de

Daniel Baier is Professor of Innovation and Dialog Marketing at the University of Bayreuth. He completed his dissertation and habilitation in business administration at the University of Karlsruhe and was Professor for Marketing and Innovation Management at Brandenburg University of Technology Cottbus-Senftenberg. His research interests are in market-oriented design and pricing of products and services as well as theory, methods, and applications of data science with a special focus on data analysis. He has published in journals such as Advances in Data Analysis and Classification, Journal of Econometris, Journal of Retailing and Consumer Services, or Technological Forecasting and Social Change. He has led many publicly or privately funded research projects at the interface between computer science and marketing and now is also part of the Project Group Business & Information Systems Engineering of Fraunhofer FIT.

Alexandra Rese is Assistant Professor at the Chair of Innovation and Dialogue Marketing at the University of Bayreuth, Germany. She completed her dissertation in sociology and entrepreneurship at the University of Karlsruhe and her habilitation in business administration at Brandenburg University of Technology Cottbus-Senftenberg. Her works have appeared in journals such as R&D Management, Creativity and Innovation Management, International Journal of Innovation Management, Technological Forecasting and Social Change, as well as Journal of Retailing and Consumer Services. Her current research focuses on the acceptance of innovative applications in retailing, e.g. augmented reality, as well as interfirm cooperation and open innovation.

Nikita Nonenmacher is Product Owner for Order (Checkout) at empiriecom GmbH & Co. KG. He completed his master's degree in economics at the Otto Friedrich University Bamberg. His main task is to create with the developer team the best checkout experience for the user/customer of baur.de, imwalking.de, universal.at, jelmoil-shop.ch, quelle.at, quelle.de, quelle.ch, ackermann.ch and ottoversand.at.

Steve Treybig is Head of all B2B cooperations and market research at BAUR Versand. He holds a degree in business management and economy law at university of Schmalkalden. His main task is to trade with big data, keyaccount management with important partners from industry and retail trade as primary and secondary market research with focus on mobile devices.

Benjamin Bressem is Human Resources Officer for University Marketing at BAUR Versand. He completed his master's degree in economics at the University of Bielefeld. His main task is the recruitment, selection and supervision of students for the Baur Group. In addition, he is responsible for the organization of student research projects.

Applying Sound-Based Analysis at Porsche Production: Towards Predictive Maintenance of Production Machines Using Deep Learning and Internet-of-Things Technology

Matthias Auf der Mauer, Tristan Behrens,
Mahdi Derakhshanmanesh, Christopher Hansen,
and Stefan Muderack

Abstract

(a) **Situation faced**: All mechanical and mechatronic devices are subject to wear, tear and breakdown. Failure of such devices can cause significant costs, e.g., in automotive factories. Established predictive maintenance approaches usually require deep integration with the specific machine. Such approaches are not practically feasible because of technical, legal and financial restrictions. A non-intrusive, lightweight and generic solution approach is desired.

(b) **Action taken**: A solution concept was developed which, at its heart, is based on deep learning algorithms that monitor sound sequences captured from a microphone, analyze them and return classification results for use in further steps of a control loop, such as planning actions and execution steps. We named this approach the 'Sound Detective' and it was evaluated by retrofitting a coffee machine using simple microphones to capture production sounds. The sound sequences are subsequently analyzed using neural networks developed in Keras and TensorFlow. During prototyping, multiple kinds of neural networks and architectures were tested and the experiment

The case is a result of research conducted by the authors in the scope of the Porsche Digital Lab Berlin. This lab is operated by MHP—A Porsche Company.

M. A. der Mauer (✉) · T. Behrens · M. Derakhshanmanesh · C. Hansen · S. Muderack
Porsche Digital Lab, Berlin, Germany
e-mail: matthias.aufdermauer@porschedigitallab.com; tristan.behrens@porschedigitallab.com; mahdi.derakhshanmanesh@porschedigitallab.com; christopher.hansen@porschedigitallab.com; stefan.muderack@porschedigitallab.com

© Springer International Publishing AG, part of Springer Nature 2019
N. Urbach, M. Röglinger (eds.), *Digitalization Cases*, Management for Professionals, https://doi.org/10.1007/978-3-319-95273-4_5

was realized with two different kinds of coffee machines to validate the generalizability of the solution to different platforms.

(c) **Results achieved**: The prototype can analyze sounds produced by a mechanical machine and classify different states. The technical realization relies on cheap commodity hardware and open-source software, demonstrating the applicability of existing technologies and the feasibility of the implementation. Especially, it was described that the proposed approach can be applied to solve predictive maintenance tasks.

(d) **Lessons learned**: The present work demonstrates the feasibility of the Sound Detective's reference architecture and discusses challenges and learnings during implementation. Specifically, key learnings include the importance of data quality, preprocessing and consistency, influences of the experimental setup on real-world prediction performance and the relevance of microcomputers, the target hardware and type of the programming language for complex analyses.

1   Introduction

The Porsche Digital Lab in Berlin is a collaboration of MHP Management- und IT-Beratung GmbH and Porsche AG (Mhp.com 2018; Dr. Ing. h.c. F. Porsche AG – Porsche Deutschland 2018). The goal of the technology lab is to support digitalization at Porsche, by applying agile methods, creating and disseminating knowledge bases and building prototypes to raise awareness about the most modern technologies with a focus on Artificial Intelligence (AI), Blockchain and Internet of Things (IoT). In this paper, we will elaborate on one of these prototypes.

It is important to stress that prototypes developed at the Porsche Digital Lab are used to raise awareness and understanding of what is possible with current technologies in the Porsche context, as opposed to creating deployment-ready software. This is particularly useful for C-level-management and other stakeholders. All of the prototypes built at the Porsche Digital Lab challenge the status quo of current research activities. This includes business models, technical infrastructure, development processes and even existing skillsets and mindsets, just to name a few.

All mechanical and mechatronic devices are subject to wear and failure. Outages of such devices cause significant costs. This is for example the case due to fixed maintenance intervals in production environments. Predictive maintenance is being pursued with the intent to reduce the number and cost of unplanned downtime created by machine-train failures (Mobley 2002). Established approaches usually focus on deep integration with the machine of concern. Unfortunately, such approaches are prone to a number of implementation limitations. In automotive manufacturing, these typically include regulatory, juridical and financial restrictions related to integrating new technologies into existing machines.

Deep Learning as a subfield of AI focusses on designing, training and deploying deep neural networks to both supervised and unsupervised learning tasks (LeCun et al. 2015). Recently there has been a surge in successful deep learning use cases, mainly due to increasing availability of data and computing power—and a willingness to explore AI-based solutions to real-world problems. The active developer community has also made deep learning very accessible via a number of open-source deep learning software frameworks (Theano, TensorFlow, Keras, Caffe, Torch) (Keras.io 2018; TensorFlow 2018). Until only recently it was almost impossible to train neural networks that solve complicated tasks. Now, this technology is available to a large audience of software developers.

IoT is an emergent technology that, amongst other things, deals with Ambient Intelligence (Gubbi et al. 2013). The overall idea is establishing a network of interconnected physical devices, or so-called 'Smart Devices'. The general IoT infrastructure consists of a set of sensors and actuators, plus communication technologies that enable interoperation of sensors, actuators and other smart devices. In this paper, we introduce and elaborate on a general architecture to detecting failure—acute and impending—in production. The core is a novel neural network model that is capable of classifying acoustic data in a production setting.

The developed neural network model is a sequence-to-one model that uses a series of preprocessed sound samples as input and generates a prediction of the state of the monitored machine (Sutskever et al. 2014). The preprocessing of the sounds mainly involves extracting features from short audio samples. For example, spectrograms and chromagrams of short audio snippet samples can be extracted and used to reduce the task of sound classification to image classification. Using a series of such pre-processed samples allows us to deal with sounds that are non-repeating or potentially rhythmical in nature.

We embed this neural network into a network of smart devices, distributing tasks including sound recording, sound classification, storing results and providing means for analysis, both manually and automatically. Details of the architecture are provided in the solution concept (see Sect. 4.2).

We complement the description of the Sound Detective's reference architecture with one specific use case for evaluation purposes. In order to start with prototyping quickly in a lab environment, first a demonstrator based on components that are available at a favorable price was implemented. Therefore, a coffee machine was chosen as the first test case. We implement a system that uses a neural network in order to differentiate between different hot beverages produced by a coffee machine. The beverage classification is then used to count the produced goods. This example use case is situated in our laboratory environment, but nevertheless can be mapped to other domains in a systematic way.

2   Situation Faced

Porsche AG is a German car manufacturer. The company has been created in 1931 and now has around 30K employees. Similar to many companies of such high age and large size, Porsche permanently needs to transform itself, embracing the current era of Digitalization. There is a need for gathering extensive knowledge and expertise in modern fields. These fields include but are not limited to know-how on a technical level. Reforming a company that grew over 80 years takes considerable time and effort, e.g., due to established rigid structures and processes that may hinder progress towards Digitalization.

The most relevant technical field at Porsche AG for the presented use case is production. The company's car-manufacturing process is highly facilitated by Information Technology. A major challenge with respect to Digitalization is choosing which technologies should be injected into the existing infrastructures and how this can be done in the most optimal way.

Time-based maintenance of production machines is based on the idea that necessary maintenance tasks on a machine are conducted in regular cycles. Experience has shown that this approach is insufficient in many cases since it is difficult or almost impossible to predict the time to failure of mechanical components. For this maintenance approach, it is likely that unnecessary maintenance is conducted (Hashemian and Bean 2011). Additionally, upcoming failures are often not detected in advance and the production machine and subsequently the entire following production process breaks down.

In contrast to time-based approaches, predictive maintenance is a well-known technique of monitoring system behavior to prevent failure and to conduct maintenance only when necessary. Manual visual inspection is the oldest version of predictive maintenance and still one of the most powerful approaches. In recent years, different automated predictive maintenance solutions have been developed that are based on techniques like pattern recognition, empirical and physical modelling, neural networks or fuzzy logic (Wu et al. 2007).

Many of these techniques work well and enable the desired monitoring of the system. However, their implementation is often associated with technical limitations related to solution complexity as well as to legal and financial restrictions.

Predictive maintenance approaches typically utilize different types of sensors, like vibration, pressure or acceleration sensors to monitor system conditions and measure failure critical parameters. Some of these solutions require deep integration into the monitored system, leading to large installation efforts. Sensors generate a large amount of data, which is often processed by one central unit. Transferring this data inside the factory networks can cause blockages and break downs.

Accurate and secure monitoring of production machines requires often specialized and expensive hardware. Another technical issue of many current predictive maintenance solutions is the lack of transferability between the production machines. These hardware costs combined with technical integration can lead to high costs of predictive maintenance solutions (Yang et al. 2014).

Legal constraints are also critical. The invasiveness of predictive maintenance approaches often violates warranty and leasing conditions of production machines. An iPhone for example, loses its warranty once it was opened by the user. This is similar for production machines and in some cases, implies hurdles for implementations of new solutions.

Many machines already have integrated sensors that could be used as an input for monitoring solutions. This would be a simple approach for predictive maintenance because it does not require additional hardware. Nevertheless, in many cases leasing conditions of the machine only include usage of the machine, but not access to integrated sensor data. Therefore, this approach is also not always feasible and additional hardware is necessary.

The predictive maintenance solution presented in this work is based on audio data that addresses the afore-mentioned technical, financial and legal restrictions of implementing predictive maintenance solutions in production settings.

3   Action Taken

In order to accelerate Digitalization in production at Porsche AG, it is imperative to (a) gather enough knowledge about the problem domain, (b) create a working prototype and (c) create a reference architecture as a basis for the final system. A working prototype is an effective mean for communication. First, it shows the feasibility of technological approaches. Second, it is a tool to inspire stakeholders about potential opportunities. When proposing ambitious projects using new technologies, it is beneficial to ensure awareness at the higher levels of a corporate hierarchy, i.e., C-level management.

Here we elaborate on one technical prototype—the Sound Detective—having the aim to digitalize the production domain.

3.1   General Idea

In general, every system consisting of moving and non-moving parts generates a unique acoustic footprint. This sound profile can be used to differentiate one system from another and even systems of identical construction (Wright and Wright 2015). In the automotive industry, these systems include a range of complex production lines such as robots, hydraulic lifting platforms and forklifts, to comparably more delicate entities like motors and gear boxes. Similar examples of machines used by workers include power tools or even copying machines. Depending on the mode of operation, these systems generate acoustic footprints that are distinguishable by humans and therefore—as we hypothesize—possibly also by smart computing entities.

In a production environment, different states of operation—such as running, standby, offline and failure—generate acoustic sound profiles that are usually clearly distinguishable. It is possible to detect changes and potentially predict damages in a running system by analyzing changes in the sound profile over time. A car engine provides a good example: A driver is able to hear if something is wrong and is able to decide when he needs to switch gears by listening to the engine sounds. Skilled and experienced technicians are capable of classifying different states of systems simply by listening to them. Additionally, they are able to hear whether a system is functioning accurately and in case of a problem, they are able to locate the origin and cause of the problem.

The basic concept of the presented case is to generalize this idea and to transfer it into a digital technology that is capable of differentiating different working states of a (mechanical) system and predicting failure states before they occur using only the system's acoustic profile. In order to achieve this goal, a prototype was developed that captures sound data with a microphone and processes it using a neural network running on a low-cost and low-power computer.

The hardware architecture of the system consists of two main components. A standard off-the-shelf USB microphone and a Raspberry Pi, which is a low-power and low-cost computer (Upton and Halfacree 2014). The recorded data is processed with a trained neural network on a Raspberry Pi and only valuable insights from the analysis are transferred to the backend to ensure that only a minimum amount of data is transferred within factory networks.

Utilizing standard off-the-shelf components keeps the costs for this solution very low. These standard components have the benefit that they are easy to use and do not require additional expertise. Since the data is processed on the Raspberry Pi and only small amounts of data enter factory networks, technical issues are minimized. Microphones can record data without a physical connection to the monitored production machine, therefore the solution is non-invasive and maintains the structural integrity of the observed system; thus, addressing the above mentioned legal issues.

3.2 Neural Network Model

In the present work, a neural network model was used to process the acquired data on the Raspberry Pi. Specifically, a deep recurrent neural network was utilized, since these kinds of networks have proven useful for a wide range of problems involving time-series data. Due to the availability of high-level application programming interfaces (APIs) like Keras, complex and complicated networks are straightforward to implement and experiment with (Keras.io 2018). This helped us quickly validate different model architectures and (hyper-)parameters. In order to realize this, we chose a standard sequence-to-one model. As shown in Fig. 1 this form of a neural network takes a fixed length of inputs and returns one prediction of the classified class per sequence of sound data that is analyzed. Each slice is fed into the feature extraction algorithm, yielding a vector that encodes the sample as seen in Fig. 2 After

Fig. 1 Scheme of a sequence-to-one neural network model

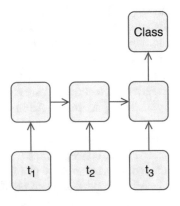

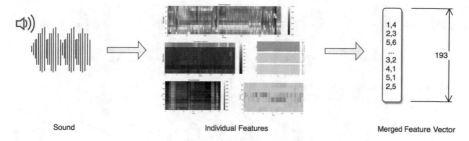

Fig. 2 Conversion of sound to feature vectors

that, training data is generated and consists of ordered sequences of those vectors. The length of the sequences is represented by the number of slices.

Before we elaborate on the algorithmic and architectural details, the neural network hyper-parameters are specified (Goodfellow et al. 2016):

- **Sampling rate:** Sampling is the reduction of a continuous-time signal to a discrete-time signal. The rate is usually in samples per second.
- **Slice length:** Our model maps sequences of audio-data and performs a prediction. We call the length of such pieces of audio data, the slice length.
- **Number of slices:** This is the number of slices that are fed into the neural network as input. This is basically the length of the sequences.
- **Number of features:** The model can extract variable numbers features from any given sound sample, which can be defined by this factor.
- **Training/testing ratio:** Datasets are usually split into a 'training set' for training the model and a 'test set' for evaluating the model.
- **Dropout:** This is the probability of a node in the neural network being dropped during training, which prevents 'overfitting'.
- **Learning rate:** Determines how quickly a neural network learns new knowledge.
- **Number of epochs:** An epoch is a single training run using the entire training set.
- **Batch size:** This is the number of training examples used in one step of training. To clarify, with a dataset of 150 data points and a batch size of 10, a single epoch can contain 15 training runs (determined by the number of data points/batch size).

The neural network model is facilitated by a number of pre-processing and feature extraction steps (Piczak 2015).

(i) In the first step, a sound-sample of arbitrary length and sample rate—both are hyper-parameters of the neural network—are the input to generate a set of features (Fig. 1). These features include Chromagram (Chroma), Mel-frequency Cepstral coefficients (MFCC), Spectral Contrast and Tonal Centroid Features (Tonnetz) (Librosa.github.io 2018). All of these features are represented as images, thus transferring the problem from the acoustic domain to the visual domain.

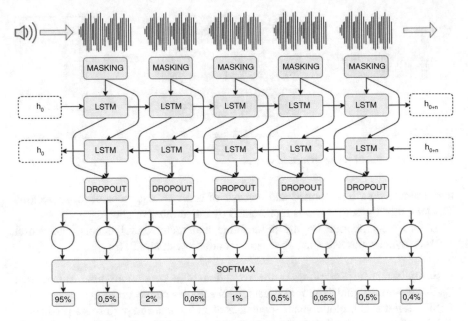

Fig. 3 The neural network model developed for the Sound Detective case

(ii) In a second step, a straightforward dimensionality reduction is applied to the features. This is done by computing the mean of the image rows.

(iii) Following this, a second algorithm preprocesses the data-set. Given a set of labelled sound samples, the algorithm first cuts each sample into slices of a specific length (Slice length, e.g. 1 s). This length is one of the afore-mentioned hyper-parameters.

The structure of the neural network includes the following layers, as seen in Fig. 3.

- **Masking:** Ignores entire time steps in computation if the input value is zero. Here, it is required for short recordings of sound.
- **Bidirectional LSTM:** Facilitates the sequence-part of the model. This is a layer of stacked long short-time memories (LSTMs) that reads the input sequence from left-to-right and right-to-left. With this, inspecting a time-step yields information about its complete surroundings and not only information from one direction (Sundermeyer et al. 2012).
- **Dropout:** Randomly removes nodes from the network in order to prevent overfitting during training (Srivastava et al. 2014).
- **Dense:** Dense means that the layer is fully connected, in addition it uses the softmax activation function to generate the probability for each class.

Fig. 4 Every second an audio slice is recorded; these slices are joined to give a single sequence that can be interpreted by the neural network

Preprocessing and training phases are complemented by a real-time algorithm that computes predictions during live operation of the observed machine. This real-time prediction activity includes the following steps:

(i) It records and preprocesses one-second-slices of audio (using the same algorithm as for the training data) and merges them to produce a sequence of pre-defined length (according to the model hyper-parameters).
(ii) The sequence is given to the model to predict and classify the sound class.
(iii) The computed predictions for each sequence is recorded by a count algorithm and used to give an overall classification of the type of beverage produced according to pre-defined thresholds; for example, five consecutive predictions for the class 'coffee', means the beverage being produced is a coffee.
(iv) The data about predicted beverages is published on a broker component, thus made accessible for further visualization steps.

When dispensing a beverage, several overlapping audio sequences may contain recordings of the beverage being produced, as seen in Fig. 4. Therefore, the algorithm has to take into account that the same beverage is not classified multiple times during a single dispense. During prototyping, multiple kinds of neural networks were experimented with. Describing their structure is out of the scope of the current work.

3.3 Specialized Use Case

In a typical production environment, many different sound-generating machines are present. All of these machines have a unique acoustic footprint and could be used as a test use case in order to test the developed neural network model. Examples include assembly belts, pumps, engines and further machines. A coffee machine was chosen as the first test case. Similar to any machine in production, it has its own acoustic footprint depending on its operational state. Furthermore, it is a machine that needs regular and semi-predictable maintenance; including refilling of beans, water and milk and cleaning. Hence, it is a feasible alternative to the more complex and hard to reach production machines in factories.

In order to train a neural network to detect a failure of a system, it is necessary to acquire labeled system data of failures. In the case of the Sound Detective, this means sound data recorded before and during system failure. In order to test the algorithm and easily acquire data, we decided to start with differentiating between different hot beverages, because it is much faster to acquire necessary data of different beverages than data of machine failure. If the algorithm is able to differentiate coffee types—and therefore different states of the machine—it should also be possible to recognize the change of a machine before it breaks down, assuming that there is a significant acoustic change associated with events leading to machine failure.

Similar to most automated coffee machines, our selected coffee machine is capable of producing a multitude of different beverages. We limited our research in the first instance to these classes: coffee, cappuccino, tea and ambient sound. The ambient sound class contains sounds that are typical for working environments, like air-conditioning and people chatting. For the training of a neural network, it is important to train the model with a large dataset that provides from a wide range of situations for the neural network to 'learn' from. Initially, fifty data samples were collected for every class. During preprocessing of the data, distortion was automatically applied to the sound files that adds effects like reverb. This preprocessing step enhances the robustness of the model because by increasing the amount of data and by adding more sound variations.

The basic idea was to develop a solution that is built on top of a reference architecture that can easily be applied to different production machines. In order to validate the generic nature of the developed solution architecture, the neural network was transferred and applied to a second coffee machine from a different manufacturer. Since the involved hardware (especially the microphone) is easily transferable, almost no installation effort was necessary.

However, a different coffee machine has a different acoustic footprint because the hardware and the production process of the same coffee produced with a different coffee machine might be different. Hence, for the model to be effective on a different production machine, new training data has to be acquired and the model needs to be re-trained. This is the most significant adaption effort when transferring the model to another production machine. The neural network itself only requires a few changes. For example, some of the hyper-parameters may need to be changed, because the length of the data changes.

4   Results Achieved

One of the major goals of the present development was to help digitalization in the production at Porsche AG by building a prototype that shows the feasibility of sound-based condition monitoring. This running prototype was used for communication inside the company and inspired further stakeholders about potential application areas. The proposed approach is assumed to be a viable enabler for realizing predictive maintenance and further solutions in the manufacturing of cars. Out of the development of this prototype and showcase, a number of different projects were identified at Porsche AG where a sound detection and classification system could add major value for quality, process stability and machine operation.

4.1 Identified Use Cases at Porsche AG

Process Control for Manual Assembly Procedures

A major issue during manual assembly is the missing immediate feedback to the person who is assembling, whether a task was performed successfully or not. Often the assembly procedure is performed without visual contact and usually under time pressure. For example, this is the case with electronics connections that are assembled manually. When these connections snap-in they generate a clear sound, that indicates that the connection was successful. However, under the condition of a very loud production environment this loud snap-in sound is not recognizable for the person that is performing the assembly. Additionally, the connections are normally performed within the car or overhead, so a visual confirmation is not possible either. Through this sound-based solution, it is possible to analyze the sound of the connection and give a feedback to the assembly person on whether or not the connection was successful. In case the feedback is negative, the connection has to be checked and clicked again. This quality control drastically improves process control in production and can lead to a decrease in errors and breakdown of cars after shipping and therefore cost reduction.

Quality Analysis and Control of Parts Provided by Suppliers

An electric vehicle consists of significantly less moving parts than a vehicle with a combustion engine. This highlights the remaining moving parts and the sounds generated by them. A challenge for automotive manufacturers is, for example, the design and assembly of gearboxes for electronic vehicles using parts of third-party suppliers. The Sound Detective concept can be applied to monitor the sound generated by different gearboxes. Through sound analysis, it is possible to draw conclusions about the quality of the supplied parts to ensure that the components delivered by suppliers conform to the specified standards of the car manufacturer and generate the desired sound profile for the end customer while driving the vehicle. Additionally, it is possible to observe which physical design parameters of the gearboxes have influence on the sound profile and therefore improve on them.

Assistance in Repetitive Quality Assurance Procedures

Sounds are a major quality characteristic in the automotive industry which is manifested during active and passive usage of the car, e.g., noises of the door mechanisms, screeching noises during car rides, etc. Additionally, the sound profiles of the power-lifts of car windows or windshield wipers define a part of the perceived quality for the customer. The automotive industry invests a lot of time and resources in quality assurance.

Semi-automated testbeds for car doors are a concrete example for quality assurance tests. These tests consist of robots which open and close doors in a variety of environmental conditions during long running tests. Doors are opened and closed hundreds of thousands of times and are closely monitored by sound engineers. A tool like the Sound Detective can be used to analyze the sounds of the door hinges automatically and detect when a screeching hinge or a grinding noise as the door rubber starts to unfold.

Autonomous Driving
The fastest way to detect and locate an approaching emergency vehicle today is the recognition through the siren of the vehicle. Autonomous vehicle also need to distinguish emergency vehicles to act accordingly. Since human drivers and autonomous vehicles will share the road in the foreseeable future, a mechanism needs to be found which enables the recognition of emergency vehicles by both human and autonomous drivers. The Sound Detective can create another layer of perception in addition to camera and laser-based systems—and the human eye.

4.2   Generalized Architecture

The hardware architecture was developed to facilitate the effortless application of the solution to different production machines. The system consists of three main components: A standard off-shelf USB microphone and two Raspberry Pi. The recorded data is processed with a trained neural network on one Raspberry Pi and only valuable insights of the analysis are transferred to a second Raspberry Pi that stores the data in a database and visualizes it. An overview over our architecture is given by Fig. 5.

The centerpiece of the architecture consists of the production machine; in the present case: the coffee machine. A USB microphone is simply clipped inside the coffee machine and sends the recorded sound data to the first Raspberry Pi. Three algorithms (explained in Sect. 3.2) are running on the Raspberry Pi to perform

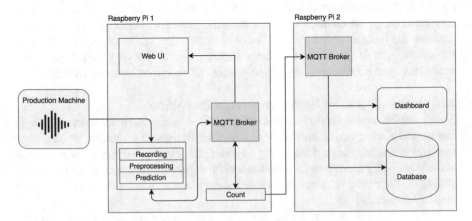

Fig. 5 Draft of the generalized architecture implemented

recording, preprocessing of data and predictions. The results of this analysis consist of probabilities that the analyzed sequence is a specific class (in this case a beverage type). The probabilities for each class are sent over a local MQTT (Mqtt.org 2018), broker on the Raspberry Pi to a user interface that displays the results. Once the neural network detects a sequence as a class of interest, the prediction results are published to a second WIFI-connected MQTT broker that visualizes historical data, such as how many and what kind of beverages were produced. These visualizations create data transparency between the production level (shop floor) and management and controlling (top floor).

As mentioned in Sect. 2, current predictive maintenance approaches face several technical, financial and legal implementation issues. A major goal during development was to address the problems of current predictive maintenance approaches.

Data Transfer In order to keep data traffic as low as possible, an edge-computing approach was followed. Edge-computing describes the procedure of processing data at the edge of the network, in this case, the Raspberry Pi. Only necessary information is transferred from the machine and via the network to the second Raspberry Pi.

Generalizability Generalizability issues of current solutions were tackled by building a generic solution that allows easy installation and setup of both hardware and software. Hardware installation is simplified by the usage of microphones, which are non-invasive and relatively inexpensive. An additional benefit is that warranty or leasing conditions are not violated. Software and model setup are simplified by the nature of sound data. When analyzing sound data, similar parameters are of importance and therefore the neural network model does not need to be changed significantly whenever the production machine is changed.

In order to confirm the transferability of the developed solution, a second coffee machine from a different manufacturer was tested. The hardware installation took only a couple of minutes. The adaption of the algorithms was limited to changes of the hyper-parameters to account for different sequence length of beverages from the new coffee machine. As described earlier, the main challenge of changing to a new production machine is the necessity of new training data for the neural network model.

Financial Since the microphones we used are standard off-the-shelf components and setup is simple, our solution is also cost-effective.

Legal The proposed approach is non-intrusive and additive. It does not require any kind of deep integration with the production machine to be observed.

4.3   Future Work

Although our prototype returns good results and has helped to reveal many interesting practical use cases, it still requires more work. Further improvements and challenges with our current approach are described subsequently:

- First, for every data point, a beverage has to be produced. This means that data acquisition uses a lot of time and resources. Due to the excessive amount of resources required to collect data, a validation of our neural network on a large dataset is still in process. This challenge will apply to full-scale car production systems, as well.
- Second, the presented neural network model is limited to distinguishing different types of beverages. This is only the first step for predictive maintenance—the ideal use case will be for predicting machine failure and enabling a better maintenance schedule. This will require gathering training data and training the model to learn failure or maintenance states. In the coffee machine case, empty coffee beans, milk or water containers are examples for failure states.
- Third, the training of the model currently follows a supervised learning approach, which required correctly labelled data. Data acquisition and labelling is biggest challenge associated with changing to a new production machine, because a trained person has to manually label the data. Therefore, in the future it would make sense to develop an unsupervised or semi-supervised learning approach to label data more efficiently and save time during data acquisition.
- Finally, it is possible to extend the current solution to include a wider variety of sensors beyond microphones.

All in all, the sound detective is an excellent basis for further research on the application of deep learning algorithms and IoT architectures in real-world production environments. Our ongoing work is especially focused on transferring the introduced solution concept to full-scale applications in the factory and beyond.

5   Lessons Learned

During the development process the following lessons were identified:

1. Data quality and consistency has a major influence on model performance.
2. The integrity of the setup needs to be guaranteed.
3. Microcomputers are sufficient for sound analysis with neural networks.
4. It is imperative for IoT projects to start using the target hardware as early as possible.
5. General-purpose programming languages are not sufficient for specialized tasks.

Lesson 1: Data Quality and Consistency

Achieving optimal results with neural networks requires large amounts of data and consistent data quality. The coffee machine which was used to showcase the experimental solution featured a compartment close to the brewing chamber. This space was utilized for the microphone because it offered a certain degree of noise reduction from the outside environment. However, we found unexpected alterations of temperature and humidity in the brewing chamber influenced parts of the training data and altered the quality and consistency of the data over the entire dataset. This affected real-time performance as our training data was not completely representative of volatile real-world conditions—humidity and temperature within the brewing chamber varies quite significantly, depending on coffee machine usage and setup on any given day. One obvious solution is to collect more data, which was done in various production conditions of the coffee machine. Another key learning in this domain was that insufficient training data can be augmented by artificially enhancing recorded data with ambient sounds present during production.

Lesson 2: The Integrity of the Setup Needs to Be Guaranteed

During the course of the project, training data from two coffee machines had to be collected. Machine A was the regular coffee machine of the Porsche Digital Lab and thus available from the start of the project. We analyzed the coffee machine to determine optimal positioning of the microphone and gathered a large amount of training data. However, Machine A lacked mobility because of its fixed water supply. Halfway through the project, the team was supplied with the mobile coffee machine, Machine B. This featured a compact design and water tank and was deployable in mobile scenarios and could thus be presented in various internal presentations and innovation fairs. Changing to Machine B resulted in several days' worth of debugging and error handling because Machine B produced noise in a non-deterministic manner because of the missing fixed water supply, efflux, compact design and not optimized software. A major lesson learned was that the integrity of the setup needs to be saved at all costs especially when neural networks are involved and time for experiments is limited.

Lesson 3: Microcomputers Are Sufficient for Sound Analysis with Neural Networks

Sound processing and analysis, as time-series analysis, is a resource-intensive task and has traditionally been reserved for workstations and laptops. In this project, we learned that a standard off-the-shelf Raspberry PI can compute complex tasks like sound (pre-)processing, TensorFlow applications and an MQTT Broker in parallel utilizing a programming language like Python. Given the availability of such small general-purpose computing devices and their ability to execute state of the art software for embedding neural networks into applications, many IoT applications can be prototyped and deployed in various scenarios easily. This way it is possible to move from cloud-based computing to edge computing which is carried out at the point of interest.

Lesson 4: Early Use of Target Hardware
IoT projects are limited by the available hardware despite the advancements in raw processing power. Limitations comprise but are not limited to speed, chip architecture and available software libraries. The Raspberry PIs feature (like most embedded devices) a CPU in ARM architecture. The speed of the Raspberry PI is sufficient for almost all everyday applications, but the preprocessing of recorded sounds overloaded the PI, especially because Python can only utilize one core for the execution (see "Lesson 5"). Moreover, the ARM architecture does not support the usage of certain standard Linux packages, which were initially used during development but could not be implemented on the Raspberry PIs. Since package limitations do not occur on usual development machines (which normally feature fast processing speeds, x64 architecture), errors and the lack of compute power only becomes obvious after deployment on the target architecture is done. Differing sound qualities due to variable sound processing techniques and hardware between laptop and Raspberry PI proved to be cause of errors since neural network rely on input data being processed in a similar manner to the training data.

Lesson 5: General Purpose Programming Languages Are Not Sufficient for Specialized Tasks
Python as a programming language has several benefits like ease of use and the large number of available and actively maintained packages. Nevertheless, some Python libraries are too slow to be utilized for production applications. Additionally, the 'Global Interpreter Lock' (GIL) in Python prevents efficient multi-threading for most cases. Effectively, this means only one CPU core is used resulting in a significant slowdown in performance. This problem occurs in every processing heavy script. Hardware-intense tasks should be done with a programming language which is compiled before the execution and closer to the hardware. This is not a surprising fact but, given that Python has evolved into the primary language for developing neural networks, we feel that it is worth mentioning.

Acknowledgements The presented work was, in parts, funded by MHP Management—und IT—Beratung GmbH and Dr. Ing. h.c. F. Porsche AG. In no particular order, the authors thank Alice Chan, Judith Gabbert, Belal Chaudhary, Claudio Weck and Roman Siejek for their valuable input.

References

Dr. Ing. h.c. F. Porsche AG – Porsche Deutschland (2018) Dr. Ing. h.c. F. Porsche AG – Porsche Deutschland. Available at: http://www.porsche.de. Accessed 31 Jan 2018

Goodfellow I, Bengio Y, Courville A, Bengio Y (2016) Deep learning, vol 1. MIT Press, Cambridge

Gubbi J, Buyya R, Marusic S, Palaniswami M (2013) Internet of Things (IoT): a vision, architectural elements and future directions. Future Gener Comput Syst 29(7):1645–1660

Hashemian HM, Bean WC (2011) State-of-the-art predictive maintenance techniques. IEEE Trans Instrum Meas 60(10):3480–3492

Keras.io (2018) Keras Documentation. Available at: https://keras.io/. Accessed 31 Jan 2018

LeCun Y, Bengio Y, Hinton G (2015) Deep learning. Nature 521(7553):436–444

Librosa.github.io (2018) LibROSA—librosa 0.5.1 documentation. Available at: http://librosa.github.io/librosa/index.html. Accessed 31 Jan 2018

Mhp.com (2018) MHP – a Porsche company. Available at: http://www.mhp.com Accessed 31 Jan 2018

Mobley RK (2002) An introduction to predictive maintenance. Butterworth-Heinemann, Amsterdam

Mqtt.org (2018) MQTT. Available at: http://mqtt.org/. Accessed 31 Jan 2018

Piczak KJ (2015) Environmental sound classification with convolutional neural networks. In: 2015 I.E. 25th international workshop on Machine learning for signal processing (MLSP), September 2015 (pp. 1–6). IEEE

Srivastava N, Hinton G, Krizhevsky A, Sutskever I, Salakhutdinov R (2014) Dropout: a simple way to prevent neural networks from overfitting. J Mach Learn Res 15(1):1929–1958

Sundermeyer M, Schlüter R, Ney H (2012) LSTM neural networks for language modeling. In: Thirteenth Annual Conference of the International Speech Communication Association

Sutskever I, Vinyals O, Le QV (2014) Sequence to sequence learning with neural networks. In: Advances in neural information processing systems, pp 3104–3112

TensorFlow (2018) TensorFlow. Available at: https://www.tensorflow.org/. Accessed 31 Jan 2018

Upton E, Halfacree G (2014) Raspberry Pi user guide. Wiley, Chichester

Wright GL, Wright MA (2015) U.S. Patent No. 8,983,677. Washington, DC: U.S. Patent and Trademark Office

Wu SJ, Gebraeel N, Lawley MA, Yih Y (2007) A neural network integrated decision support system for condition-based optimal predictive maintenance policy. IEEE Trans Syst Man Cybern Part A Syst Hum 37(2):226–236

Yang W, Tavner PJ, Crabtree CJ, Feng Y, Qiu Y (2014) Wind turbine condition monitoring: technical and commercial challenges. Wind Energy 17(5):673–693

Matthias Auf der Mauer is the Topic Owner of Industry 4.0 at the Porsche Digital Lab in Berlin. Currently, his research activities are concerned with Internet of Things Technologies with a focus on predictive maintenance applications. Mr. Auf der Mauer received a M.Sc. degree in Micro and Nano Technologies and a B.Sc. degree in Mechanical Engineering from ETH Zurich. During his academic career, he conducted research on the development CMOS flow cytometers at UC Berkeley. Additionally, he gained practical experience with distributed air quality sensor networks with Clarity, a Berkeley based sensor startup.

Tristan Behrens holds a PhD in Computer Science, granted by Clausthal University of Technology in 2012. In his thesis, he focused on software engineering in the multi-agent-systems domain. After university, Dr. Behrens went into industry, where he worked for clients such as Volkswagen AG, HeidelbergCement AG and Porsche AG. There, he contributed to accelerating digitalization in the fields of mobility, client-server software architecture, and artificial intelligence. From mid-2016 until the end of 2017 he was a core-member of Porsche Digital Lab Berlin. Currently, Dr. Behrens works as a freelancing AI expert.

Mahdi Derakhshanmanesh is the Director of the Porsche Digital Lab in Berlin. His current research and consulting activities span many aspects of software engineering and CIO advisory with a focus on applications in the automotive industry. Doctor Derakhshanmanesh received Ph.D. and M. Sc. degrees in Computer Science from the University of Koblenz-Landau as well as a B.Sc. in Computer Science from the Johannes Gutenberg University Mainz.

Christopher Hansen is a working student at the Porsche Digital Lab in Berlin and writing his Bachelor Thesis. He is currently conducting research with a focus on artificial intelligence and Internet of Things technologies.

Stefan Muderack is a Senior Consultant at MHP—A Porsche Company and currently responsible for building a team for the SoundDetective in the MHPLab Berlin. His present research and consulting activities span over many aspects of innovations in the fields of Internet of Things, artificial intelligence and CIO Advisory with a focus on the automotive and manufacturing industry. From February 2017 until the beginning of 2018 he was the Topic Owner of Industry 4.0 in the Porsche Digital Lab Berlin. Mr. Muderack received a university diploma in Computer Science from the University of Rostock.

Part II

Digital Business

Industry 4.0 Enabling Smart Air: Digital Transformation at KAESER COMPRESSORS

Maximilian Bock, Martin Wiener, Ralf Gronau, and Andreas Martin

Abstract

(a) **Situation faced**: The case company, KAESER, is a leading manufacturer of compressed air systems and services with worldwide operations. The air compressor industry is characterized by high competition and has undergone significant changes over the last three decades. In response to shifting customer demands, KAESER started to transform and expand its traditional business model.

(b) **Action taken**: KAESER introduced a service-based operator model, called SIGMA AIR UTILITY. In this model, customers no longer purchase the customized air compressors but pay a monthly base only for the compressed air they used. KAESER remains owner of the system, building and operating the compressors on the customer's behalf. Industry 4.0 technologies play a key role in the success of this new operator model by enabling operational efficiencies resulting from big data analytics and predictive maintenance.

(c) **Results achieved**: The SIGMA AIR UTILITY operator model leads to numerous benefits for both KAESER and its customers. Key benefits from a customer perspective include reduced cost and increased flexibility, the transfer of operational risks, increased transparency, and improved

M. Bock (✉)
Friedrich-Alexander Universität, Nürnberg, Germany
e-mail: maximilian.bock@fau.de

M. Wiener
Bentley University, Waltham, MA, USA
e-mail: mwiener@bentley.edu

R. Gronau · A. Martin
KAESER KOMPRESSOREN, Coburg, Germany
e-mail: ralf.gronau@kaeser.com; andreas.martin@kaeser.com

© Springer International Publishing AG, part of Springer Nature 2019
N. Urbach, M. Röglinger (eds.), *Digitalization Cases*, Management for Professionals, https://doi.org/10.1007/978-3-319-95273-4_6

operational planning. From KAESER's perspective, main benefits are the reduction in service cost, the development of a long-term partnership with customers, and synergies in product development and innovation.

(d) **Lessons learned**: KAESER learned numerous lessons from the successful introduction of its service-based operator model. Key lessons learned relate to a lack of cost transparency on the customer side, the changing role of the sales department, the importance of partnerships, the emergence of new risks, the offering of a 'mixed' model as an intermediate step, the role of data privacy and security concerns, and a need for interdisciplinary teams.

1   Introduction

When building a new production facility, most companies would probably not consider purchasing their own power station and generating their own electrical power; rather they would simply sign a utility contract with an electricity supplier. However, when it comes to compressed air—which is just like electricity a utility vital for a wide range of industries, from producing water bottles to spray painting—it today is still common practice in many companies to operate and maintain their own air compressors. Within KAESER COMPRESSORS, the case company, this prompted the central question of what their customers really need—compressors or compressed air—and eventually led to a significant transformation of their business model.

KAESER operates in the mechanical engineering industry and is specialized in designing and producing compressed air systems. Founded in 1919 and headquartered in Coburg, Germany, KAESER is a family-owned business that produces its compressors exclusively in Germany with a high vertical range of manufacturing. Its product portfolio ranges from small, partly mobile, air compressors used by carpenters, dentists, and construction firms to large stationary compressors with a power of up to 500 kW, generating air pressure of up to 15 bar and weighing up to 10 tons. To sell its air compressors, KAESER uses both direct and indirect sales channels. For the latter, it relies on a wide network of sales and service partners worldwide. In addition to selling compressors, KAESER also offers a wide range of services such as installation and maintenance. For this purpose, KAESER employs internal service technicians and cooperates with service partners spread all over the world. In 2016, KAESER marketed its compressors and related services to customers from more than 140 countries and generated revenues of 798.6 million €. In total, KAESER employs more than 5500 employees worldwide, of which around 1900 are located in Coburg (KAESER 2017a).

KAESER's traditional business model was based exclusively on selling and installing customized air compressor stations (consisting of one or multiple compressors, dryers, etc.) to customers from a broad range of industries as well as on providing these customers with after-sales services (e.g., maintenance). However, more recently, KAESER expanded its market offerings by a service-based operator model called SIGMA AIR UTILITY. In this model, customers no longer buy the (customized) air compressor station but pay KAESER a usage-based service fee for providing them with a set amount of compressed air in a defined quality and with an assured availability. SIGMA AIR UTILITY also means that KAESER stays owner of the technical equipment (installed at the customer's site) and performs all maintenance services in the form of an all-around carefree package for the customer (KAESER 2017b).

The new service-based operator model is one key cornerstone of the digital transformation at KAESER. This transformation aims at adopting Industry 4.0 technologies and trends—such as digital metering, big data analytics and predictive maintenance—in order to provide customers with 'Smart Air' (Lasi et al. 2014; Wortmann and Flüchter 2015).

In the following, we present the case of how KAESER leveraged Industry 4.0 technologies to transform and expand its traditional business model. In particular, our case study sheds light on the factors driving KAESER's decision to introduce a service-based operator model (SIGMA AIR UTILITY) as well as on the benefits realized and the lessons learned from the introduction of this new model.

2   Situation Faced

Over the last three decades, the air compressor industry has undergone several substantial shifts, mainly driven by changing customer demands (market pull). For example, back in the 1980s, customers used to buy all the components needed for an air compressor station (i.e., one or multiple compressors, dryers, etc.) and put them together on their own. This started to change in the 1990s, when customers started to look for system solutions. For KAESER, which until then was mainly focused on the technological development of compressor components and equipment, this led to the addition of a broad range of services (e.g., installation and maintenance) to its product portfolio.

On a related note, the air compressor industry is characterized by high competition among four globally operating manufacturers—with KAESER being one of them—and a considerable number of niche players. Consequently, customers have a relatively high bargaining power. Specifically, when a company identifies the need for one or multiple new air compressors and releases an invitation to bid, it can collect offers from numerous different suppliers. Here, since basic technical parameters are usually clearly specified, the customer can easily compare the different offers and make a decision mainly dependent on the prices offered. Examples for such technical parameters are the volume and quality of compressed air, as well as the required pressure and energy consumption. Moreover, the modular architecture of air compressors enables customers to combine equipment from different suppliers, further increasing their bargaining power.

Regarding the provision of after-sales services, the market is even more competitive. Since all manufacturers use similar technologies for the generation of compressed air, market players are often able to offer basic services (e.g., maintenance) for the compressors of their competitors. In other words, the customer's use of an air compressor by one specific manufacturer does not result in a technological lock-in regarding after-sales services; rather, customers typically invite numerous suppliers to bid on the provision of maintenance services, repair services, etc. Such bidding usually also involves sales distributors and service firms, which contributes to a further increase in competitive pressure. For example, it is not unusual that a manufacturer (e.g., KAESER) sells and installs a customized air compressor station, but then loses the bid for maintenance services to a sales distributor or competitor.

Given the highly competitive industry environment, it becomes even more important for market players to quickly respond to shifts in customer demands. Here, one specific instance of an, at least at that time, somewhat unusual customer inquiry had a lasting effect on KAESER. In 1991, a large German conglomerate with high demands in compressed air was struggling with maintaining its air compressors, leading to major production problems such as production disruptions and stoppages. This company thus asked KAESER to provide them with compressed air, just like they buy electricity. Back then, this inquiry was far out of scope of KAESER's daily business and far beyond what was common in the market. After careful consideration and extensive manual calculations, KAESER decided to offer this customer a fixed-price contract providing a defined amount of compressed air, in a certain quality and with a set pressure. This marked the birth of a new operator model, which is today marketed under the name SIGMA AIR UTILITY.

3   Action Taken

Given their positive experiences with offering a fixed-price contract to one of its customers, KAESER managers started to ask themselves: What is it that our customers really need—compressors or compressed air? Just as in the case of electrical power, the obvious answer is the latter. Nevertheless, after issuing the first fixed-price contract, KAESER waited until the mid-2000s to offer its service-based operator model on the market. Until then, it used the experiences gained from the first customer contract to further develop this model and make it ready for the market. The development and market introduction of the new operator model was mainly driven by KAESER's sales department, which also observed a general shift in market demand from individual components to complete solutions. Recognizing the significant market potentials of the service-based operator model early on, the family owners of KAESER, who continue serving on the company's management board, have granted extensive support for this initiative from 'day one.'

For KAESER, the operator model entailed the shift to a completely new market offering, as it changed the focus of the company from selling machinery to offering a utility service, namely compressed air. This, in turn, gave rise to a new set of business requirements. For example, standard contracts for the new operator model had to be designed; reliable methods for calculating the service fee based on past maintenance cost had to be developed; etc. Also, the introduction of the new operator model affected KAESER's organizational structure. For example, a new organizational unit was established within the service department. This unit was held responsible for managing all service orders originating from SIGMA AIR UTILITY contracts. Relatedly, the model introduction required the service and sales departments to collaborate more closely.

For customers, the new service-based operator model means that they no longer buy a compressor station, but that they pay KAESER a monthly fee for providing compressed air in a defined quality. This monthly fee is based on the actual usage of compressed air. As indicated above, for KAESER, this means that they expand their value creation from manufacturing, installing and servicing air compressor stations to actually operating such stations. Here, one key difference between the operator model and the traditional model is that, in the aforementioned, KAESER is also responsible for the assurance of operator obligations that come with operating technical equipment. These obligations are legally binding and, for example, include the regular inspection of pressure tanks and other technical parts as well as the assessment of operational risks.

As of today, KAESER is one of the market leaders in offering compressed air in the form of a pure operator model and operates a large number of SIGMA AIR UTILITY compressor stations worldwide. With these compressor stations, KAESER generates more than 2 billion cubic meters of compressed air per year. This accounts for a total installed electrical power of more than 75 MW, which equals the output of a small nuclear power plant. Even though it is up to KAESER how they generate and deliver the compressed air to the customer, they are limited by technological restrictions and the cost of energy production. Most importantly, in contrast to electrical power, compressed air cannot be transported via long wires or pipes. Therefore, offering the service-based operator model (SIGMA AIR UTILITY) still requires KAESER to install customized compressor stations at the customers' site. In this context, KAESER has introduced numerous Industry 4.0 technologies to support its new operator model. These digital technologies play a critical role in enabling KAESER to optimize service provision along the entire lifecycle of a SIGMA AIR UTILITY contract. In the following, we will describe the three major lifecycle phases of the new operator model (development, installation, and operation) alongside key technologies for each phase.

Development After a potential customer has indicated its interest in one or multiple new compressors, the first step for KAESER is to analyze the specific demand of compressed air of this customer with regard to amount, pressure, quality, and availability. Here, a critical step is the so-called Air Demand Analysis (ADA). During this analysis a data-logger is connected to the existing compressor station of the potential customer and collects information on air pressures and usage amounts over a period of at least 10 days. Given the importance of the data-loggers, KAESER decided to enter into a partnership with T-Systems in order to equip data-loggers with network technology. This enables KAESER engineers to accurately track the position and status of each data-logger (e.g., battery charge level). In addition to the logged data, KAESER sales engineers collect further information at the potential customer's site. The collection of additional information is facilitated by checklists and, among other things, concerns the space available for the new compressor station as well as external factors that influence the production of compressed air. An example for such an influencing factor is the amount of dust in the production facility. All collected information is then gathered at KAESER headquarters in Coburg, where engineers develop a technical concept for the new compressor station. Another important tool in the development phase is the so-called KAESER Energy Savings System (KESS). This tool helps engineers simulate different technological configurations for the to-be-developed air compressor station, based on data gathered during the ADA as well as past experiences. Since up to 80% of the cost for generating compressed air come from electricity costs, the focus of these simulations lies on the energy efficiency of the compressor station. The simulation results allow KAESER to guarantee its SIGMA AIR UTILITY customers a certain level of energy efficiency in the contract. The energy costs along with the expected investment and technical service costs also build the basis for calculating the contract lifecycle costs. Here, a detailed IT-supported analysis of past contracts, including maintenance services, allows KAESER to automate cost calculations. As a result, KAESER is able to determine the offered price per cubic meter compressed air within less than an hour.

Installation If the customer accepts KAESER's offer and opts for a SIGMA AIR UTILITY contract, KAESER will install the technical equipment required for the generation (and purification) of compressed air at the customer's site. In addition, KAESER will install industry PCs, a control device for the air compressor station, and network technology including a SAP Internet of Things (IoT) client. This IoT client connects the compressor station with a central SAP HANA database at KAESER headquarters in Coburg (see Fig. 1). More specifically, every machine in the compressor station (e.g., an air compressor or dryer) is equipped with an industry PC, which allows for the regulation of the technical equipment and for the gathering of relevant data. The PCs of all machines of a compressor station are then linked to one so-called SIGMA AIR MANAGER 4.0 (SAM) via an Ethernet-based data connection, referred to as SIGMA NETWORK. The SAM is a tablet-like device and has two core functions. First, it controls the machinery in the SIGMA NETWORK to ensure that the compressor station produces the current demand of compressed air in the most energy-efficient way. Second, it collects data from the different machinery of a compressor station and sends them to the central database in Coburg. This data transfer is realized via an Ethernet connection between the SAM and the IoT client, which in turn is connected to the central database. For the connection between the IoT Client and the database, there are currently three options available: (1) via the customer network, (2) via a separate DSL connection installed by KAESER, or (3) via a mobile connection. For security reasons, the database connection works in only one direction (from the SAM to the database); this ensures that it is not possible to control the compressor station from outside of the customer's production facility.

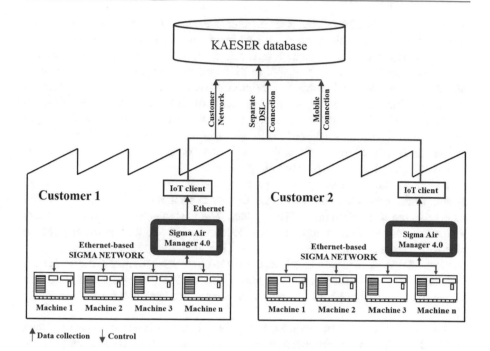

Fig. 1 Technical infrastructure of SIGMA AIR UTILITY model

On a related note, only the IoT client is able to communicate with the central database to minimize the risk of data manipulation. As of recently, KAESER has started to equip all air compressor stations of SIGMA AIR UTILITY customers with the above-described network technology.

Operation Once the technical and network equipment has been installed at the customer site, the so-called KAESER Plant Control Center—a dedicated organizational unit in the service department—monitors the operation of the deployed air compressor stations. To do so, KAESER engineers working at the Plant Control Center can see a graphical map of all SIGMA AIR UTILITY compressor stations worldwide with colored icons indicating the operational status of each station. Here, an orange icon indicates that a planned service is coming up and a red icon indicates that there is a problem with a compressor station. In the latter case, engineers can look into the affected plant, get a detailed overview of relevant parameters, and then decide on whether a service technician is needed to fix the problem.

In addition to monitoring the operational status of the installed compressor stations, the Plant Control Center also analyzes the data collected from the individual machines with the goal of identifying and anticipating operational issues. The Plant Control Center collects and monitors numerous operating metrics per machine, which are for example related to power consumption, machine temperatures, pressures and vibrations. The relevant data are automatically transferred to the central database. In this context, a key metric is the so-called 'reserve level' (*Reservegrad*), which indicates how much compressed air a particular station would be able to produce in response to a demand increase. Such an increase might for example result from the addition of new machinery to the customer's production facility or from an increase in output of an existing production line. On this basis, KAESER engineers can identify bottlenecks of compressor stations early on; that is, before a SIGMA AIR UTILITY customer may have to halt production processes. Another key metric is the customer's consumption of compressed air, which is required for the monthly billing cycle.

Based on the analysis of key operating metrics, planned service orders are automatically generated and distributed to service technicians through KAESER's enterprise resource planning (ERP) system. The system-generated service orders include all contract and compressor-specific information that the technician needs to perform the required maintenance services. This integration was realized in collaboration with SAP, which provides both the HANA database and the ERP system used by KAESER. The two companies have been working together closely for more than 20 years, and KAESER has been serving as a reference customer for SAP for many years.

The actual execution of service orders is based on an advanced service concept, which KAESER has introduced over the last years. In this concept, service technicians carry about 80% of standard spare parts in their vehicle. All other spare parts needed for a specific service order are either sent directly to the customer via a logistics service provider, or are delivered to a service container where the service technician can pick them up. These service containers are comparable to a post office box.

In this context, another important goal of KAESER's Plant Control Center is to convert unplanned service orders into planned ones. To reach this goal, engineers conduct sophisticated data analyses to predict maintenance intervals of air compressor stations installed in the field.

4   Results Achieved

The introduction of the service-based operator model SIGMA AIR UTILITY resulted in several benefits for both KAESER and its customers. Key benefits for both sides are discussed in the following.

4.1   Benefits for Customers

Reduced Cost and Increased Flexibility From a customer perspective, an obvious benefit of the SIGMA AIR UTILITY operator model is the reduction in fixed cost. This results from the fact that the customer does not buy the compressor station and does not have to employ dedicated staff for its maintenance; rather, the customer

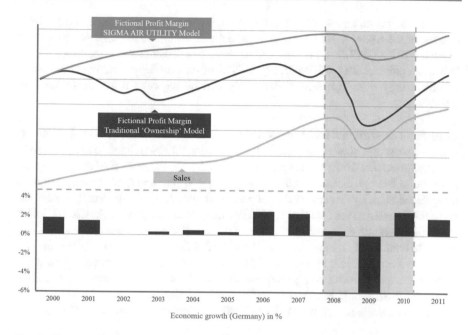

Fig. 2 Financial benefits of SIGMA AIR UTILITY model (illustration) (KAESER 2017b)

pays only a monthly fee. Given that this fee largely depends on the actual consumption, the customer's cost for compressed air will be more directly related to the production output. Figure 2 illustrates this benefit by comparing the development of the profit margins of a fictional customer firm in the SIGMA AIR UTILITY model versus the traditional 'ownership' model.

For example, let's assume that, as a result of the economic crisis in 2009, total sales of the fictional company decreased significantly for this year. In the case of the traditional ownership model, this decrease would have led to an even more significant decrease in the company's profit margin, since, for example, the depreciation costs of the purchased technical equipment would have remained constant (see Fig. 2). In contrast, in the SIGMA AIR UTILITY case, the decrease in profit margin would have been less significant. On a related note, in comparison to the traditional model, the service-based operator model can also be beneficial from an accounting viewpoint. This is because the SIGMA AIR UTILITY service fees are operating expenses that affect only the customer's profit and loss statement but not its balance sheet.

In addition, SIGMA AIR UTILITY customers benefit from reduced indirect costs. For example, since KAESER owns and operates the air compressor station, it is also required to cover all costs resulting from operator obligations such as costs for periodical technical inspections, etc. Also, the operator model enables customers to free up internal resources bound to the management and maintenance of the compressor station, and to reassign these resources to other, more important tasks, such as the optimization of the production facility. Finally, another cost-related benefit of the SIGMA AIR UTILITY model concerns the fact that, due to its rich experience, KAESER can be expected to operate the customer's compressor station in a more efficient way. Given that up to 80% of the cost for generating compressed air are energy cost, operational efficiency can be regarded a key lever for cost reduction.

Transfer of Operational Risks Another benefit of the SIGMA AIR UTILITY model from a customer's view is that it transfers operational risks (related to the generation of compressed air) from the customer to KAESER. For example, KAESER is legally required to bear all risks related to complying with the above-mentioned operator obligations, such as the certification of pressure tanks. Another important operational risk factor relates to the fact that KAESER can guarantee its SIGMA AIR UTILITY customers a certain energy-efficiency level of the installed compressor station, which is tied to bonus and malus payments. This implies that KAESER also bears all risks related to the inefficient operation of the compressor station. In other words, if the energy efficiency of the compressor station falls below the contractually specified level, KAESER would have to cover the additional electricity costs. This transfer of operational risks is in line with prior scientific findings (e.g. Ehret and Wirtz 2016).

Increased Transparency For customers, the SIGMA AIR UTILITY model also contributes to an increase in cost transparency. According to a company-internal survey, 9 out of 10 customers that operate their own air compressor station do not know the exact total cost associated with the generation of compressed air. This can be explained by the numerous indirect cost factors affiliated with owning and operating an air compressor station. These factors include tasks such as compressor maintenance and the assurance of operator obligations. In the SIGMA AIR UTILITY model, all these indirect costs are included in the monthly service fee.

In addition, KAESER performs a wide range of analyses concerning the operation of the air compressor stations, which contributes to a further increase in customer transparency. For example, KAESER engineers meet with representatives of each SIGMA AIR UTILITY customer at least once per year and give them an update on their company's use of compressed air over time, possibilities regarding energy savings, and the current *Reservegrad* of their compressor station. This information enables customers to further optimize their production processes.

Improved Operational Planning Relatedly, the SIGMA AIR UTILITY model enables customers to better plan their future demand of compressed air. In parts, this follows from the above-described benefits regarding the transfer of operational risks and the increase in transparency. Also, SIGMA AIR UTILITY customers benefit from planning certainty since KAESER guarantees them a fixed price per cubic meter of compressed air for the complete duration of the contract, which is usually around 10–15 years.

4.2   Benefits for KAESER

Reduction in Service Cost KAESER gathers extensive and detailed data from the SIGMA AIR UTILITY compressor stations it operates. The goal of collecting this data is on the one hand to prevent unplanned outages and on the other hand to synchronize planned service intervals with the actual lifecycle of the technical equipment. Here, the constant analysis of the collected data helps KAESER reduce service cost. For example, data analyses for predictive maintenance enable KAESER to prolong planned service intervals (e.g., if a compressor was used less than anticipated) as well as to reduce the number of costly unplanned services (e.g., during the weekend or at night) by combining them with planned services.

Moreover, the integration of different data pools (e.g., data on compressor operations and ERP data) enables KAESER to provide its service technicians with detailed information on each service order. Further, automated analyses of this integrated data make sure that all necessary spare parts are available before a service order is generated. In doing so, KAESER is able to increase the productivity of its service technicians, for example, by avoiding that a technician wastes its valuable time with driving to a customer's site despite lacking some of the parts needed for completing the requested service.

Long-Term Partnership with Customers For KAESER, another major benefit of the SIGMA AIR UTILITY model is the development of a close and long-term relationship with its customers. For example, all services for the complete contract duration are included in the monthly service fee. The close customer relationship often also leads to the renewal of the service contract once the initial contract has expired. A related benefit is that the establishment of a long-term partnership enables KAESER to better plan its service business (e.g., in terms of staffing).

In this context, the collection and analysis of data on the current status and performance of the customers' compressor stations serves KAESER as a basis for further intensifying the relationship with its customers. For example, the data analysis allows KAESER sales agents to stay in close contact with customers as well as to provide them with additional insights. Specifically, the analysis results may indicate that the customer's demand of compressed air has been constantly increasing for a certain time period. In this case, KAESER would offer the customer to 'upgrade' the SIGMA AIR UTILITY contract accordingly (e.g. by adding an additional compressor).

Product Development and Innovation In terms of benefits related to research and development, the massive data collected and analyzed as part of the SIGMA AIR UTILITY operator model again play a pivotal role. For example, insights gained from data analysis help KAESER identify the root causes of serial defects, which may stem from problems with parts delivered by certain suppliers or from design errors during engineering. This, in turn, also facilitates the quick resolution of corresponding defects. Adding to this, data analysis results, e.g., on the energy efficiency of existing compressor products, provide important input for the design and further improvement of future products.

---

5   Lessons Learned

While SIGMA AIR UTILITY offers numerous benefits to customers and has helped KAESER reap several benefits for itself, the transition to this service-based operator model was far from being easy and is still ongoing. In the following, we present a set of seven key lessons learned derived from KAESER's experiences with the introduction of its novel operator model.

1. **Lack of cost transparency on customer side:** As noted above, many companies do not know the total cost of owning and operating a compressor station, which includes several indirect cost factors such as regular maintenance and legal compliance costs (e.g., related to operator obligations). For KAESER, this lack of cost transparency created the challenge that some potential SIGMA AIR UTILITY customers find it difficult to compare the offered service fee against the cost associated with alternative buying options. Here, some potential customers also seem to be concerned that KAESER may use its service-based operator model to disguise the actual price of the compressor station. In response, KAESER developed extensive training programs to 'educate' its sales engineers on the pros and cons of the new operator model. Also, with the new model, sales engineers are encouraged to devote even more time to closely interacting with their customer contacts in order to explain and discuss customer-specific benefits (and potential drawbacks) of the SIGMA AIR UTILITY model.

2. **Changing role of sales department:** From a sales perspective, one may argue that a SIGMA AIR UTILITY customer has already signed up for the all-round carefree package and therefore requires less attention than a customer purchasing a compressor station. In KAESER's experience, however, it is just the opposite. In essence, this is because of the close partnership between KAESER and its SIGMA AIR UTILITY customers and the significant efforts required for cultivating this partnership (e.g., preparation of regular meetings). For KAESER, it is thus of critical importance to keep 'investing' in the relationship with each and every SIGMA AIR UTILITY customer. Otherwise, the contact to the customer is likely to break off during the contract duration—which may range from 10 to 15 years—and the customer will be unlikely to renew its contract (even if KAESER fulfilled all contractual obligations). In this regard, the scheduling of regular review meetings represents a vital tool for fostering the customer relationship by offering KAESER sales engineers the opportunity to provide customers with new insights and show interest in their concerns and problems.

   Relatedly, with the introduction of the SIGMA AIR UTILITY operator model, KAESER's focus as a company shifted, at least partly, from a pure technology focus to a stronger business focus. This shift also affected the daily work of sales engineers. In particular, in the past, sales conversations tended to focus on the discussion of technical aspects. In contrast, nowadays, business aspects play an increasingly important role in such conversations. For KAESER's sales department, this change had two major consequences. First, sales engineers had to be sensitized for, and educated on, the unique features of the service-based operator model and the importance of a partnership-like customer relationship for this model. Second, for sales engineers, it became important to not only talk to their 'traditional', more technical customer contacts (e.g., in plant maintenance), but to also involve business-oriented people (e.g., division heads, accountants) in sales conversations. Typically, the latter are more accessible when it comes to the business benefits of the service-based operator model.

Although the introduction of SIGMA AIR UTILITY led to significant changes in work processes and practices for many KAESER employees (e.g., sales engineers—see above), most employees are highly committed to this model, as they see it as an important chance for the company, as well as for themselves. To further employee commitment, the KAESER management board has also created financial incentives, e.g., for sales engineers, related to the adoption of the new service-based operator model.

3. **Importance of partnerships:** For KAESER, the introduction of SIGMA AIR UTILITY entails entertaining partnership-like relationships with customers as well as close partnerships with key technology suppliers including SAP and T-Systems. For example, serving as a SAP reference customer, KAESER was among the early adopters of the SAP HANA database, which serves as the backbone of the data analyses performed at KAESER's Plant Control Center. Further, KAESER and SAP collaborated closely on further developing the database functionalities, which led to a win–win situation for both firms.

   Similarly, the operator model allows KAESER to equip its air compressor stations with the latest technologies, enabling the collection of 'big data' from these stations. This data in turn are used to further improve the availability and efficiency of compressor stations and to increase their availability, which also benefits KAESER's customers and thus again creates a win–win situation for both parties.

4. **Emergence of new risks:** Given that KAESER keeps ownership of the air compressor stations in the SIGMA AIR UTILITY model, several additional risks emerge that need to be carefully managed. One such risk relates to the solvency of SIGMA AIR UTILITY customers. For example, for each customer, KAESER has to make significant upfront investments (e.g., development and production of customized compressor station, installation of compressor station at customer site) to be amortized over the lifespan of the customer contract. However, if a customer goes bankrupt before the expiration of the contract, this will result in a loss for KAESER. In consequence, KAESER now performs a detailed solvency analysis for each customer before signing a SIGMA AIR UTILITY contract.

   A new operational risk of KAESER's service-based operator model concerns the external conditions at a customer's production facility. For example, high dust levels in production halls accelerate the clogging of air filters, requiring KAESER to replace filters more frequently and thus driving maintenance cost. To mitigate this risk, KAESER performs a detailed analysis of customer facilities and their environment during the development phase of a SIGMA AIR UTILITY project. The results of this analysis represent a critical input for the calculation of the customer-specific service fees. A related operational risk for KAESER concerns unforeseen contingencies. For example, in a worst-case scenario, an incident such as the complete failure of a compressor station in the last week of a service contract might jeopardize the profitability of the entire contract. Here, KAESER uses sophisticated data analyses performed by the Plant Control Center and continuous financial controlling of all contracts to reduce this risk to a minimum. In addition, the considerable number of SIGMA AIR UTILITY contracts helps KAESER diversify the risks associated with each individual contract.

5. **Offering of 'mixed' model as intermediate step:** To further mitigate the risks described above, KAESER has defined clear and strict rules for SIGMA AIR UTILITY contracts. For example, such a contract will only be offered if the customer requests a new compressor station that consists exclusively of original parts manufactured by KAESER. On the other hand, potential customers of the SIGMA AIR UTILITY model sometimes fear the loss of know-how regarding the operation and maintenance of air compressors, and therefore decide against this model. Against this backdrop, KAESER decided to introduce an additional operator model, called SIGMA FLEX (KAESER 2017c), which can be seen as a light version of the SIGMA AIR UTILITY model. This 'mixed' model is primarily targeted at companies that have purchased their own air compressor station just recently (e.g., 3–4 years ago) and would like to add another air compressor to this station (e.g., due to an increasing demand in compressed air).

   In the SIGMA FLEX model, the customer rents the compressors and KAESER takes on responsibility for all services. However, in contrast to the SIGMA AIR UTILITY model, with this model, operator obligations stay with the customer and installation cost are not included. Due to the reduced scope and lower operational risk of the SIGMA FLEX model, KAESER is able to offer customers short-term contracts for this model and also allows them to terminate the contract for economic reasons. For KAESER, the key advantage of offering this 'mixed' model is that it can serve as an intermediate step between the traditional owner-ship model and the adoption of the SIGMA AIR UTILITY model, since SIGMA FLEX enables customers to become familiar with the benefits of an operator model.

6. **Data privacy and security concerns:** KAESER's service-based operator model centers on the remote collection of massive operational data from air compressors installed at customer sites. Thus, unsurprisingly, data privacy and security become of particular concern to customers. Consequently, KAESER goes to great lengths in securing the network infrastructure that connects the air compressor stations with KAESER's central database in order to prevent unauthorized data and network access. For example, the database connection works in only one direction and only the SAP IoT client is able to communicate with the database.

This high importance of security is in line with prior research on the Internet of Things (e.g., Wortmann and Flüchter 2015).

On the other hand, data privacy—with regard to the operational data gathered from the compressor stations—seems to be less of a concern to most of KAESER's customers. This can be explained by the fact that the collected raw data are not of particular value to anybody except for KAESER.

7. **Need for interdisciplinary teams:** The introduction of the SIGMA AIR UTILITY operator model affected virtually all organizational units of KAESER—from research and development to marketing and sales to service—and therefore necessitated close collaboration across these units (e.g., Dremel et al. 2017). For example, the new operator model requires engineers working at the KAESER Plant Control Center to work hand-in-hand with service technicians and sales engineers. Eventually, this has led to a major change in KAESER's organizational structure from a focus on working in vertical departments with clearly defined interfaces to an emphasis on forming interdisciplinary project teams. The latter enables KAESER to bring together the expert knowledge from highly specialized departments, and project team members to see and understand the 'bigger' picture.

The 'digital revolution' has had and will continue to have a significant impact on traditional manufacturing companies worldwide by forcing them to rethink established ways of doing business. In this context, KAESER is a prime example of an established company that leveraged Industry 4.0 technologies to expand its traditional business model by a service-based operator model, called SIGMA AIR UTILITY. Centering on big data analytics and predictive maintenance, this novel operator model enables KAESER to provide its customers with 'Smart Air.' In summary, even though the digital transformation of KAESER's business model resulted in numerous challenges requiring substantial technical and organizational changes, SIGMA AIR UTILITY clearly represents a success story for KAESER. Success indicators include, for example, the continuous growth in total revenues generated from SIGMA AIR UTILITY contracts and the expansion of this model from the German market to a global customer base. It is thus our hope that the lessons learned derived from KAESER's experiences can assist other manufacturing companies with the digital transformation of their business models.

References

Dremel C, Wulf J, Herterich MM, Waizmann J-C, Brenner W (2017) How AUDI AG established big data analytics in its digital transformation. MIS Q Executive 16(2):81–100

Ehret M, Wirtz J (2016) Unlocking value from machines: business models and the industrial internet of things. J Mark Manag

KAESER (2017a) KAESER KOMPRESSOREN – company profile. http://www.kaeser.com/int-en/company/about-us/ (visited on 07/15/2017)

KAESER (2017b) Operator model: SIGMA AIR UTILITY. http://www.kaeser.com/int-en/products/sigma-air-utility-operator-model/ (visited on 07/15/2017)

KAESER (2017c) Operator models. http://www.kaeser.com/int-en/solutions/operator-models/ (visited on 07/15/2017)

Lasi H, Kemper H-G, Fettke P, Feld T, Hoffmann M (2014) Industry 4.0. Bus Inf Syst Eng 6 (4):239–242

Wortmann F, Flüchter K (2015) Internet of things – technology and value added. Bus Inf Syst Eng 57(3):221–224

Maximilian Bock is a Research Associate and Ph.D. student at the Chair of IT-Management at Friedrich-Alexander University Erlangen-Nürnberg (Germany). His research concerns digital business models and has been published in major Information Systems conference proceedings (International Conference on Information Systems). His doctoral thesis deals with the enablers, value potentials and challenges of pay-per-use business models with a particular focus on the manufacturing industry. Maximilian Bock holds a Bachelor and Master degree in industrial engineering from the Friedrich-Alexander University Erlangen-Nürnberg (Germany).

Martin Wiener is an Associate Professor in the Information and Process Management (IPM) Department at Bentley University (USA), as well as an Affiliated Researcher at the Stockholm School of Economics Institute for Research (Sweden) and the Friedrich-Alexander University Erlangen-Nürnberg (Germany). His research concerns digital business models, IS project control and IT-mediated control, global IT sourcing, and ICT-related overload, and has been published in top-tier journals such as Journal of Management Information Systems and MIS Quarterly. He currently serves as Associate Editor for Information Systems Journal and as Editorial Review Board Member for Information & Management and Journal of the Association for Information Systems.

Ralf Gronau is Head of Project Sales at KAESER KOMPRESSOREN SE in Coburg. He began his professional career with a technician training at KAESER and later advanced training as a state-certified technician (mechanical engineering). Since 1990, he has been working in the sale of capital goods requiring intensive consulting. His responsibility includes among others, turn-key-projects in the German market, as well as the development, market implementation and realization of operator models with a high degree of digitalization.

Andreas Martin, M.Sc., works as a project engineer at KAESER KOMPRESSOREN SE since 2015, where he is responsible for the realization of compressed air projects, as well as for the development of business models for pay-per-use and predictive maintenance. Andreas Martin studied industrial engineering (B.Sc.) and (M.Sc.) at the Friedrich-Alexander University Erlangen-Nürnberg. In his master thesis, he dealt with the conception, implementation and realization of energy controlling tools. During his studies, he gained practical experience in the automotive industry and at KAESER KOMPRESSOREN SE.

Dual-Track's Strategy for Incumbent's Transformation: The Case of Danske Bank Adopting a Platform Business Model

Kalina S. Staykova and Jan Damsgaard

Abstract

(a) **Situation faced**: The traditionally stable and conservative financial service industry is undergoing a process of transformation where contenders utilizing new technologies and relying on novel business models challenge the role of incumbent financial organizations. The changing preferences of customers, who demand customized services at convenient for them time, and the shifting regulatory environment, which encourages the entry of fintech start-ups, threaten the dominant position of these traditional actors.

(b) **Action taken**: Instead of observing passively this ongoing trend, Danske Bank, one of the leading banks in Northern Europe, took a proactive approach to digitalization by launching pre-emptively a number of disruptive digital initiatives in order to protect itself from disruption. Danske Bank correctly read the market dynamics in Denmark in connection to consumer readiness, technology maturity and competitors' actions and decided to venture into the mobile payment area in order to position itself as first mover. By launching its solution MobilePay, which functions as digital payment platform, Danske Bank also adopted a platform business model, which differs from the traditional banking products.

(c) **Results achieved**: Leveraging its first mover advantage, MobilePay gained momentum and has successfully defended its dominant position in the Danish market, which other local and international mobile payment solutions tried to threaten. Four years after its launch, MobilePay is currently being used by more than 90% of the Danes, has established a growing ecosystem of partners, and has expanded to other Nordic markets.

K. S. Staykova (✉) · J. Damsgaard
Copenhagen Business School, Danske Bank, Copenhagen, Denmark
e-mail: kss.digi@cbs.dk; jd.digi@cbs.dk

© Springer International Publishing AG, part of Springer Nature 2019
N. Urbach, M. Röglinger (eds.), *Digitalization Cases*, Management for Professionals, https://doi.org/10.1007/978-3-319-95273-4_7

MobilePay's success has helped Danske Bank improve its brand image and reduce customer churn. It has also demonstrated Danske Bank's ability to be at the forefront of digital innovation by proving the bank's capability to address the changing preferences of its private customers and to deliver on the digitalization agenda of its corporate customers.

(d) **Lessons learned**: This case demonstrates how an incumbent financial organization can successfully protect its core services by venturing into disruptive digital initiatives, such as the launch of platform business model, which requires the adoption of different business thinking. The success of such initiative depends upon the timely launch of a customer-centric solution with focus on simplicity, ease of use and strong value proposition. Despite the short-term gains, the long-term sustainability and profitability of such a solution operating in constantly changing environment requires its continuous development. Its success also depends on achieving a certain level of organizational autonomy from the traditional business, while at the same time establishing synergy to it in order to gain access to the incumbents' core resources.

1 Introduction

In the recent years, the rapid advancement of digital technologies has led to the disruption of a number of traditional industries, such as music (e.g., iTunes), print media (e.g., Guardian), and transportation (e.g., Uber) (see, e.g., Karimi and Walter 2015). Similarly, the emergence of new actors who offer disruptive financial services by utilizing novel digital technologies (e.g., TransferWise, Square, LevelUP, Zopa, etc.) have recently challenged the traditionally stable and conservative financial industry.

Observing closely this ongoing trend, Danske Bank, the leading bank in Denmark and one of the largest banks in Northern Europe, was contemplating the long-term consequences of this shift. Headquartered in Copenhagen, Denmark, Danske Bank operates in 16 markets and serves more than 2.7 million private customers, app. 240,000 small and medium-sized business customers and around 1800 corporate and institutional customers. With its history tracing back to late nineteenth century, Danske Bank has always been at the forefront of financial service innovation. For example, in 1881 the bank introduced for the first time in Europe safe deposits. It was also among the first in Europe to incorporate payment cards and online banking to its portfolio of financial products. In 1999, the bank launched the first mobile banking service in the world by utilizing the new Wireless Application Protocol (WAP) technology, which allowed its Finnish private customers to connect to their online banking accounts via mobile phone devices.

The present situation, however, was different. Novel digital technologies, such as smartphones, which had absorbed services offered previously by multiple physical devices (e.g., camera, mP3 players, navigation devices), were rapidly adopted by significant part of the population in Northern Europe [e.g., 59% of the Danes had a smartphone in 2013 (Statista 2016)]. This led to a change in consumer preferences, with customers requiring on-demand services tailored to their individual needs. The traditionally strict regulatory environment was also altering as an aftermath of the 2008 financial crisis with regulators demanding a transformation of the financial sector. Thus, Danske Bank, similarly to other incumbent banks, found itself in a fast-paced changing environment, with its competitive advantages eroding significantly.

Instead of awaiting disruption, Danske Bank adopted a proactive approach towards digitalization by pursuing disruptive initiatives within its own business units, which challenged the current modus operandi of the bank. The venturing into a platform business model, which facilitate the interaction between distinct types of actors in a process of value creation and exchange (Hagiu and Wright 2011; Parker et al. 2016), constituted one of the most successful digital disruption initiatives. In particular, Danske Bank launched a mobile payment platform, MobilePay, around which an ecosystem of actors formed over time. MobilePay proved to be a huge success immediately after its release in May 2013. Four years after its launch, app. 90% of the Danish population and app. 75,000 merchants use the platform, which facilitates peer-to-peer (P2P) and consumer-to-business (C2B) payment transactions. MobilePay also has a growing customer base in Finland and, until recently, in Norway.

Although Danske Bank managed to launch successfully a disruptive payment platform, it had to overcome various external and internal challenges, such as establishing viable business model, improving platform resilience and scalability, and addressing increased competitive pressure, in order to ensure the long-term sustainability of the solution. As a result, MobilePay had to evolve constantly by adding new types of participants and by increasing its value proposition towards them. Thus, based on the evolutionary journey of MobilePay, we argue that the success of a digital payment platform requires not only identifying and launching appealing functionalities, but it also evokes its continuous managing and optimization.

In this case, we investigate how a traditional company can successfully launch and manage a digital platform business model and how such a disruptive initiative can help the incumbent protect itself from disruption. To this end, we draw upon first-hand observations, semi-structured interviews and archival documents, which we have collected since the launch of MobilePay—first, by acting as consultants on key strategic decisions, and later, by conducting a 2-year fieldwork on site. We use an inductive approach to analyze the gathered data, based on which we synthetize several key learning points for practitioners and academics alike.

2   Situation Faced

As an incumbent financial institution operating in rapidly changing environment, Danske Bank faced many uncertainties in 2012. The regulatory environment, in which financial institutions operated, altered as an aftermath of the financial crisis in 2008. The already strictly regulated financial industry was subjected to more regulatory requirements in a bid to mitigate the consequences of the financial crisis (Danske Bank 2013). At the same time, the provisions of the new Payment Service Directive 2 (PSD2), with which the European Union (EU) aimed at transforming the payment area in the Single Market, required incumbent banks to open their infrastructures in order to give non-discriminatory access to new actors (European Union 2013). Even though the PDS 2 is about to come into effect in late 2018, it already became a central topic for Danske Bank when it was first proposed in 2013 mainly due to the uncertainty of the consequences, stemming from its implementation for the bank's business model.

The 2008 financial crisis also significantly eroded the consumers' trust in the financial institutions around the world. At the same time, the altering consumer preferences towards easy to use, innovative and real-time solutions also led to banks' customers substituting traditional financial products and services for novel, customer-centered offerings of fintech start-ups. In 2012, these new players, some of whom had managed to achieve significant global user base (e.g., Mint, Zopa, etc.), were about to enter the Danish market as well. For example, iZettle, which delivered innovative Point-of-Sale solutions to small and medium-sized businesses, announced its plans to enter the Danish market in 2012.

In 2012, Danske Bank also faced customer backlash due to the implementation of its new strategy "New Normal-New Standards", which, although emphasizing on introducing new standards for financial services by providing state-of-the-art digital solutions (Danske Bank 2012), failed to deliver optimal results. As result of an ill-planned new customer program, part of the new strategy, and the fiasco of the corresponding marketing campaign, Danske Bank was rapidly losing its private customers, who decided to switch to other financial institutions.

Thus, Danske Bank found itself into a state of flux facing changing consumer preferences, new competitors, rapid spread of emerging technologies (e.g. NFC, dongles, real-time analytics, etc.) and stricter regulatory environment. To tackle these challenges, the financial institution had to undertake a new approach in order to protect its core services, restore its tainted image and remain relevant to the needs of its customers.

3   Action Taken

Observing closely these ongoing trends, in 2012, Danske Bank decided to put focus on customer-centric solutions, digitalization, and increased transparency and trust (Danske Bank 2012). Although top managers perceived digitalization as an ongoing and overarching effort in the bank, they concluded that to protect Danske Bank from disruption, they should also focus on radical digital initiatives, which deviated from the traditional approaches towards innovation. Thus, Danske Bank adopted a dual-track strategy to digitalization—being a classical bank, which embraces digitalization incrementally, while, at the same time, experimenting with disruptive initiatives. Radical, consumer-centric, utilizing novel technologies and relying on agile innovation processes, these disruptive digital initiatives aimed at turning upside down the modus operandi of the bank. To fulfil this vision, Danske Bank was on a quest to identify projects, which would disrupt the bank from within.

Developing and offering a mobile payment platform around which an ecosystem of actors emerges constituted one of these digital disruptive initiatives. Venturing into this new type of digital business models, however, required the adoption of different capabilities and thinking. Thus, instead of relying on traditional business processes and strategies, building a digital platform business model called for the adoption of platform logic (Parker et al. 2016).

3.1   Launch of MobilePay

Situation

In 2013, mobile payments were gaining momentum. Due to increased consumer demand from its private customers, Danske Bank had already been exploring the opportunity to launch a joint sector solution for mobile payments together with other Danish banks. The assumption was that payments via smartphone were to become a fast growing financial channel with significant long-term opportunities for both private and business customers. The common efforts, however, progressed slowly due to various technical issues. In late 2012, the major Danish telecom operators openly announced their intention to enter jointly the mobile payment area. At the same time, fintech start-ups (e.g., iZettle) also revealed their plans to enter the Danish market. Thus, with the shift in the competitive dynamics, various actors engaged in a race to dominate the untapped mobile payment market in Denmark.

Actions Taken

As the competitive environment changed and the talks for joint bank sector solution stalled, Danske Bank decided to leave the common initiative in order to ensure that it launched the first mobile payment solution in the Danish market. Danske Bank's solo venture in this area begun with the set-up of a small, dedicated team of employees, whose task was to develop and launch a mobile payment solution within 6 months. The team had the freedom to explore different innovation methods than the ones usually applied in Danske Bank. Adopting agile principles, business analysts worked closely together with IT specialists in conceptualizing, prototyping and testing the solution. During the development phase, the team considered multiple technologies enabling mobile payments—from Near Field Communication (NFC), QR codes and dongles to solutions utilizing the existing bank infrastructure through pre-paid accounts and even integration to the existing Danske Bank's mobile banking app.

After 6 months of work, in May 2013, Danske Bank launched its mobile payment app, MobilePay, which allowed users to transfer money to their friends and split the bill in various situations. The solution functioned as one-sided platform, enabling the interactions among one distinct group of platform participants, namely private customers, who wanted to send one another money (Hagiu and Wright 2011; Parker et al. 2016). Designing MobilePay as easy to use, simple and intuitive solution, while still maintaining high level of security, reflected Danske Bank's new strategy, which focused on consumer centricity. Instead of developing a complex solution with multiple offerings, the team decided to solve one particular problem, which private customers faced, namely exchanging money with peers. The mobile payment platform utilized the existing card-based infrastructure by allowing users to add their cards to the app and transfer money to their friends via mobile phone numbers. Thus, instead of adopting complex technology, which would have required significant investment and longer development time, MobilePay took advantage of the existing payment infrastructure by leveraging Danske Bank's key assets and expertise.

Results Achieved

The initial strategy estimated that app. 250,000 users would adopt MobilePay within a year after its launch, but the digital payment platform proved to be hugely popular with the Danes. In just 9 months, app. one million users (1/5 of the Danish population), both Danske Bank and non-Danske Bank customers, used the platform, with the number of transactions amounting to more than 134 million euros (MobilePay 2015). In fact, non-Danske bank customers accounted for app. 70% of the total user base of MobilePay. Thus, instead of designing a bank-specific solution, Danske Bank offered open to all users mobile payment platform in order to solidify its position in Denmark. The openness on user level strengthened MobilePay's same-side network effects (that is, the value of MobilePay for existing users increased with the inclusion of new users and vice versa, see, Shapiro and Varian 1999).

Due to the fast market entry, Danske Bank managed to secure a first mover advantage by acquiring large number of private customers within a relatively short time span. This put the bank in advantageous position in comparison to its competitors (that is, other Danish banks, telecom operators and fintech start-ups) as the large and growing user base constituted a significant barrier to entry.

Key Learning Points from MobilePay's Launch Phase

Being a first-mover in a new and not yet defined market, such as mobile payments, is important for ensuring the long-term success of a digital disruptive solution. To share the risks and manage uncertainties, collaborating with other relevant actors is preferable, but in case, there is high consumer demand, intensified competitive environment and various coordination issues associated with a multi-partner initiative arise, developing and launching solo such a solution is advisable.

Instead of offering a complex digital payment platform targeting various participants (e.g., private customers, merchants, etc.) and offering multiple functionalities, managers should focus on initially addressing the needs of one distinct group of participants (e.g., private customers). This allows them to speed the entry to market as it reduces development time and to focus on solving efficiently an existing customer pain point. For example, instead of relying on complex technological set-up, managers can build upon existing technology, thus leveraging the key assets and strengths of an incumbent when developing disruptive solutions. MobilePay's disruptive potential, for example, stems from offering a novel service, allowing private users to execute P2P transfers more efficiently than existing solutions (such as online banking) rather than adopting new technologies. The simplicity (in terms of design and functionalities), easiness of use and high level of security of this digital payment platform, designed with a customer-centric mindset, are the main reasons for the fast adoption of the solution.

Instead of only focusing on catering to its own customer base, an incumbent launching a novel digital platform with disruptive potential should also try to incorporate a large number of users outside its traditional customer base. Both Danske Bank and non-Danske Bank customers have free access to MobilePay, which allowed the incumbent bank to start building relationships with customers outside its own scope.

3.2   MobilePay Expansion

Situation

Despite its initial success in terms of rapid user adoption, MobilePay's first mover advantage could easily come under threat as other players also launched competitive mobile payment platforms in response to Danske Bank's move. Just few months after the launch of MobilePay, 81 Danish banks launched a common banking sector solution, Swipp, which functioned as an account-based P2P platform incorporated as a separate feature in the mobile banking apps of the participating banks. Approximately half a year after the launch of MobilePay, the four major telecom operators in Denmark introduced their own competing solution, Paii, which allowed users to execute web and app purchases and transfer money to their peers. The payment platforms developed by Swipp and Paii were similar to MobilePay's offerings, but differed significantly in terms of ease of use and simplicity. Thus, as the competitive environment continued to change, Danske Bank needed to solidify further MobilePay's dominant market position.

Apart from the challenges posed by other competitive solutions, MobilePay also faced a number of internal issues, which jeopardized the long-term sustainability of the solution. Despite its growing user base, the payment platform had not identified a viable business model as private customers used the solution free of charge. In addition, as it utilized the existing card payment infrastructure, MobilePay incurred cost per transaction, which Danske Bank decided to subsidize. As this initial decision was not sustainable in long term, Danske Bank needed to identify stable revenue streams. In addition, MobilePay faced internal inefficiency with regards to the resilience of its own IT systems. Although the digital payment platform relied on the existing payment infrastructure in order to shorten time to market, the legacy of the bank's existing IT systems, built largely in silos, posed threats to the scalability and agility of the solution as well as to the speed with which MobilePay could innovate.

Actions Taken

The threat posed by competitive solutions prompted MobilePay to evolve further by incorporating novel functionalities in order to increase the value proposition towards its private customers (e.g., increased daily payment limits, introduced photos and personal messages when users sent money, etc.). MobilePay also evolved by incorporating merchants through the launch of business version of the MobilePay app, which allowed small merchants, such as street vendors and coffee shop owners, to receive mobile payments from private customers (Danske Bank 2014a). Thus, by adding merchants as second distinct group of platform participants, MobilePay transformed into being a two-sided platform (that is, facilitating the interactions between two distinct groups of participants, namely users and merchants).

The opening to business customers proved to be successful move and MobilePay continued to launch novel functionalities with the aim to expand its base of merchants. To this end, MobilePay introduced a number of different payment methods (e.g., in-app payments, online payments, in-store payments) in order to address the various payment contexts, in which the different merchants operated. For example, unlike the solutions for small merchants and online shops, MobilePay transactions in large retail shops needed to be executed faster due to the specificity of this payment context. To this end, MobilePay upgraded the platform architecture by introducing NFC and Bluetooth technology. Apart from offering solely mobile payments, MobilePay also included value-added services such as loyalty cards, discount-based loyalty programme, receipts, etc. Thus, by enabling the interactions between private and business customers and by introducing novel functionalities to both of them, MobilePay increased their level of engagement. Consequently, MobilePay managed to defend its dominant market position from the aspiration of new competitors.

The introduction of merchants as second distinct group of platform participants allowed MobilePay to establish stable revenue stream. Attracted by the large number of private customers using MobilePay, business customers also wanted to gain access to the platform ecosystem and were willing to pay a fee for acquiring it. Thus, the fees, which merchants paid to participate in the platform ecosystem, constituted a stable revenue source for MobilePay.

With the growth of the platform ecosystem, the speed with which innovative offerings were released to various heterogeneous participants became of paramount importance for MobilePay. In order to guarantee the rapid launch of new functionalities, a business unit within Danske Bank was set up, with the sole purpose to guide the future development of MobilePay. The team could adopt significant level of independence from the bank's strategy, processes and approaches towards innovation. At the same time, the MobilePay team had access to key Danske Bank's resources such as IT development, customer support and marketing, which it utilized to develop and provide new offerings in the fastest and the most efficient manner.

The increasing number of functionalities incorporated in the platform architecture required the optimization and further development of the underlying IT architecture. For this purpose, a special IT unit within Danske Bank was set up to support solely MobilePay. The new team also focused on ensuring the platform architecture's resilience and scalability and on supporting the development and maintenance of various platform functionalities. For example, a stand-in procedure, which allowed for reducing the downtime for processing a payment transaction, was introduced in order to allow the efficient execution of MobilePay transactions. The optimization of the platform architecture also included the gradual migration towards a more cost-efficient account-to-account infrastructure.

Results Achieved

Less than a year after opening for business customers, app. 4000 small businesses, such as coffee shops, clothing companies, hairdressers, bike repair shops, etc., had adopted MobilePay's business solution (Danske Bank 2014b). With the release of more functionalities towards various types of merchants, MobilePay's base of business customers grew rapidly. By the end of 2015, 17,500 merchants enabled the use of MobilePay in their shops (MobilePay 2015). In May 2016, app. 3 years since the launch of MobilePay, more than 25,000 small and medium-sized merchants and app. 37,000 online shops adopted the solution (Danske Bank 2016). In fact, the usage of MobilePay for C2B transactions continued to grow with double-digits since 2016. The incorporation of various merchants corresponded to the continuous growth of the private customers, which was influenced by the presence of strong cross-side network effects [that is, the more merchants join MobilePay, the more value private customers have from the solution and vice versa (see, Shapiro and Varian 1999)]. In May 2016, app. 85% of the Danish population used MobilePay to execute app 738,000 transactions on daily basis (Danske Bank 2016).

Learning Points from the MobilePay's Expansion Phase

In a rapidly shifting competitive environment, contenders can easily challenge the initial success of a digital platform. To prevent the erosion of the previously gained competitive advantages (e.g., huge user base) and to stay ahead of competitors, managers should constantly evolve the digital platform by incorporating new types of participants (e.g., business customers) and functionalities. However, as business customers, for example, operate in different contexts; managers should cater to their specific needs by providing customized solutions instead of delivering one-size-fits-all functionality.

The inclusion of additional platform participants, who wish to gain access to the already existing user base on the platform, allows managers to identify a revenue source in order to cover operational and innovation costs (see also, e.g., Evans and Schmalensee 2016). However, the quest for identifying a viable business model is far from being over as more often than not the revenue streams are not enough to ensure profitability.

The openness of the digital platform leads to the establishment of a vibrant ecosystem of multiple actors that challenge the optimal functioning of the digital platform. To amend for this, managers should invest in IT resilience and scalability. The explosive growth also calls for the establishment of different organizational set-up to better support the performance and future development of a digital platform.

3.3   Building a Nordic Vision

Situation
Due to the rapid adoption from both private and business customers, MobilePay
gained significant advantage over its competitors—the common bank sector solution, Swipp, and Paii, operated by the major Danish telecom operators. Swipp, which
was the biggest MobilePay's competitor in the Danish market, did not manage to
acquire significant customer base. In 2016, Swipp had only 900,000 registered
private customers and app. 16,000 business customers (Finans 2016; Skjærlund
2016). Swipp could not erode significantly the competitive advantage of MobilePay
due to its complicated sign-up process, consumer unawareness of the solution, and
lack of coordinated actions between the participating banks as each of them set their
own strategies, including different prices towards merchants for using Swipp. The
other contender, Paii, operated as two-sided platform and aimed at getting both users
and merchants on board simultaneously—a task, which proved to be challenging.
After Paii struggled to ignite, Swipp acquired the solution in November 2014 in
order to boost its online payment capabilities.

The competitive environment, however, shifted significantly since the launch of
MobilePay. In particular, the team behind Swipp had been preparing new design of
the solution and of its organizational set-up. Depending on their scale and nature, the
planned changes could threaten MobilePay's leading position. At the same time, the
global, regional and domestic competition from both financial and non-financial
actors continued to build up. For example, on a regional level, Nets, a Nordic-based
payment service provider, launched white-label wallet in Norway. On international
level, tech giants such as Apple and Samsung introduced their own mobile payment
platforms, Apple Pay and Samsung Pay, while the card company Visa collaborated
with Facebook to enable P2P transactions. Thus, MobilePay needed to defend once
again its position from new potential contenders with different business models and
global reach.

Action Taken
In order to solidify further its position, MobilePay expanded its reach by venturing
into several Nordic markets. The strong presence of Danske Bank in the region and
the similarity between the consumer preferences across the Nordic countries, combined with the possibility to gain first mover advantage due to weak competition,
provided good foundation for the successful export of MobilePay to selected Nordic
markets.

In December 2013, MobilePay entered the Finish market by launching a P2P
mobile payment platform, which mimicked fully the design of the Danish version.
The expectation was that the smooth registration flow, ease of use and overall
simplicity of the solution would lead to its fast adoption among users. The initial
uptake of MobilePay, however, proved to be not as expected as a key factor for
the success of MobilePay in Denmark was not present in Finland. In particular,
the easiness with which users could sign-up for MobilePay was not feasible in
Finland, which resulted in cumbersome registration process. In Denmark,

MobilePay's sign-up process required the input of bank account number, which is indicated on the users' payment cards. In Finland, however, this was not the case; thus, users needed first to find their bank account details, usually by accessing their online banking, and then entered them as part of the MobilePay's registration flow. To mitigate this, MobilePay improved the registration process, but, despite these efforts, the adoption rate remained relative low (e.g., in 2015, MobilePay had 148,000 registered users in Finland). Despite the slow adoption rate, MobilePay became the leading mobile payment platform in the country as other competitors also struggled to ignite.

In Sweden, a banking sector solution, Swish, which launched in 2012, had already earned a significant market share. Launching a standalone competitive solution in this market was not considered a viable strategy, and thus, Danske Bank decided to join the other banks in the Swish initiative (note: Danske Bank was not part of common banking solution Swipp in Denmark).

The Norwegian market constituted the next potential option for expansion. Various legal and technical constraints postponed the launch of MobilePay in Norway. One of the impeding issues turned out to be the rather low payment limit for receiving payments, which, when reached, prevented users from receiving money unless they authenticated themselves with an ID. The integration of such ID authentication process slowed down the launch of the solution in the Norwegian market. While MobilePay contemplated on the different options and the potential risks associated with each of them, the largest Norwegian bank, DBN, launched a P2P mobile payment platform, Vipps, in May 2015; thus, changing significantly the competitive environment in Norway. Although other mobile payment platforms had existed in Norway prior to the launch of Vipps, such as Valyou and mCash, their user adoption rates had been low due to their limited value propositions. Vipps, which is similar to MobilePay's design, however, managed to attract one million users in just 5 months after its launch. In response, MobilePay entered the Norwegian market in August 2015. Even though MobilePay supported both P2P and C2B transactions (Vipps initially enabled only P2P transactions), it could not overcome the strong first mover advantage, which Vipps had acquired. Thus, MobilePay needed to adopt a different strategy for conquering the Norwegian market.

In order to gain ground in Finland and Norway, individual country teams were established, which worked in close cooperation with the MobilePay team in Denmark. While these local teams focused on designing and executing marketing campaigns and forging strong relations with local customers and partners, the team in Denmark was responsible for providing innovative features and rolling them out to all relevant markets.

Results Achieved

MobilePay's fast adoption rate in Denmark could not be replicated in other Nordic markets. In 2016, 210,000 private consumers had MobilePay in Norway, while 180,000 private consumers utilized the digital payment platform in Finland (MobilePay 2016). The initial struggles led to re-formulation of the strategies for each market, and even though the growth rates improved, there was strong competition from local players. In Finland, for example, Pivo, a mobile wallet operated by the largest Finnish bank OP-Pohjola, amassed more that 500,000 users as of 2015 (OP-Pohjola, 2015). MobilePay's user base, however, was growing with 40% in the second half of 2016 (MobilePay 2017) and it was largely expected to gain a market dominance. In Norway, the dominance of Vipps, which reported over 2.1 million private customers in 2016 (Vipps 2016), seemed to be difficult to overcome.

Learning Points from Building a Nordic Vision Phase

Despite the dominance of MobilePay in the Danish market, Danske Bank could not easily replicate this success story in other markets even if there are a number of similarities across the Nordics. In particular, when entering new geographical markets, managers need to start building the platform's user base from scratch. Applying similar adoption strategies across different markets, however, do not lead to replication of the initial success. At the same time, due to local characteristics, the technological set-up and customer journey of the Danish version of MobilePay, which largely contributed to the success of the solution, could not be replicated to all markets (e.g., MobilePay in the Finnish market), and instead, required adaptations. Furthermore, the lack of interoperability between the MobilePay-branded digital payment platforms in the three markets (in Denmark, Finland and Norway) prevent any network effects between the three solutions, which could constitute a driver for further adoption. To govern successfully the entry and subsequent development of a digital payment platform in different markets, local teams should be set up with focus on distribution and marketing, while the innovation efforts remained in the central team.

3.4   Building an Ecosystem of Partners

Situation

In 2016, MobilePay continued to grow in size and scope by attracting more than 3.2 million private users and approximately 35,000 business customers (MobilePay 2016). To keep this large customer base active, MobilePay needed to increase their engagement rate by continuously launching novel functionalities, which required resources and the ability to read quickly the ever-changing consumer preferences and competitive environment. In addition, MobilePay had to balance the heterogeneous interests of multiple stakeholders—from private customers to different types of business customers (e.g., small and medium sized to large retail groups), who also operated in different payment contexts—online, in-store, in-app, etc. As a result, the MobilePay team faced constant demands for delivering various functionalities addressing the needs of specific merchants, which they needed to balance against the demand for innovative features by private customers.

MobilePay also struggled to ignite in Finland and Norway due to lack of clear vision how to win these markets and shortage of necessary resources to ensure rapid expansion. In 2016, MobilePay yet again operated in an increasingly disruptive payment landscape with new international competitors closing in the Nordic markets (e.g., Apple Pay's indications to launch in the Nordics). As a result, MobilePay contemplated how to build up its capabilities in order to outpace the innovation speed of its main competitors. Ultimately, the team faced the decision whether to continue MobilePay's journey as a sole quest or to establish a collaboration with other regional or international players in order to conquer the Nordics.

Action Taken
As the Nordic expansion as standalone payment platform proved to be a difficult and fruitless endeavor, the MobilePay team decided to join forces with other incumbent banks across the Nordic region. Nordea was the first bank to join the new initiative, which led to its exit from the common sector solution Swipp. The majority of the other Danish banks also followed and left Swipp in order to enter into agreement with MobilePay. A number of banks in Finland and Norway also decided to participate in the new venture.

Under the terms of the collaboration, partner banks were to act as local distributors of MobilePay towards their business customers. Danske Bank retained full ownership of MobilePay, but the existing business unit was to be carved out into a separate company operating under an E-Money license. Partner banks also agreed to invest in MobilePay in order to spur continuous innovation, which would be at MobilePay's discretion.

Apart from forging alliances with banks, MobilePay also entered in dialogue with numerous local and regional partners, most of which, such as the PoS vendor Verifone, operated across the Nordics and aimed at solidifying their market positions. Perceiving MobilePay as the most advanced and innovative mobile payment platform in the Nordics, various actors view potential partnership as a driver for their own digitalization agenda. For example, one of the largest retail groups in the Nordics, Rema 1000, cooperated with MobilePay on launching on-demand delivery app, Vigo, which utilized MobilePay as sole payment method.

Results Achieved
The opening of MobilePay to external partners resulted in solidifying the position of the digital payment platform in the Danish market. Currently, more than 70 banks have joined MobilePay as distribution partners, which allowed MobilePay to expand its ecosystem by acquiring new business customers. The opening to external banks have also implications for the platform's architecture as this allows for moving from the existing card-based infrastructure to more efficient and cheaper account-to-account set-up. The stable revenue stream also gave MobilePay the opportunity to innovate at increased speed. Multiple technology providers, independent app developers, and businesses from various sectors and industries also approached MobilePay seeking a potential collaboration.

Learning Points from the Building an Ecosystem of Partners Phase
As the dynamic competitive environment requires the continuous delivery of high quality innovative functionalities, this can puts serious constraints on the innovative

capabilities of a digital platform. To secure more resources for development, a digital platform should open up to various types of partners, who can boost its capabilities [e.g., distribution partners (banks); technology providers (Verifone as terminal provider), etc.] (see also, Parker et al. 2016). Such co-innovation in particular with incumbent actors in industries, which also face digital disruption (e.g., retail, transportation, etc.), for example, helped MobilePay explore multiple innovation paths simultaneously and thus, increase its innovation potential. Working with various types of partners, however, requires the set-up of dedicated governance regimes for each type of platform partners (e.g., vendors, other banks, technology providers), which regulate issues with regards to revenue sharing, intellectual property rights protection, data ownership, etc. and serve as mechanisms for preventing and resolving any potential conflicts (see also, Evans and Schmalensee 2016).

4   Results Achieved

In 2017, 4 years after its launch, MobilePay continues to dominate the Danish market, while also expanding its reach to selected Nordic markets. The user base of MobilePay continued to grow rapidly and by end of 2017, it amounted to 3.7 million users (more than 90% of the Danish population) and more than 75,000 physical stores and app. 8000 Danish online shops (see Table 1 for overview of the growth of MobilePay's private and business customers in Denmark). The total sum of the executed daily transactions via MobilePay amounts to app. 18,000 €. The collaboration between MobilePay and various business customers also turned to be successful. For example, 74% of the tickets sold in the Danish State's railway app are purchased through MobilePay. As of beginning of 2018, more than 70 partner banks also have joined MobilePay as distribution partners. Despite this development and the presence of stable revenue streams, MobilePay is still in search of a viable business model.

MobilePay's popularity led to the closure of its main competitor in the Danish market, Swipp. New contenders, both local and international, however, have emerged, prompting MobilePay to continue evolving in order to stay ahead. In 2017, the Nordic payment service provider Nets, for example, launched its own mobile wallet in selected Danish stores in direct competition with MobilePay.

Table 1 Overview of MobilePay's private and business customers in Denmark

Phase	Number of private customers (app.)	Number of business customers (app.)
Launch of MobilePay	870,000 (2013)	Solution not offered
MobilePay expansion	1.8 million (2014)	4000 (2014)
Nordic expansion	2.7 million (2015)	17,500 (2015)
Building an ecosystem of partners	3.2 million (2016)	35,000 (2016)

ApplePay also entered the Danish market in 2017, but due to its technical set-up, merchants have to pay higher fees when using it in comparison to using MobilePay.

Across the Nordics, MobilePay is still trying to gain traction. In Finland, the popularity of MobilePay across both private and business customers increases, (e.g., 40% user growth in Finland). Despite all the efforts to establish MobilePay in the Norwegian market, the digital payment platform was shut down in January 2018 as the competitor Vipps managed to attract the majority of the Norwegian banks as distribution partners. As a result, MobilePay's strategy for Norway changed from going solo to seeking collaboration with Vipps.

The success of MobilePay has helped Danske Bank achieve a number of non-financial benefits. In particular, the success of MobilePay contributed to Danske Bank's efforts to protect itself from disruption by gaining a first mover advantage in the mobile payment area, improving its brand image and reducing the churn among its customers. MobilePay is also a proof case demonstrating the innovation capabilities of Danske Bank, which various business and corporate customers of the bank can utilize in order to deliver on their own digitalization agenda. The success of Mobile Pay has also led to the emergence of several other disruptive initiatives within Danske Bank, which also adopt new approaches to innovation.

5 Lessons Learned

Facing the possibility of disruption by the entry of various contenders both fintech start-ups and established companies (e.g., Apple, Samsung) operating at local and global level, Danske Bank, an incumbent financial organization, decided to embrace digitalization. While digitalization is an ongoing and incremental process within the bank and permeates throughout all its business units and projects, Danske Bank also adopted a radical approach towards digitalization by launching initiatives with high disruptive potential. In particular, Danske Bank aimed at revolutionizing the way people pay by offering a mobile payment platform, MobilePay, which quickly gained dominance in Denmark and expanded to other Nordic markets.

In this case, we investigate how an incumbent financial institution succeeded at developing a digital payment platform—an endeavor, which required the adoption of platform thinking and different approach to innovation. Below, we summarize the main findings, which practitioners need to take into account when launching and further developing a digital platform.

Pursuing a platform business model deviates significantly from the business logic associated with traditional banking products [e.g., managing the interactions among various distinct groups of participants (see e.g. Hagiu and Wright 2011; Parker et al. 2016, etc.), identifying a subsidy and revenue side (Evans and Schmalensee 2016), creating a robust ecosystem of external partners (Parker et al. 2016)]. To succeed with this disruptive initiative, Danske Bank relied on different from usual approach when it comes to organizational set-up and innovation processes. In particular, a small, agile and cross-functional team of employees (e.g., IT developers, business analysts, legal experts, etc.) carried out the initial development of MobilePay as a

6-month project. To ensure the continuous development of the digital payment platform in a fast, innovative and agile manner, Danske Bank established a separate business unit, characterized by high degree of autonomy in terms of innovation processes, strategies and business models. In addition, an IT unit dedicated solely to the development and maintenance of MobilePay was established.

While the new organizational set-up fostered autonomy, MobilePay also established close synergies with other units in Danske Bank in order to benefit from bank's key resources (e.g., access to payment infrastructure, legal and technical expertise in the payment area, IT and marketing resources, etc.). The challenge, however, is to leverage the benefits stemming from being associated with an incumbent, while trying at the same time to reduce those dependencies, which can create inefficiencies and stifle innovation (e.g., slow decision-making process, being risk-averse, etc.). Thus, the development of MobilePay required a careful balance between autonomy and synergy when it comes to the relations with Danske Bank. The evolutionary journey of MobilePay also demonstrated that as the digital platform matures and its ecosystem grows, it bolsters higher degree of autonomy (e.g., the carving out of MobilePay as separate company in 2017) and less synergy due to the need to pursue new opportunities and establish collaborations with various heterogeneous actors.

The timing of digital platform's market entry is of importance as indicated by MobilePay's launch in Denmark and by the subsequent entries in Finland and Norway. Observing closely the market dynamics, Danske Bank decided to speed up its venturing into the area of mobile payments due to increased demand from private customers and the preparations from various contenders, both incumbents and fintech start-ups, to launch their own solutions. By identifying the window of opportunity for market entry, Danske Bank managed to attain a first mover advantage, which led to MobilePay's dominance in the Danish market and constituted high barriers to entry, which various contenders (e.g., Swipp, Paii, etc.) could not overcome. This Danish success story, however, could not be easily replicated to other markets, as the factors determining the popularity of MobilePay in Denmark were not present there.

MobilePay's strategy included first the launch of a customer-centric state-of-the-art digital payment platform, followed by efforts to build critical mass of private customers and later of various types of merchants and only then, seeking to make the solution financially sustainable for the bank. As part of its evolutionary journey, MobilePay also expanded its services from payment transactions to include value-added services such as receipts, loyalty cards and programs, and established a vast network of partners, which contributed to its expansion into selected Nordic markets. Thus, despite the initial high adoption rate, attributed to the simplicity, ease of use and strong value proposition of MobilePay, its continuous success and long-term sustainability remained elusive as the digital platform ecosystem faced many challenges (e.g., technology trends, consumer preferences, regulations, competitors, etc.). To address them, MobilePay needed to evolve constantly in search of new opportunities. This indicates that the success of a digital platform requires ongoing efforts, which stretch beyond the launch phase and consist of casting multiple bets on various innovation efforts. We recommend adopting an incremental approach to evolution, where the digital platform ecosystem starts small (in terms of types of platform participants and value proposition) and scales later. The quest for finding a viable business model can take place at a later stage.

In this case, we trace Danske Bank's endeavors to develop and evolve MobilePay over time. As a result, we provide a number of practical recommendations how incumbent organizations can successfully venture into a digital platform business. By doing so, we contribute to the literature on Multi-Sided Platforms and on digitalization. In particular, we shed light into the execution of a dual-track strategy towards digitalization and prove its suitability for incumbent organizations. We also offer a number of advancements in the platform literature. First, we outline how a traditional business can adopt a digital platform business. Although researchers has previously dealt with this issue (see, Gawer and Cusumano 2014), they have mainly studied the transformation of physical products into digital platforms. In this case, we account for an incumbent launching and managing a digital platform from scratch. Second, we study the success of digital platform ecosystems beyond the initial launch phase. Third, we offer rare insights into the organizational set-up of successful digital platform, which is currently under researched area (Altman and Tripsas 2014). Finally, we also outline the endeavors of a digital platform to expand in geographic markets, of which currently few studies exists (see, e.g., Watanabe et al. 2017).

While Danske Bank aims to be at the forefront of digitalization, its core belief is that digital innovation should be first consumer-centric, even if this means slow-paced digitalization. Thirty percent of the private customers of Danske Bank, for example, have not yet used the bank's digital products, but as Jesper Nilsen, Head of Personal Banking in Danske Bank, states it is "ok not to be super digital" (Børsen 2017). Instead, the digitalization of these customers could be slow-paced and should occur when they found a strong value proposition for themselves to adopt digital solutions.

References

Altman EJ, Tripsas M (2014) Product to platform transitions: organizational identity implications. Harvard Business School Research Paper No. 14-045. Available at SSRN: https://ssrn.com/abstract=2364523 or https://doi.org/10.2139/ssrn.2364523

Børsen (2017) Danske Bank: "De sidste kunder skal være digitale". Can be found here: https://www.pressreader.com/denmark/dagbladet-b%C3%B8rsen/20170803/281956017867315

Danske Bank Group (2012) Annual report. Can be found here: https://www.danskebank.com/en-uk/ir/Documents/2012/Q4/Annualreport-2012.pdf

Danske Bank Group (2013) Annual report. Can be found here: https://danskebank.com/en-uk/ir/Documents/2013/Q4/Annualreport-2013-parent-company.pdf

Danske Bank (2014a) First Danish mobile payment solution for businesses. Press release. Can be found at: https://danskebank.com/en-uk/press/News/news-archives/Pages/mobile-payment-solution-for-businesses.aspx

Danske Bank (2014b) Mobiltelefonen er fremtidens betalingsløsning. Can be found at: https://danskebank.dk/da-dk/erhverv/nyheder/pages/danske-business-december-2014.aspx

Danske Bank (2016) Three million people in Denmark are now using MobilePay. Can be found at: https://danskebank.com/en-uk/press/News/news-archives/Pages/3-million-use-mobilepay-in-denmark.aspx

European Commission (2013) Proposal for a Directive of the European Parliament and the Council on payment services in the internal market and amending Directives 2002/65/EC, 2013/36/EU and 2009/110/EC and repealing Directive 2007/64/E, COM

Evans DS, Schmalensee R (2016) Matchmakers: the new economics of multisided platforms. Harvard Business Review Press, Watertown, MA

Finans (2016) Danskerne valgte MobilePay frem for Swipp. Can be found at: https://finans.dk/live/erhverv/ECE9149552/danskerne-valgte-mobilepay-frem-for-swipp/?ctxref=ext

Gawer A, Cusumano MA (2014) Industry platforms and ecosystem innovation. J Prod Innov Manage (3):417–433

Hagiu A, Wright J (2011) Multi-sided platforms. Harvard Business School Working Paper 12-024

Karimi J, Walter Z (2015) The role of dynamic capabilities in responding to digital disruption: a factor-based study of the newspaper industry. J Manage Inf Syst 1:39–81

MobilePay (2015) MobilePay 2015 – året i tal. Can be found at: https://www.mobilepay.dk/da-dk/Nyheder/artikler/Pages/MobilePay-2015-aaret-i-tal.aspx

MobilePay (2016) Nordea tilslutter sig MobilePay. Press release. Can be found at: https://www.mobilepay.dk/da-dk/PDF/Pressemeddelelser2016/20161013-pressemeddelelse-nordea-tilslutter-sig-mobilePay.pdf

MobilePay (2017) MobilePay is heading towards 1000 webshops in the Nordics. Press release. Can be found at: https://www.mobilepay.dk/da-dk/PDF/Pressemeddelelser/Checkout-MobilePay-PressRelease-20170419.pdf

OP-Pohjola (2015) OP brings easy contactless payment to the Pivo mobile wallet. Can be found at: https://www.pohjola.fi/pohjola?cid=-1691

Parker G, van Alstyne M, Choudary SP (2016) Platform revolution: how networked markets are transforming the economy and how to make them work for you. WW Norton, New York

Shapiro C, Varian H (1999) Information rules. Harvard Business School Press, Boston

Skjærlund S (2016) Swipp og MobilePay dukker op i flere og flere lokale butikker. Can be found at: https://frdb.dk/erhverv/Swipp-og-MobilePay-dukker-op-i-flere-og-flere-lokale-butikker/artikel/89864

Statista (2016) Percentage of people who use a smartphone in Denmark from 2012 to 2016. Can be found at: https://www.statista.com/statistics/488341/smartphone-penetration-denmark/

Vipps (2016) Over 100 norske banker satser sammen på Vipps. Press release. Can be found at: https://www.vipps.no/pressemelding.html

Watanabe C, Naveed K, Neittaanmäki P, Fox B (2017) Consolidated challenge to social demand for resilient platforms-lessons from Uber's global expansion. Technol Soc 48:33

Kalina S. Staykova is Industrial PhD fellow. She is primarily investigating digital payments as multi-sided platforms and their ecosystems in close collaboration with MobilePay, a leading Nordic digital payment platform. Kalina is also studying the disruption in the financial service area caused by new technologies and changing regulatory environment. Her research interests also focus on studying multiple issues related to multi-sided platforms (e.g., design, adoption, monetization, strategy, regulation, etc.) in various other contexts (e.g., sharing economy, social media, etc.). Kalina holds a joint Elite Master's degree in International Law, Economics and Management from Copenhagen Business School and University of Copenhagen.

Jan Damsgaard is Professor of Digitalization at Copenhagen Business School as well as Head of Department of Digitalization. During his academic career, he stayed at the Case Western Reserve University, Jyvaskyla University, Aalborg University and Curtin University,and Curtin University. Jan Damsgaard's personal research focuses on the business aspects of digitalization and disruption including platform economics, IoT and Big Data. Jan is member of the Danish Government's "Disruption Council" that is headed by the Danish Prime Minster along with 7 Cabinet Ministers and 30 representatives from leading Danish institutions and companies. In 2014, the Danish Academy of Technical Sciences appointed Jan to "National Digital Advisor".

Digitalization Partnership: How GKN Established a Digital Platform with 3YD to Realize the Disruptive Potential of Metal Additive Manufacturing

Klaus Wildhirt, Claudius Seidel, Udo Bub, Markus Josten, and Stephan Kühr

Abstract

(a) **Situation faced**: GKN Powder Metallurgy, a leading manufacturer for high precision parts for the automotive industry (GKN Sinter Metals) as well as for metal powder (GKN Hoeganaes), faced the question of how to deliver the future technology of metal additive manufacturing successfully to the market. The potential which stems from disruptive technologies, such as 3D printing to established structures of the industry, was supposed to be realized through an innovative business model before other competitors or new entrants would claim the market.

(b) **Action taken**: GKN connected with start-ups to gain access to innovative ideas and digital know-how. But it also realized that thinking differently makes it necessary to act differently. Therefore, a separate unit was created, which was detached from the established organizational structure. Together with 3YOURMIND (3YD), a start-up in the area of 3D printing, GKN not

K. Wildhirt · C. Seidel
EIT ICT Labs Germany GmbH, Berlin, Germany
e-mail: klaus.wildhirt@eitdigital.eu; claudius.seidel@eitdigital.eu

U. Bub (✉)
EIT ICT Labs Germany GmbH, Berlin, Germany

Eötvös Loránd University Budapest, Budapest, Hungary
e-mail: udo.bub@eitdigital.eu

M. Josten
GKN Sinter Metals Engineering GmbH, Radevormwald, Germany
e-mail: markus.josten@gkn.com

S. Kühr
3YOURMIND GmbH, Berlin, Germany
e-mail: sk@3yourmind.com

© Springer International Publishing AG, part of Springer Nature 2019
N. Urbach, M. Röglinger (eds.), *Digitalization Cases*, Management for Professionals, https://doi.org/10.1007/978-3-319-95273-4_8

only realized a platform and business model, but also digitalized the related back-end processes. Based on the initial success and the grown relationship, the digitalization partnership was furthermore instructed to question the status quo at GKN in more fundamental ways.

(c) **Results achieved**: With InstAMetal, a digital platform and brand has been developed through which the potential of Metal additive manufacturing (MAM) could be realized at the front-end. Due to innovative services as well as the high scalability and reach of the platform, not only existing customers could be inspired with the new offer, but completely new customers and markets could be won. The platform also triggered the digitalization of the related back-end processes, and while technology and procedures changed, the culture also began to transform with regard to the daily work with 3YOURMIND. Inspired by this success, traditional manufacturing technologies are now being successively investigated for their digital potential and platform capability.

(d) **Lessons learned**: Four central aspects turned out to be important parameters in the digitalization partnership of GKN and 3YOURMIND: (i) plan digital projects "by sight", but with a vision, (ii) start in market niches and corporate niches to gain experience and legitimacy, (iii) set up a shelter, in order to decouple the digital initiative from established organizational patterns of action and thought, and (iv) actively engage in co-innovation by systematically opening and networking with start-ups, customers and corporates— because digitalization does not stop, but rather starts at corporate boundaries.

1   Introduction

Metal additive manufacturing (MAM), a new technology that has the potential to disrupt existing production processes and business models across industries is pushing into the market (Frazier 2014; Huang et al. 2015). While plastic remains the most commonly used 3D printing material, this case refers to MAM which is supposed to become an increasingly important application of 3D printing due to the wide range of possible applications for e.g. the production of small batches as well as to realize significant cost reductions due to comparatively high basis material costs of precious metals (Muller and Karevska 2016; Sculpteo 2017). Trend analyses emphasize the growing importance especially for industry sectors with a high demand to manufacture e.g. prototypes or low numbers per batch of goods such as is the case in "mechanical and plant engineering, where products contain mainly metal components" (Muller and Karevska 2016). Furthermore, it is forecasted that the global MAM market will grow tremendously due to two factors: higher demand in the global luxury market, dental market, market for hip and knee implants, the already mentioned automotive sector (Attaran 2017) as well as reduced costs and

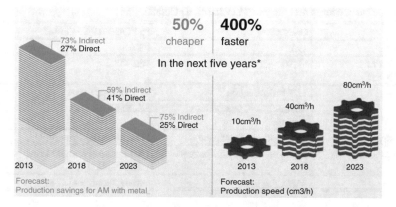

Fig. 1 Forecast: Production savings and speed for AM with metal (Siemens 2014)

increased production speed in the MAM technology (Siemens 2014; Fig. 1). Currently, this market is dominated by four big players offering MAM machines and services: Arcam Group; 3D Systems Corporation; EOS and Concept Laser GmbH (Daedal Research 2016).

Beside the potential of MAM, even long standing, traditional companies are challenged as to how to bring such a disruptive digital technology to the market through building a coherent and sustainable business model—especially confronted with established organizational structures, patterns of thought and action.

Thereby it can occasionally be observed that start-ups take on the role of digitalization partners that guide traditional companies through the digitalization process or at least successfully bring it into motion. By doing so, the companies are trying to gain access to new technologies and out-of-the-box thinking in order to launch innovative business models swiftly or to develop innovative applications for future-oriented technologies (Weiblen and Chesbrough 2015; Kollmann et al. 2016). Besides the mindset, the application of entrepreneurial methods is playing an increasingly important role for companies in order to develop their digital market offers and survive in today's competitive environment.

The following case study illustrates how the long-established company GKN successfully developed a digital solution and applied a disruptive technology through the partnership with the technology-driven start-up 3YOURMIND (3YD).

GKN's Powder Metallurgy division consists of GKN Sinter Metals and GKN Hoeganaes. GKN Sinter Metals is not only a globally leading manufacturer of precision car parts, but also produces parts for industry customers. GKN Hoeganaes is one of the biggest producers of metal powder, the important raw material in powder metallurgy. GKN Sinter Metals has more than 30 locations worldwide with approximately 7500 employees. In total, more than 58,000 people work in various GKN sub-companies and in joint ventures in more than 30 countries.

Compared to GKN, a global engineering company with a 258-year history, 3YD is a young Berlin start-up that has developed an industrial 3D printing software platform for work sequences that enables the digitalization of industrial processes through additive manufacturing (Table 1). The platform enables the analysis and

Table 1 Comparison: GKN plc and 3YOURMIND GmbH

	GKN plc	3YOURMIND GmbH
Founded	1759	2013
Number of employees	59,800	ca. 40
Revenue	11.7 billion euros	1.5 million euros
HQ	Redditch, Worcestershire, England	Berlin, Germany
Industry	Automotive, Aerospace	Industrial 3D Printing
Core products	Vehicle, aircraft components	3D Platform and 3D Print Consultation
Website	www.gkn.com	www.3yourmind.com

optimization of 3D data, which is necessary for printing at the touch of a button, and offers, for example, help with the search for service contractors through price comparisons. Currently 3YD is in the scale-up phase and employs about 40 people in its locations in Berlin, Wroclaw and San Francisco. Among its customers are German DAX-companies as well as other innovative businesses from all over the world.

2   Situation Faced

As described MAM is a disruptive technology that is pushing into the market. During the process that is based on digital 3D models, components are printed from stratified material layer by layer. As part of the so-called *powder metallurgy processes*, a process of laser sintering, components are designed on the computer and printed into metal components from metal powder (Leupold and Glossner 2016). This powder metallurgy process allows the construction and printing of metal components, which until now was deemed impossible. At the same time, the process allows the printing of very light but still very stable components, e.g. by the imitation of biological patterns such as the structure of honey combs. Since during the metal sintering the melted metal powder is built layer by layer and only the amount of metal powder that is actually needed is used, it is also a very resource-efficient process. It allows entirely new shapes for rapid prototyping and rapid manufacturing as well as shapes for mass customization of complex metal components (Fig. 2). MAM is therefore considered not only promising, but compared to existing technology and manufacturing processes, a disruption, which will fundamentally change the existing business models and production processes.

In light of this, the people at GKN had to ask themselves how powder metallurgy can contribute and be delivered successfully to the market and how its features in comparison with existing production methods can be exploited. The goal was to develop an innovative business model that includes the disruptive potential of

Fig. 2 GKN powder metallurgy—a bottle opener as an example of additive manufacturing (GKN 2017)

additive manufacturing, i.e. one that realizes and at the same time opens up access to new markets and customer groups. Since GKN's structures had until then been traditional and above all shaped by the traditional automotive market and distribution structure, a cooperation with start-ups was favoured to gain access to disruptive technologies, digital know-how and innovative business models. GKN has been trying to connect specifically with start-ups and divergent thinkers who deliberately question the established structures of GKN. As part of the process, the board gained an initial and sustainable impression during a journey to Silicon Valley—this journey generated an understanding within the board of the importance to take unusual, unfamiliar paths to stay competitive in the future. In a next step, office space was rented in RocketSpace, a prestigious co-working space with accelerator services in downtown San Francisco,[1] and individual key persons were dispatched to establish contacts to such offices, learn a new mindset and thereby promote digitalization within their own company.

Through employees in the EIT Digital network who were in Silicon Valley at that time and who were likewise renting office space in RocketSpace, GKN became aware of the start-up 3YD as a potential cooperation partner (Heger and Bub 2012). 3YD has qualified before as a recipient of Business Development services by EIT

---

[1]http://www.rocketspace.com

Digital Accelerator. One aspect of particular interest to GKN was that they believed to have found a partner in 3YD with whom they could start working with quickly and closely. What convinced GKN was the statement "let's start right away" and first develop a Minimum Viable Product (MVP) (Ries 2011) fast and cheap, based on the existing platform solution of 3YD, which could then gradually be developed further in cooperation with lead customers. As a result of this, GKN has a highly conceptual influence on the development of the platform and, at the same time, can reduce the project risk to a minimum by adapting the platform over the course of time. Decisive for establishing a partnership with 3YD was ultimately the realization that 3YD's vision of their own platform's further development and GKN's vision regarding a solution for additive manufacturing were similar in many ways. At the core remained the initial idea to provide a B2B-customer platform and an "Amazon-style" experience.

3   Action Taken

After the common vision of the platform had been determined, the realization followed seamlessly. But instead of utilizing traditional planning approaches—i.e. first drafting the entire platform in a conception phase and then realizing it as part of the next phase—planning and implementation were carried out instantaneously, and only the goals to be achieved in the next step were planned *on sight*. The main goal was to rapidly develop a MVP with rudimentary but reliable functions in order to gain direct customer feedback as early as possible. Following the entrepreneur's claim *fail fast and cheap*, this should avoid running in the wrong direction for too long or working past the customer needs and thereby causing unnecessary development costs. Because even if the digital initiative, unlike many start-ups, could rely on considerable financial resources, GKN was breaking new ground and therefore, the investment risk was hard to calculate. Additionally, this prototype-based approach enabled initial results to be presented to company-internal stakeholders soon after the kick-off. This was essential since the digital unit did not generate turnover on their own right from the beginning, but was financed through funds of those units whose territories they would be expanding into one day. Therefore, they relied on strong internal support from the corporate board.

The prototype did not need to be developed from scratch as it was based on 3YDs' white label solution of their 3D printing platform, which represented a significant advantage. This solution had already proven itself in several application contexts and was one reason for working with 3YD, but it did not include GKN's specific requirements so far, i.e. in terms of printing metal components. Therefore, one major step included the requirement that the processes of virtual 3D printing—which were initially designed for plastic connections—had to be adapted to the requirements of laser sintering. In this context, it was necessary to pay attention to the optimization of the support structure of the components, to optimize the alignment during printing and implement some functions that were only relevant to metal printing. These knowledge-intensive adaptations and specifications were realized in direct cooperation using joint project teams with experts from GKN and 3YD.

Parallel to the development of the prototype, the brand image was already designed right from the start, too. In doing so, the online appearance was supposed to be different from GKN's traditional brand in order to differentiate from the existing corporate identity and to be able to bring the potential that MAM has to offer with a new face to the market. More importantly, the digital market presence aimed to draw the attention of entirely new industries and customer groups to the platform's services, which were not covered by the previous umbrella of GKN's reputation. Furthermore, separation from the previous brand should avoid or reduce possible negative effects on GKNs core reputation in case the digitalization would not be as successful as hoped. Last but not least, the intention of approaching GKN's existing business areas in the future using its own digital offer could be communicated more credibly to the market and potential customers with a separate brand image.

Even if the brand building was strongly supported or driven by an external agency, it was still merely a cooperative process that took into account the ideas and notions of the employees from the digital unit. The significant influence in the design of the brand ensured a high level of employee identification with the digital online presence right from the beginning. Additionally, GKN was able to draw on 3YD's experience in the digital economy regarding questions such as drafting and choosing the logo. 3YD thereby acted as a sparring partner or digital mentor, providing valuable advice from their considerable experience in the digital world.

The tasks were worked out together in mixed project teams. In the beginning, the digital unit comprised 12 members of staff with various areas of expertise, put together cross functionally by GKN. In particular, employees with an affinity for new media and the ability to think out-of-the-box were sought in-house. The main reason for this was that employees who think (too) strongly in the usual patterns and processes could reduce the flow of the project as brakemen or doubters. Moreover, it was considered important that they demonstrate "entrepreneurial thinking and acting" and, even with persistent resistance, keep fighting to ensure sustainable success.

The project team was supported or strengthened by 3YD employees who had worked with agile approaches in the start-up environment and—beside their specific platform know-how—provided a strong entrepreneurial mindset. Through the close cooperation, GKN staff were confronted with the agile approach from the very beginning, they immersed themselves in the digital culture and adopted it successively. For example, the employees of GKN had direct access to 3YD's development and project management tool Jira and were thus directly involved in the processes and working methods. While the employees of the digital unit continued to be involved, individual experts or teams were gradually consulted as required. Accordingly, communication of the methods and cultures that were central building blocks of the digital transformation was accomplished through an implicit learning-by doing process, as training measures could only have taught explicit knowledge (Nonaka and Takeuchi 1995).

Following the basic idea of agile project management, regular feedback loops or reviews were scheduled in intervals of approximately 2–4 weeks. On the one hand, these review meetings were used to jointly reflect customers' feedback and demonstrate modifications and learnings of the latest sprint. On the other, the reviews served to provide improvements and new functions, which were discussed by a wide range of experts, and which could then possibly be included as a new requirement or function in the product backlog for the purpose of an application and development memory. Only the project team responsible for implementations could make decisions during the sprint, according to which priority, tasks and functions in the product backlog were implemented (Gloger 2008). Overall, provision of the prototype needed just five sprints: three sprints for the adaptation of the platform in line with the characteristics of metal printing, and for programming GKN-specific services and functions; as well as two quality sprints, which only served to fix errors and make optical adjustments, and not provide any functional extensions. Through this approach, it was possible to supply a first rudimentary MVP however, with regard to the core functions, only a few weeks after the project kick-off—with manageable investments. All further adaptations and functions were then developed during the beta phase, in direct exchange with test users.

Following this, the prototype was validated by test users in an open beta phase, which enabled them to obtain initial experience and provide feedback. This not only allowed to outsource learning costs. At the same time, the circle of digitalization partners was extended with the most important segment—the future customers. From this point in time, lead customers were able to influence the ongoing design process of the platform just a few weeks after the start of the project. However, InstAMetal was not yet open to everybody or linked on the GKN website. Rather, the beta phase was carried out with a limited user group. Therefore, 25 top customers, selected jointly by the digital unit and 3YD based on criteria such as media fitness, relevance of prototyping in small batches or stability of the business relationship, were asked whether they were interested in participating in the test phase and wanted to try out the platform during the early stage. The majority of these companies responded to this invitation and were accompanied by a support team during the beta phase.

The test phase lasted a total of 2 months and consisted of a cycle of recurring feedback and development phases: Identifying new applications based on feedback from expert meetings, implementing the favoured functions, releasing the functions on the beta platform, customer testing and, partly divided into different customer groups (A/B-tests), the continuous collection of feedback, followed by reflection and, if needed, adaptation or changing of those functions. During this time numerous additional functions were developed and implemented based on customer feedback. The regular coordination in-between sprints, during which the status quo was reported, were identified as essential. Later on, first customer feedback was reflected on, and the targeted approach for the next sprint was announced. Essentially, it was important that all required experts came together for the coordination meetings like a task-force: besides metal experts and marketing staff, technicians, programmers and content designers were also present so that the discussion could have a wide basis and incorporate all areas and employees in the development. As a result of this, meetings provided comprehensive feedback and also enabled so-called show-stoppers to be identified at an early stage.

The early use and integration of test users is rather common among start-ups, but differs strongly from the classic approach of innovation management within established companies and industries. Many companies fear the possible damage to their reputation during a test phase—a fear that is counteracted by the creation of a digital brand in advance.

Three things had to be kept in mind: first, it was important to choose lead users from existing customers and include digital experts from 3YD in the feedback rounds. Secondly, it was important to take customers seriously or to give them feedback for their feedback. This helps to ensure customers are not disappointed and stop their cooperation as soon as all their proposals are not (immediately) implemented. Finally, the circle of feedback providers could not be restricted solely to customers, because often they do not know all the available possibilities. For instance, various ideas and suggestions for services or functions have also arisen from discussions between the different experts during the actual feedback rounds.

A further factor that was identified as important for the described successful project was putting the digital unit into a kind of *internal shelter* within the MAM team structure. In other words, the area of MAM, which was still in the building phase, was taken out of the established structures and relocated in a geographically and structurally separated unit that was positioned directly under the board. Through the direct connection to the board and the relocation of various areas of responsibility into the digital unit, the latter was able to make most of the decisions in a fast and independent manner. This allowed the company to keep up with the speed of the decision-making and agility of a start-up like 3YD. Here, the digital unit also acted as a *translator* or *bridge builder* between the two worlds when it was necessary that specialist departments or GKN experts exchange their views directly with employees at 3YD (Cohen and Levinthal 1990).

Obstacles came up when the classic functions of the company, e.g. sales or legal department, were integrated and thereby "the old world" seeped through. Therefore, know-how and resources that were essential to the project were made available. For example, a marketing employee was included in the digital units' team so that they did not to have to compete with other units of GKN for the scarce resources of the central departments like marketing. The immediate availability of the experts enabled the digital unit to (re)act fast and to plan the market presence of InstAMetal on a greenfield beyond the traditional corporate identity. Furthermore, the direct connection to the board was helpful in providing the necessary vigour regarding time-sensitive decisions and to meet the often tight deadlines.

Besides designing an unconventional structural position, independent key performance indicators (KPIs) and decision-making processes were established that took into account the particular requirements of the explorative character of the internal shelter. While the KPIs of established divisions focused on efficient acting in established markets, in this case it was important to intensify the exploratory, entrepreneurial character. Therefore, from the beginning onwards, it was permitted to make errors or to try out new things, even if they might fail. This time of nurturing was limited or was dependent on the long-dated goals while, together with the management, the progress was continuously and critically compared with the previously defined quality gates. Up to the end of the beta phase, the primary focus was on achieving mainly qualitative goals: has a sustainable digital vision been developed? Has it been possible to develop a coherent business model? Has progress been made with regard to content since the last report, or if not, did learning from mistakes and reflection take place? Can a prototype be provided or when does the beta phase start? Once the beta phase had been successfully completed, however, growth-based targets geared towards capacity utilization were defined; such as the number of customers or machine utilization. However, against the backdrop of MAM, the transition from mass production to single-part production of a batch had to be taken into account here.

The beta phase was accompanied by coverage in the trade press in order to draw attention to the digital solution at an early stage. According to the motto "Do good things and talk about them", the innovative offer was brought to the attention of customers at an early stage and quickly generated demand after a successful beta phase. After the successful beta-phase, the go-live of InstAMetal took place in June at the "RAPID + TCT" fair in Pittsburgh. From this moment on, all existing and new customers were able to register on the platform. At the same time, the go-to-market phase was now being promoted strongly by GKN's sales and marketing experts to push up the number of users rapidly—both via traditional offline and online channels. In addition to reports in industry forums and trade journals, targeted advertising was placed, regular webinars were held for free participation and specific "experience and tech" days were held in companies. At the "experience and tech" days, representatives from the digital unit, together with employees from the engineering and additive manufacturing departments, held in-house exhibitions at selected major customers in order to demonstrate the potential of MAM live.

According to GKN's competence-based view, laser sintering was initially a disruptive technology of MAM, which could have been brought to the market faster and more customer focused by realizing a digital platform concept. Following this successful digitalization test run, a team of employees from GKN and 3YD was set up, which is now examining the connection of traditional technologies and business units to the platform. During the implementation it became clear that the platform does not only facilitate the connection of MAM, but could also serve additional GKN in-house manufacturing techniques that should be extended by other possible services. Therefore, in the current phase, not only established processes and units are being tackled by InstAMetal and MAM, as the digitalization is also gradually making its way through the organization in small, clearly arranged projects in order to drive the border of GKN's digitalization efforts further into other corporate units.

4 Results Achieved

By building InstAMetal hand-in-hand with 3YD, GKN was not only able to realize the potential of MAM on the front-end, but also trigger the automatization of the back-end processes. As a result, GKN is now able to offer a new kind of service and manage an individualized ordering process with high speed and a high degree of efficiency. The extensive geographical reach and the inherent logic of the platform also opened up completely new markets and customer groups. But above all, the digital lighthouse project InstAMetal was able to successfully initiate the digital transformation at GKN, which, following the successful implementation and go-to-market of MAM, will be successively extended to traditional technologies and processes—hand-in-hand with 3YD.

Due to the constant availability of the platform via the internet and the high degree of automatization, customers can initiate their order process "anytime" from "anywhere" and manage the process autonomously without being dependent on the availability of service employees. E.g. it is possible to conduct a feasibility analysis of the parts that are to be produced by uploading a digital 3D model and initiating the automated process. Besides the general feasibility analysis, a so-called part selector provides customer proposals for conceptual improvements for the design of the print template based solely on algorithms. The automated order procedure also supports customers in their choice regarding material selection and production sites, in relation to realizing projects on time and budget. Design engineers only have to intervene in a few exceptional cases for the final review of some print templates, instead of having to check all templates comprehensively and individually as before. And even the previous and expensive calculation of offers is now performed by corresponding algorithms and presented to the customer at the touch of a button.

The digitalization of the customer interface has also triggered the packaging, structuring and optimizing of back-end processes, because it was only possible to realize the digital business model in its entirety by removing interfaces and connecting the 3D printing technology directly to the digital platform. Due to these end-to-end solutions, customers will be able to directly address and control the 3D printers and manage their own printing jobs (Fig. 3). This allows automotive

Fig. 3 InstAMetal web interface and price comparison (3YD 2017)

suppliers and manufacturing businesses to order individual metal parts in small batches directly from the manufacturer using the platform interface right from their desk. The linking of machines also allows GKN to transfer information regarding workload, status and completion of the current print jobs. In doing so, the workload can be ensured and optimized across several machines, and printing jobs can be changed between various sites with the click of a button.

All in all, 90% of all time-consuming, manual and therefore error-prone ordering processes and the processing itself could be automated. Besides a high degree of automatization, the digital platform also gained in transparency and speed. Thus, on individual request, the prices and delivery times of various printing centres or suppliers can be accessed directly from the GKN network, compared with one another and presented to the customer. Due to the end-to-end solution, the order process as well as the execution of highly complex building parts can be performed in a minimum of time compared to former technologies and processes—with almost the same speed and simplicity as we are accustomed to when ordering commodities online, such as books.

Owing to the innovative services and digital process transformation, the new offerings convinced numerous existing customers of GKN to handle 3D printing orders via InstAMetal. The platform also has a previously unattained geographical reach and high scalability. The linking of platforms between companies, which has been a part of the common vision from the beginning and lead to further opening, networking and digitalization partnerships, played a central role. This is because 3YD's collaboration with other companies, e.g. from the automotive industry, enables the establishment of cross-company digital production or industry networks.

As a result, numerous potential new customers have been acquired by connecting other platforms of companies and business associations that are also working hand-in-hand with 3YD, but which do not have their own production or MAM facilities. For example, by connecting a platform operated by medium-sized companies, thousands of potential new customers were won in one fell swoop. This high degree of scalability cannot be achieved via established businesses or sales and not even by large OEMs. Through various cooperation activities, numerous new customers were acquired in the first few months and the entry into new markets was successfully taken up. These cooperation activities are to be further expanded and early market entry is to be developed into a first-mover-advantage.

In addition to these obvious successes and countable results, there has also been a silent change in the way of working together. Because with the change of technology and procedures, the business culture has also started to transform. In the course of the development of InstAMetal, the agile approach and strong customer orientation used to create new offers or services was successively adopted into the daily work by staff in the digital unit. Here, in particular, the close and intensive cooperation with 3YD throughout the projects' daily routine contributed immensely to gaining access to the world of digital cultures and instruments in the form of on-the-job training.

According to GKNs competence-based view, laser sintering was initially a disruptive technology of MAM that has been brought to the market by realizing a digital platform concept. The initial success of InstAMetal achieved with MAM also caused a stir among GKN's higher management levels. After the MVP had been launched successfully, a project team consisting of existing employees from the digital unit and 3YD was put together to analyse additional GKN-technologies, beyond MAM, regarding their *digitalization fit* and evaluate their possible integration into the platform. The digitalization initiative is thus supposed to link other technologies with InstAMetal and also to automate the related back-end processes step-by-step. In the future, even traditional manufacturing processes should be complemented by innovative digital services. In a nutshell, existing processes and distribution structures should be successively tackled, according to the motto *if you don't cannibalize yourself, someone else will*. This digital attack will be accomplished under the brand InstAMetal, the specifically created digital appearance, and in doing so, traditional and innovative distribution structures will be able to compete immediately for new but also existing customers. Instead of thinking in cycles for a limited time, as in most traditional consulting services, the described innovation and digitalization partnership between GKN and 3YD has been developed to last. A win-win situation for both players as 3YD is profiting as well from this cooperation, e.g. reputational gain or through ideas developed during this digitalization partnership and, for the first time, realized through InstAMetal—and adopted for existing and future 3D printing platforms. Therefore, in the current phase, not only are established processes and units being "attacked" by InstAMetal and MAM now, as the digitalization is gradually making its way through the organization in small, clearly arranged projects in order to push digitalization further in other corporate units of GKN.

5   Lessons Learned

The following part reflects the milestones of the digitalization partnership between GKN and 3YD and summarizes the key learnings. Initially, the digitalization initiative was triggered by the question of how the face to the customer resp. the digital customer interfaces have to be designed so that the MAM's disruptive potential could be transferred into a sustainable, coherent business model and realized extensively on the market. Right from the start it became clear that the established distribution approaches would have to be reconsidered from the ground up. InstAMetal was therefore developed as a digital e-commerce platform that—in connection with 3D printing technology—facilitated an innovative business model for the metal construction industry. The realization of the digital business model resulted in the necessity to adapt internal processes accompanied by a cultural change.

Lesson 1: Planning by Sight—But with a Vision
Digital transformation projects are often unpredictable and complex for corporations which lack the necessary experience for reliable planning. Additionally, numerous ideas are worked out first during realization and in close cooperation with lead customers. Pivots associated with this, i.e. fundamental directional changes in the

development approach, cannot be predicted or planned. Moreover, the required time and staff needed for such schemes can rarely be reasonably calculated beforehand. In view of these facts, the traditional planning approaches with sequential phases, fixed resource planning and a time horizon of up to several months or years could not be established in the digitalization domain.

Instead, the agile approach, predominantly applied by start-ups, has proven itself in GKN's digitalization projects. Here, two planning and time horizons were important: on the one hand, the technologically driven vision, i.e. where do we want to go, was the decisive compass and, at the same time, an expression of the company's ambitions. In doing so, a shared picture of the future was also developed that the company's own employees could identify with, and from which external interested parties could gain a quick impression of the overall scheme. On the other hand, however, the road towards this vision could not be completely determined in advance, as it was strongly driven by the identified customer problems and targeted product-market-fit. Hence the second planning horizon often did not exceed the next 3 months and, particularly in product development, it was strongly driven by the contents of the product backlogs, in the sense of a topic-developmental memory.

Accordingly, it has proven successful in the approach chosen by GKN to set a relatively short time limit for the digital planning horizons, which are mainly driven by the market pull, respectively by product development. Complementarily, the digital vision, in the sense of the shared picture of technological potentials, was also of high importance for success and provided the decisive argument for cooperating with 3YD.

Lesson 2: Starting in Niches—Gain Experience and Legitimacy
The digitalization initiative has been triggered by the question of how to apply the disruptive potential of MAM. Therefore, it was specifically decided to use a still young, but very promising and seminal technological procedure, which was neither "prejudiced" by established internal business units or perspectives nor formed by already existing market structures or leading competitors outside. Accordingly, a promising technological niche—inside as well as outside the company—was specifically chosen to initiate the digital transformation.

The start in a protected niche market, or niche segment, is a mark of success of numerous start-ups and can be recognized (ex post) with disruptive innovations, too (Christensen 1997; Friedrich von den Eichen and Matzler 2012). In such a niche, it is possible to make experiences with new technology and lead customers as well as to build an innovative reputation within a territory that has little or no competition and attention by competitors (Friedrich von den Eichen et al. 2016). This advantage in experiences and cost allows companies to push forward into previously unreachable market segments, including the advantage of being ahead of the rest.

This logic can be recognized in this particular case of digitalization. The disruptive potential of 3D printing offered the chance to turn already existing business processes completely upside-down and to actuate the potential of digitalization within the company. By focusing on MAM, GKN has developed a digital solution in a previously "unoccupied area" of the company. There was no threat of resistance by established and previously successful departments, the profits of which finance the digital unit. At the same time, the external market of MAM was still under construction. This allowed the completion of a cost-intensive test run without falling behind in terms of price with established suppliers. Due to this initial success, the procedure's internal legitimacy rose also, so that the linking of further technologies and internal processes could be tackled with the necessary support from the board. Thus, the digitalization initiative began on a small scale and is now gradually being rolled out within the organization.

Lesson 3: Setting up a Shelter—Give Space to the New

Digitalization projects usually have an explorative character, which, in its core, is clearly delimited from company divisions like production or the distribution of established products that are geared towards exploitation. Rather, digitalization projects can be compared with innovation, research or development projects via which new knowledge is acquired and new technology is developed. In light of its explorative character, the unit commissioned with the digital transformation must be equipped with adequate growth orientation and development-oriented guidelines as well as incentive schemes—if the participants' commitment is not to be nipped in the bud from the start (O'Reilly and Tushman 2008, 2016). At the same time, this disconnection also offers protection against the fight for scarce company resources as well as against the internal, persisting powers and inertia of established divisions (Wildhirt 2011). Because the profit from the (still) successful business units are usually used to finance the digital projects, which will then attack the established departments and their *analogous* distribution channels.

The creation of such an independent digital division at GKN, which successively pushes the border of digitalization within the company, has turned out to be an instrument that is necessary as well as successful. Besides the objective that is geared towards long-term growth, the unit was equipped with an independent budget and high decision-making powers. Due to the short decision-making channels and high autonomy of action, the digital unit gained agility and speed, which turned out to be important to keep up with the fast pace of the start-up. The direct link between the board and unit also provided the necessary support, in order to overcome internal resistance and persisting powers. The digitalization initiative could thus be equipped with adequate firepower, and the responsible employees were chosen according to their entrepreneurial thinking and acting. This made it possible to create *start-up-like* conditions and realize advantages, like short decision-making processes and speed and agility, in an internationally active major corporation.

Lesson 4: Living Co-innovation—Systematic Opening and Networking

With MAM, GKN seized a disruptive technology, which in its core functions is entirely different compared to previous solutions. Nevertheless, GKN was still operating within its own sphere of technological key competences. This meant that the connected potentials and technological possibilities could be estimated and realized in-house. However, this was not the case for the customer front-end and the concomitant process digitalization. The possibilities of the digital world as well as the logic of the platform were still rather unknown. Also, in view of the existing market appearance and the established distribution channels, the employees were not really able to see what the entirely new services and innovative business model could offer.

In light of this, the early opening and networking with 3YD, who have been a successful pioneer in this market for a while, was an important and decisive step. Because in doing so, not only did GKN gain digital know-how, but also brought in a white-label-solution, which was used to develop a shared company-internal platform for 3D metal printing. This immensely shortened the development time for the platform. But even more so, beyond the actual task, it was possible to draw from the digital expertise of 3YD's employees and gain creative input, e.g. for the development of the digital brand and the business model. During the shared development process, it became clear that the cooperation with the start-up was much more than a mere commissioned work in the classic sense—which was partly due to the fact that 3YD was able to advance its own platform solution during the joint work. Furthermore, the targeted opening and the decision to bring the lead customers into the development process provided valuable knowledge that was needed for the further development and, at the same time, it enabled the first customers to be won at an early stage in the process. A further decisive step was the link to additional platform partners which don't have the metal 3D printing capabilities in-house, in order to digitalize the cross-company supply chain in full length and integrate partners. Accordingly, it is essential to think about digital approaches and strategies beyond the borders of the own company and involve various digitalization partners for the subsequent development with the right objective at the right time.

In addition to the contributions provided by the various partners, the close and intensive cooperation between corporate and start-up employees was especially relevant for the identity of the digital unit. GKN employees were able to learn the methods and procedures relevant to digitalization in a shared development process within an intensive and close cooperation process with the 3YD experts. But they did not only exchange explicit knowledge and project-management tools in the joint project teams. They also observed and learned in particular implicit knowledge, work routines and cultural practices. This "digital knowledge and mindset" cannot be bought externally, it can only be experienced within the scope of direct, everyday cooperation. In the meantime, spill-over effects from the digital unit to other areas in GKN have become visible. The stone that has been set in motion by the digitalization partnership should thus continue to gain momentum and push forward the digitalization process in the company.

Acknowledgement We would like to thank Josh Norman who helped to build InstAMetal and gave us valuable contributions.

References

3YD (2017) InstAMetal web interface & price comparison. https://www.3yourmind.com/de/enter prise. Accessed 20 Dec 2017

Attaran M (2017) The rise of 3-D printing: the advantages of additive manufacturing over traditional manufacturing. Bus Horiz 60(5):677–788

Christensen CM (1997) The innovator's dilemma: when new technologies cause great firms to fail. Harvard Business School Press, Boston

Cohen WM, Levinthal DA (1990) Absorptive capacity: a new perspective on learning and innovation. Adm Sci Q 35(1):128–152

Daedal Research (2016) Global metal additive manufacturing market: size, trends & forecasts (2016–2020)

Frazier WE (2014) Metal additive manufacturing: a review. J Mater Eng Performance 23 (6):1917–1928

Friedrich von den Eichen S, Cotiaux N, Wildhirt K (2016) Open Innovation – ein Erfahrungsbericht. In: Granig P, Hartlieb E, Lingenhel D (eds) Geschäftsmodellinnovationen. Springer Gabler, Wiesbaden, pp 107–118

Friedrich von den Eichen S, Matzler K (2012) Disruptive Innovationen erfolgreich managen. Symposium Publishing, Düsseldorf

GKN (2017) GKN powder metallurgy – a bottle opener as an example of additive manufacturing. http://casellasdesign.de/portfolio/flaschenoeffner-additive-manufacturing. Accessed 20 Dec 2017

Gloger B (2008) Scrum: Produkte zuverlässig und schnell entwickeln. Hanser Verlag, München

Heger T, Bub U (2012) The EIT ICT Labs – towards a leading European innovation initiative. Inf Technol Methods Innov Anwend Inf Inf Tech 54(6):288–295

Huang Y, Leu MC, Mazumder J, Donmez A (2015) Additive manufacturing: current state, future potential, gaps and needs, and recommendations. J Manuf Sci Eng 137(1):014001

Kollmann T, Stöckmann C, Hensellek S, Kensbock JM (2016) European Startup Monitor 2016. http://europeanstartupmonitor.com/fileadmin/esm_2016/report/ESM_2016.pdf. Accessed 5 Sept 2017

Leupold A, Glossner S (2016) 3D-Druck, Additive Fertigung und Rapid Manufacturing. Rechtlicher Rahmen und unternehmerische Herausforderung. Franz Vahlen, München

Muller A, Karevska S (2016) How will 3D printing make your company the strongest link in the value chain? EY's global 3D printing report 2016. Ernst & Young, Mannheim

Nonaka I, Takeuchi H (1995) The knowledge-creating company: how Japanese companies create the dynamics of innovation. Oxford University Press, New York

O'Reilly C, Tushman M (2008) Ambidexterity as a dynamic capability: resolving the innovator's dilemma. Res Org Behav 28:185–206

O'Reilly C, Tushman M (2016) Lead and disrupt: how to solve the innovator's dilemma. Stanford Business Books, Stanford

Ries E (2011) The lean startup: how today's entrepreneurs use continuous innovation to create radically successful businesses. Crown Business, New York

Sculpteo (2017) The state of 3D printing – 2017. https://www.sculpteo.com/en/get/report/state_of_3D_printing_2017/. Accessed 20 Dec 2017

Siemens (2014) 3D Printing: facts & forecasts. https://www.siemens.com/innovation/en/home/pictures-of-the-future/industry-and-automation/Additive-manufacturing-facts-and-forecasts.html. Accessed 20 Dec 2017

Weiblen T, Chesbrough HW (2015) Engaging with startups to enhance corporate innovation. Calif Manage Rev 57(2):66–90

Wildhirt K (2011) Wissensmanagementstrategien zur Steigerung der Innovationsfähigkeit von Unternehmensberatungen – Eine empirische Analyse am Beispiel der Detecon International GmbH, Kölner Wissenschaftsverlag, Köln

Klaus Wildhirt is Head of Industry at EIT ICT Labs Germany GmbH, a company dedicated to driving digitalization with a service offering ranging from Consulting, Business Development and Acceleration, a portfolio of Innovation Projects, and academic Education. Shareholders are SAP SE, Deutsche Telekom AG, Siemens AG, DFKI gGmbH, Fraunhofer-Gesellschaft e.V., and Technical University of Berlin. At the same time, he is member of the Industry Engagement Program at EIT Digital, an initiative within the European Institute of Innovation and Technology. Klaus Wildhirt studied economics at the Ruhr-Universität Bochum and Ludwig-Maximilians-Universität Munich; he received a PhD in innovation and knowledge management from University of Cologne and including a stay at RWTH Aachen. He worked as a Co-Founder and many years as a management consultant in the areas of strategy and organization, innovation and entrepreneurship. Author of numerous book and essay publications and lecturer at conferences.

Claudius Seidel holds an M.Sc. in Innovation Management and Entrepreneurship by TU Berlin (DE) as well as a M.Sc. in Business Administration by University of Twente (NL). After his studies he worked on business model development and business plan creation followed by a deep dive into the field of E-Government and E-Governance as a Research Associate at Hertie School of Governance. Currently Claudius works as an Innovation Manager and German Node Corresponding Officer in EIT Digital. He is responsible for the running of the German network with its members which are a.o. SAP SE, Deutsche Telekom AG, Siemens AG, Technical University Munich and Technical University of Berlin. Prior to that he worked as a Business Developer in EIT Digital's Business Development Accelerator (BDA) program. There he successfully supported startups from various locations in Europe and beyond, including being deployed at EIT Digital's Silicon Valley hub in RocketSpace/San Francisco in 2016.

Udo Bub is the founding CEO of EIT ICT Labs Germany GmbH, a company dedicated to driving digitalization with a service offering ranging from Consulting, Business Development and Acceleration, a portfolio of Innovation Projects, and academic Education. Shareholders are SAP SE, Deutsche Telekom AG, Siemens AG, DFKI gGmbH, Fraunhofer-Gesellschaft e.V., and Technical University of Berlin. At the same time Udo is the director of EIT Digital for Germany. Before, he was co-founder of Deutsche Telekom Innovation Laboratories (T-Labs) in Berlin and its long-time Vice President of Innovation Development. Before that he served 6 years as a management and technology consultant and as visiting scientist at Carnegie Mellon University in Pittsburgh, PA. He has received both his Master's and PhD degrees (Dipl.-Ing./Dr.-Ing.) in Electrical and Computer Engineering from Technical University of Munich and his habilitation degree (Dr. habil.) in Computer Science from Eötvös Loránd University (ETLTE) in Budapest where will be serving from the beginning of 2018 on as tenured Associate Professor of Innovation and Information Systems Engineering at the Faculty of Informatics.

Markus Josten is the Global Sales Director Disruptive Technologies, which has the intention to lead the grow initiative outside automotive market at GKN Powder Metallurgy. During his professional career, he was responsible for several OEM's and 1st Tier automotive customers and gained experience in customer development and managing projects on a global basis. In 2016 he was part of the RocketSpace/GKN Powder Metallurgy collaboration team to gain more experience outside the conventional business and find innovative ways of thinking and working in the Silicon Valley. He is also the commercial lead for 3D printed metal components which enables GKN to start it's E-Commerce journey.

Stephan Kühr is CEO and Founder of 3YOURMIND who provides software-solutions for companies around the world to capture the potential of additive manufacturing (industrial 3D printing). After graduating with a diploma in Physics and Business, he gathered practical experience as an Engineer and Team Leader of Service Sales Department at Vestas Wind Systems A/S. In 2014, Kühr founded 3YOURMIND to radically simplify access to 3D printing. He has developed streamlined software solutions that fuel efficiency and growth at every stage of the Additive Manufacturing workflow. The company was awarded the "German Innovation Prize" in 2016 and entered the elite StartX Accelerator network in Silicon Valley in 2017. Kühr is an expert on digital transformation in industry and speaker on this topic at key international conferences.

Socio-technical Complexity in Digital Platforms: The Revelatory Case of *Helix Nebula*: *The Science Cloud*

Michael Blaschke

Abstract

(a) **Situation faced**: The digitalization case reported here refers to the digital platform *Helix Nebula—The Science Cloud*. Early after the go-live in 2014, *Helix Nebula* aimed to compete with leading digital platforms such as those of *Microsoft* and *Alphabet*. To this end, *Helix Nebula* extended its scale and scope of inter-organizational collaboration toward a digital ecosystem. In effect, four leading European information technology (IT) providers started cooperating with partners over a shared digital platform to deliver cloud services to client organizations. Value-destroying high levels of socio-technical complexity resulted. This complexity increasingly inhibited the digital platform *Helix Nebula* from thriving and growing.

(b) **Action taken**: *Helix Nebula* implemented four consecutive and interrelated actions to counteract complexity. *First*, it modelled its digital ecosystem entailing platform owners, partners, clients, and subcontractors. *Second*, it agreed on a shared understanding of socio-technical complexity comprising four constituents: structural organizational, dynamic organizational, structural IT, and dynamic IT complexity. *Third*, it identified manifestations of these constituents in its digital ecosystem. *Fourth*, it took according countermeasures to reduce these manifestations. While two countermeasures (*orchestration* and *standardization*) reflect the need of maintaining organizational and technological integrity, the other two (*autonomization* and *modularization*) reflect the need of maintaining organizational and technological elasticity in digital ecosystems.

(c) **Results achieved**: *Helix Nebula* has reduced its digital ecosystem's socio-technical complexity to value-adding levels. This reduction contributed to

M. Blaschke (✉)
University of St. Gallen, St. Gallen, Switzerland
e-mail: michael.blaschke@unisg.ch

© Springer International Publishing AG, part of Springer Nature 2019
N. Urbach, M. Röglinger (eds.), *Digitalization Cases*, Management for Professionals, https://doi.org/10.1007/978-3-319-95273-4_9

realizing three interrelated improvements. First, *Helix Nebula* has scaled more effectively from initially 10 partners to currently 40. Second, *partly* owing to reduced socio-technical complexity, *Helix Nebula* has improved its efforts in *co*-creating value through more effectively exchanging, adding, and even synergistically integrating resources. Third, in implementing the countermeasures against socio-technical complexity, *Helix Nebula* has developed four capabilities for facilitating a thriving digital platform. These capabilities deal with the intricacies of digital ecosystems that substantially complicate digital platforms' state of continued existence.

(d) **Lessons learned**: *First*, facing considerable challenges in analyzing its evolving digital ecosystem, capturing all dimensions and characteristics of socio-technical complexity in digital platforms proved intricate. In effect, *Helix Nebula* managers have favored the parsimonious and succinct framework presented in this work conversely. *Second*, *Helix Nebula* managers adopt an ambidextrous approach to reducing complexity. That is, successful digital platforms balance (i) top-down, central *control* imposed by platform owners and (ii) bottom-up, decentral *generativity* imposed by platform partners, clients, and subcontractors. *Third*, complexity in digital platforms can pose both *good effects* (enabling, rewarding, value-adding, required, desirable) and *bad effects* (constraining, unrewarding, value-destroying, unrequired, undesirable).

1   Introduction

This case description sheds light on socio-technical complexity as *one* reason for weak scaling, inhibited value co-creation, and fugacious existence of digital platforms. The overarching goal of this case description is thus to provide practical guidance in *reducing* socio-technical complexity of an implemented digital platform. As such, while the case description at hand does *not* offer a method on how to *launch* a digital platform, it aims to offer practical guidance on how to reduce socio-technical complexity in any given digital platform. Specifically, the digitalization case reported here refers to *Helix Nebula—The Science Cloud*, an exemplar of a digital platform (Reuver et al. 2017). *Helix Nebula* was founded during a 3-year pilot phase from 2011 to 2013. It has grown out of a pioneering European public-private partnership between leading information technology (IT) providers (e.g., Atos, SAP, and T-Systems) and Europe's biggest research centers (e.g., CERN, EMBL, and ESA). *Helix Nebula* has been established to build a multidisciplinary digital ecosystem for data-intensive, large research organizations. Its digital self-service marketplace denoted *HNX* facilitates the marketing of *Helix Nebula*'s cloud computing services. By means of an innovative broker technology, *Helix Nebula* aims to deliver easy and large-scale access to a range of commercial cloud computing services (e.g., storage, processing, or high performance computing). Target groups are both publicly-funded as well as commercial organizations of diverse sectors (e.g., healthcare, oil and gas, financial, high-tech, and manufacturing). From the outset, *Helix Nebula* aspired to compete with digital platform incumbents such as *Microsoft*. Consequently, it aimed to extend its scale and scope of inter-organizational collaboration toward a loosely-coupled digital *ecosystem*.

However, while the needs of *Helix Nebula*'s target group's IT were and still are underserved and first client organizations were satisfied with their pilot use cases, *Helix Nebula*'s initially targeted levels of scaling, value *co*-creation, and platform permanence were significantly inhibited. The intricacies and constraints imposed by socio-technical complexity (Xia and Lee 2005), *one* reason for digital platform failure (Hanseth and Lyytinen 2010; Tiwana 2015; Reuver et al. 2017), contributed to this disillusioning episode. In what follows, socio-technical complexity refers to the "*state of consisting of many varied organizational and technological elements that are interrelated and change over time*" (Xia and Lee 2005, p. 54). *Helix Nebula* managers learned that complexity per se is not a problem *if* it is well balanced and harnessed, which was at first not achieved in *Helix Nebula*. In effect, *Helix Nebula*'s unbalanced complexity eventually culminated in partially failed cloud computing services, little platform scaling, and limited value *co*-creation. Neither explicit formal targets nor implicit individual organization's commercial targets were fully met. *Helix Nebula* has not scaled as initially targeted. *Helix Nebula* managers increasingly understood that digital platforms' unique *structure* (i.e., multiplicity, variety, and interdependency of elements), *dynamics* (i.e., varied rates and patterns of change over time), and *socio-technical* nature (i.e., organizational *and* IT elements) contribute to pervasive socio-technical complexity in digital ecosystems.

Against this backdrop, the case narrative of *Helix Nebula* is presented hereafter to serve digital platform analysts, designers, and managers as a consultable record. That is, this case description can be valuable for other organizations that may be motivated to implement a new (or improve a given) digital platform, but may not be aware of inherent complexity and related managerial countermeasures to cope with this complexity. I am hopeful that such organizations would benefit from reflecting on *Helix Nebula*'s experiences with socio-technical complexity, and consciously utilizing relevant actions taken and lessons learned as reported in this work.

Recognizing that it is impossible to capture all dimensions and characteristics of socio-technical complexity, this digital platform description seeks to make two contributions.[1] First, promising 8 years of empirical evidence shed light on socio-

---

[1] This study builds on a prior study (Huntgeburth et al. 2015), co-authored by the author of this work at hand. The prior study was presented and discussed at the 23rd European Conference on Information Systems. For the avoidance of doubt, after transparent communication with the previous co-authors, the author declares no conflicts of interest with respect to the idea, research, authorship, or publication of this article. Both studies draw on the same underlying single case study data, but they fundamentally differ in their topics of interest. While the prior study (Huntgeburth et al. 2015) uncovers *modes of value co-creation* predominantly for digital platform *researchers*,

technical complexity manifested in a revelatory digital platform. To this end, this work reports a classification framework that synthesizes and integrates four countermeasures against socio-technical complexity in digital platforms. Second, the case's narrative itself serves as consultable record of how socio-technical complexity manifests and consequently constrains the benefits of digital platforms. Thereby, this work addresses (i) *researchers* interested in digital platforms, digital ecosystems, socio-technical complexity, and cloud computing; and (ii) *practitioners* in organizations acting as platform owners, partners, clients, or subcontractors—all mutually seeking to establish a thriving digital *ecosystem* (Parker et al. 2017).

2   Situation Faced

While few digital platforms thrive and grow, such as those of Alphabet (*Android*), *Amazon.com*, Apple (*iOS*), or Microsoft (*Windows*), most others fail to survive in the long run (Parker et al. 2017). A prominent example is Microsoft's *Windows Phone*. In 2013, Microsoft acquired Nokia's *Devices and Services* division in an attempt to leverage its extant mobile operating system. In 2017, Microsoft discontinued its support for *Windows Phone* (Briegleb 2017) with less than 0.2% of all smart-phones running *Windows Phone* (Gartner 2017). *Helix Nebula* faced a similar destiny of platform failure in its three evolution phases: analysis phase (2011–2013), design phase (2014–2015), implementation phase (2016–today). Client and competition challenges in these phases impeded *Helix Nebula*'s growth.

Regarding **clients**, *Helix Nebula* faced a set of intricate client service requests, meeting each of which increased complexity. *Compute and Storage Services* support a range of virtual machines and container configurations working with datasets in the petabyte range. *Network Connectivity and Federated Identity Management Services* provide high-end network capacity for the whole platform with common identity and access management. *Payment Services* offer a range of purchasing options to determine and configure the most appropriate option for the scientific application workloads at hand to be deployed.

Regarding **competition**, prominent IT service providers, such as *Alphabet*, *Amazon Web Services*, *IBM*, *Microsoft*, *Oracle*, *Salesforce.com*, or *SAP*, had already started building up digital *ecosystems* by that time. These organizations act as orchestrators at the core of their digital ecosystem (Iansiti and Levien 2004; Ceccagnoli et al. 2012). Notably, *Alphabet*, *Amazon*, *Apple*, and *Microsoft* have become world's most valuable companies (Statista 2017). Each is marked by an extensible codebase to which complementary third-party modules can be added—a *digital platform* (Tiwana 2015; e.g., Parker et al. 2017; Reuver et al. 2017).

---

the article at hand reports *socio-technical complexity countermeasures* predominantly for digital platform *practitioners*. Consequently, due to different topics of interest, the study at hand differs in its conceptual foundation, coding scheme, data analysis, and results. Reused and adapted figures and tables are cited accordingly.

Consequently, (i) owing to pervasive evolution and adoption of cloud computing (client pressure); and (ii) owing to effectively compete with incumbents' omnipresent digital platforms (competitive pressure), *Helix Nebula* decided to also adopt the digital platform model. *Helix Nebula* thereby aimed to scale significantly beyond its extant three clients and to shift to a more dynamic process of value *co*-creation in a digital ecosystem (Ceccagnoli et al. 2012). This shift is seen as a "decisive factor in competition for tomorrow's distributed world of 'cloud computing'" (Williamson and De Meyer 2012, p. 32). It conforms to a shift in the economy toward service ecosystems (Vargo and Akaka 2012; Lusch and Nambisan 2015).

Helix Nebula's extended scale and scope of inter-organizational collaboration with a myriad of platform partners sparked different complexities:

- Multiple, varied, and interdepend elements (*structural* complexity);
- Organizational *and* technological elements (*socio-technical* complexity);
- Varied rates and patterns of element changes over time (*dynamic* complexity).

Resulting high levels of socio-technical complexity constrained and risked the digital platform's benefits. Consequently, *Helix Nebula* faced a situation of complexity and uncertainty—both factual and perceived—that were found to be negative factors in IT-outsourcing and cloud-sourcing decisions (Schneider and Sunyaev 2014). Cloud computing customers "desire to receive a service which is simple to understand and use" (Venters and Whitley 2012, p. 180). Therefore, complexity emerged as *Helix Nebula*'s major concern in scaling its digital platform.

Helix Nebula managers lacked a thorough understanding of complexity in digital platforms. Since literature on digital platforms is scarce and its investigation from a *socio-technical complexity* perspective is lacking, digital platform managers do not find actionable advice on how to cope with complexity. Existing studies employ perspectives of *risk* (Hauff et al. 2014), *business models* (Leimeister et al. 2010), and *value co-creation* (Huntgeburth et al. 2015). Therefore, in line with Tilson et al.'s call for understanding and guiding "IT ecosystem dynamics" and "complex service ecologies" (2010, p. 757), *Helix Nebula* faced a situation of *how to reduce its socio-technical complexity to facilitate platform scaling, value co-creation, and platform permanence.*

3 Action Taken

Helix Nebula opted for four consecutive and interrelated actions to reduce its pervasive socio-technical complexity. Table 1 synthesizes these actions. In what follows, each section specifies one of the taken actions.

Table 1 *Helix Nebula*'s four-stage process in reducing socio-technical complexity

Action	Input	Brief description	Output
1. Ecosystem analysis	Documentary evidence on *Helix Nebula*'s components	Conceptually modelling *Helix Nebula*'s ecosystem to shed light on undisclosed complexity amongst platform owners, partners, clients, and subcontractors	*Conceptual model* of *Helix Nebula*'s digital ecosystem
2. Complexity definition	Complexity as identified root-cause of absent platform scaling	Agreeing upon a mutually shared understanding of socio-technical complexity	*Quadripartite framework* of socio-technical complexity (Xia and Lee 2005)
3. Complexity evaluation	(1) Digital ecosystem model (2) Complexity framework	Interviewing representatives from platform owners, partners, clients, and subcontractors in the quest for unpacking the complexity construct in *Helix Nebula*	*Identified manifestations* of socio-technical complexity in *Helix Nebula*
4. Complexity reduction	Manifestations of socio-technical complexity in *Helix Nebula*	Deriving and implementing countermeasures to reduce the identified manifestations of socio-technical complexity	Reduced socio-technical complexity; increased scaling of *Helix Nebula*

3.1 Action 1: Ecosystem Analysis

Two SAP employees seconded *Helix Nebula* as technology partners to analyze *Helix Nebula*'s digital ecosystem. They drew on fragmented documentary and verbal evidence on *Helix Nebula*'s architecture. This action aimed to shed light on undisclosed complexity amongst platform owners, partners, clients, and subcontractors. The resultant conceptual model of *Helix Nebula*'s digital ecosystem (see Fig. 1) highlights a complex setup of *four* leading European public cloud Infrastructure-as-a-Service (IaaS) providers. They deliver IT services to client organizations in cooperation with platform partners and subcontractors over a shared digital platform. These organizations also operate a digital marketplace *HNX* to offer their cloud services. With *four* platform owners orchestrating *numerous* interdependent partners with different roles, a partner program focuses on helping licensed consulting, technology, and financial partners to build platform-based businesses by providing them with technical and marketing support. Moreover, *Helix Nebula* engages in a complex business model. That is, four federated IaaS providers mutually install a shared European digital platform based on distributed cloud computing technology and act as one integrated orchestrator to provide storage and processing capacities with a scale and complexity far beyond what can be provided by any single organization.

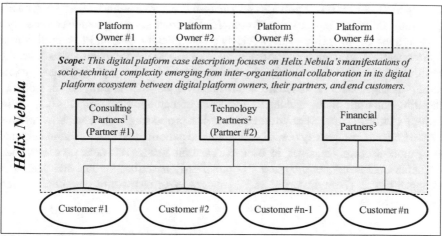

1 System Integrators, Consultancies, Resellers, Agencies, and Value-added resellers
2 Cloud Brokerage, Independent Software Vendors, SaaS, PaaS, Management and Security Vendors
3 Governments, Payment Services, Investors, and Financial Services

Fig. 1 The relationship between infrastructure providers, their partners, and customers (adapted from Huntgeburth et al. 2015)

	Structural	Dynamic
Organizational	Structural Organizational Complexity (SORG)	Dynamic Organizational Complexity (DORG)
Technological	Structural IT Complexity (SIT)	Dynamic IT Complexity (DIT)

Fig. 2 Constituents of socio-technical complexity (Xia and Lee 2005)

3.2 Action 2: Complexity Definition

Drawing on an understanding that the complexity inherent in *Helix Nebula*'s architecture is *one* root-cause of absent platform scaling, the organizations started a 4 months lasting process of researching, discussing, defining, and agreeing upon a mutually shared understanding of socio-technical complexity. Specifically, Xia and Lee's (2005) conceptualization framework of information systems (IS) complexity[2] (see Fig. 2) was and still is employed—covering both *organizational* and *technological* complexity (organizational vs. technological complexity) (i.e., socio-technical

[2]From a scientific perspective, Helix Nebula's action two combines *socio-technical theory* (Bostrom and Heinen 1977a, b) and *complexity theory* in organization science (Anderson 1999) to explore manifestations of socio-technical complexity in the context of digital platform ecosystems. The resultant *socio-technical approach* emphasizes joint optimization of social and technical subsystems to maximize performance of an overall organizational system (e.g., a digital platform ecosystem) by recognizing the interdependency of the social and technical subsystems.

complexity). Moreover, it provides a *structural* (i.e., cross-sectional) and a *dynamic* (i.e., longitudinal) perspective on IS complexity (structural vs. dynamic complexity). Through the combination of these views on complexity, Xia and Lee outline four components of IS complexity: *Structural organizational* complexity describes the multiplicity and interdependency of organizational elements (e.g., end users, project team, management, or external contractors/vendors). *Structural IT* complexity describes the multiplicity and interdependency of technological elements (e.g., technology platform, software environments, or data processing requirements). *Dynamic organizational* complexity describes the rate and pattern of changes in organizational environments (e.g., changes in user information needs, business processes, and organizational structures). *Dynamic IT* complexity describes the rate and pattern of changes in the IT environment (e.g., changes in infrastructure, architecture, and development tools).

3.3 Action 3: Complexity Evaluation

Drawing on both (i) the conceptual model of *Helix Nebula*'s digital ecosystem (see Sect. 3.1) and (ii) the framework of socio-technical complexity (Xia and Lee 2005) (see Sect. 3.2), two *Helix Nebula*-affiliated analysts intensively collected data from April 2013 to February 2014. These analysts are SAP employees, a *Helix Nebula* technology partner at that time. Specifically, they documented manifestations of complexity in *Helix Nebula* in semi-structured interviews, pilot studies, strategy workshops, weekly alignment meetings with all partners, informal bilateral calls with platform partners, and other documentary evidence. Specifically, ten semi-structured interviews were conducted in November and December 2013 including representatives from platform owners, partners, clients, and subcontractors. The SAP analysts ensured that interviewees have cloud computing and digital platform knowledge. *Helix Nebula*'s complexity evaluation efforts ensure a *quadripartite* perspective on digital platforms (owner, partners, end user organizations, subcontractors). Table 2 underscores the four different perspectives. This *multi*-perspective approach has proofed particularly valuable in evaluating socio-technical complexity of digital platforms. For instance, what *one* organization (e.g., a platform owner) perceives as value-adding complexity, *another* organization (e.g., a technology partner) perceives as value-destroying complexity. Since the data covers socio-technical complexity well, it presents an enormously rich source for unpacking the complexity construct in ecosystems.

3.4 Action 4: Complexity Reduction

Drawing on the complexity evaluation (see Sect. 3.3), the platform owners implemented countermeasures in four categories: *orchestration*, *standardization*, *autonomization*, and *modularization*. These countermeasures have been implemented to reduce the identified manifestations of socio-technical complexity.

Table 2 Organizations and profiles of the interviewees (Huntgeburth et al. 2015)

Organization	Brief description	Position/role
Client #1	European intergovernmental big science (2250 employees) Research in space and earth surface exploration	Satellite Mission Manager (C1_M)
Client #2	European intergovernmental big science (1900 employees) Research in life science	Head of IT Services (C2_M)
Owner #1	Multinational IT services corporation (78,000 employees) Solid track record in developing and delivering cloud services Leads the cloud platform and provisioning in *Helix Nebula*	Principal Solutions Architect (O1_M)
Owner #2	Pure public IaaS provider (40 employees) Enterprise-class cloud servers and cloud hosting solutions Leads the user and service requirements in *Helix Nebula*	Manager Enterprise Solutions Architecture (O2_M)
Partner #1	Multinational IT services corporation (100,000 employees) IT infrastructure and managed services experience Leads the flagship deployment as technology partner for IT infrastructure brokerage in *Helix Nebula*	Solutions Architect (P1_M)
Partner #2	Cloud and distributed system solution provider (20 employees) Specialized in agile delivery and process automation Leads the technical architecture track in *Helix Nebula*	Co-Founder (P2_M)
External #1	Multinational software and IT services corporation (2600 employees) Cloud-based applications with the largest web-based trading ecosystem	Vice President of Business Network Strategy (E1_M)
External #2	Multinational enterprise software corporation (8000 employees) Industry's only in-memory cloud platform ecosystem	Senior Director of Global Business Development (E2_M)
External #3	Multinational management consulting (425,500 employees) Technology services and outsourcing professional service provider Worldwide leading consulting experience in cloud service integration	Platform ecosystem Alliance Channel Director (E3_M#1) Lead Architect of Agile IT (E3_M#2)

Table 3 presents a classification framework to synthesize the four categories of employed countermeasures—serving *Helix Nebula* as an organizing, simplifying, and steering framework to (1) classify its manifestations of complexity and (2) reduce

Table 3 A classification framework of countermeasures against socio-technical complexity in digital platforms

Type	Structural organizational (SORG) complexity	Structural IT (SIT) complexity	Dynamic organizational (DORG) complexity	Dynamic IT (DIT) complexity
Challenge	Multiplicity, variety, and interdependency of actors and relations in digital ecosystems	Multiplicity, variety, and interdependency of IT in digital ecosystems	Varied rates and patterns of *organizational* changes in actors and relations in digital ecosystems	Varied rates and patterns of *technological* changes in actors and relations in digital ecosystems
Action	Orchestration	Standardization	Autonomization	Modularization
Result	Organizational integrity	Technological integrity	Organizational generativity	Technological generativity
Mechanism	(1) *Central organizational* actions undertaken by the digital platform owner(s) (2) In response to the multiplicity, variety, and interdependency of actors and relations (3) To control the digital ecosystem's organizational integrity; and to extract value from the ecosystem for the platform owner(s), partners, and clients	(1) *Central technological* actions undertaken by the digital platform owner(s) (2) In response to the multiplicity, variety, and interdependency of existing IT arrangements (3) To stabilize the technological integrity of the ecosystem; and to capitalize on resource diversities for digital service innovation	(1) *Decentral organizational* actions undertaken by distributed, loosely coupled actors (2) In response to environmental stimuli and competitive pressures causing varied rates and patterns of *organizational* change in the ecosystem (3) To (re)configure organizational structures to align actors in different ways	(1) *Decentral technological* actions undertaken by distributed, loosely coupled actors (2) In response to environmental stimuli and competitive pressures causing varied rates and patterns of *technological* changes the ecosystem (3) To synergistically co-create value in arbitrary n-lateral ways to suit varied innovation opportunities
Techniques	• Resolving coopetition tensions • Control mechanisms for maintaining/increasing ecosystem stability • Designing macro logic of	• Supplementary IT resource integration • Complementary IT resource integration	• *Business/contractual flexibility* for customers and partners • Leakage/exploitation of proprietary knowledge • Self-reinforcing, informal	• Context-specific, dynamic resource integration for value co-creation in ecosystems • *Functional/technical flexibility* demanding scalability,

(continued)

Table 3 (continued)

	network structure • Managing micro logic of network processes		mechanisms • Formal and more warily mechanisms	interoperability and modularity
Implication	The greater the multiplicity, variety, and interdependency of actors, the greater the need of orchestrating the digital ecosystem	The greater the multiplicity, variety, and interdependency of IT, the greater the need of standardizing the digital ecosystem	The more varied the rates and patterns of organizational change in actors, the greater the need of autonomizing the digital ecosystem	The more varied the rates and patterns of technological change in actors, the greater the need of modularizing the digital ecosystem

them through according countermeasures. The framework's contextual, empirical understanding in the case of *Helix Nebula* as well as the generalized four categories of countermeasures against socio-technical complexity are presented hereafter.

Orchestration Selected empirical evidence highlights the results of *Helix Nebula*'s evaluation of structural organizational complexity (see Sect. 3.3). This type of complexity refers to the multiplicity, variety, and interdependency of actors and relations in *Helix Nebula*.

> It is also contractually and process wise an orchestration challenge. [. . .] Helix Nebula is not one commercial or one organization [sic!] entity that we can talk to [. . .] and that we can receive bills from or that we can contract. It is rather an aggregation of different partner organizations under one umbrella and operated by one operator organization. [. . .] following individual terms and conditions [. . .] is another level of **complexity** in terms of orchestrating all these things together. (C2_M)

> It is both. [. . .] So it is not only the **complexity of requirements** that are posed by the user side but also the **complexity** by introducing difference from completely different vendors and aggregating them under one umbrella. That is a challenge in the complexity from both sides. (C2_M)

> [. . .] the complexity comes because the service is then being offered by so many organizations. So we have P1 offering the EC2 Bridge. We have F2 who are hosting the blue box which is being offered by P2. Also the service support is then being offered by P3. And then also there is a web portal, which is being offered by F3. [. . .] **complexity** comes because there are so many organizations involved. (P1_M)

Helix Nebula platform owners increasingly orchestrate their digital ecosystem through central control. Thereby, they reduce the outlined manifestations of structural organizational complexity and increase their ecosystem's organizational integrity. Its foundational mechanism is that top-down, regulative control through central governance by the orchestrators facilitates organizational integrity. Orchestration is required due to the multiplicity, variety, and interdependency of actors in *Helix Nebula*. One or more hub firm(s) and a myriad of loosely coupled partners collaborate in digital ecosystems. These partners vary in their roles—technology, consulting, regulation, or financial partners (see Fig. 1). For all actors to collaborate efficiently and effectively, a set of central organizational actions (*orchestration*) is required to control the ecosystem's organizational integrity (Lusch and Nambisan 2015).

Standardization Selected empirical evidence highlights the results of *Helix Nebula*'s evaluation of structural IT complexity (see *Action 3*). This type of complexity refers to the multiplicity, variety, and interdependency of *Helix Nebula*'s IT.

> We need to find a way for Oracle and MySQL and MSSQL and Mongo and Apache and all of these other different data providers to work together. It is possible, but very complex. There are technologies that exist in the world that are prepared to sit above multiple sources of data and to provide a global catalogue and a global access methodology to that data; but this is a **very, very complex piece of infrastructure**. (O2_M)

> It introduces **complexity** as the individual vendors not all have the same underlying infrastructure. So compared to the big global players who have [. . .] just one infrastructure or only few infrastructures to cater for, in Helix Nebula [. . .] that is different. [. . .] Building the blue box [a brokerage tool] and seeing that there are some different levels of complexity from the different vendors that offer cloud computing resources [. . .] is certainly a challenging piece of work. (C2_M)

Helix Nebula platform owners increasingly standardize their ecosystem's IT through central control. Thereby, they reduce the outlined manifestations of structural IT complexity and increase the ecosystems technological integrity. The platform owners impose top-down, regulative standardization of extant IT arrangements. Its foundational mechanism is that standardization facilitates technological integrity. A digital ecosystem's actors inherently contribute unique IT resources. For all actors to collaborate efficiently and effectively, *Helix Nebula* now operates a set of central technological actions to facilitate technological integrity (Lusch and Nambisan 2015).

Autonomization Selected empirical evidence highlights the results of *Helix Nebula*'s evaluation of dynamic organizational complexity (see *Action 3*). This type of complexity refers to the varied rates and patterns of organizational changes in actors and relations in *Helix Nebula*.

> One of them is the **complexity of data ownership** and intellectual property and so on. [. . .] Whose information is it? Whose data is it? Who is paying for it? People have these ideas that selling the information will pay for the storage of the data which ultimately it might do. But we are a long way from that [. . .]. (F1_M)

> These [customer] organizations have a complex procurement process which means they have to consider things such as geo return, so that the countries which fund these

organizations get back a fair share of work. [. . .] then there are **all these kinds of complex rules** that then determine how they can procure things. So in Helix Nebula we are coming up with a complex approach, which will allow them to procure things which then align with those rules. (P1_M)

Helix Nebula platform owners increase their digital ecosystem's generativity through granting partners, clients, and subcontractors decentral and local autonomy only in *certain* decisions. That is, it has gained the "capacity of a self-contained (digital) system to generate new outputs, structures, or behaviors endogenously through the participation of uncoordinated third-party actors without deliberate planning from the originator of the system" (Lyytinen et al. 2016, p. 7). Thereby, they control the outlined manifestations of dynamic organizational complexity and increase the ecosystem's organizational generativity. The platform owners grant certain degrees of freedom to foster decentral, local bottom-up emergence, commonly referred to as generativity. Digital ecosystems comprise a diverse set of loosely coupled actors that are relatively free to enter and exit the ecosystem and form different n-lateral configurations with other actors for the delivery of a specific IT service to serve a given client's needs. To this end, a fair degree of actor agency is required to provide for organizational generativity (Lusch and Nambisan 2015) in digital ecosystems.

Modularization Selected empirical evidence highlights the results of *Helix Nebula*'s evaluation of dynamic IT complexity (see *Action 3*). This type of complexity refers to the varied rates and patterns of technological changes in actors and relations in *Helix Nebula*.

> [The partners] have to find a way of matching what the customer requirements are, the particular unique set of resources to a range of possible provisions and do so in a structured and reasonably deterministic way. [. . .] That is not as simple as it may sound. [. . .] we know that aligning resources is a **complex** process. (F1_M)

> The other aspects are [. . .] technology. Its [IaaS] needs certainly offer much more flexibility than one individual organization can leverage and handle. Flexibility is key. It will be key to have elasticity of individual infrastructures. It will be **much more complex** than the ones [. . .] provided by individual resources. (C2_M)

> So there is complexity there around the **large amount of data** which we are going to be storing. [. . .] Then around the description of what data is available and how that data is stored and how you interface with that data; it is unlikely that we will ever see one common approach to that. (P1_M)

Helix Nebula platform owners increasingly modularize the ecosystem through decentral autonomy. Thereby, they reduce the outlined manifestations of dynamic IT complexity and increase the ecosystems technological elasticity. Thus, the digital platform's modular IT architecture balances top-down, central control and bottom-up, and decentral emergence. Modularity refers to the separation and recombination of infrastructure components. Its foundational mechanism is that a modular architecture facilitates a digital ecosystem's technological generativity. Actors can trigger IT changes within their organizations and across the network due to a fair degree of agency (Lusch and Nambisan 2015). For this reason, *Helix Nebula* has ensured to become more generative.

4   Results Achieved

Helix Nebula's four-stage process in reducing socio-technical complexity (see Sect. 3) contributed to improvements in three areas. First and foremost, after the countermeasures' implementation in 2014, socio-technical complexity has decreased to a value-adding level, while *Helix Nebula* has scaled more successfully.

4.1   Result 1: Increased Platform Scaling

Since its creation in 2011, *Helix Nebula* has overcome its complexity challenges and grown to become a leading public-private partnership between public research organizations and cloud service providers. The outlined countermeasures resulted in a new governance structure entitled *HNSciCloud*. In 2017, the initiative has undertaken its first joint pre-commercial procurement (PCP) tender called *HNSciCloud* to support the deployment of high-performance computing and big-data capabilities for scientific research. This 5.3 million euros PCP tender is sponsored by ten of Europe's leading public research organizations (CERN, CNRS, DESY, EMBL-EBI, ESRF, IFAE, INFN, KIT, STFC, SURFSara) and co-funded by the European Commission. Beyond, a wider range of organizations has shown interest in participating in the procurement group.

The streamlined governance structure *HNSciCloud* simplifies the multiplicity, variety, and interdependency of actors and IT as well as the varied rates and patterns of organizational and technological changes in *Helix Nebula*'s digital ecosystem. *HNSciCloud* refers to a procurement of innovative IaaS solutions before they are commercially available (see Fig. 3). In November 2016, four consortia won the *HNSciCloud* PCP tender for further implementing *Helix Nebula*. This clarification of actors and relations has reduced complexity significantly. *HNSciCloud* involves the current 40 platform owners, partners, and clients that all compete through different phases of development. The risks and benefits are shared between the platform owners, partners, and clients under market conditions. For PCPs, risk-benefit sharing under market conditions is when platform clients share the benefits and risks with platform owners and partners at market prices. R&D is split into phases (exploration, design, prototyping, pilot) with the number of competing R&D providers being reduced after each evaluation phase.

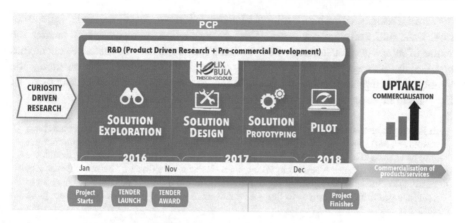

Fig. 3 *Helix Nebula*'s simplified governance structure *HNSciCloud*

4.2   Result 2: Increased Value Co-creation

Reducing its socio-technical complexity has allowed *Helix Nebula* to more effectively *co*-create value in three areas (Huntgeburth et al. 2015). First, the federated four platform owners started bartering and pooling IT infrastructure resources (i.e., networking, storage, servers, visualization, processing). This effort co-creates the value of higher scale and elasticity of the digital platform and reduces cloud vendor lock-in due to the choice between four IT infrastructure providers. Peak demands by one IT infrastructure provider request higher scale and elasticity of the digital platform. This effect can be mitigated due to an hourly compensated exchange on an internal *Helix Nebula* storage and capacity market. Further, inter-organizational, technological standards reduce cloud vendor lock-in. This is illustrated as follows.

> The requirements of the existing demand side could not be handled solely by one of the providers [. . .]. By working together, we are able to build toward a scale which [. . .] no single cloud provider can offer. [. . .] We are able to offer large amounts of cloud computing resources. (P1_M)

Second, consulting and technology partners layered additional services on *HNX*, *Helix Nebula*'s self-service marketplace. These partners thereby gain global reach and signal effects through collaboration with the platform providers. This effort co-creates the value of the existence of a European-wide integrated, trusted cloud computing marketplace. This marketplace allows for hybrid and multi-cloud deployment scenarios appropriate to clients' existing business processes and in-house IT. The marketplace provides clients with a larger service pool including especially hybrid and multi-cloud deployment scenarios. This is illustrated as follows.

> What we end up with is in essence a marketplace where cloud vendors—again a small chosen group to begin with, but eventually a larger group of cloud vendors—will be able to come and offer their [. . .] services in a way that will be understandable to the potential user community and will be governed by a set of service and business and technology rules. (F2_M)

Third, reduced complexity allows platform clients to amalgamate IT infrastructure, data, and software resources. This amalgamation of resources co-creates the value of integrated, customized new information services. For instance, clients are enabled to manage the risks posed by ground deformations. Furthermore, the synergistic integration of cloud firms yields in cross-fertilization and analysis of big data in heterogeneous formats. This is illustrated as follows.

> It is complementation and aggregation of data and information from public, quite unrelated resources, and [Helix Nebula] pools and puts that together and arrives at new opportunities and new insights. [...] That is one. If we focus on the future and why we would see information as a service being important, then that was one driver. The other driver was partly also kind of an outsourcing argument that we could use external capacities in order to facilitate providing IT sources in times of peaks or in times of very fast deployment [...].
> (C2_M)

4.3   Result 3: Capabilities for Digital Platform Permanence

In the process of reducing its socio-technical complexity, *Helix Nebula* developed four capabilities to permanently ensure its digital platform survival. Capability refers to the ability to repeatedly perform or achieve certain actions or outcomes which relate either directly or indirectly to a firm's capacity for creating value (Grant 1999). For instance, a hospital's capability in cardiovascular surgery is dependent on integrating the specialist knowledge of surgeons, anesthetist, radiologist, operating-room nurses, and several types of technicians. With the same token, *Helix Nebula*'s capability in leveraging digital platform permanence is dependent on integrating the owner's, partners', clients', and further stakeholders' resources.

Orchestration Maintaining organizational integrity in the ecosystem is an orchestrator's central capability (Lusch and Nambisan 2015). First, the orchestrator needs to balance the tension between simultaneous cooperation and competition across different types of organizational roles and resources over time mitigating the tensions caused by *coopetition* (Ritala 2012). Second, the orchestrator needs to manage the strategy, architecture, co-learning, value co-creation/capture, and processes. For instance, certifying the reliability of interrelated IT service providers is a complex endeavor (Schneider and Sunyaev 2015). In fact, the removal of the orchestrator(s) will in many cases result in a collapse of the ecosystem (Iansiti and Levien 2004). Third, digital platform ecosystem orchestration demands to simultaneously focus both on the macro logic of network structure and the micro logic of network processes (Venkatraman and Lee 2004). The orchestrator needs to *design* the macro logic of network structure by recruiting and aligning further partners (membership, structure, and market position). Conversely, the orchestrator needs to *manage* the micro logic of network processes that facilitate value co-creation (knowledge mobility, innovation appropriability, and network stability) (Dhanaraj and Parkhe 2006).

Standardization *Helix Nebula* managers have developed the capability of integrating supplementary and complementary resources by means of effective standardization. First, *supplementary* resource alignment refers to pooling similar kinds of resources—that is, homogeneous or horizontal ecosystem (Lavie 2006; Han et al. 2012). Platform owners intend greater scale, enhanced competitive position, economic efficiency, and strategic, organizational, and operational compatibility in their industry (Das and Teng 2000). Within *Helix Nebula*, the four IaaS providers (e.g., Focal #1, Focal #2) federate, barter, and exchange storage, processing, and network resources to build a common digital infrastructure (Tilson et al. 2010). The scale, interdependency, and complexity of that digital infrastructure reaches far beyond what any single platform owner could provide on its own. Second, *complementary* resource alignment refers to integrating resources with diminutive intersections—that is, inhomogeneous or vertical ecosystem (Lavie 2006; Han et al. 2012). Organizations seek to access resources that are otherwise hard to obtain (Hill and Hellriegel 1994). Within *Helix Nebula*, organizations synergistically integrate digital infrastructure, data, and software resources. IaaS providers cross-fertilize and exploit data hosted by customer's (e.g., Customer #1, Customer #2) with the help of the technology partners for data analysis to provide integrated, customized new IT-enabled information services.

Autonomization *Helix Nebula* managers have learned how the digital platform best adapts "to new environmental stimuli and competitive pressures and, in turn, create new service innovation opportunities" (Lusch and Nambisan 2015, p. 164). Decentral organizational changes require business/contractual flexibility (Benlian et al. 2011) covering the degrees of freedom that actors have in changing actor-generated institutions and institutional arrangements (Vargo and Lusch 2016). Specifically, *Helix Nebula* needs to take care of complex open and restricted tender rules that determine how the customer can procure IT resources. Further, the dynamic, context-specific aggregation, mining, and analysis of interfirm information sources raises complex security and privacy considerations. On the one hand, self-reinforcing, informal mechanisms of coevolving trust, goodwill, and commitment are required. On the other hand, reality often demands formal and more warily isolation mechanisms such as patents, trademarks, or contracts to protect strategic resources (Lavie 2006).

Modularization Ultimately, *Helix Nebula* managers have learned how to design the platform more flexible. *Functional/technical flexibility* refers to scalability, interoperability, and modularity (Benlian et al. 2011). Scalability depends on the time in which resources can be (de-)allocated as required and the maximal number of simultaneously available resources (e.g., user accounts, instances, functions, or services). Interoperability describes the integration degree between services of the same provider and services of different providers. In *Helix Nebula*, customers' capacity requirements vary that much in terms of scale of requested IT resources that *Helix Nebula* needed to establish an internal storage and capacity market to reach a better scale and elasticity of the platform. Further, *Helix Nebula* clients' requests for information and data services are unpredictable. This requires an adaptability of infrastructures, tools, and data sets in capturing, processing, analyzing, and archiving heterogeneous data.

5 Lessons Learned

Helix Nebula managers learnt how to reduce socio-technical complexity manifested in their digital ecosystem in the quest for increased platform scaling, value *co-creation*, and permanence of their digital platform. The outlined digital platform case *Helix Nebula* was reported from a socio-technical complexity perspective. Specifically, the conceptualization of socio-technical complexity by Xia and Lee (2005) was applied. Reflecting the overall digital platform case, *Helix Nebula* analysts, designers, and managers have learnt the following lessons.

Lesson #1: Simplified Governance Structures Reduce the Socio-technical Complexity of Digital Platforms In 2016, *Helix Nebula* started its implementation phase. To this end, it employed a simplified governance structure denoted *HNSciCloud* (see Sect. 4.1 and Fig. 3). This structure contributed to simplifying the multiplicity, variety, and interdependency of platform-affiliated actors and IT as well as the varied rates and patterns of changes in *Helix Nebula*'s digital ecosystem. This governance structure has considered the performance, security, and management aspects of a hybrid cloud platform, including technical standards, interoperability, portability, as well as building trust and confidence in cloud computing services—all in the context of large public research organizations.

Lesson #2: An Early Adopter Program Reduces Perceived Complexity and Insecurity for Platform Clients In its design phase (2014–2015), *Helix Nebula*'s beta version suffered from a lack of early adopters. Early adopters are crucial for reaching a digital platform's critical mass of both platform partners and platform clients (Parker et al. 2017). *Helix Nebula*'s complexity reduction efforts unveiled that interested organizations perceived the platform as too complex and uncertain. To this, *Helix Nebula* installed an early adopter program for research organizations. This program offers a legal framework and access conditions to make the adoption of the digital platform as simple as possible. For instance, interested research organizations can fund the use of *Helix Nebula* services via their regional, national, or European commission projects. This made the purchase of the cloud services way simpler. Early adopter group members benefit from evaluating the use of commercially supported cloud services that were selected and tested against a range of use-cases that are directly relevant for the research community.

Lesson #3: Succinct Statements Serve as Guiding Principles in Reducing Socio-technical Complexity in Digital Platforms *Helix Nebula* managers have translated their experiences and learnings in reducing socio-technical complexity in digital platforms to succinct principles. Each implication covers one of the four constituents of socio-technical complexity in digital platforms. They serve as starting point to quantify and manage an otherwise hard-to-grasp management problem: digital platform complexity. While two guiding principles (*orchestration* and *standardization*) reflect the need of maintaining organizational and technological integrity, the other two (*autonomization* and *modularization*) reflect the need of maintaining organizational and technological generativity in digital ecosystems.

1. **Orchestration**: The greater the multiplicity, variety, and interdependency of actors, the greater the need of orchestrating the digital ecosystem.
2. **Standardization**: The greater the multiplicity, variety, and interdependency of IT, the greater the need of standardizing the digital ecosystem.
3. **Autonomization**: The more varied the rates and patterns of organizational change in actors, the greater the need of autonomizing the digital ecosystem.
4. **Flexibilization**: The more varied the rates and patterns of technological change in actors, the greater the need of modularizing the digital ecosystem.

Lesson #4: Accessing Socio-technical Complexity is Highly Challenging Helix Nebula faced "the huge challenges in studying large-scale complex phenomena" (Tilson et al. 2010, p. 751), such as its digital ecosystem. These challenges constrain the exploration and understanding of the dimensions and characteristics of socio-technical complexity that are important and relevant for management—and therefore should be captured by a classification framework like the one presented in this case description. Moreover, these challenges in studying socio-technical complexity constrain the understanding of which complexity characteristics are beneficial and which are constraining. Against this backdrop, *Helix Nebula* managers soon learnt that interpreting and applying the complexity constituents reported here should be done cautiously. While *Helix Nebula*'s systematic complexity evaluation (see Sect. 3.3) guided by a theoretical framework reflects the most critical aspects of socio-technical complexity (Xia and Lee 2005), *Helix Nebula*'s complexity evaluation showed the huge challenges of studying large-scale complex phenomena. By drawing on a *single European-based* case study which was *not* analyzed over its entire life-cycle—much rather its design and implementation phases—, parts of the understanding of socio-technical complexity can be refined in their generalizability. Moreover, given the customer's importance in digital ecosystems, the customer facet in the complexity construct and how customers may contribute to complexity in ecosystems is considered too implicitly. Overall, the lesson to be learnt is that it is impossible to capture all dimensions and characteristics of complexity.

Lesson #5: Reducing Socio-technical Complexity Requires Parsimonious and Succinct Approaches While studying and limiting socio-technical complexity in digital ecosystems involves huge challenges due to the scale and scope of complex phenomena (see *Lesson #4*), *Helix Nebula* learnt that to effectively communicate and limit its socio-technical complexity, it needed to identify a parsimonious and succinct conceptualization of its socio-technical complexity. This is because more sophisticated classification frameworks than the one presented turned out to be hard to understand and neither mutually exclusive nor collectively exhaustive. As such, other attempts of framing *Helix Nebula*'s socio-technical complexity raised more questions among employees than they answered. Owing to this learning—that is, a parsimonious and succinct classification framework is more effective—, four constituents of socio-technical complexity along with their second-order theoretical understanding (Lee 1991; Walsham 2006) emerged from *Helix Nebula*'s complexity reduction efforts (see Sect. 3). While two constituents (i.e., *orchestration* and *standardization*) reflect the complexity of maintaining organizational and techno-logical integrity, the other two constituents (i.e., *autonomization* and *modularization*) reflect the complexity of maintaining organizational and technolog-ical elasticity in digital platform ecosystems. Each constituent comprises a succinct managerial proposition that captures *Helix Nebula*'s learning regarding the constitu-ent. Overall, the lesson to be learnt is that effective communication and management of complexity demands parsimonious and succinct approaches.

Lesson #6: A Complexity Sweet Spot Balances Required and Unrequired Socio-technical Complexity While *Helix Nebula*'s complexity analysis started under the naïve premise that complexity is *always* bad, *Helix Nebula* learnt that complexity can be advantageous for a digital platform ecosystem's success. As such, complexity in digital platform ecosystems can pose both *good effects* (enabling, rewarding, value-adding, required, and, desirable) and *bad effects* (constraining, unrewarding, value-destroying, unrequired, and undesirable). Notably, complexity is of different kind in digital platform ecosystems than in IS development projects.

Specifically, regarding *good effects*, socio-technical complexity turned out to be advantageous through the exchange, addition, and synergistic integration of distributed and heterogeneous resources. Competitive advantages far beyond what any single organizations can achieve on its own resulted. In *Helix Nebula*, multiple IT infrastructure providers federate, barter, and pool IT infrastructure to build an integrated, standardized digital infrastructure facilitating value co-creation. Beyond, multiple officially licensed technology and consulting partners add further layers of IT skills, resources, and experiences on the digital infrastructure to build a digital platform marketplace. Ultimately, multiple complementary resource integrators amalgamate infrastructure, data, and software resources in a mutually reinforcing manner to design computing and information services.

Conversely, regarding *bad effects*, socio-technical complexity turned out to be disadvantageous through organizing the exchange, addition, and synergistic resource integration of resources unnecessarily complex. Specifically, decreasing infrastructural connectivity inhibited resource mobilization and demobilized plat-form partners. Thus, less computing and information services were available on the online marketplace *HNX*. Beyond, *Helix Nebula*'s reach decreased as existing and prospective partners' marketplace modules deteriorated due to unbalanced complex-ity. Ultimately, less users adopted the *Helix Nebula* platform as less resources were invested. This decreased the usefulness of the platform ecosystem. Overall, the lesson to be learnt is that future research and management approaches should carefully differentiate between *good* and *bad* complexity. Potentially, future approaches find ways to even identify a complexity sweet spot. Multiple case studies could validate, refine, and enhance the proposed constituents.

Lesson #7: An Ambidexterity Sweet Spot Balances Structural Integrity and Structural Elasticity Digital platform design needs to enable associated digital platform ecosystems to become ambidextrous. That is, digital platform ecosystems require a balance between (i) top-down, central *control* through the platform owners' *orchestration* and *standardization*; and (ii) bottom-up, decentral *emergence* through partners' *autonomization* and *modularization*. In that respect, if structural complexity remains uncontrolled and goes beyond certain limits, it will significantly constrain the elasticity of digital platform ecosystems. Reversely, if dynamic complexity remains uncontrolled and goes beyond certain limits, the structure of the digital platform ecosystem will diverge. Thus, while digital platform owners should exert (i) top-down, central *control* (to account for structural complexity and to maintain structural integrity), digital platform owners should allow for (ii) bottom-up, decentral *emergence* (to account for dynamic complexity and to main structural elasticity). Overall, the lesson to be learnt here is that digital platform owners should allow for both control and stability as well as for autonomy and change.

Lesson #8: Helix Nebula's Case Narrative Serves as Consultable Record Finally, to conclude, the case narrative of *Helix Nebula* itself is an important learning for researchers and practitioners, serving as a consultable record. The case highlights socio-technical complexity of an exemplary digital platform ecosystem with four federated IT organizations orchestrating an extended, dynamic actor-to-actor network. Reflecting this model can be valuable for other organizations that may be motivated to implement a digital platform ecosystem but may not be aware of inherent socio-technical complexity and managerial actions to cope with it. The author is hopeful that such organizations would benefit from reflecting on *Helix Nebula*'s experiences with socio-technical complexity, and consciously utilizing relevant conceptual knowledge embedded in this work.

Acknowledgement This work has been supported by the Swiss National Science Foundation (SNSF).

References

Anderson P (1999) Perspective: complexity theory and organization science. Organ Sci 10:216–232

Benlian A, Koufaris M, Hess T (2011) Service quality in software-as-a-service: developing the SaaS-Qual measure and examining its role in usage continuance. J Manage Inf Syst 28:85–126

Bostrom RP, Heinen JS (1977a) MIS problems and failures: a socio-technical perspective part I: the causes. MIS Q 1:17–32

Bostrom RP, Heinen JS (1977b) MIS problems and failures: a socio-technical perspective part II: the application of socio-technical theory. MIS Q 1:11–28

Briegleb V (2017) End of life: Windows Phone ist offiziell tot. Heise Online. https://www.heise.de/ho/meldung/End-of-Life-Windows-Phone-ist-offiziell-tot-3769434.html. Accessed 24 Nov 2017

Ceccagnoli M, Forman C, Huang P, Wu DJ (2012) Cocreation of value in a platform ecosystem: the case of enterprise software. MIS Q 36:263–290

Das TK, Teng B-S (2000) A resource-based theory of strategic alliances. J Manage 26:31–62

de Reuver M, Sørensen C, Basole RC (2017) The digital platform: a research agenda. J Inf Technol:1–12. https://doi.org/10.1057/s41265-016-0033-3

Dhanaraj C, Parkhe A (2006) Orchestrating innovation networks. Acad Manage Rev 31:659–669. https://doi.org/10.5465/AMR.2006.21318923

Gartner (2017) Gartner says worldwide sales of smartphones grew 9 percent in first quarter of 2017. https://www.gartner.com/newsroom/id/3725117. Accessed 24 Nov 2017

Grant RM (1999) Prospering in dynamically-competitive environments: organizational capability as knowledge integration. In: Knowledge and strategy. Elsevier, pp 133–153

Han K, Oh W, Im KS et al (2012) Value Cocreation and wealth spillover in open innovation alliances. MIS Q 36:291–316

Hanseth O, Lyytinen K (2010) Design theory for dynamic complexity in information infrastructures: the case of building internet. J Inf Technol 25:1–19

Hauff S, Huntgeburth J, Veit D (2014) Exploring uncertainties in a marketplace for cloud computing: a revelatory case study. J Bus Econ 84:441–468. https://doi.org/10.1007/s11573-014-0719-3

Hill RC, Hellriegel D (1994) Critical contingencies in joint venture management: some lessons from managers. Organ Sci 5:594–607. https://doi.org/10.1287/orsc.5.4.594

Huntgeburth J, Blaschke M, Hauff S (2015) Exploring value co-creation in cloud computing platform ecosystems: a revelatory case study. In: Proceedings of the twenty-third European conference on information systems (ECIS). Münster

Iansiti M, Levien R (2004) The keystone advantage: what the new dynamics of business ecosystems mean for strategy, innovation, and sustainability. Harvard Business Press, Boston

Lavie D (2006) The competitive advantage of interconnected firms: an extension of the resource-based view. Acad Manage Rev 31:638–658. https://doi.org/10.5465/AMR.2006.21318922

Lee AS (1991) Integrating positivist and interpretive approaches to organizational research. Organ Sci 2:342–365. https://doi.org/10.1287/orsc.2.4.342

Leimeister S, Böhm M, Riedl C, Krcmar H (2010) The business perspective of cloud computing: actors, roles and value networks. In: Proceedings of the 18th European conference on information systems. Pretoria

Lusch RF, Nambisan S (2015) Service innovation: a service-dominant logic perspective. MIS Q 39:155–175

Lyytinen K, Yoo Y, Boland RJ Jr (2016) Digital product innovation within four classes of innovation networks. Inf Syst J 26:47–75

Parker G, Van Alstyne M, Jiang X (2017) Platform ecosystems: how developers invert the firm. MIS Q 41:255–2A4

Ritala P (2012) Coopetition strategy – when is it successful? Empirical evidence on innovation and market performance. Br J Manage 23:307–324. https://doi.org/10.1111/j.1467-8551.2011.00741.x

Schneider S, Sunyaev A (2014) Determinant factors of cloud-sourcing decisions: reflecting on the IT outsourcing literature in the era of cloud computing. J Inf Technol. https://doi.org/10.1057/jit.2014.25

Schneider S, Sunyaev A (2015) Cloud-Service-Zertifizierung. Springer Gabler, Wiesbaden

Statista (2017) Most valuable companies in the world 2017. Statista. https://www.statista.com/statistics/263264/top-companies-in-the-world-by-market-value/. Accessed 22 Nov 2017

Tilson D, Lyytinen K, Sørensen C (2010) Digital infrastructures: the missing IS research agenda. Inf Syst Res 21:748–759. https://doi.org/10.1287/isre.1100.0318

Tiwana A (2015) Evolutionary competition in platform ecosystems. Inf Syst Res 26:266–281. https://doi.org/10.1287/isre.2015.0573

Vargo SL, Akaka MA (2012) Value cocreation and service systems (re)formation: a service ecosystems view. Serv Sci 4:207–217. https://doi.org/10.1287/serv.1120.0019

Vargo SL, Lusch RF (2016) Institutions and axioms: an extension and update of service-dominant logic. J Acad Mark Sci 44:5–23

Venkatraman N, Lee C-H (2004) Preferential linkage and network evolution: a conceptual model and empirical test in the U.S. video game sector. Acad Manage J 47:876–892. https://doi.org/10.2307/20159628

Venters W, Whitley EA (2012) A critical review of cloud computing: researching desires and realities. J Inf Technol 27:179–197. https://doi.org/10.1057/jit.2012.17

Walsham G (2006) Doing interpretive research. Eur J Inf Syst 15:320–330

Williamson PJ, De Meyer A (2012) Ecosystem advantage: how to successfully harness the power of partners. Calif Manage Rev 55:24–46

Xia W, Lee G (2005) Complexity of information systems development projects: conceptualization and measurement development. J Manage Inf Syst 22:45–83

Michael Blaschke is a research assistant and doctoral candidate in information systems at the University of St. Gallen, Switzerland, at the Institute of Information Management as well as researcher at the SAP Innovation Center Network. During his academic career, he studied information systems at the University of Augsburg and Chung-Ang University, Seoul. He also gathered practical experience as consultant with Senacor, Accenture, and SAP. In his foundational research supported by the Swiss National Science Foundation, Michael Blaschke has been working on value co-creation in the context of digital platforms for several years. His work has been published in scientific journals and in the proceedings of key international conferences. In his applied research, he investigates business intelligence in system-relevant banks. He co-heads DACH's largest doctoral association, the Doctoral Network at the University of St. Gallen. He won Deutsche Studienstiftung's and the University of St. Gallen's start-up competitions.

Sitecore: Retaining Technological Leadership Through Digital Tech Acquisitions

Stefan Henningsson and Nishu Nishu

Abstract

(a) **Situation faced**: In 2011, Sitecore was the market leader in web content management industry. Sitecore envisaged that the web content industry was about to converge with the e-commerce industry as one unified industry. To remain competitive in this new market, Sitecore would need to provide integrated commerce and a content platform in its product portfolio. To build this unified platform, Sitecore would require a commerce engine. Sitecore's competitors also recognized this gap in the market and started actively exploring options for making this industry convergence. Thus, the competition to be the first one to offer a unified platform in the industry was in full throttle.

(b) **Action taken**: Sitecore considered the different options of the building, buying (acquiring), and partnering to cover up the e-commerce gap in its offering. Building the commerce engine would involve complex development, and take a longer time to market. Sitecore, therefore, shortlisted the different options for partnering and acquiring. During this shortlisting phase, a company named SMITH—with one of the leading e-commerce engine in their product portfolio—approached Sitecore with a selling proposition. Sitecore decided to acquire the e-commerce unit. Sitecore established the strategic rationale for the acquisition, investigated its feasibility, and eventually integrated both the technology and the development team of the e-commerce engine into a coherent platform.

(c) **Results achieved**: As a result, Sitecore achieved technology leadership in the converged industry including both e-commerce and web content management—commonly referred to as omni-channel retailing. Being the first

S. Henningsson (✉) · N. Nishu
Copenhagen Business School, Frederiksberg, Denmark
e-mail: sh.digi@cbs.dk; nn.digi@cbs.dk

© Springer International Publishing AG, part of Springer Nature 2019
N. Urbach, M. Röglinger (eds.), *Digitalization Cases*, Management for
Professionals, https://doi.org/10.1007/978-3-319-95273-4_10

one to be able to combine commerce and content, Sitecore has been successful in maintaining its leadership position in Gartner's magic quadrant for web content management for four straight years since the acquisition of Commerce Server in 2013. Altogether, Sitecore has held this leadership position in quadrant for 8 consecutive years now. By providing a unified platform, Sitecore has been able to increase customer satisfaction and successfully established a partner eco-system around the unified platform.

(d) **Lessons learned**: Sitecore learned valuable lessons for what it takes to retain technology leadership through acquisitions that are of value to all companies seeking to compete on technological innovation. Five critical learnings extracted are: First, when speed matters, acquisition can be the right thing instead of building or partnering with technology. Second, the cultural fit is essential, and to ensure this fits the organization, it must invest in the acquisition process. Third, acquiring something that is not overlapping makes integration easier. Fourth, a tech acquisition creates technological debt that needs to be paid off. Fifth, it is never too early to think about integration in the acquisition process.

1 Introduction

In digital technology industries, such as the enterprise-software industry, technological innovation has always been an important means to address competition (Zahra et al. 1995; Li et al. 2010; Taganas and Kaul 2006). For Sitecore, a company that was born in Denmark in 2001 as a web-development company, technological change has become part of their DNA by innovating and staying ahead of its competitors repeatedly.

During the early years, Sitecore displayed its innovation capabilities by delivering dynamically assembled web pages and content when the major players in the market were publishing static HTML files. When web-development tools matured, making Sitecore's main business services redundant, the company went through its first strategic transformation to focus on software products for web content management.

Between 2007 and 2011, Sitecore evolved to become a market leader in web content management. By introducing OMS—Online Marketing Suite in 2009, Sitecore became the first in the industry to integrate web content management capabilities, web analytics, and marketing automation into one integrated platform (Guarnaccia 2009).

However, despite persistent growth and market leadership, around 2011, it became gradually clear to Sitecore that, to retain its position, they needed to move on. Sitecore projected an industry transformation, where Sitecore's web content management industry would converge with the e-commerce industry. Within a short time, technological leadership in the sector would mean integrated offerings covering both spaces.

This case story is about Sitecore's decision to meet this strategic challenge through the acquisition of a company that held the technical and organizational capabilities to help bridge this gap. The unattractiveness of the other strategic options drove the decision—to develop the product internally or to partner up with an e-commerce provider—in combination with the strategic opportunity of a suitable acquisition target emerging on the market in the form of *Commerce Server*.

Commerce Server, was both the name of a business unit and a piece of software for e-commerce; it was initially developed by Microsoft (Borck 2000) who had divested the business to US-based SMITH (formerly Ascentium). SMITH had plans of expanding their digital experience agency into a software business with *Commerce Server* as one of the pillars, but got caught in the swells of the financial crisis and struggled to identify resources for the future development and commercialization of the software. Therefore, SMITH approached Sitecore with a proposal to sell the *Commerce Server* business unit (including the development team).

The acquisition process started formally in February 2013 with a 2-week workshop between Sitecore and SMITH to determine the possibilities for technology integration. Extensive due diligence followed technology integration to investigate and assess the match between the two firms. The next step was visualizing an integration roadmap and minimally-viable product. After that, negotiation took place and eventually the deal was closed in November 2013.

Post-acquisition integration lasted for 9 months. It was done by bridging the *Commerce Server* catalog system[1] with Sitecore's content tree[2] and then building a new business experience for merchandisers on the top. The integrated product '*Sitecore Commerce Engine*' became the first unified platform that combined commerce and content functionality. With this product release, Sitecore confirmed itself as the technology leader in the industry. This new engine contributed to Sitecore's continued expansion of market share, growth in revenues, and further improvement of customer satisfaction.

Having addressed the quest for technological leadership, previously achieved through internal innovation, making a so-called "technology acquisition" was a new experience for Sitecore. In the process, Sitecore learned many lessons for what it takes to retain technology leadership through acquisition that is of value to all companies seeking to compete on technological innovation.

---

[1]A Catalog System lets you import, export, create and manage online catalogs. Developers use the Commerce Server Catalog System APIs to define products, categories, base catalogs, and virtual catalogs.

[2]A Content Tree is another way of describing the hierarchical repository structure that contains your site content, information architecture, and system settings.

2 Situation Faced

In 2011, Sitecore could envisage that the web content management industry was going to converge with the commerce industry, forming one unified sector. Sitecore sensed the need for making a strategic shift and started working out with its strategic mapping processes.[3] Evidently, one thing became sure to Sitecore: They would require a *Commerce Server* to develop a unified platform.

This section of the case story portrays the journey of Sitecore from starting the business in 2001, to deciding on acquiring *Commerce Server,* to overcoming the situation faced by a need to bridge physical and digital channels.

2.1 Sitecore: From Web-Development to Omni-channel Commerce

At the inception of Sitecore in 2001, companies were increasingly turning to the Internet as a storefront and marketing channel for their business. Some pioneering firms used the internet for necessary electronic commerce. Because of the technological maturity at the time, most internet sites were, at the time, dependent on high degrees of customization and specific developments. This web development became the initial business model of Sitecore.

As the technology matured, the need for web-development services decreased. Therefore, Sitecore made its first strategic repositioning to focus on content management—the process of creating material through different communication channels such as websites, email and traditional physical channels. Sitecore evolved to become the market leader in this industry and enjoyed almost a decade of prosperous business.

However, despite continued growth and increasing profit, Sitecore declared the content-management industry dead internally in 2007. One reason was that content-management was developing into a commodity service with little possibility to differentiate offerings from competitors. The Sitecore web content management system became more about editing, managing and publishing the content with a bit of business value generated from it. The declining value triggered the development of the digital marketing suite which was released in 2009 with advanced web analytics, web content management and marketing automation in one piece of software (Guarnaccia 2009). According to Lars Fløe Nielsen, co-founder and CDO at Sitecore, Sitecore used the transformation proactively to strengthen the market position:

> In 2007, predicting the future of web content management, we made a strategic decision to declare web content management dead internally in the company. We decided to strategically reposition our business by focusing on the concept of context. We reinvented our platform by closely coupling content, context, and omni-channel automation. By adding omni-channel to our technology stack, we brought a disruptive mechanism to the market, which gave us a leadership position in the Gartner's magic quadrant in 2009–2010.

---

[3]Sitecore developed strategic maps that they use to model future market developments.

Following this strategic shift, business continued to prosper, with growth both in sales and profits. However, in 2011, Sitecore started to experience the need for another strategic change; this was based on Sitecore predicting that the web content industry would be converging with commerce in the very near future. The envisionment increased the need to bridge Sitecore's customer and marketing-oriented content-management solutions with a solution for e-commerce. Until this time, content management and e-commerce had evolved as independent services. Bridging of these services was to the extent that it was at the customer's side with suboptimal patch-work integration. This meant that the industry was just providing a content management platform, and business users would create bridges to couple their commerce functions with the content platform according to their individual needs. Lars Fløe Nielsen saw this as another opportunity to differentiate Sitecore from its competitors:

> Whenever we sense a need for strategic drift, we follow our strategic and iterative processes. In these processes, we always try to understand how are we positioned in the market and how are our competitors positioned in the market and what can we do to differentiate our self in the product stack compared to anyone else. So, the decision to move in commerce was based on the perception that any business that will sell the physical product in the future, they will, at some point, take into considerations of selling them online.

In addition to that, the growth of e-commerce made this phenomenon of convergence even more attractive for Sitecore. The consumers were moving fast to an online environment. Therefore, the businesses also needed to move there, which created a whole new market for content management in online commerce.

3   Action Taken

In the previous section, we described the situation faced by Sitecore: the need to unify the commerce and content functions on one platform. In this part, the aim is to provide a clear picture of what Sitecore did to address the situation faced. To give a better context to the story, a short description of what the web content industry looked like at that time is made. This description is then followed by the description of different options available for Sitecore; then, the possibility Sitecore chose, and, finally, the acquisition process of the selected option.

3.1   The Web Content Industry

In 2010, the web content management industry was characterized by fragmentation, where a large number of actors were holding market shares and jockeying for market leadership. According to Gartner's magic quadrant for web content management between 2010 and 2013 (MacComascaigh et al. 2010, 2011, 2012, 2013), Oracle,

SDL, Sitecore, Opentext, HP (Autonomy)[4] and Adobe (DAY)[5] were positioned as leaders in the market. Following the leaders, Episerver and Ektron were positioned as the visionaries, and IBM and Microsoft were placed as the challengers because of their ability to execute and their completeness of vision. The leaders were already competing to maintain their leadership position. However, with a maturing web content management industry, the need for innovation at the industry level was prevailing.

Among the actors in the market, Episerver, Adobe, and Sitecore were the first ones to act on the necessity to integrate content management and e-commerce. Episerver was the first mover in offering a suite that combined both product lines, but they did not integrate the systems into one coherent suite. Instead, customer data was stored in the two separate databases, called, 'content database' and 'commerce database.' The consequence of this setup can be explained with an example: Based on the customer touchpoints such as website visitation, the customer was known by its business in content database, for instance—even though the customer had not made any purchases yet. However, the other database, 'commerce database,' did not have any clue that the customer was already known for that business and would only recognize customers when a purchase was made. This issue was all because of the lack of integration between two databases. This whole set up resulted in reduced customer experience, as customer touchpoints were missed; this meant that the business was not able to tailor the marketing content to the customers until the purchase was made. Although it was a revolutionary solution, the web content management market was still waiting for a unified commerce and content platform which enables the business to know the customer from touchpoints even before they had made any purchase—subsequently allowing the firm to tailor and deliver the marketing content to specific customer needs.

The second actor, Adobe, which was the most direct competitor of Sitecore for technological leadership in the content management industry, was working with the e-commerce provider Hybris to develop a unified platform with commerce and content. Adobe strongly preferred to acquire Hybris because of its market position in e-commerce—where Hybris was emerging as the preferred e-commerce provider among large enterprise customers. However, Adobe was not successful in acquiring Hybris. Industry analysts have claimed that Adobe tried to buy Hybris on a couple of occasions, but they rejected the offers as Adobe underestimated the market value of Hybris and made acquisition bids far below it. Sitecore could not think of acquiring Hybris at that time because of the strategic conflicts, as Adobe was already working together with Hybris in other domains other than commerce. So, the option of partnering or acquiring Hybris was ruled out.

In the future, SAP would go on and acquire Hybris in the same year as Sitecore acquired *Commerce Server* (in year 2013).

---

[4]HP acquired enterprise software company Autonomy in 2011.
[5]Adobe acquired web content management software company DAY in 2010.

For the third actor Sitecore, the various options at hand are discussed in the (next) Sect. 3.2, where they had to make a rational choice between building, partnering, or buying the commerce solution.

3.2   Build, Partner or Buy into Omni-channel?

Analyzing the industry and its competitors, Sitecore evaluated the options of the building, partnering or acquiring its way into the converging industry whose trend was becoming known as the 'Omni-channel' industry.

The first option was building the missing products by themselves to complete the omni-channel offering. Sitecore did the internal review and decided on not making a commerce engine by themselves, as it was not a viable option. The decision was because of two main reasons: One was complexity. The commerce space was very complicated and broad in nature to be understood, and it would relatively be an extensive process for Sitecore because they did not possess any knowledge of commerce space. The second reason was time pressure. Although Sitecore could develop the missing product itself, by the time it would be built and ready for full integration with the rest of the technology stack to attain any leverage, it would be too late for Sitecore in a highly-competitive environment.

The second option was partnering with a mature e-commerce provider. Hybris could have been the right partner, but, as discussed in the last section, it was ruled out. Other options were still available in the market, but they were either owned by large enterprise software companies like SAP (which Sitecore did not want to partner up with as they would face the same situation as Episerver) or they would be lagging in the technological development of their products as well as in the market shares.

The third option was an acquisition. With no proper options available in the market to partner with, Sitecore started shortlisting candidates for acquisition. The purchase would allow Sitecore to attain the control of the organizational unit behind the e-commerce technology. Sitecore would be able to conduct resource development to ensure that the product evolved at the pair with the rest of the e-commerce and possibly grow the market share by promoting the product to existing Sitecore customers.

Sitecore was still in the process of shortlisting options when *Commerce Server* became available in the market. The owner of *Commerce Server*, the SMITH company, approached Sitecore with the proposal to sell its e-commerce business unit, including the development team, and sales organization. Sitecore could not resist this offer and jumped right into acquiring the technology.

3.3   About Commerce Server and Why It Was the Best Option for Sitecore

Commerce Server had its roots in the tech startup 'Ink development,' founded in 1991. In 1993, Ink Development Corporation was renamed to eShop, and focused on developing electronic commerce software for the B2C marketplace. In 1996,

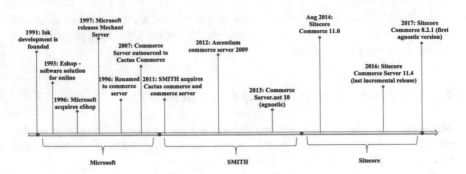

Fig. 1 Commerce server's product lifecycle

Microsoft acquired eShop for the software's intellectual property rights (Microsoft News 1996). The reason behind it was that it would save Microsoft on development time[6] required for introducing a merchant server in the market. Based on redeveloped eShop technology, Microsoft launched a new product called 'Microsoft Merchant' server in 1996. In 2001, the server was re-named as *Commerce Server*, and in following years, Microsoft released several incremental versions of the product.

In 2007, Microsoft outsourced the development work of *Commerce Server* to Cactus Commerce. Despite the outsourcing, Microsoft's ambition was still to tightly couple it with Microsoft's other enterprise software SharePoint. However, the SharePoint product developed into a different direction than commerce, and *Commerce Server* became more of a problem child for Microsoft.

In 2011, SMITH (then Ascentium) acquired Cactus Commerce, and Microsoft decided to sell off the *Commerce Server* to SMITH (Walker 2011). After the acquisition, SMITH re-coded the *Commerce Server* to make it agnostic by decoupling it from the deep integration with SharePoint and other Microsoft enterprise software. However, because of financial constraints and an inability to further develop the product, SMITH decided to divest the *Commerce Server* product and related business functions. The product lifecycle of *Commerce Server* is depicted in Fig. 1 later in this story.

For Sitecore, the acquisition of *Commerce Server* was an opportunity that immediately felt compelling. Sitecore already had a partnership with SMITH and was continually updated on the technical architecture of the *Commerce Server*. They knew that SMITH had redeveloped the *Commerce Server* product with modern architecture and, at the same time, had not added any content functionality to the commerce engine. No addition meant that SMITH was offering a pure transaction

---

[6]According to an interview with the Vice President of Microsoft Paul Maritz from June 17, 1996, Microsoft saved 12–24 months on development time.

software[7]—precisely what Sitecore needed. It would be relatively easy for Sitecore to do the full integration at the later stages as there would be no overlapping with Sitecore's web content management (customer experience) architecture. According to Lars Fløe Nielsen, the match was apparent:

> The acquisition of Commerce Server seemed to be a perfect strategic marriage. We were the undisrupted leader in the customer experience, and commerce engine was the most solid piece of pure transaction technology at the time. Both software were top notch in their respective spaces. SMITH had not added any experience functionality after refactoring the engine; it was the perfect match. With this marriage, we would achieve two things: first, to complete our platform and second, to enhance another platform with our platform, so it was the best option we could ever get.

Another reason that made the offer of acquiring *Commerce Server* compelling was that *Commerce Server* was a mid-market actor, attracting mostly medium-sized businesses. This mid-size segment was also Sitecore's principal business segment in the content management space. Thus, an option became available for Sitecore to offer a new unified platform to an existing customer segment. Moreover, this acquisition would come with a list of clients for Sitecore; these clients would come along with the *Commerce Server* due to the subscription-based business model used by *Commerce Server* creators.

Lastly, at face value, there were seemingly technological similarities between Sitecore and *Commerce Server*. Both companies' offerings were already supported with Microsoft's .net framework and the long-term development vision behind both technologies was same: to move entirely to Microsoft's .net framework called Azure.[8] *Commerce Server* was coded in Python with additional C++ plugins. Although possible to connect to the Sitecore technology stack already, the existence within the same technological regime made the prospect of tight coupling between the Sitecore technology stack and the *Commerce Server* software made this acquisition even more compelling.

3.4   The Acquisition of *Commerce Server*

Acqusitions are an important driver of technological innovations and firms often decide to acquire in quest to innovate faster (Ahuja and Katila 2001; Lee and Kim 2016; Makri and Hitt 2010). Sitecore decided to move forward with the option of leaping into the converging market space with an acquisition of *Commerce Server*. This decision was based on working out the strategic rationale, investigating the feasibility of achieving the strategic aspirations in the due diligence process, and,

---

[7]In transaction-based software, search engine optimization (SEO) is the primary transaction driver, with little focus on user identity, meaning no personalized marketing, etc.

[8]Microsoft Azure is an open, flexible, enterprise-grade cloud computing platform.

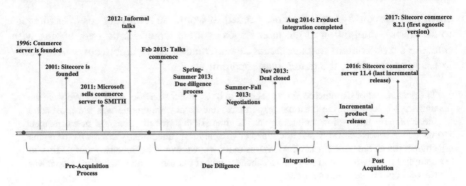

Fig. 2 Acquisition timeline

finally, to realize intentions in the integration of the two business units and the two software products. How this process unfolded is depicted in Fig. 2.

3.4.1 Strategic Rationale

Starting to explore the option of an acquisition, Sitecore established the strategic rationale that could make this purchase a pleasant prospect:

- **Creating customer value**: Before the acquisition, *Commerce Server* clients were using Sitecore as the software in the content space, which meant that they had to deal with two separate tool sets for commerce and content. By integrating commerce and content, Sitecore would create value for the existing (*Commerce Server* came with a book of customers) and new customers by providing one toolset.
- **Market leadership aspirations**: Sitecore's strategic purpose had always been to be one step ahead of its competitors. The market for e-commerce was growing faster than web content management. From the market growth perspective, there were clear signs that vendors in the commerce space would slowly turn into the experience management space. Sitecore needed to move into the integrated commerce and content space before customers or competitors did. By acquiring *Commerce Server*, Sitecore could maintain its leadership position in the market by being the first integrated solution provider.
- **Time and cost savings**: Sitecore weighed in the option of building the commerce engine by them self, which included extensive financial investments and more extended 'Time to Market'[9] period. Deciding to acquire seemed like the right decision as the MVP (minimum viable product) looked promising with shorter 'Time to Market' in the due diligence process. Moreover, the seller of *Commerce Server* 'SMITH' was in financial constraints and Sitecore had the opportunity to gain from this financially as they had the leverage to negotiate knowing situation

---

[9]The length of time it takes from a product being conceived until its being available for sale.

of SMITH; Sitecore was a partner with SMITH before their acquisition of *Commerce Server* from Microsoft.

- **Architectural fit**: the long-term strategy of Sitecore was to move their core cloud infrastructure to 'Microsoft Azure' which was a technology based on the .net framework. *Commerce Server* was also developed on the .net framework as Microsoft initially designed it. Therefore, the decision to go for the acquisition of *Commerce* Server grew more compelling due to software architectural fit between two technologies.

3.4.2   Planning, Due Diligence, and Negotiations

The decision to acquire *Commerce Server* form SMITH was formed over a period. Microsoft exiting the commerce space ignited the interest of Sitecore in *Commerce Server*. Sitecore's interest in commerce grew, and they had first informal talks about the future of commerce engine with *Commerce Server* team in November 2011 at a workshop organized by SMITH. Following which, Sitecore became more engaged in discussions with SMITH, and these talks continued through 2012. Sitecore participated in another SMITH workshop in 2012 as a part of the pre-acquisition process, where both parties were able to visualize customer scenario's, market requirements and a rough idea of how technical journey might look like for the new product; this was formalized later in due diligence process.

At the beginning of 2013, SMITH approached Sitecore to sell *Commerce Server*. The official acquisition process started after a meeting between the CEO of Sitecore and Chief Technology Officer of *Commerce Server* in Copenhagen. Ascentium received the formal letter of intent for the acquisition from Sitecore in February 2013.

Sitecore started the due diligence process by flying a team to Ottawa for 2 weeks to participate in a workshop organized by SMITH. The focus of this workshop was to come up with an integration roadmap and a minimal viable product (MVP) that will be introduced as the first integrated platform after the acquisition. Sitecore spent a substantial amount of time with the *Commerce Server* team to cover the technical depths to make sure that it was the right match for Sitecore. By doing so, they also established that technology was robust enough for their business. The due diligence process ran through spring and summer of the same year, uncovering the many dimensions of the deal. As Ryan Donovan, Head of product management, explains:

> Typically, technology-driven businesses do the acquisitions either for technology or talent. For example, Microsoft usually acquires for Intellectual Property or Technology. Contrary to that, Sitecore's acquisition passed through the multiple dimensions of technology, talent, revenue, market share, customer base, brand, and marketing position. So, this acquisition stands out because of the multiple dimensions.

The negotiation process started in the summer and lasted until the fall of 2013. Sitecore was aware of the financial constraints of SMITH. During the negotiation process, they used this knowledge as a tactic and deliberately delayed, and prolonged negotiation talks. Sitecore was aware that if they could move the process to the next financial quarter, they would have more leverage over SMITH, as pressure to close the acquisition deal was building up on SMITH because of the economic situation. As Lars Fløe Nielsen explains:

> If you can manage to spend more time with the new team in due diligence process, it gives you leverage as a buyer. The key tactic is to delay the negotiations if possible, but also stick around at the same time. This tactic created some financial pressure on the seller, and at the same time, we got an opportunity to learn more about what we were buying. We managed not only to negotiate financially but also managed to figure out cultural match during the time spent with the team.

Using the tactics of delaying the negotiations, Sitecore managed to spend a lot of time close to *Commerce Server* team. This time spent enabled them to develop a relationship between employees of both companies. The effect of which was that Sitecore was successful in creating inclination in Commerce Server team towards joining the Sitecore. In this way, the *Commerce Server* team was themselves advocating the sell to Sitecore.

Microsoft also played a role in negotiations because the original contract between Microsoft and SMITH (which came along Commerce Server) restricted Sitecore to sell *Commerce Server* in the future. This restriction was because Microsoft retained the intellectual rights of *Commerce Server* software even after selling it to the SMITH. Sitecore negotiated a new contract with Microsoft to be able to use the code base during an interim period before Sitecore would be able to remove all the remnants of Microsoft technology from the *Commerce Server* code base.

3.4.3   Integration

Technology Integration

The integration process lasted for 9 months. Sitecore started the integration process by building a bridge between the *Commerce Server* catalog system and the Sitecore content tree. They then built a business user experience that included merchandising manager, catalog manager, inventory manager, marketing manager, and so forth on top of the bridge solution, as shown in Fig. 3. According to Ryan Donovan:

> After the acquisition, we had two sets of users, one set as Commerce Server user and another set as Sitecore content management user. The challenge was to bridge them together. To do so, we separately wired in user profile management of two sets together so that the user in Sitecore was same as the user in Commerce Server. At that point, all the e-commerce aspects were still being handled by Commerce Server, but to a business user complete content management and merchandise experience was holistically one. So, the user was now using integrated commerce and content platform.

After this initial coupling, the link between the formerly-independent products evolved through several iterations, while building next-generation commerce engine. Sitecore released the renamed *Commerce Server* as 'Sitecore Commerce Server 11.0' as the first new version in August 2014, which underpinned much of the commerce functionality in Sitecore's product portfolio. Version 11.1 of the Sitecore *Commerce Server* that was released in October 2014 had a codebase that was the first

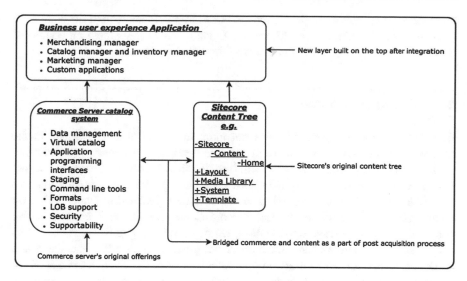

Fig. 3 Post-acquisition integration

built entirely in Microsoft .net framework, eliminating C++ runtime dependencies for peripheral plugins, thus removing the last Microsoft remnants in the code base.

Organizational Integration

Regarding customer base overlapping, Sitecore was, by far, most over-lapping with the *Commerce Server* customers. After the acquisition, Sitecore kept most of the development team in Canada, and only a few employees were moved across business units in Denmark and North America. Sitecore has been expanding the organization in North America ever since because of the growth potential in the North American market.

With just the geography being a factor, instead of moving people across the continent, Sitecore moved employees onto other areas of the product. The Sitecore team that spent a lot of time in Ottawa working alongside the Commerce Server team was integrated into the original Commerce Server team after the acquisition. And eventually, Sitecore's acquisition team started primarily working in the commerce domain. Many Commerce Server's team members took prominent roles in Sitecore because they had the unique experience. For example, the primary person who leads the cloud transformation in Sitecore was from the Commerce Server team, another employee from the commerce team was given the global portfolio responsibility and was given the designation of a free mover to coordinate activities between Denmark and North America by working at both places simultaneously.

Sitecore acquired the *Commerce Server* team along with the *Commerce Server* deal. Sitecore did not have any understanding of the commerce domain. Therefore, it was rational for Sitecore to make sure commerce team was part of the acquisition. The *Commerce Server* team became a part of Sitecore's competitive space, and they used the team to their strategic advantage. For example, Sitecore used the commerce team to build a connector for Microsoft X-retail, which gave them an additional opportunity to develop a strategic partnership with Microsoft.

4 Results Achieved

Regarding results achieved, Sitecore got more than what they envisioned in the rationale behind the acquisition. The main achievements are discussed as follows:

The first achievement was successful introduction of Sitecore *Commerce Server* 11.0 as a tightly coupled, fully-integrated commerce platform post-integration process (the technical architecture of the new platform is depicted in Appendix). Two meaningful solutions offered in this Sitecore *Commerce Server* deal were Native personalization and Native optimization, which closed the gap between customers and businesses. Native personalization is designed to enable merchandisers and marketers to deliver persona-driven content not only in the checkout phase of the shopping experience, but throughout the customer journey. In this way, marketers and brands can offer their online visitors recommendations and contextualized content based on user behavior, such as clicks, page views, and purchases, as well as demographic data, such as location, language, job role, and industry. Native optimization refers to a process by which a business can test and optimize everything from content to discounts. With such integration, more sophisticated intelligence is available to learn about each individual and the company can provide the right content with right context in real time (Tamturk 2017).

The second achievement was market leadership. When Sitecore's competitors, Oracle and IBM, were providing a commerce platform with a subset of limited content management capabilities (where a customer had to get used to complicated integration and use two different set of tools), Sitecore provided a product with one toolset which reduced a substantial amount of work and created value for Sitecore's customer. As Ryan Donovan explained:

> With the new Sitecore solution, when an enterprise adds a new piece of catalog data in merchandising, they can now either edit it in merchandising, or they can edit in the experience editor, or they can edit it in the content editor. There will be no duplication of data which will transcend into reduced time to market. Traditionally, if enterprises want to edit, they must do it separately in all three merchandising, experience and content. Having to do so, most of the benefit goes away and time to market increases. However, with the Sitecore solution, [the] main value preposition for the customers will be that the two capabilities of commerce and content will function together for their benefit of the customer.

This new solution enabled Sitecore's clients to deliver a personalized and relevant digital shopping experience from the customer acquisition phase to the post-sales experience via a single platform. This new platform included integrated digital marketing, e-commerce, a multichannel customer experience and big data analysis applications. Now, the businesses can have a single, connected administration, with all product catalog information available within Sitecore, and that was without any data duplication or synchronization hassles. Also, customers now had unified content and campaigns, which enabled them to quickly search and edit all assets, view campaigns from end-to-end and access the customer's insights across all touch points. The integrated solution also allowed for measurements of conversions into sales and customer value. Furthermore, the digital technology acquisition of *Commerce Server* helped Sitecore efficiently leverage the convergence of content and commerce to strengthen its position towards its rivals. Out of three leading players in the convergence—Episerver, Adobe, and Sitecore—Sitecore drove the convergence and gained a competitive edge over its competitors. Because of an ability to visualize market trends, capacity to execute on the vision and to develop go-market strategies, Sitecore has been able to maintain its technological leadership in Gartner's magic quadrant for 4 straight years. In other terms, this means that since the acquisition of *Commerce Server* in 2013, Sitecore has been able to enhance the customer experience by providing an integrated platform of commerce and content together.

The third achievement came in the shape of intangible assets that were skills and capabilities the *Commerce Server* team brought along to Sitecore. Apart from the business opportunities created by the new product, the team also created great value for Sitecore in terms of bringing new business opportunities. As Ryan Donovan explains:

> [The] commerce team has proven to be very valuable for Sitecore. After the acquisition of Commerce Server, the Commerce Server team brought a lot of used case scenarios to the table which drove improvements in other aspects of Sitecore's product portfolio. For example, Sitecore's user interface (UI) framework ended up taking a lot of feature requests as a result of the commerce team's used case scenario. Commerce had a lot of complex user interface (UI) necessities for complex merchandising operations that did not exist in a traditional content management environment. So, the merchandising operations had to find a way to the user interface (UI) framework; that is where Sitecore derived quite a bit of benefit from [the] commerce team's skills and expertise.

The fourth achievement was the establishment of Sitecore's new partners' eco-system. *Commerce Server* came with the large established partner base, and there was a high degree of overlap between their partners and Sitecore's partner because many clients using *Commerce Server* had moved from SharePoint to Sitecore for their content management service after *Commerce Server's* divorce from SharePoint in the past. The new eco-system did not start from scratch, but was instead built on an existing eco-system. Some of the partners of *Commerce Server*, like Episerver, were not happy with the acquisition by Sitecore, while others got on board. Some of the Sitecore partners retreated as well, and they got together with Episerver. However, for the most part, Sitecore established a successful partner eco-system after the acquisition.

The fifth achievement was opening up the same product to new segments by recoding the *Commerce Engine*. When Microsoft owned *Commerce*, they had to develop the software architecture in a certain way due to antitrust laws in the United States. As a result, the codebase was redundant. After acquisition Sitecore removed the unwanted code and developed the same code with a much more modern architecture. The original code of 3 million lines was reduced to the 1.7 million lines. By doing so, Sitecore converted *Commerce Server's* software architecture into a very pluggable architecture, which was a microservice architecture that opened the same product to other segments. The original product with the Microsoft technology was only targeted at the upper-mid to enterprise-level segment (regarding the size of the firm). However, with micro-architecture, the same product can be aimed at the mid- to small-cap market firms as well. Ryan Donovan and Lars Fløe Nielsen explained the need to recode the engine consecutively:

> We decided to recode the commerce engine partly because of two main reasons. First, the outdated coding technology. Parts of the code of Commerce Server dated back to 1990s and was coded using a technology called COMPASS, which was outdated. Second, Microsoft was moving into a modular, open source multi-platform of the .net framework, which was in alignment with Sitecore's long-term strategy of moving core cloud infrastructure into the .net framework. Thus, we recoded the engine to make it more modular and ultimately reap the benefit of efficiency of the .net core in a cloud environment in future.
>
> The acquisition of the commerce engine from SMITH came with some of Microsoft's technology and its peripheral components. SMITH had the contract with Microsoft to develop the commerce engine in a certain way, and the agreement was passed on to us. This contract implied that we could never sell the commerce engine in future without having Microsoft's say in it. So, to pay our technical debt, we decided to recode and remove much of the Microsoft technology from our platform and develop it in-house as a Sitecore commerce engine and make it more pluggable.

The sixth achievement came in the form of a strategic partnership with Microsoft. Apart from all the results regarding product development, market growth opportunities, and so forth, Sitecore has been able to develop a strategic partnership with Microsoft. With the acquisition of *Commerce Server*, the critical asset *Commerce Server* team was also acquired. Microsoft approached Sitecore to build a connector for MS Dynamics x-retail, which is a product that is meant for alignment of how organizations sell across the different physical stores. Microsoft had a lot of experience doing physical outlets, and Sitecore had tons of experience doing the online stores. The integration process of Dynamic AX-retail was not just pure coding processes; it rather required the more in-depth understanding of the fundamentals of running commerce, and Microsoft saw the *Commerce Server* team as the most suitable for doing this job. The connector bridged the gap between online and physical stores. Hence, this gave opportunities to the business owner to manage the end-to-end omni-channel retail platform and enabled them to deliver the right product, at the right time, in the right context. Sitecore saw the opportunity to get hands-on experience in business with brick-and-mortar stores—also known as online and offline stores—because that was something Sitecore wanted to provide its clients in the long run as well. It was more of a strategic gain for Sitecore.

The seventh achievement was steady revenue growth. Sitecore's growth ambitions have, by far, a more highly-compounded growth rate than the annual growth rate in the CMS market. Sitecore's aim to grow its content management software business higher than market growth by expanding into new territories

Fig. 4 Post-acquisition revenue growth of Sitecore

and new markets was achieved after acquiring the *Commerce Server*. Sitecore *Commerce Server* has been by far the strongest content and context story together in commerce, which gave them a competitive advantage over competitors, like Adobe, as they still lacked a commerce platform. Since the acquisition of *Commerce Server*, Sitecore has had steady growth in revenue as shown in Fig. 4.

5   Lessons Learned

For Sitecore, strategic transformation of the company to stay ahead of market developments has been a vital characteristic of the company since its inception, and a critical feature to keep the company relevant. However, when acquiring *Commerce Server*, it was the first time in the company's short life that a digital technology acquisition played an instrumental role in enabling the transformation. As such, the company learned about making complex acquisitions to access new technology and innovative people that are relevant also for other prospective acquirers. We have extracted five key lessons for technology-driven businesses on how they can learn from this acquisition. These lessons can be implemented by any industry working with the technology.

Lesson 1: When Speed Matters, Acquisition Can Be the Right Thing
One of the fundamental reasons for Sitecore to go with the option of the acquisition was that they estimated shorter 'Time to Market' for the integrated content and commerce platform. Although Sitecore had the capability and ability to build the commerce engine in-house from scratch, this was not the right strategic choice in a rapidly-maturing IT market. Organizations should be able to decide on what options are the best in the early stage of the process and weigh in the rationale and logical reasoning's for three different options of building, partnering and, buying. Sitecore demonstrated that they not only made the right strategic decision of not building

in-house, but also chose the best option of buying. This was in contrast to partnering where they saw the strategic risk of a close relationship between the potential target and their main competitor.

Lesson 2: The Cultural Fit Is Essential

Organizations must invest in the acquisition process to make sure that acquisition target is ready. Even if the technical match looks perfect in the due diligence process, ignoring the fact that there is a need to measure the readiness of the target organization can delay the final integration process. If the organization does not pay attention to this scope of the acquisition, the acquired team might spend more time in getting used to the new working environment or, worst-case scenario, might not be able to become accustomed to the new organizational structure.

Unlike acquisitions for customer stock, market share or technical IP, acquisitions that involve innovative people need people that are willing and able to work with the new owner. One of the ways to establish the compatibility of people is by doing a culture match. There are many ways of doing it, but Sitecore did it by using two approaches. First, Sitecore used an external consultant to do a culture fit of the acquired company's culture and people's culture. Second, Sitecore spent much time with the *Commerce Server* team in the due diligence process to get to know their working culture and managed to test their capabilities by stress examining them to come up with different integration models.

It is worthy to note here that most mergers and acquisitions fail in the long run because of failure to couple different cultures in the organization. Sitecore's management has understood the importance of cultural fits through its history of successes and failures in M&A and, therefore, had been paying closer attention to cultural fit as an integral part of Sitecore's acquisition strategy now. One of the key criteria for Sitecore to go ahead with the acquisition is that if the culture does not fit, one should back off. It is not possible to achieve synergies if something is culturally wrong.

Lesson 3: Avoid Overlapping Whenever You Can

Acquiring something that did not overlap made integration easier for Sitecore. One of the strategic decisions Sitecore made before looking at the available option of *Commerce Server* in the market, was to look for someone who had not invested anything or added any experience functionality in the commerce engine. By setting their path from the beginning, Sitecore could achieve two main things. First, no technical overlap concerning the architecture of the product meant no need to redesign the architecture; the commerce engine was classic commerce architecture and Sitecore only had to integrate it with experienced architecture. Secondly, regarding workforce capabilities, there was no overlapping regarding skills and terminology; the commerce engine team was skilled in commerce architecture and the experience team was skilled in experience architecture. This lack of overlapping made integration easier and saved Sitecore time because teams from two different domains did not contradict each other in the decision-making process.

Lesson 4: Tech Acquisition Creates Technological Debt that Needs to Be Paid Off

Technical debt is a metaphor used to evaluate the situation of whether to use a quicker way by adding functionality to the acquired software and getting the product as soon as possible to the market. Alternatively, to use a clean and systematic approach by doing complete integration may take a long time, but it lays down solid foundations and makes it more natural for the organization to add any new functionality in the later stage.

The *Commerce Server* acquisition came with a technical debt for Sitecore. When Sitecore acquired *Commerce Server*, Microsoft still had the intellectual property rights in parts of the software. Sitecore decided to recode the whole commerce engine to move out any of the Microsoft remnants, but, more importantly, to clear off its technical debt.

A valuable lesson to be learned for future tech acquisitions is that one should not compromise with the integrity of the product. The shorter way may give you an advantage by reducing time to market for the new product, but in the longer term, it will create a technological debt. Eventually, the organization will need to clear off the technical debt and the only way would be following a clean and systematic approach. In some cases, you may have to recode the whole thing. A perfect industry example of technical debt is when Adobe acquired DAY. Adobe followed quick and easy approach and did not do the full integration at the early stages, which, of course, lead to the accumulation of technical debt and the repercussions were a sizeable, unsatisfied customer base. Eventually, Adobe had to do full integration by following a clean and systematic approach.

Lesson 5: It Is Never Too Early to Think Integration

Most of the firms think about integration after they have closed the acquisition deal. Even though Sitecore started to think about the integration very early in the process already before signing the deal, they recognized that they could have started even earlier. Because, in these acquisitions, speed is what you are after, it is never too early to think of integration. Sitecore's technical integration process got delayed because they did not involve people from different departments in the early stage of the process. As Lars Fløe Nielsen explains, there are consequences of not doing so:

> One of the important lessons Sitecore has learned is that speed is crucial in an acquisition process; speed is an imperative. Sitecore lost many opportunities because we were not fast enough to complete the whole acquisition process, especially integration. As a consequence of it, we lost the momentum of approximately 6 months in a market which is growing at the rate of 100–130% per year.

Appendix: The Technical Architecture of *Sitecore Commerce* 7.2, the First Post-integration Product Release

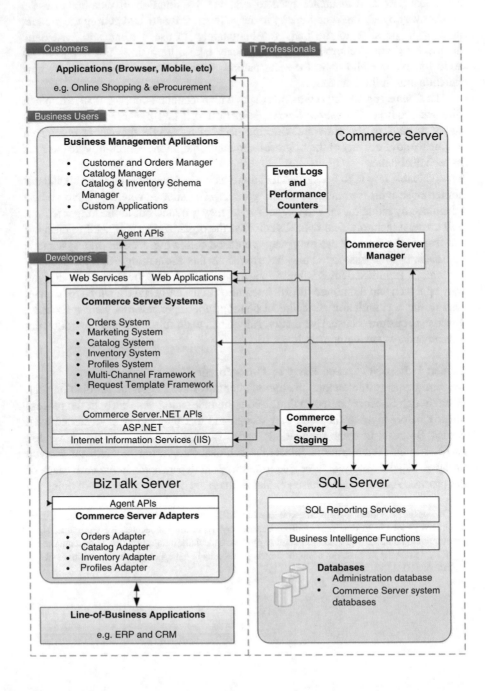

References

Ahuja G, Katila R (2001) Technological acquisitions and the innovation performance of acquiring firms: a longitudinal study. Strateg Manage J 22(3):197–220

Borck J (2000) Commerce server delivers ammo for business-level decision making. InfoWorld 22(36):49

Guarnaccia D (2009) The thinking behind Sitecore's Online Marketing Suite (OMS). Sitecore blog, Copenhagen

Lee J, Kim M (2016) Market-driven technological innovation through acquisitions: the moderating effect of firm size. J Manage 42(7):1934–1963

Li S, Shang J, Slaughter S (2010) Why do software firms fail? Capabilities, competitive actions, and firm survival in the software industry from 1995 to 2007. Inf Syst Res 21(3):631–654

MacComascaigh M, Bell T, Murphy J (2010) Magic quadrant for web content management. ID: G00201300

MacComscaigh M, Gilbert M, Tay G, Murphy J (2011) Magic quadrant for web content management. ID: G00233574

MacComscaigh M, Gilbert M, Tay G, Murphy J (2012) Magic quadrant for web content management. ID: G00233574

MacComscaigh M, Gilbert M, Murphy J, Tay G (2013) Magic quadrant for web content management. ID: G00250615

Makri M, Hitt M (2010) Complementary technologies, knowledge relatedness, and invention outcomes in high technology mergers and acquisitions. Strateg Manage J 31(6):602–628

Microsoft news (1996) Microsoft acquires eShop Inc. Redmond, Washington

Taganas R, Kaul V (2006) Innovation systems in India's IT industry: an empirical investigation. Econ Pol Wkly 41(39):4178–4186

Tamturk V (2017) Sitecore connects content management with eCommerce. CMS-Connected

Walker B (2011) Microsoft folds its hand and abandons commerce server: what it means. Forrester blog 279

Zahra S, Nash S, Bickford D (1995) Transforming technological pioneering into competitive advantage. Acad Manage Exec 9(1):17–31

Stefan Henningsson is an Associate Professor at Copenhagen Business School, Department of IT Management. His current research addresses managerial aspects of IT in contexts that include corporate mergers and acquisitions, digital payments and international trade processes. Previous publications include peer-refereed papers published in journals such as Journal of Management Information Systems, Information Systems Journal, Journal of Strategic Information Systems, European Journal of Information Systems and Management Information Systems Quarterly Executive.

Nishu Nishu is an M.Sc. student at Copenhagen Business School, currently pursuing his master's degree in Business Administration and Information Technology. He works as a research assistant under Associate Professor Stefan Henningsson at Department of Digitalization, Copenhagen Business School. His core area of research is Information Infrastructures.

Development of Strategies and Transformation Paths for Structured and Targeted Digital Change: The Case of the Presbyterian Church of Ghana Trinity Congregation

Sylvester Tetey Asiedu and Richard Boateng

Abstract

(a) **Situation faced**: The Church, irrespective of its steady growth from 4 members in 1965 to 2910 members in 2015, struggles to reach out to larger (newer) communities and improve money collection. It struggles as well in reaching its local community especially its members at the right time with the right message. In brief, for the Church to engage its members and the public with respect to worship service, publicizing its social activities (evangelism, donations to the needy, visits to prisons, etc.) and payment of voluntary contributions, it had to count on their physical presence on its premises.

(b) **Action taken**: The Church developed an interactive online presence (website) with payment integration for payment of tithe, offertory, voluntary thanksgiving, etc. Social media accounts were established to help create an online community with the secondary objective of driving traffic to the website and engaging the congregation remotely outside church service hours. Mobile money and a point of sale (POS) device were used to facilitate cashless transactions. Supportive committees were set up while interconnecting existing ones. Some of the pastors upload videos to social media as supplement to morning devotions. Events were promoted on the website and social media.

(c) **Results achieved**: Amongst the lot, there is currently an increase in social media engagements through event posts, live streaming, image and other post formats and also an increase in participation of church events by almost 50% on average as well as an increase in the number of website visitors from 2558 (901 unique visitors) in the first year after deployment to 11,612

S. T. Asiedu (✉) · R. Boateng
University of Ghana Business School, Accra, Ghana
e-mail: stetey@st.ug.edu.gh; richboateng@ug.edu.gh

© Springer International Publishing AG, part of Springer Nature 2019
N. Urbach, M. Röglinger (eds.), *Digitalization Cases*, Management for Professionals, https://doi.org/10.1007/978-3-319-95273-4_11

visitors (5841 unique visitors) in the third year as at September 2017. Even though membership statistics surprisingly indicated a 638 decline in 2017, which is worth investigating.

(d) **Lessons learned**: Although deploying the online system was successful, it came with its lessons drawn from challenges which cannot be ignored. These include trust in electronic payments, the need for strategic framework in the adoption of technology, the need to educate users. Other lessons include the need for management support and readiness of employees/volunteers and resource availability as a precursor to achieving strategic IS innovation objectives.

1   Introduction

Information technology (IT) entails significant investments. Such investments are complex and difficult decisions must be made within a strategic context such as IT governance. This case discusses the strategic digital transformation efforts made by the Trinity Congregation of the Presbyterian Church of Ghana located in Community 4, Tema—Ghana (PCGC4), to ensure that scarce resources are optimized, the full benefit of initiative and other projects are realized, the risks are mitigated and the business functions of the Church are supported. The investment made is the development of an online presence via an interactive website with the objective of streamlining the interaction between its respective stakeholders with regards to communication alternatives and payment transactions via electronic means using the Internet as the main underlying technology.

PCGC4 is an interdenominational Church that welcomes people from all other denominations and all walks of life with a mission to uphold the centrality of the Word of God, and through the enablement of the Holy Spirit, adopt a holistic development of her human and material resources to:

* Improve church growth through evangelism and nurture
* Attain self-sufficiency through effective resource mobilization
* Address all factors that inhibit development through advocacy and effective delivery of social services, and uphold the reformed tradition and cherish partnership with the worldwide body of Christ.

Its vision is to be a Christ-centered, evangelistic, disciplined, democratic, united, self-sustaining, and growing Church.

This case explores how the Ghanaian religious institution sustained and increased its congregational market share through digitalization of its social services via the internet by deploying an interactive website integrated with digital payment. It highlights the significance of electronic payments and interactive websites as strategic tools in the delivery of improved corporate service management provided at the convenience of respective stakeholders; the challenges that are likely to affect such strategic advancements and the efforts at addressing them. Lessons could help organizations interested in harnessing the power of the internet to extend their services and responsibilities dialogically.

The case also highlights ongoing discussions on how online digital technologies facilitate opportunities for organizations in such a way that interaction between stakeholders and business processes are greatly improved.

2   Situation Faced

The Church had previously been using manual means of processing, storing and retrieving information till it acquired database software to handle these tasks while still using hard files for most of its information requirements largely due to backup reasons. With the influence of technology on service delivery coupled with the ever rapid changing trends in consumer behavior, management of the Church sort to develop and deploy a website to fill the information dissemination gap that exists in reaching out to members at their convenience in a form that best suits them. A seven member committee was set up to materialize this project out of which the Interactive Church Management System (ICMS) was born. The system was sourced from a local vendor who was an email and phone call away and happens to be a member of the Church. The following highlights briefly the history of the Church in reflection of the basis of the ongoing digital transformation efforts.

During the first half of the 1960s, the establishment of many industries in Tema (a city located in the Greater Accra region of Ghana), led to an influx of people from all parts of the country into the city for various reasons. These included Presbyterians who felt the need to worship in accordance with their doctrine and as close as possible to their place of abode. There was however, only one Presbyterian Church then, at Community 1 (one of the communities of the city).

On 30th July, 1965, an itinerant small group (Presbyterian neighbors) staying in and around "C" and "D" Roads at Community 4, led by Mr. G. Owusu Dokyi (deceased) decided to team up with Mr. Emmanuel Armah Tagoe (deceased) and his family who were on transfer to Tema from Kumasi (one of the ten regions in Ghana) and had by then taken up residency in the neighborhood and had started regular morning and evening prayer sessions in his house at House number C41, Community 4 in Tema.

Mr. Tagoe was an organist whose accomplishments on the organ coupled with the melodious Presbyterian Hymns attracted more people to worship with the small group. The Hymn singing—and now the amalgamated group—which culminated in morning and evening devotions and prayers, drew others to increase their number from four (4) in July 1965 to thirteen (13) in August 1966.

This continued till 30th July, 1967 when permission was sought from the then District Minister, Rev. E. A. Adjei (deceased) for the first formal Presbyterian Sunday forenoon service which was held in the house of Mr. E. A. Tagoe. Mr. - Owusu-Dokyi (deceased) was the preacher and Mr. E. A. Tagoe (deceased) was the

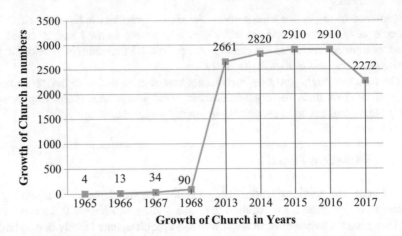

Fig. 1 Growth of church from its inception in 1965 to 2017

organist. After this service, an interim 7 member committee was set up to manage the affairs of the Church. Offertory at this service amounted to 29 Ghana pesewas (0.02 USD).

By December of 1967 when the first Christmas Forenoon Service was held, the membership had grown to 34. Thirty members further joined the group by the beginning of April 1968, making it desirable to look for a more spacious place of worship. Amongst other events that unfolded, the first Baptismal Service was conducted on 25th December 1968 at which time seven infants made up of two females and five males were baptized into the Church by Rev. E. A. Adjei. After the Baptismal Service, members of the Congregation christened the new Church "Tema North Presbyterian Church" to reflect its geographical location in relation to the other two Presbyterian Churches in Tema then i.e. Communities One and Two/Five Presbyterian Churches. It was also to encourage other Presbyterians then residing in other nearby Communities—7, 8, 9 etc., to join the Church to save them the trouble of travelling the comparatively longer distances to either Community One or Community Two/Five for the same purpose. As presented in Fig. 1, the membership has grown steadily over the period and currently stands at 2272 as at the end of 2017.

The Church, irrespective of its steady growth from 4 members in 1965 to 2910 members in 2015, struggles to reach out to larger (newer) community and improve money collection. It struggles as well in reaching its local community especially its members at the right time with the right message mostly because almost everyone is busy with a lot to do each day. Some of the members especially the youth relocate to other places for academic reasons and related. Others relocate permanently because of work and family. These members of the Church are unable to physically worship with the Church and are often left out only to be told how the Church is faring when they return or have conversations with other members on phone and through social media. Payment of contributions becomes a problem as those geographically located far away from the Church most often rely on others who are physically located close enough to the Church to fulfill these voluntary obligations for them. This puts many of these loyal members in the position of not being able to pay such contributions. Besides contributions, staying connected and keeping in touch with members had been a challenge. Some of the members in the diaspora have had issues with staying updated regularly and committed to the Church. The Senior Presbyter prior to deploying the online information system (IS) commented:

> We understand the communication challenges associated with ministering the word of God and reaching out far beyond our physically located presence, service excellence expectation and its associated cost implications on productivity of staff and volunteers and reputation that PCGC4 is faced with and recognize the unique opportunity to develop a web application which will serve the information needs of the church and general public in reaching out especially to members in the diaspora who per their circumstances, cannot be physically present at the church premises to worship with us as well as fulfill other obligations as includes tithes and other financial contributions.

Service excellence and the word of God at the fingertips of the church members and the public is the objective of this project. With technology at the center of all forms of social and business activities, innovation has come to be the order of the day. Targeted customers and existing ones are online, on their computers at work with audio and video playing at the background, on their phones browsing for information on the internet or on social media getting connected to friends and family, and always going somewhere, accessing data here and there. With all the social communication channels available to keep people more "connected," meaningful messages most often gets lost and are reduced to white noise. The thought of how many church members have travelled yet have the desire to interact with the church, how much funds are lost because of the absence of a convenient and secured remote means of payment contributions done without the inconvenience of going to the bank, how many church members are lost through relocations due to school, job and related reasons has been the basis for the deploy of the ICMS. Through its website committee, the Church opted for a bespoke online system intended to keep members from far and near connected with a web interactive software/application that has social media and digital payment features that is efficient, easy to use, and mobile friendly. Silva Soft Solutions (www.silvasoftsolutions.com) was contracted to build the ICMS.

3   Action Taken

The Church having assessed the challenges limiting the realization of its full potential put measures in place to address these challenges with the development of the website service as one of core measures. Others include setting up of respective supportive committees while interconnecting existing ones to help the website committee which was not dissolved after the launch of the website, but mandated instead to train members of the editorial committee on data entry and report generation techniques amongst other measures taken.

Initially, the focus was to develop an informative website to make available to the public and congregation, information about the Church as includes its history, management, projects (past, ongoing and scheduled), events and other announcements but through recommendations that drew insights from the Times Square Church website (http://tsc.nyc) given by the developers of the website on other possibilities that could be harnessed from the website in addition to its informative purpose, the website committee with the approval from supervising authorities agreed to incorporate other interactive features to the informative website, which in this case are the payment options that allows users to voluntarily fulfill financial obligations to the Church online and recently a scheduled integration of vehicle tracking system.

Management of the Church recognized the need to prioritize coming up with a strategic information technology and systems (IT/IS) plan that recognizes the online IS as a key strategic tool for corporate communication that adds extra value through engagements and its digital transactions portal and have since incorporated it into its strategic plans with ongoing efforts to fully realize its potential. Some of such efforts include the provisioning of a digital video equipment to aid the live streaming agenda, setting up an editorial committee and changing the status of the website committee from ad hoc to permanent, creating social media accounts and synchronizing data and information flow amongst the respective committees and departments.

The Church commissioned new committees which included an editorial board mandated to manage the information going in and out of the website as well as branding of the church online. The temporal website committee assigned to oversee to the development and deploy of the information system was not dissolved but mandated to be the main body responsible for the website with specific role emphasis on its technical functionalities. To educate the congregation on the alternative digital options of fulfilling their obligations to the church, a member of the website committee is periodically invited to give an overview of how the system works to the church midway through Sunday services where majority are gathered for worship.

> During such training sessions, the general feedback is that one can easily tell that the elderly who form the majority are mostly interested in the live video coverage of the active church service projected on the flat LED screens during ongoing service. Most of the other congregational members who fall within this category are quite interested as well in the live streaming so their relatives, colleagues, friends, other members and the general public both far and near can join the church service remotely.

The respective committees have been assigned user accounts to help offer better relationships with the public and congregation members. This feature reflects positively on Kent and Taylor's dialogic loop element proposed as a strategic website feature for corporate online communication and branding.

Also, social media accounts have been created for the church with selected social network platforms namely YouTube, Facebook, LinkedIn and Twitter with efforts made to synchronize these platforms to help grow them into online communities. A strategic approach that is aimed at generating traffic for the church's website and possibly converting unique and other visitors to church members who would turn out to be virtually or physically present at respective worship services and other activities of the church.

Discussions have been done with plans made to link the online system with the local standalone database system to reduce data redundancy challenges and to offer the accounts and finance departments more opportunities to manage members in the diaspora along with those who prefer digital transactions and communications to the manual means of interactions and payments and new members who sign up online.

To help boost confidence in the safety and security of the online payment system, a request to purchase a Secure Sockets Layer (SSL) certificate for the website had been submitted to the authorities for consideration. This is to add extra layers of encryption in a bid to prevent unauthorized access and/or hackers from denying service to any of the system's features. Although the system redirects to a secured trusted third-party payment gateway (e.g., Hubtel Ghana) using an Application Program Interface (API) to handle digital transactions, this is to help assure users of the safety of their information provided.

One more initiative to help encourage inclusiveness within the entire congregation is the introduction of the Unstructured Supplementary Service Data (USSD) which is a protocol most often referred to as short codes, quick codes, feature codes, etc. used by Global System for Mobile communication (GSM) cellular telephones to communicate with the service provider's computers and can be used for callback prepaid services, menu-based information services, WAP browsing, mobile-money services, location-based content services, and as part of configuration services for mobile handsets provided by their respective networks (Victor 2014). The USSD (*713*3840#) is in response to providing alternate means for members of the church, other stakeholders and the society with limited knowledge in internet and the use of internet enabled smart communication devices like mobile phones, tablets, etc. to have a means of making digital payments through mobile money and likewise for those without smart phones or internet enabled phones and tablets but have active mobile wallet subscriptions. Another basis for this initiative is the fact that it was realized that most of the Church members do not have credit and debit cards especially members based in Ghana with almost every member within this category using a mobile phone. Also at least half of this group has an active mobile money account even though they do not necessarily have smart phones.

As at the time of this write up, the website committee had noted that a mobile application with an easy to use interface running on software as a service (SaaS) cloud computing model had been scheduled to be configured with credit and debit card processing features along with the mobile money integration to provide the mobile experience where members in the country and abroad can install as apps on their smart phones and tablets to aid in the transactional relationships with the church without having to log on to the website each time as is the case now.

In consideration of those who prefer to engage physically with the church with regards to fulfilling their financial obligations, the accounts department has secured a point of sale (POS) device acquired through Ecobank, one of the church's banks, to offer digital payment transaction service. Another reason given by the finance committee for this payment medium is the need to reduce the amount of physical cash handled at the church.

4   Results Achieved

The deployed online ICMS has placed the church on the digital global map and is drawing traffic to its content, giving it the recognition as one of the first to deploy an online presence where one can have a similar experience as that in the church premise and be able to offer contributions in real-time online as well. Although conversion of visits is quite slow at the moment, the deployed system is continually encouraging and influencing the public positively which is a reflection of the extension of the church's social responsibility beyond its limited physical environment.

The senior Presbyter comments:

> We have some of our members who travelled to the UK and other parts of the world checking out the website and giving us positive feedback. As happy as we are to come this far, they are happier to see such developments in the church commending on the technology integration into the church's strategic vision especially being able to follow the activities of the church and the knowledge of being able to contribute to the church easily on the internet.

The system provides a one stop archive through an easy to use front and backend interface for both management of the church specifically the finance and accounts departments, and congregational members. This offers the opportunity to access history of transactions made to the respective committees and groups that one belongs to (see Fig. 2). This system makes it easy for members to easily print out their payments and contributions as proof of membership and dedication to the church when the time is due to prove to the church authorities, one's dedication and commitments to the church during specific periods such as weddings, naming ceremonies, funerals amongst others where members of the community depend on the church's role in fulfilling their social responsibilities.

> Both members and management can now keep track of tithes, contributions, offerings and pledges, print contribution statements, accept online donations, scholarship and contributions as well as other development funds.—Senior Presbyter

To allow for easy access, both backend and frontend are responsive thus the interface changes in response to which device is being used to access the system. An important feature included because of the recent increase in portable means of accessing the internet. The online portal offers the opportunity to upload respective church service sessions through video and audio as well as text and images via its blog component. Plans have been made to include live streaming soon as the system supports this service. These features comply with Kent and Taylor's dialogic

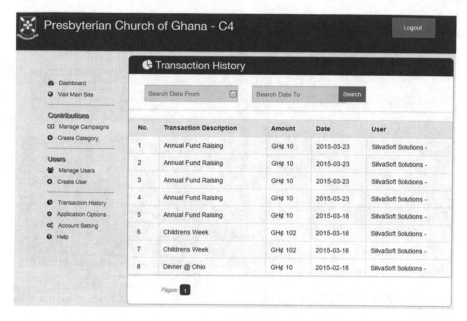

Fig. 2 Authorized moderator/administrator interface with sample (dummy) data indicating history of payments and what category payments belong to

communication framework for online corporate representation that posits that for organizations to improve organizational public and community relationships and subsequently realize their full social responsibilities, communication as an ethical practice has to be dialogic (Kent and Taylor 1998; Madichie and Hinson 2014).

Prior to deploying the online system, there was less of digital communication. Information reached the congregation through announcements made during church services with selected notifications placed on notice boards. But using the website and social media as communication tools has helped in improving dissemination of information to the general public as well as church members. The level of interactions as at now has increased which is evident for instance in the turnout of participants of church events and feedbacks from online social subscribers most of who follow published updates remotely. Out of the lot, an instance of a weekly event that had a high turnout compared to the usual turnout is presented in Fig. 3. From this event overview, even though only 14 out of the people reached indicated interest in attending the event, at least close to 150 more participants turned up, an indication that most of who attended did not necessarily indicate their decision online as attending the event but showed up at the event. Bulk SMS is used to communicate information to church members but only at the general group levels. Personalized SMS are sent out based on matters that pertain to the respective groups and once in a while information which concerns the entire church body based on its priority rating.

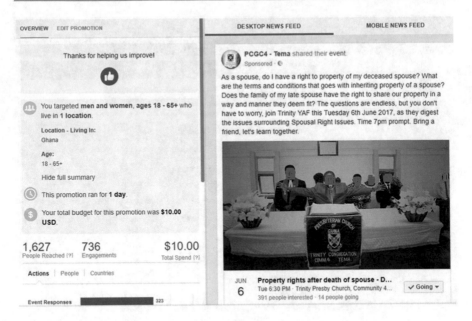

Fig. 3 Snapshot of a sampled Facebook event overview

> It is now easier to communicate our event schedules and other information to everyone and invite them to attend and participate which is encouraging active membership and socialization. —Senior Presbyter

The website complements the above communication mediums by connecting and registering people to events via online announcements and other notifications, social media integration, newsletter signups, and Google map integration that offers direction guidance to the church and church event venues as well.

On the next steps, the management of the church has plans of transforming the control room, which is currently responsible for audiovisual projection and care of media gadgets, into an ultra-modern production studio responsible for all prerecorded and live streaming content through the online system and social media although in the meantime live streaming is done via Facebook's live streaming feature using internet enabled mobile phones during church services and other events of the church. Efforts have been made to purchase a high definition HD camera with streaming features to aid in the streaming and recording of high quality media.

From the website statistic in Table 1, it can be deduced from the viewed traffic of unique visitors that there is a steady growth of unique online visitors over the period from the year 2015 through 2016 to 2017 with this increasing from 901 through 3513 to 9256 unique visitors respectively. However, as presented in the table, the number of pages accessed per visit indicates a reduction over the period from 29.02 pages per visit for 2015 through 12.8 pages per visit in 2016 to as low as 9.84 pages per visit for 2017. A follow up on this via random interactions with the congregation indicates the demand for content in their variations over the period that reflects more

Table 1 Website statistics reflecting total visits from Jan. 2015 to Dec. 2017

Reported period	Unique visitors	Number of visits	Pages	Hits	Bandwidth
2015	901	2558	74,256	134,399	2.69 GB
		2.83 per visit/ visitor	29.02 Pages/ visit	52.54 hits/ visit	1103.98 kb/visit
2016	3513	9123	116,818	174,600	4.91 GB
		2.59 per visit/ visitor	12.8 Pages/ visit	19.3 hits/ visit	564.65 kb/visit
2017	9356	22,916	225,851	418,625	6.44 GB
		2.47 per visit/ visitor	9.84 Pages/ visit	18.26 hits/ visit	294.86 kb/visit

Table 2 A breakdown of the number of visits for the year 2017

Visits duration		
Number of visits: 22,916—Average: 566 s	Number of visits	Percent
0 s–30 s	16,825	73.4
30 s–2 mn	806	3.5
2 mn–5 mn	339	1.4
5 mn–15 mn	701	3
15 mn–30 mn	756	3.2
30 mn–1 h	1574	6.8
1 h+	1918	8.3

of recent activities in the form of images from events and video (where available) with social sharing options to allow posting of content through visitor's social network accounts such as Facebook, WhatsApp, Twitter, amongst others. This feedback reflects in the website report on time spent on the site as presented in Table 2 for the year 2017. It can be noticed that the majority of visitors (73.4%) spend at most 30 s on the site. In other words, the short stay of visitors on the website can be related to frequency of updates where there isn't much to read upon each subsequent visit. Thus, as seen from the report, there is an inverse representation where the site is getting more traffic but losing out on engagement due to lack of variety resulting in shorter times spent on the site. The decline in bandwidth (amount of data downloaded per visit) over the period further explains this with less content (pages) viewed per subsequent visit. This reflects the need for regular updates and an indication as well on the likelihood of further increase in the number of visits and time spent on the site.

On the other hand, as reflected in Fig. 1 and presented in detail in Table 3, an observation made is that, comparing the total number of active members of the church for the periods 2015/2016 and that of 2017, there seem to be a considerable reduction in membership from 2910 to 2272 reflecting a 638 reduction in number of active congregational members implying that less people are going to the church to be together as a community in a physical way. As to whether this reduction in main

Table 3 Congregational
statistics

Generational groups	2015/2016	2017	Gain/loss
Children service	288	284	−4
Junior youth	140	172	+32
Young people's guild	623	362	−261
Young adult's fellowship	687	449	−238
Adults	1172	1005	−167
Total	2910	2272	−638

church service attendance is linked to the increasing engagements online is worth another investigation. This decrease in church visits as discussed in literature can be recognized as a potential downside of new technological developments (Reimann 2017; Wielstra 2012). An issue which needs to be investigated as this loss of membership cannot be assumed to be directly related to a shift from physical engagements to the digital communication channels most specifically social media (with emphasis on Facebook).

5 Lessons Learned

Investments in IT can be complicated and strategic decisions are required to mitigate the associated risks. Out of the steps taken by PCGC4 to digitally transform are some challenges and lessons that cannot be ignored in this discussion. These include absence of a strategic framework that stipulates the roadmap for integrating the online system deployed into the strategic vision of the church and the recommended need for one in technology adoption; digital divide within the congregation concerning knowledge and use of internet; trust and security of online system to protect user information and implications of change of administration from one tenure of office to the other.

5.1 Challenges in the Transformation Process

Digital Divide
A greater number of the congregation are not accustomed to the world of digital transactions that involves debit and credit cards, digital currency, internet banking and related although mobile money is widely accepted. This to some extent can be attributed to the levels of education and age where the youth are more familiar with social media and digital transactions than the old. This cultural limitation can be seen from research findings (Junadi and Sfenrianto 2015; Ruiz-Martínez et al. 2012) where there is likely to be a difference in culture between one region and the other with regards to factors that limit the adoption of IT/IS as includes availability of internet connectivity infrastructure and access, computer knowledge and usage, traveling habits, region (where one resides), mobile phone, amongst others (Dahlberg and Öörni 2007). Hiram Ting et al. (2016) reports in their research that age, gender,

computer experience, and level of education have significant effect on the desire to use online payment systems and that the adoption of electronic payments is thus affected by knowledge and use of internet (Ting Yacob et al. 2016). A member of the technical subcommittee to the website committee comments that:

> Only a fraction of the congregation—40 percent perhaps—are knowledgeable in the use of internet and digital transactions with about 30 percent of this group willing to actually use the online payment system. The lots amongst the latter are those in the diaspora.

As a result of the above, some of the members do not have access to digital tools as such are yet to sign up for online banking solutions from their respective banks or third party payment gateways.

Trust as a Challenge

> Who built the payment aspect of the website? Are you sure our hard earned cash is safe? By using the system am I not exposing my credit card details to the developers? Will the system keep my credit card and bank information?

The above questions came as feedbacks from some members of the congregation who happen to have active credit card issued by both local and international banks when the system was deployed. These reflect a problem of trust as a limiting factor to the successful adoption of electronic payments in literature where one is less likely to adopt the system because one does not trust the system or have reservations with the security of the proposed system and one's safety as end user(s) (Ha 2004; Kim et al. 2008, 2009; Tsiakis and Sthephanides 2005). Concerning online payment, there was the initial issue of who should absorb the cost of transactional charges that are deducted when digitally transferring funds from one account to the other till the church accepted to be at the losing end.

Data Sharing/Communication Between Online System and Standalone Church Database

Another challenge with the deployment of the ICMS had to do with data communication between the already sourced desktop based church management database system, the accounts management system used by the finance and accounts department and the online deployed system under the auspices of the website committee. This problem became evident after the website was successfully deployed and some of the congregation members indicated their preference for the manual way of submitting payments to the church because they felt the newly introduced system does not reflect their previous transactions with the church. This challenge translates into the issue of mental resistance as discussed further below.

Ama, a member of the church currently residing in the USA, upon an enquiry to know the process of becoming a "distant" member of the church through the church's website (via the corporate email), had to resort to sending her mom to physically deliver her request. In a reply mail to a conversation with her, she stated:

Thank you so much for the information but I was able to get a letter to my mum to give to the church.

This reflects the problem of having to physically handle data processing which is mostly compounded by different schedules of service representatives involved and the response rate to online conversations. Response to Ama's request required the physical services as offered by her mom—to go to the church office in order to acquire a new membership ID. This compounds the challenge because in the end, the final consumer (church member) is not able to access his/her full profile along with other transactions that reflect complete history of membership and payment contributions online.

Resistance to the Use of the Online System

Currently evident as well on the issue as stated above is the interest in using the online payment system by majority of the congregation (mostly the youth) who find themselves in the position of being able to do so but the actual behavior not reflecting such because it conflicts with long standing policies of the church as perceived by the congregation and trust as discussed above.

This is in the sense that whereas the church leadership seeks to be ethically responsible and accountable in their dealings with the congregation and the public by placing participation and documentation at the core of affairs, and in a bid as well to promote cashless transactions, some of the church members have the perception that their tithe and other books for recording their contributions has to be manually signed by a representative of the church leadership each time a contribution is made, a tradition done over the years. This perception shifts their preference from the digital platform to the traditional means.

This implementation challenge reflects the discussion on resistance to information systems implementation and use where some of the reasons behind information systems adoption failures or success to a greater extent can be related to the tendency of a user to either postpone the use of a system to a later date, decide not to use the information system (reject), or initially protest or mildly reject such system till more information is gained on the value to be attained from the use of such system (Chang and Greenleaf 2017; Klöcker 2015; Salih et al. 2012).

5.2   Discussion of Lessons

Lesson 1: The Need for a Strategic IT/IS Framework

With the constantly evolving advancements in innovations, organizations are compelled to respond by adapting to the changing trends as a result of the dynamics of market with respect to high levels of uncertainty and economic conditions. This makes the role of IT/IS crucial in the proposition of adding value to business and the means through which such value is harnessed (Cuenca et al. 2010). This places a strategic IT/IS framework as a tool for managing changes in a critical position that bridges business strategy with innovation such that issues involved go beyond that of an IT one to that of organizational strategic one (Chen et al. 2008). Aligning strategic business and IT/IS becomes critical in maintaining business value as such alignments are mostly not easily executable with respect to conceptualization and subsequent accomplishment. As evident in this case, the absence of such strategic alignments accounts mostly for unachieved expectations of IT/IS investments (Chen et al. 2008; Henderson and Venkatraman 1993). This case highlights the need for a consistent and integrated strategic framework which incorporates the information, resources, data, and technological views to facilitate strategic planning of IT/IS and its alignment with business strategy. This research presents a significant contribution to enterprise architecture field. As a guide for other organizations interested in following this roadmap, starting with a strategic IT/IS framework that aligns with the business strategy is recommended.

Lesson 2: The Need for Management Support (Leadership)

Well-established within change management literature are the relevance and benefits of support from top management and strong leadership. Evident in literature is the discussion that organizations that tend to positively influence the likelihood of IT/IS implementation success are those that are able to articulate their strategic vision and communicate as well the value of IS to respective stakeholders of the organization representing the most important IS users. The readiness of top management can be explained to reflect the ability to anticipate, manage, and execute the adoption and implementation of information systems solutions (Basole and Rouse 2009). Top management support also reflects the level of support, encouragement, commitment and strategic vision that is offered by management with regards to implementation and use of IS. As evident in this case, the risk orientation, knowledge, innovativeness and level of skill of an organization's leadership is critically relevant to the success of IS adoption.

Lesson 3: The Need to Create Awareness When Introducing a New System

As some of the perceptions of the congregation to a larger extent has led them to resist the use of the online payment system, lessons here reflect the need to educate the congregation on the significance of processes as carried out within the church through periodic awareness campaigns with respect to administrative policies and their implications and benefits to the church as suggested in literature on the need for awareness in systems implementation as a measure of mitigating resistance and other limiting factors to adoption of technology (Ahmadi et al. 2017; Bhattacherjee and Hikmet 2007; Liu 2015). As pointed out by Liu (2015), there is the need to provide awareness not just on the introduction and existence of a new technology but also awareness on the changes and implications it has on the existing processes and outcomes (Liu 2015).

Lesson 4: Resource Availability

Prior research indicates that organizations with social, financial, and human resources are better positioned for the adoption and implementation of an information system

(Wielstra 2012). To this, appropriate resource availability and allocation of IS is often carefully weighed an absolute necessity to enterprise readiness where resource readiness can be explained to refer to an organization's ability to allocate necessary resources as includes social (e.g. partnerships, alliances, vendor support, training), human (e.g. consultants, expertise, innovation influencers, support staff), and financial assets (e.g. funds for training, budget), to support the adoption, implementation, continued use, and maintenance of IS solution/innovation. From this case, it can be deduced that the church was not well resourced as a pre-cursor in their quest to achieve strategic growth. This is evident in the use of mobile phones to stream church sessions for one and the church after 3 years of going online, now making arrangements after recently sourcing/allocating funds (under a new leadership for the period 2018 onwards till another change is due) to purchase advanced streaming camera's to provide quality images and live audiovisuals for streaming both online and in the church while service is going on.

Lesson 5: Employees/Volunteers Readiness

The extent to which an IS is used and the extent to which it has infused into the processes of an organisation determines the rate of success of technology adoption and implementation of—as is the case of this study—online interactive websites and use of social media as strategic communication tools. Employee readiness which determines the extent of IT/IS usage can be explained to refer to the respective characteristics of individuals as includes learning capabilities, previous experience, level of computer skill, risk orientation, motivation and attitude towards change and innovation which are relevant for the successful adoption of IS. From this case, it can be deduced as discussed in literature, that it is essential to establish the readiness of employees (paid staff by church) and volunteers and their levels of commitment towards the bigger picture of aligning strategic IT/IS framework with the strategic vision of the church (Ahmadi et al. 2017; Cresswell and Sheikh 2012; Mwafise and Stapleton 2012; Sena et al. 2016).

As discussed above, it can be realized that the evolution and future of the digital transformation efforts by the church was influenced by a number of factors. The lessons from the church's experience highlight the choices of delivery channels and levels of sophistication that organizations in developing countries are faced with in making strategic technology adoption decisions. Amongst the varied options of engaging stakeholders, the delivery channel decision depends on the level of sophistication of the service an organization intends to deliver. The final decision is subject to the strategic choice of which service can be effectively deployed and managed over which services to provide by assessing the constraints of their context of business and capabilities.

In summary as illustrated in Table 3, this study represents a typical reflection of the introduction of a digital technology (website) that was initially introduced to provide common information about the Church, but went further to provide interactive community collaboration and engagement, a disruption to traditional ways that people are used to communicating and paying their contributions (Digital Disruption) which was followed by the development and initial increase in their congregational market share (Digital Business), and has led to the digital transformation of the church. The study highlights the inhibiting factors to corporate online success and how such challenges were managed. Lessons from the challenges and results achieved through the technologically informed organizational change can serve as benchmark of lessons for practice and pointers as well for future research.

With all economic and societal sectors being challenged by disruptive digital technologies, the essence of this case most importantly illustrates how organizations leverage their capabilities to create disruptive innovation, develop digital business models, and digitally transform themselves. It contributes to discussions on best practices and lessons learned from organizations that succeeded in tackling the challenges and seizing the opportunities of the digital world by providing insightful discussions for practitioners and interesting case and discussion themes for researchers, teachers, and students alike. This case is further summarized in Table 4 below.

Table 4 Summary of strategic decisions and lessons

Strategic decisions	Influencing factors/ challenges	Actions/efforts at addressing challenges	Lessons
Strategic communication channel	• Operational constraints • Diffusion of ICT in Ghana • Capabilities of organizational online presence	Decision to develop an online system and use of social media as strategic communication tools	Organizational capabilities, external constraints, customer needs and channel operation costs are critical in digital transformation
Website development approach	• Human resource • Organizational learning • Vendor support and relation • Lack of internal IT/IS structure • Electronic transactions development in Ghana	• In-house development leveraging on internal skill sets • Assigning responsibilities to respective set up committees	• Starting small with available resources is critical to developing adequate organizational learning before running full scale • Investment in the right technology and in the right human resource is critical to a successful technology adoption
Engaging the congregation/ public	• Resource availability • Sophistication of digital communication • Objective of the digital payment implementation • The problem of trust	• Periodic mention of the availability of the website and its other features during church gatherings along with its secured nature • Use of POS device at the premises to facilitate cashless transactions • Providing mobile	E-payment success also depends on efforts aimed at educating congregation on ease of use and assured safety of online transactions with the church

(continued)

Table 4 (continued)

Strategic decisions	Influencing factors/ challenges	Actions/efforts at addressing challenges	Lessons
	• Digital Divide • Resistance to online payment	money as alternative digital payment	
Managing resources and channel conflict	• Management goal for digital transformation • Limited investments to harness full potential of digital transformation agenda. • Data silos and integration within respective systems	Potential plans to integrate online and local information systems	Aligning strategic business and IS/IT is critical in maintaining business value

References

Ahmadi H, Nilashi M, Shahmoradi L, Ibrahim O (2017) Hospital information system adoption: expert perspectives on an adoption framework for Malaysian public hospitals. Comput Hum Behav 67:161–189. https://doi.org/10.1016/j.chb.2016.10.023

Basole RC, Rouse WB (2009) Enterprise readiness for IT innovation: a study of mobile computing in healthcare. Icis-Rp. Retrieved from http://aisel.aisnet.org/icis2009/104/

Bhattacherjee A, Hikmet N (2007) Physicians' resistance toward healthcare information technologies: a dual-factor model. In: Proceedings of the annual Hawaii international conference on system sciences, pp 1–10. https://doi.org/10.1109/HICSS.2007.437

Chang HY, Greenleaf WJ (2017) Determinant of resistance for ERP system in private companies in Yemen. J Sci Tochnol 21(2):14–36 https://doi.org/10.16288/j.yczz.17-199

Chen D, Doumeingts G, Vernadat F (2008) Architectures for enterprise integration and interoperability: past, present and future. Comput Ind 59(7):647–659. https://doi.org/10.1016/j.compind.2007.12.016

Cresswell K, Sheikh A (2012) Organizational issues in the implementation and adoption of health information technology innovations: an interpretative review. Int J Med Inform 82(5):e73–e86. https://doi.org/10.1016/j.ijmedinf.2012.10.007

Cuenca L, Ortiz A, Boza A (2010) Business and IS/IT strategic alignment framework. In: Camarinha-Matos LM, Pereira P, Ribeiro L (eds) Emerging trends in technological innovation: IFIP advances in information and communication technology, vol 314, pp 24–31. https://doi.org/10.1007/978-3-642-11628-5_3

Dahlberg T, Öörni A (2007) Understanding changes in consumer payment habits – do mobile payments and electronic invoices attract consumers? In: Proceedings of the annual Hawaii international conference on system sciences. https://doi.org/10.1109/HICSS.2007.580

De Sena R, Naomi S, Fernando D (2016) Intention of adoption of mobile payment: an analysis in the light of the unified theory of acceptance and use of technology (UTAUT). IMR Innov Manage Rev 13:221–230

Ha H-Y (2004) Factors influencing consumer perceptions of brand trust online. J Prod Brand Manage 13(5):329–342. https://doi.org/10.1108/10610420410554412

Henderson JC, Venkatraman H (1993) Strategic alignment: leveraging information technology for transforming organizations. IBM Syst J 32(1):472–484. https://doi.org/10.1147/sj.382.0472

Junadi, Sfenrianto (2015) A model of factors influencing consumer's intention to use E-payment system in Indonesia. Proc Comput Sci 59:214–220. https://doi.org/10.1016/j.procs.2015.07.557

Kent ML, Taylor M (1998) Building dialogic relationships through the world wide web. Public Relat Rev 24(3):321–334. https://doi.org/10.1016/S0363-8111(99)80143-X

Kim DJ, Ferrin DL, Rao HR (2008) A trust-based consumer decision-making model in electronic commerce: the role of trust, perceived risk, and their antecedents. Decis Support Syst 44 (2):544–564. https://doi.org/10.1016/j.dss.2007.07.001

Kim DJ, Ferrin DL, Rao HR (2009) Trust and satisfaction, two stepping stones for successful E-commerce relationships: a longitudinal exploration. Inf Syst Res 20(2):237–257. https://doi.org/10.1287/isre.1080.0188

Klöcker P (2015) Resistance behavior to national EHealth implementation programs. Springer, Cham. https://doi.org/10.1007/978-3-319-17828-8

Liu Y (2015) Consumer protection in mobile payments in China: a critical analysis of Alipay's service agreement. Comput Law Secur Rev 31(5):679–688. https://doi.org/10.1016/j.clsr.2015. 05.009

Madichie NO, Hinson R (2014) A critical analysis of the "dialogic communications" potential of sub-Saharan African Police Service websites. Public Relat Rev 40(2):338–350. https://doi.org/10.1016/j.pubrev.2013.10.009

Mwafise AM, Stapleton L (2012) Determinants of user adoption of mobile electronic payment systems for microfinance institutions in developing countries: case study cameroon. In: IFAC proceedings volumes (IFAC-PapersOnline) (vol 45). IFAC. https://doi.org/10.3182/20120611-3-IE-4029.00010

Reimann RP (2017) Uncharted territories: the challenges of digitalization and social media for church and society. Ecum Rev 69(1):67–79. https://doi.org/10.1111/erev.12267

Ruiz-Martínez A, Reverte ÓC, Gómez-Skarmeta AF (2012) Payment frameworks for the purchase of electronic products and services. Comput Stand Interfaces 34(1):80–92. https://doi.org/10.1016/j.csi.2011.05.007

Salih SH, Dahlan HM, Hussin ARC (2012) User resistance factors in post ERP implementation. J Res Innov Inf Syst 19–27. Retrieved from http://seminar.spaceutm.edu.my/jisri/download/F_FinalPublished/Pub19_UserResistance_PostERP.pdf

Ting H, Yacob Y, Liew L, Lau WM (2016) Intention to use mobile payment system: a case of developing market by ethnicity. Proc Soc Behav Sci 224:368–375. https://doi.org/10.1016/j.sbspro.2016.05.390

Tsiakis T, Sthephanides G (2005) The concept of security and trust in electronic payments. Comput Secur 24(1):10–15. https://doi.org/10.1016/j.cose.2004.11.001

Victor D (2014) On the user-centric evolution of mobile money technologies in developing nations: successes and lessons. In: AMCIS (Americas Conference on Information Systems), pp 1–11

Wielstra S (2012) Social media and the Church: a systematic literature review. Retrieved from http://referaat.cs.utwente.nl/conference/17/paper/7333/social-media-and-the-church-a-system atic-literature-review.pdf

Sylvester T. Asiedu is a Doctoral Researcher at the Operations and Management Information Systems Department of the University of Ghana Business School. From 2013 to present, he has been an Adjunct Lecturer at the School of Technology with the Ghana Institute of Management and Public Administration, GIMPA. During 2009 to 2015, he was a Tutor with the University of Ghana distant education program. He is the founder of Eudemonia International Foundation, an NGO focused on quality community healthcare advocacy through research, preventive, and educational initiatives and where possible, curative interventions. He is a dedicated, resourceful and goal-driven professional leader and educator interested in sustainable initiatives driven by business needs and social impact. Sylvester's research interest covers e-marketing, e-commerce, governance and management of IT, e-learning, social media, entrepreneurship, ICT for development, ICT and health care, electronic business, gender and ICT, and mobile commerce at global, national, industrial, organizational and community levels.

Richard Boateng is a technology researcher who focuses on developing, promoting and protecting ideas and concepts into sustainable projects of commercial value and development impact. Richard is an Associate Professor of Information Systems and the Head of the Department of Operations and Management Information systems at the University of Ghana Business School. He is the associate editor of the Information Technologies and International Development Journal and also serves on the editorial board of the Information Development Journal. Richard was a British Chevening scholar and a Dorothy Hodgkin's Doctoral Scholar during his postgraduate education at the University of Manchester, United Kingdom. Richard's research experience covers e-learning, ICT for development, electronic governance, social media, electronic business, gender and ICT, mobile commerce, and ICT and health care at the national, industrial, organizational and community levels. Since 2006, Richard has published more than 30 articles in international journals, refereed conferences and book chapters.

Creating a Digital Consulting Solution for Project Management Assessments at Dr. Kuhl Unternehmensberatung: Development and Initial Demonstration of a Fully Automated Asset-Based Consulting Approach

Volker Nissen, Jochen Kuhl, Hendrik Kräft, Henry Seifert, Jakob Reiter, and Jim Eidmann

Abstract

(a) **Situation faced**: Consulting provider DKUB GmbH & Co. KG was looking for options to achieve a positive marketing effect with only moderate effort, to raise the profile of the company through innovative consulting services, and to supplement the existing portfolio with digital services, which represent a "door opener" for the classical consulting business. Due to a personal contact between the first two authors of this contribution, the idea of a joint project emerged. It was decided to develop a digital assessment tool. The chosen pilot application area was project management assessment, as project management issues account for the core of DKUB business.

(b) **Action taken**: Since a software system should be created, a design-science (DS) approach was employed. Within design and development, a prototype-oriented process model was used. The project took place without a particular client. Instead, the basis was a jointly developed business concept. Furthermore, a study of Nissen et al. (2017) on quality requirements for virtual consulting services and general features of advisory consulting were considered. The process within the web-based system should reproduce an expert report by gathering data from the client company and linking these with

V. Nissen (✉) · H. Seifert · J. Reiter
University of Technology Ilmenau, Ilmenau, Germany
e-mail: volker.nissen@tu-ilmenau.de; henry.seifert@infosys-consulting.com;
jakob.reiter@tu-ilmenau.de

J. Kuhl · H. Kräft · J. Eidmann
Dr. Kuhl Unternehmensberatung GmbH & Co. KG, Hardegsen, Germany
e-mail: JKuhl@DK-UB.de; HKraeft@DK-UB.de; JEidmann@DK-UB.de

© Springer International Publishing AG, part of Springer Nature 2019
N. Urbach, M. Röglinger (eds.), *Digitalization Cases*, Management for
Professionals, https://doi.org/10.1007/978-3-319-95273-4_12

digitally stored expert knowledge to produce a well-founded assessment on the given subject.

(c) **Results achieved**: The assessment is today available to clients on the initial website of the consulting firm via an online shop. After all participants (which might have different roles in the respective project) have successfully taken part in a survey related, the client can call up an expert report. As a result, he or she receives an approximate overview on the status of project management in this particular project. Moreover, recommendations for action to improve the situation are given. Currently, the system is being evaluated for use in a multinational company to assist in continuously monitoring internal projects.

(d) **Lessons learned**: It is possible to create a flexible architecture for virtual assessments on in principle any conceivable subject. Whether virtualization is the right approach for a specific client or project should be clarified based on appropriate criteria, such as the ones proposed by Nissen and Seifert (2017a). The early integration of clients into design and development of digital consulting products is important to economic success. Consulting providers should get involved early and build up experience and knowledge in virtualizing own services without expecting immediate breakthroughs. We estimate that virtual consulting will not generally replace conventional on-site consulting, but rather supplement it.

1   Introduction

The case study presented here is to be placed in the context of the digital transformation of business consulting.[1] Even though the total turnover in the consulting industry is increasing year after year, the competitive playing field for consultancies is changing rapidly. This is due to recent developments in potentially disruptive technologies used by successful digital newcomers, but also substantial changes and evolving requirements on the client side. Although consulting firms strengthen the competitiveness of their clients through innovative solutions and are decisively involved in the development of new concepts and the use of digitalization, traditional face-to-face approaches are mostly applied in the consulting process. To remain strong in the market, established consultancies need to critically evaluate their business models as well as the way they provide their services to clients. Technology-fueled tools and digital products can distinguish a provider from its competitors by optimizing and sustainably extending the service-portfolio. Asset-based consulting services can offer new starting points to lower ones' own costs and recover marginal scope. Through rethinking the delivery-process of consulting itself, consultancies can reshape the interaction with the client and open up segments of new customers.

---

[1]This text builds on Nissen et al. (2018).

A promising approach to achieve these goals is virtualization (Overby 2008, 2012). Central virtualization mechanisms are digitalization and networking. The aim of virtualization in consulting is to reasonably reduce the amount of face-to-face interaction between consultant and client by the suitable use of information and communication technologies (ICT) (Christensen et al. 2013; Greff and Werth 2015; Nissen et al. 2015). It can thus be referred to as the strategy for digital transformation of the consulting business. Virtualization can introduce new digital business models of consulting which increase the efficiency, flexibility and effectiveness of consulting services. In combination with a standardization of the consulting service, the door to fully automated consulting solutions is opened in some fields. In practice, the strongly virtualized forms of business consulting, for instance self-service consulting, have only been used occasionally so far (Nissen and Seifert 2016).

In our case study, we provide an account of the creation of a fully virtualized consulting solution in the context of project management by the Dr. Kuhl Unternehmensberatung GmbH & Co. KG (DKUB), Hardegsen, Germany. This consulting firm specializes in small and medium-sized customers and exists since 2003. DKUB is a small consulting provider with below ten employees. The consulting portfolio centers around project management issues. Frequent mandates concern the management of client projects on behalf of medium-sized companies. Other consulting areas are covered as well, such as data warehousing and controlling, as well as restructuring consulting, but project management themes are at the core of the business model.

To strengthen sales and raise the innovative image of the consultancy, the CEO of DKUB, Dr. Jochen Kuhl, entered into a development partnership with the Chair of Information Systems Engineering in Services of Ilmenau Technical University, Germany (Wirtschaftsinformatik für Dienstleistungen—WID), Prof. Dr. Volker Nissen. This partnership was initiated through a previous common academic history of both. Moreover, a major research focus at WID is the digitalization of consulting services, which was exactly the focus of this joint project with DKUB. The project team consisted of four members from DKUB and three members of WID. The internal project started in July 2015, and continues up to now with pilot client rollouts. The project was carried out on both sides in addition to day-to-day business and without a particular client background.

The technical project goal was to design and implement an IT framework that allows the straightforward provision of fully virtualized assessment products for a range of different themes. Assessing the quality of project management at DKUB's clients was chosen as the particular area for a pilot implementation. Assessments are a form of advisory consulting and particularly suited for virtualization as they rely only on a structured low-level interaction with the client (Deelmann 2012). From the perspective of DKUB, a practical target is to extend the consulting service portfolio with a virtual project management service that complements the classical face-to-face consulting usually provided to clients of DKUB. For WID the objective is to put scientific results on the virtualization of consulting services into practice and scientifically accompany the usage thereof.

In the following sections, it is explained why a virtual consulting solution was pursued, how the conception and development took place in terms of a prototyping-based approach, and what results were achieved.

2   Situation Faced

Consulting businesses intensively need to deal with questions of how their core business will run in the future. In the current situation, this demands analyzing mega-trends such as digitization and big data with respect to own processes and service portfolios. For small consulting providers like DKUB, competition is intense and large fluctuations in the occupancy rate can be dangerous for the survival of the company. Thus, professional marketing and sales activities are necessary, but apart from the time-consuming day-to-day business, they are difficult to carry out. More-over, there is frequently a lack of knowledge and time to develop innovative new consulting products, although this could lead to a competitive advantage. In this situation, the CEO of DKUB, Dr. Kuhl, was looking for possibilities

- To achieve a lasting positive marketing effect with moderate effort,
- To raise the profile of his company in the consulting segment through innovative consulting services,
- To supplement the existing consulting portfolio with digital services, which represent a "door opener" for the classical consulting business, because they generate follow-up orders.

The interest in asset-based consulting products was further fueled by the aca-demic background of the CEO in computational intelligence, and a current shortage of qualified staff to push traditional marketing and sales activities. Due to a long-established personal contact between the CEO of DKUB and the professor of WID, the idea of a joint project emerged to develop a digital assessment tool to provide innovative automated consulting.

Digital assessments are a form of advisory consulting. In general, four different approaches of business consulting can be differentiated: advisory consulting, expert consulting, organizational development/coaching and systemic consulting (Walger 1995). Advisory consulting presents a form of content-oriented consulting, where a consultant, based on specific knowledge, suggests a solution to a client problem in the form of a report (Bamberger and Wrona 2012). The consultant acts as an external and neutral expert. Initially, he or she gathers information, analyzes it, and develops one or more alternatives for solving the client problem in the form of a textual elaboration. The concerned employees usually do not take part in the final expert report for decision-making. On the other hand, the consultant is usually not involved during the (optional) implementation of these proposals.

Advisory consulting is marked by relatively little, well-structured interaction between the client and the consultant, which makes it an ideal test case for the virtualization of consulting services. Project management (PM) was decided to be the area of a pilot implementation here, as this is the core area of activity at DKUB.

A quick assessment using the method to evaluate the virtualization potential of a particular consulting service proposed by Nissen and Seifert (2017a) resulted in a positive business case for the prospective project. Very briefly, this method comes in three steps. The first step, evaluation of the process-related virtualization potential, is based on the Process Virtualization Theory by Overby (2008, 2012), and investigates how features of the consulting process influence the virtualization potential. The second step, the organizational analysis, investigates key factors within the consulting company and how they influence the virtualization potential. In the third and strategical step the chances and risks of virtualization are investigated from both the perspectives of the client and the consulting provider in the scope of a business case.

As no large amounts of funding were available for the planned development project, only internal staff from DKUB (two experienced consultants and two technical staff) and WID (professor—a former consultant himself, PhD student—also consultant, and a Master student with good software development skills) were integrated into the project team.

The current state of practice with respect to high degrees of virtualization is not very advanced (Nissen and Seifert 2016). From a scientific point of view, there is moreover a shortage of research on the digital transformation of the consulting industry, and, consequently, a lack of scientifically sound artefacts to help in practical implementations, as pointed out by Seifert and Nissen (2016). However, in the project team, rich knowledge on virtualization theory and technologies, software development issues, and long-standing project management experience (the assessments' application area) was available. Furthermore, the team was highly motivated to produce a practically relevant, but also scientifically interesting outcome.

The focus in this case study is especially on the design and development, as well on as the demonstration of the usability and usefulness of the artefact. The intention is to provide other consultancies with concrete input for own virtualization activities. A broad evaluation of the virtual consulting product is not covered, as it will be the focus of future research.

3   Action Taken

3.1   General Approach

Since a software system should be created, an artefact in the sense of Hevner et al. (2004) and Hevner and Chatterjee (2010), a design-science (DS) approach was chosen for this study. More specifically, we follow the DS process model suggested by Peffers et al. (2007/2008). This process model consists of six steps: (1) Identify problem and motivate research, (2) Define objectives of a solution, (3) Design and development, (4) Demonstration of utility and usability, (5) Evaluation of artefact, and (6) Communication of results. The model can be started at various points. Furthermore steps (2)–(6) are parts of an iterative process.

A prototype-oriented process model was chosen for design and development, as it quickly produces first versions of the future IT system. Moreover, after validating the given prototype, the model allows for iterations of phases and backward steps in the overall procedure (Bunse and von Knethen 2008; Balzert et al. 2009; Kuhrmann 2012). In the context of the given objective, a prototype-oriented process model seems to be reasonable, as several obscurities regarding the system design were initially present, which could be quickly clarified by suitable prototypes.

As was mentioned before, the virtual assessment tool to be developed is mainly intended as a sales channel at DKUB. However, this background did not much affect the core design activities, as the immediate goal is to provide clients with a fitting assessment of their project management (PM) situation. It is known, though, that many (in particular small) clients do have serious issues in this domain. Thus, it can be anticipated that the assessment results will highlight areas of potential improvement for many customers of this virtual product. Given such a result, the assessment then suggests DKUB as a competent PM consulting provider to the respective client. Moreover, DKUB will learn of results that represent an opportunity to sell classical PM consulting business. After this initial "door opening", however, the further sales process currently continues as usual. Therefore, the intended use of the virtual assessment tool at DKUB has only minor influence on the system design activities. It also underlines that this application is seen as complementary to existing services at this consultancy, and not as a replacement for classical business.

3.2 Requirements Analysis

The requirements analysis took place without a particular client. Instead, the basis for this project was a jointly developed business concept. Furthermore, a study of Nissen et al. (2017) on quality requirements for virtual consulting services was used, and the general features of advisory consulting were considered. It emerged during the conception that it is clearly preferable to have client input in this process. In general, this input helps to focus activities on issues that clients value and cross-check ideas that come up in the development process. However, a pilot client will not always be present when a consulting provider decides to embark on a digital transformation initiative. In our view, this should not prevent first steps that carry a manageable risk. The complexity of modern technologies and digital transformation suggest getting involved early and building up experience that can in the long run lead to competitive advantage.

The process within the prototype should roughly reproduce an expert report by gathering data from the client's company and linking these with digitally stored expert knowledge to finally produce a well-founded assessment on the given subject. A rough system draft was already outlined in the business concept, which served as basis for the design of the prototype. Thus, this system is supposed to have a survey function, which makes it possible to conduct online surveys. In the course of these surveys, different question formats, such as open questions or scale-based questions, as well as a branching out of questions, should be possible. A further component of this system is the user account, which is necessary for the authentication and registration of a client and can store the required information on him. The data storage and data processing components include the evaluation of survey data, logics on the selection of a recommendation for action and the opportunity to define these logics by means of formulae. Furthermore, all the required data to issue an expert report, should be stored in a structured way. At the end of the survey, these data should be presented to the client in an edited form, so that he or she gets an overview of the key figures and recommendations for action.

The concrete requirements are divided into different categories. The category *user administration* includes requirements of the participants' user accounts, as an anonymized participation and the function to add several participants are necessary. The requirements in the field of *data collection* especially refer to the survey. For example, it should be possible to collect data either by an external or an internal survey, and to consolidate the results of questionnaires from different participants (with possibly different roles) for the evaluation. In the category *data processing*, key figures must be calculated on the basis of survey data and recommendations for action should be selected. Furthermore, all the required data, such as questionnaire, survey- and evaluation results, as well as user data should be permanently stored. Moreover, the evaluation results should be presented in a simple and clear way to the client, and it must be possible to print and save them. Furthermore, proposals for a data- and authorization model, as well as for the definition of suitable interfaces were part of the business concept.

Further requirements were derived from a study by Nissen et al. (2017). In this study, the quality criteria of virtualized consulting services were initially determined by a literature review, and subsequently evaluated by an expert group in a Delphi-study. In doing so, a set of quality criteria was defined that will be briefly explained in a descending order of importance. These include the general system availability of the virtualized consulting process, as well as the actuality of the gathered data. The criterion fulfillment describes the expectation of the client that the promised and expected service correlates with the resulting solution of the consulting process. In the case of mistakes or problems, the efficiency of the process, as well as the reaction capability of the responsible consulting provider, is also important. Moreover, the most sensitive company data should be adequately protected, and a simple way to contact the business consulting should be given. The chance of compensation should also be provided when there are deficiencies in the process. Furthermore, the solution should have an appealing appearance and it should be possible to use the consulting service easily.

Every requirement was then transferred into a uniform tabular structure, to be able to get a better complete overview on all requirements. In these tables requirements were classified as functional or non-functional and sorted into one of three categories. Subsequently a prioritization of the requirements took place according to their significance for the fundamental functions of the prototype and the benefit, which can be expected, when they are implemented.

Subsequently ambiguous requirements were specified more accurately. This happened by interviewing the consulting partner. More accurate specifications were needed for the above described service quality requirements as these had to be adapted and formulated on the concrete case of application. Furthermore, central elements were conceptually defined to attain a uniform understanding. The term *consulting product* was assigned to the central element of the prototype, the gathering of data and preparation of an expert report.

In the following, a concrete consulting project, acquired by the client, will be described as an *assessment*. Moreover, two groups of persons must be differentiated. On the one side is the *client*, who acquires the assessment. He or she may invite different persons to enter data, and he or she finally receives the expert report afterwards. On the other side is the *participant*, who needs to be invited by the client and only partly gains access to the data gathering. *Questionnaires* with corresponding answer options are crucial for gathering data. When the collection of data has been completed, a *report* with recommendations for action and explanatory text blocks is generated.

The requirements list, which was now completed, was finally validated in collaboration with the research group WID at Ilmenau and the consulting partner DKUB. In this process, some requirements were prioritized differently than before. As a result, some requirements are omitted and others attain a greater significance during implementation. For example, the opportunity to add more participants to a survey was more strongly prioritized. In doing so the virtual processes of advisory consulting were specifically considered in the prototype while other necessary functions for commercial use, such as web shop integration, were initially less in focus.

3.3 Design and Development

3.3.1 Process Design

The requirements implicitly refer to a web-based solution, so that web-technologies were specifically chosen. Initially the central processes of the prototype were defined to get an impression of the future user experience. The basis for this design was, in turn, the collected requirements, and a first outline of the processes within the business concept.

The first process (Fig. 1) deals with acquiring an assessment. For this purpose, the client uses an online-shop, the accurate details of which will not be part of this contribution. There he or she chooses a consulting product and consequently receives an assessment. Afterwards this acquired assessment is shown to him on an overview page. Every assessment has a detailed view, which also provides the opportunity to invite any number of participants. The participants are notified by e-mails and with a link within the e-mail they can call up the survey.

The second process (Fig. 2) deals with the participation in a survey. In this case, it is necessary to differentiate between the client and the participant, who was invited by e-mail. Whilst a participant receives the link for participating in a survey via e-mail, the client can directly access the survey from the assessment detail page.

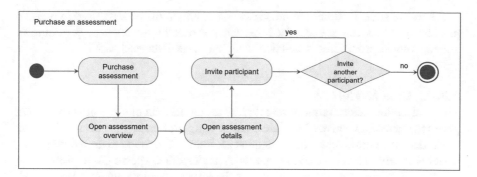

Fig. 1 Illustration of the process needed to acquire an assessment

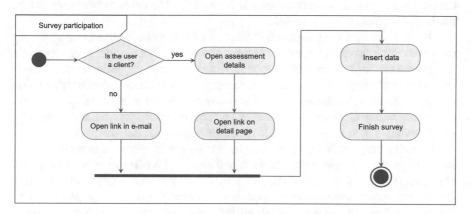

Fig. 2 Illustration of the process needed for the participation of a survey

Fig. 3 Illustration of the process to call up an expert report

Afterwards the process is the same again for both user groups. The retrieved data are entered into the online-survey and finally the data are saved, after completing the survey.

The third central process (Fig. 3) is calling up the expert report after completing the survey. In this process, the client opens the assessment in his or her assessment overview once more, chooses the particular assessment, and opens its detailed view. Within the detailed view the client can then call up the expert report and display it in the browser. Furthermore, there is the opportunity to save and print the expert report.

There are several additional processes, for example the process used to create a user account. As this process is, however, generically constructed, according to general known procedures, a detailed modelling was dispensed with.

3.3.2 Data Model

The data model includes four different areas for all the data of a potential consulting product: client data, survey templates, report templates and report data. Within the *client data*, the entities user and participant are found. According to the requirements, a user is a client, who acquired the product. A participant is a person, who takes part in a survey. For every client who takes part in the survey, a participant is also generated. Furthermore, the entity assessment exists. This entity represents a single purchase of the consulting product and can be assigned to a client. The entity answer saves all the participant's responses of a survey.

The *survey template* contains all the data, which are needed to compile a survey for a consulting product. Here there is the entity survey that describes the scope of a survey and can be assigned to a product. It also contains the entity section, which groups individual questions under a common title. Furthermore, the entity question exists, which contains the text for a concrete question and more information on the processing within an expert report. Several entities of the type option can be assigned to a question. These present individual answer options for the questions.

A similar purpose is accomplished by the *report template*, where all data are saved to provide a basic frame for an expert report of a consulting product. Every consulting product has a template, which describes the basic features of the expert report. This expert report is composed of several entities of the type block, which represent individual building blocks of the expert report. This entity can accept various types, and can derive more accurate details from the entity text-input or graph-input, which either describes text or a graphical building block.

Finally, to issue an expert report, calculated key figures have to be entered into the template and afterwards a completed report can be presented. For this purpose, the *report data* is available, which saves the concrete expert report as the entity report. In the report template variables are used, which are individually calculated from the client data, for each expert report. For this reason, the entity value is assigned to the report. The linking between the expert report and the template is presented by the entity entry, which represents a single part of the expert report. To every entry an entity calculation can be assigned, which intermediately stores the results for the graphical elements.

Beyond this core data model, there are more data structures, which, however, were outsourced. These include the data of the authentication of the client, as well as the intermediate stored survey data, which were already implemented in the used third-party survey software LimeSurvey.

3.4 System Architecture

3.4.1 General Approach

Amongst the requirements to the system architecture, a high flexibility stands out, in order to be able to react to different application areas in terms of consulting content, changed requirements, or new insights in the development process. By choosing prototyping as a model for the development, the requirements arose, that on the one hand, the opportunity for experimenting should be given to be able to validate compiled hypotheses quickly. On the other hand, a certain independency of the programming language should be guaranteed, so that the decision for a programming language can be made dependent on its suitability for the intended use.

For the implementation of the prototype, a simple but flexible form of service-oriented architecture (Barry 2013) was chosen. However, also aspects from the microservice concept were employed, where individual components of the software are disassembled in even smaller sub-components that communicate with each other by a language independent interface (Namiot and Sneps-Sneppe 2014). After the first outline, the services were roughly structured according to the required functions of the software. Initially three services were developed, which can be complemented by more services in future expansions.

As the extent of the in-house development of a survey function was too large for this scope, an available service for this work task was established within the system architecture. The implementation of functionality for the user administration and display of web pages also seemed too comprehensive. Therefore, these functions were also outsourced into their own services.

3.4.2 Architectural Components

The backend-service required the major effort during development, as this had to be implemented from scratch. It represents the core component of the architecture, as the coordination of the other services, data storage and data processing takes place there. Python was chosen as programming language. This language is suitable for a rapid development and provides efficient libraries to analyze data.

In the backend, the delivered data for an assessment and the corresponding questionnaire as well as the expert report are processed. These data are transmitted by means of a standardized Excel-file. The Excel-file is read, the data are copied into the database and afterwards they are transmitted to the survey-service via a SOAP-interface. This component was used to implement the requirements referring to the storage of formulae for the calculation of key figures and the import and configuration of questionnaires.

The backend-service is closely linked to a database-service, where all the data are deposited. Communication with the frontend takes place via a REST-interface and can only be used with a correlating API-key. The survey-service is linked to a SOAP-interface, which is also secured by a password. Figure 4 gives an overview of the system architecture.

The frontend-service provides all the functionality required for the graphical user interface. This includes the administration of assessments by the client. This service also takes over the authentication of the end user, and therefore provides the

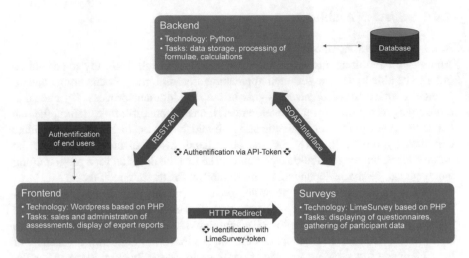

Fig. 4 Illustration of the overall system architecture with key services and links

opportunity to create a user account. *Wordpress* is used for this process, as it contains the required functionality and is freely available. This way it is possible for the client to open up a user account, and to log on to the system with an e-mail address and a password. Furthermore, pages for an overview of all purchased assessments, a detailed view of a specific assessment with a display of the participants, and the opportunity to show the expert report, were implemented.

Communication with the survey-service takes place via simple HTTP-redirects, where the user is redirected within the browser. The authentication takes place via an internal token of the survey-service.

The survey-service supplies every function for the administration and implementation of the survey. LimeSurvey was chosen as the tool to conduct the survey. LimeSurvey is a freely available and well-established open source survey tool. It supplies a comprehensive interface for the communication with other services within the architecture. Furthermore, it supplies good opportunities to expand the software and includes a large range of functions. LimeSurvey is based on the programming language PHP, which is widely spread in the Internet and uses MySQL as data storage. This database is, within the context of this prototype, only responsible for the intermediate storage of the survey data, which are transmitted to the backend, after successfully completing the survey.

The survey within LimeSurvey is automatically applied and configured by the backend-service via the SOAP-interface. Furthermore, a key is issued to every participant, which simplifies the later assignments of questions to a specific assessment and excludes multiple use of the survey by one person. Besides, a surveillance of the progress of a participant is possible, as surveys can be interrupted.

The administration within the prototype is initially limited to the construction of new consulting products. At some later point of time more administration functions could be implemented, which would be suitable to support the client or solve problems in consulting.

All the data for a concrete consulting product are essentially stored in an Excel-file, which consists of two different worksheets. The first worksheet contains all the data for a survey, and the second worksheet all data for the generation of the expert report for the client, after completing the survey. The supply of Excel-files takes place via a simple file transfer on the server of the backend-service. Subsequently a command line-tool has to be rendered, which stores the data in the database and releases the corresponding survey into LimeSurvey.

The non-functional requirements have already been looked at on this level, as they do not refer to individual functions of the software, but rather define common qualitative requirements. It was attempted to implement the requirement of system availability with distributed architecture, as in this way the individual services can partly operate independently from each other. The efficiency of the consulting service can be guaranteed by the chosen standard software, as this provides already known operating patterns, which supplies efficient processes for the user. Privacy will be guaranteed by the authentication concept. By using the API-token most attacks can already be barred. Finally, the requirements of aesthetics were considered by constructing the prototype in the design of the practice partner.

4   Results Achieved

In this section the resulting digital consulting product will be briefly demonstrated with various screen shots, to convey a first impression. The particular application area here is the assessment of the project management quality for a given project based on a survey amongst project stakeholders. These can have different roles, such as project manager and project worker or external project partner. Based on the role, the questionnaire used in the respective survey changes adaptively. This virtual assessment product was termed ProMAT (Project Management Assessment Tool).

The design of the user-frontend was based on the website of the practice partner DKUB. The assessment is available to the client on the initial website of the consulting firm (Fig. 5). Clients are then passed on to an online shop, where the digital assessment can be acquired.

The overview page of the consulting product gives some details about the product, its basic principles as well as its benefits. Furthermore, clients that have already used the tool have the option to give feedback via a feedback-form. Besides that, feedback and questions can be communicated via e-mail and telephone. Corresponding contact information is presented in the header of the website.

Once the client clicks on the shopping-cart-button, the assessment will be stored in the personal shopping cart. If the client then clicks on "proceed to checkout", he or she will be forwarded to the checkout page of the assessment where he or she must enter basic information like his or her name, address or e-mail. Furthermore, the client is asked to select a payment method. Once the client clicks on "Send Order", the assessment buying process is finished and the client will be able to use the product.

Fig. 5 The assessment is available via the website of the consulting partner (see bottom, translated from German)

The assessment overview page serves the administration of an individual assessment (Fig. 6). When an assessment has been acquired, the client can administrate the participants of the survey. For this reason, there is a set form to attach participants by means of their e-mail addresses. Afterwards they can be invited to the survey per e-mail. When the client has logged himself in as a participant, he or she can open the survey directly from the detailed view, and participate. Furthermore, every participant is shown and whether he or she has already been invited, or whether he or she has completed the survey. Finally, the client may call up the generated expert report.

The implementation of the survey is done via an online-questionnaire, which consists of various pages with grouped questions, referring to a specific topic of project management. Figure 7 displays an exemplary illustration. At the head of the page, the actual progress of the questionnaire is shown to the participant, subsequently followed by individual questions. The questions are composed of a text and the possible answer options to it. Often, only one answer can be chosen. However, in the case of multiple choice questions, several options may be chosen. After completing the survey, the participant is directed to a page in the user-front-end, where the software thanks for his or her participation. In the background, the survey data are transferred from the survey-service to the backend-service.

After all participants have successfully taken part in the survey, the client can call up an expert report via his or her detailed view of an assessment. Subsequently, the

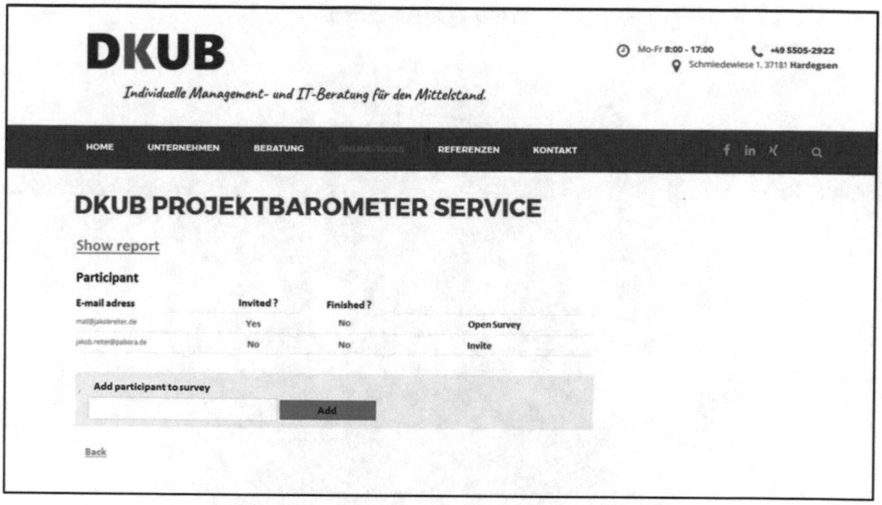

Fig. 6 Assessment overview page (translated from German)

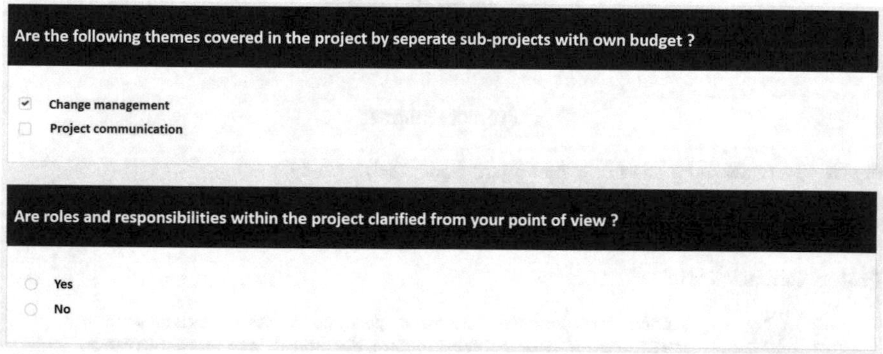

Fig. 7 Exemplary illustration of questions in the survey-service (translated)

client has the opportunity to read the expert report directly in the browser, to save it as a PDF-file, or to print it. The report is composed of an introductory radar-chart (Fig. 8), which summarizes all the key figures of the report. It is divided in six perspectives on the quality of project management.

Furthermore, the report contains various sections on these different perspectives of project management. These sections are comprised of a heading, a graph and text blocks, which are shown, depending on the answers of the participants in the survey. The text blocks are adaptively generated using rule-based expert knowledge on project management and reflect on deficiencies identified in the assessment. The key figures for the graphical elements are also generated from these data. Figure 9 shows an exemplary excerpt on project communication.

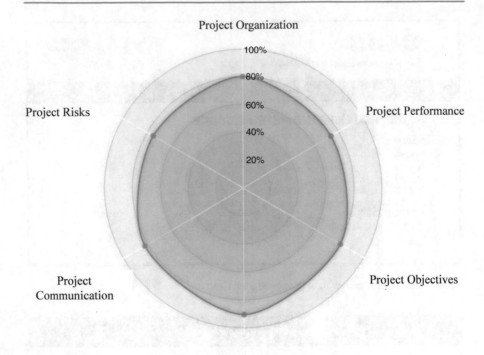

Project Organization

Project Risks

Project Performance

Project
Communication

Project Objectives

Project Contract

Fig. 8 Overview radar chart of expert report (translated)

Project communication

82%

A prompt and transparent information policy on relevant issues is an important prerequisite for successful cooperation in the project. In this way, risks can be identified and project work can be organized efficiently. At the same time, a poor information policy in the project leads to demotivation and misunderstandings.

An inappropriate and unprofessional handling and communication style in the project can be a sign of overstrain, especially in management functions, or excessive pressure to perform at the project level and can lead to a bad atmosphere in the project.

Active change management is necessary for projects that trigger a significant or fundamental change in the organization. In this way, the organization and employees can be prepared for the changes and succeed. A large number of reorganization projects are not successful, although there are neither business nor technical reasons for this. There is usually only a lack of answers to two questions: 1) How can employees be adapted to the new structures? 2) How can the old patterns in the head be replaced by new ones? Change management provides solutions to answer these questions.

Fig. 9 An excerpt on project communication, focusing on the deficient aspects of the respective client project, from a generated expert report

The expert report gives the client an approximate overview on the status of the project management in his or her project. Moreover, recommendations for action to improve the situation are given.

With the present web-based system, it is possible to conduct advisory consulting on in principle an arbitrary subject in a virtualized way. The focus of this contribution was mainly on the technical realization, while the content of the consulting product was not considered here in much detail. The first generated expert reports are promising, though. However, there is still room for improvement, and an extensive evaluation of the virtual assessment is only now starting. On the technical side, some limitations should be dealt with. For a market-ready product, the authentication concept has to be revised and different software for the frontend-service may have to be implemented, as some requirements could only be realized in Wordpress with quite some difficulties.

As far as the wider implications for the involved consulting firm are concerned, it is actually quite early to assess them properly. Currently, the system is being evaluated for use in a very large German multinational company to assist in continuously monitoring internal projects. It is fair to say that without the appeal of the described virtual consulting product, this client company would probably never have approached DKUB for services. Moreover, DKUB has now started marketing this product more actively and some smaller clients started using it. For a more general assessment of the impact on sales and market success, however, more time must elapse. Moreover, before a broad use is targeted, a technical revision will have to be performed to remove the drawbacks with some of the used tools as discussed above and lower the maintenance efforts.

In the future, a second consulting product from another topic area will be integrated. The practice partner has already indicated that he would be prepared to develop the system further, and use it in a complementary way to the classical project management consulting services offered. The projected new target area is IT agility assessments. A company's ability to change increasingly depends on the ability to change its IT, something referred to as 'IT agility' here. High IT agility can contribute to increased business agility and thus create a competitive advantage. At the Chair of Information Systems Engineering in Services, we develop a methodology to assess IT agility based on objectively measurable characteristics (see, for instance, Nissen and von Rennenkampff 2017). This research lays the foundations for a corresponding virtual assessment that will address in particular CIOs.

5   Lessons Learned

Lesson One

It is possible (and useful) to create a fully flexible architecture for virtual assessments on in principle any conceivable subject matter. Changing to a different application area in the described system only requires adapting the content of two worksheets in Excel. The first worksheet contains the data to automatically create a survey, and the second worksheet contains all the data needed to prepare the expert report later.

In the first worksheet, the title of the product is first defined and then any number of section definitions follows, each representing a separate page on which grouped questions are displayed in the subsequent survey. For each question, information on the question text, answer options and a weighting of the question for the calculations within the report is kept available.

The calculations for the later assessment can be based on a self-developed logic language, which includes simple mathematical functions such as the creation of a sum or the reading out of a value of a response. Blocks can be defined for the later assessment structure, which are shown or hidden based on their display conditions for certain responses of the participants. In addition, there is a calculation rule for the blocks with graphical elements, according to which the key figures displayed are calculated. The Excel files are made available by a simple file transfer to the server of the backend service.

We would like to point out, though, that fine-tuning the frontend appearance of the system to suit the needs of a particular user group can always be an issue to address when the application domain is changed.

Lesson Two
The digital transformation in consulting requires a methodology and decision process, based on appropriate criteria, to assess the virtualization potential within the service portfolio of the particular consulting provider. In this context, a helpful method to determine the virtualization potential of a particular consulting service was proposed by Nissen and Seifert (2017a). In three steps it evaluates the *process characteristics* of the service to be virtualized, the *organizational context* of the company, and the *strategic fit* of the virtualization initiative. This leads to a business case that helps to decide whether a consulting task can be fruitfully virtualized or not. This methodology was tested in the context of the here described development project. All criteria were positive and supported the targeted virtual consulting application. More details appear in Seifert (2018).

Although the proposed method certainly provides room for improvement (for instance, the order of the aspects looked at might be changed in more complex scenarios), the virtualization potential can roughly be identified with the proposed method. In the future, it appears useful to integrate results from process acceptance theory (Müllerleile and Nissen 2014; Müllerleile et al. 2015; Nissen et al. 2016) with this methodology on the process level.

Lesson Three
The early integration of clients into the design and development process of virtual consulting services is important to economic success. In our case, the conception and development took place without a concrete customer. A (very large) pilot customer was only acquired after an initial version of the digital assessment product was already available. Although much knowledge on typical deficiencies in project management and potential countermeasures were available in our team, it turned out, that the client demanded substantial changes and adaptions to the available assessment product to use it internally for project monitoring. It would certainly have

been very helpful to have had this client in the team right from the start to focus the conception and consecutive development efforts instead of changing a ready-to-use result. However, as a low demand for (highly) virtualized consulting services is the largest obstacle on the way to the in-depth penetration of virtualization in the consulting practice (Nissen and Seifert 2017b), it might not always be possible to choose this way of proceeding.

Lesson Four
The complexity of modern technologies, and digital transformation as a whole, suggest getting involved early and building up experience and knowledge without expecting immediate breakthroughs. In the case of our cooperating consulting partner DKUB, the focus of the virtualization initiative clearly was on sales support (digital assessment as a "door opener" for classical consulting) and raising the company profile in the consulting segment through innovative consulting services. For a small consulting provider, this appears a reasonable entry point to digital transformation. More complex virtualization projects could follow in the future with increasing experience.

Technology-based products may be ahead of current client needs, but maybe ideal to serve these clients tomorrow. This implies taking first steps in this direction today, adopting a more experimental approach instead of long-term planning, and also accepting the risk of failure in certain digital initiatives. The biggest issue here is digital leadership, i.e. active management of the transformation.

Digital transformation in the consultancy sector is a complex undertaking, creating barriers to competitors. Those who accumulate relevant knowledge early, develop a sound digital strategy, and execute successful pilot projects, can in the long term be expected to generate and defend competitive advantage. This requires a high degree of creativity, entrepreneurship, and strategic thinking.

Lesson Five
Virtualized consulting services will not generally replace conventional on-site consulting. With new technology-driven competitors and changing framework conditions, consultants should continually assess their service portfolio critically. Virtualization is a promising approach to optimize consulting processes and deliver innovative consulting products, thereby creating a sustainable competitive advantage. Using state-of-the-art ICT enables consulting firms to supply customized solutions anytime and anywhere while the individual work load of consultants can be optimized. The downside of virtualization is a reduced direct interaction of clients and consultants and thus the risk of weaker client-consultant-relationships—a critical resource of consulting companies.

It is a value-adding combination of traditional and digital approaches that consulting providers should aim for. Virtual services can supplement classical offerings of business consulting in an attempt to optimize performance, and complement the existing service portfolio as well as delivery modes.

In the simplest case, virtualization can be understood as a measure for securing efficiency and flexibility. At the highest evolution level, virtualization offers the opportunity to completely change the delivery model of the company. The consequence would be that the complete service system of the consulting business is changed, and the value chain is optimized. Each consulting company must develop its own consistent strategic vision, how virtualization and traditional consulting can be meaningfully combined in the next step of business evolution.

References

Balzert H, Balzert H, Koschke R, Lämmel U, Liggesmeyer P, Quante J (2009) Lehrbuch der Softwaretechnik: Basiskonzepte und Requirements Engineering, 3rd edn. Spektrum

Bamberger I, Wrona T (2012) Konzeptionen der strategischen Unternehmensberatung. In: Wrona T (ed) Strategische Unternehmensberatung, 6th edn. Gabler, Wiesbaden, pp 1–44

Barry DK (2013) Web services, service-oriented architectures, and cloud computing, 2nd edn. Elsevier, Waltham

Bunse C, von Knethen A (2008) Vorgehensmodelle kompakt. Spektrum, Berlin

Christensen CM, Wang D, van Bever D (2013) Consulting on the cusp of disruption. Harv Bus Rev 91(10):106–114

Deelmann T (2012) Organisations- und Prozessberatung. In: Nissen V, Klauk B (eds) Studienführer Consulting. Gabler, Wiesbaden

Greff T, Werth D (2015) Auf dem Weg zur digitalen Unternehmensberatung. IM+io – Magazin für Innovation, Organisation und Management. IMC, Saarbücken, pp 30–34

Hevner A, Chatterjee S (2010) Design science research in information systems – theory and practice. Springer, Berlin

Hevner AR, March ST, Park J, Ram S (2004) Design science in information systems research. MIS Q 28(1):75–105

Kuhrmann M (2012) Prototyping. In: Gronau N et al (eds) Enzyklopädie der Wirtschaftsinformatik, 9th edn. GITO, Berlin. http://www.enzyklopaedie-der-wirtschaftsinformatik.de/. Accessed 14 Dez 2016

Müllerleile T, Nissen V (2014) When processes alienate customers: towards a theory of process acceptance. In: Nonopoulos A, Schmidt W (eds) Proceedings of S-BPM One (LNBIP). Springer, Berlin, pp 171–180

Müllerleile T, Ritter S, Englisch L, Nissen V, Joenssen D (2015) The influence of process acceptance on BPM: an empirical investigation. In: Proceedings of the 2015 I.E. 17th conference on business informatics (CBI 2015). IEEE, Piscataway, pp 125–132

Namiot D, Sneps-Sneppe M (2014) On micro-services architecture. Int J Open Inf Technol 2 (9):24–27

Nissen V, Seifert H (2016) Virtualisierung in der Unternehmensberatung. Eine Studie im deutschen Beratungsmarkt. BDU e.V., Bonn

Nissen V, Seifert H (2017a) Evaluating the virtualization potential of consulting services. In: Nissen V (ed) Digital transformation of the consulting industry – extending the traditional delivery model. Springer, Berlin

Nissen V, Seifert H (2017b) Digital transformation in business consulting – status quo in Germany. In: Nissen V (ed) Digital transformation of the consulting industry – extending the traditional delivery model. Springer, Berlin

Nissen V, von Rennenkampff A (2017) Measuring the agility of the IT application systems landscape. In: Leimeister JM, Brenner W (eds) Proceedings Wirtschaftsinformatik 2017, St. Gallen (AISeLibrary)

Nissen V, Seifert H, Blumenstein M (2015) Virtualisierung von Beratungsleistungen: Qualitätsanforderungen, Chancen und Risiken der digitalen Transformation in der Unternehmensberatung aus der Klientenperspektive. In: Deelmann T, Ockel DM (eds) Handbuch der Unternehmensberatung, KZ. 7311, 25th edn. Erich Schmidt Verlag, Berlin

Nissen V, Müllerleile T, Kazakowa E, Lezina T (2016) Analyzing process acceptance with IT-enabled experimental research. Vestn Econ 3:109–129

Nissen V, Seifert H, Blumenstein M (2017) Chances, risks and quality criteria of virtual consulting. In: Nissen V (ed) digital transformation of the consulting industry – extending the traditional delivery model. Springer, Berlin

Nissen V, Kuhl J, Kräft H, Seifert H, Reiter J, Eidmann J (2018) ProMAT – a project management assessment tool for virtual consulting. In: Nissen V (ed) Digital transformation of the consulting industry. Extending the traditional delivery model. Springer, Cham, pp 351–369

Overby E (2008) Process virtualization theory and the impact of information technology. Org Sci 19 (2):277–291

Overby E (2012) Migrating processes from physical to virtual environments: process virtualization theory. In: Dwivedi YK, Wade MR, Schneberger SL (eds) Information systems theory. Explaining and predicting our digital society. Springer, New York, pp 107–124

Peffers K, Tuunanen T, Rothenberger MA, Chatterjee S (2007/2008) A design science research methodology for information systems research. J Manage Inf Syst 24(3):45–77

Seifert H (2018) Virtualisierung von Beratungsleistungen: Grundlagen der digitalen Transformation in der Unternehmensberatung. PhD Dissertation. Ilmedia, Ilmenau (to appear)

Seifert H, Nissen V (2016) Virtualisierung von Beratungsleistungen: Stand der Forschung zur digitalen Transformation in der Unternehmensberatung und weiterer Forschungsbedarf. In: Nissen V, Stelzer D, Straßburger S, Fischer D (eds) Proceedings of MKWI2016. Ilmedia, Ilmenau, pp 1031–1040

Walger G (1995) Idealtypen der Unternehmensberatung. In: Walger G (ed) Formen der Unternehmensberatung: Systemische Unternehmensberatung, Organisationsabwicklung, Expertenberatung und gutachterliche Beratungstätigkeit in Theorie und Praxis. Otto Schmidt, Cologne, pp 1–18

Volker Nissen holds the Chair of Information Systems Engineering in Services at Technische Universität Ilmenau, Germany, since 2005. Prior to this, he pursued a consulting career, including positions as manager at IDS Scheer AG, director at DHC GmbH, and CEO of NISSCON Ltd., Germany. In 1994 he received a PhD degree in Economic Sciences with distinction from the University of Goettingen, Germany. His current research interests include the digital transformation of the consulting industry, the management of IT-agility, metaheuristic optimization, and process acceptance research. He is author and editor of 20 books and some 200 other publications, including papers in Business and Information Systems Engineering, Information Systems Frontiers, IEEE Transactions on EC, IEEE Transactions on NN, and Annals of OR.

Jochen Kuhl studied economics with a focus on business informatics in Braunschweig and Göttingen. He obtained his PhD in Business Informatics at the University of Göttingen. Jochen is Managing Director of Dr. Kuhl Unternehmensberatung and specialized in the optimization and digitization of management and business processes in midmarket companies. Furthermore, he is Managing Director of MeyerundKuhl Spezialwäschen GmbH, which is specialized in innovative washing and impregnation processes.

Hendrik Kräft studied Social Sciences (Diplom Soz.-Wirt) with a focus on media and communication in Göttingen. He is a consultant and project manager at the Dr. Kuhl Unternehmensberatung and manages the business field of project management. His focus is the methodical development of project management and the consulting of mid-market customers in the digitization of business processes.

Henry Seifert is a graduate engineer for media technology and since 2011 working as a management consultant. His main focus is on the automotive industry and artificial intelligence, analytics, process optimization and requirements management. He works in projects in the area of sales and after sales processes as well as professional learning. He received a PhD at the Group for Information Systems Engineering in Services at Technische Universität Ilmenau (Prof. Volker Nissen), where he examined the digital transformation in the consulting industry. The goal of his dissertation was to demonstrate the opportunities and limitations of virtualization, as well as the design of artifacts that enable the realization of virtual consulting services.

Jakob Reiter is a Master student of Information Systems Engineering at Technische Universität Ilmenau, Germany. He holds a Bachelor of Science and is currently finishing his Master studies with research on digitalized consulting products at the chair of Prof. Volker Nissen. Besides his study, he works as a freelance web developer.

Jim Eidmann is a specialist in application development at the Dr. Kuhl Unternehmensberatung. His main focus is the development of software prototypes.

Building a Digitally Enabled Future: An Insurance Industry Case Study on Digitalization

Janina Weingarth, Julian Hagenschulte, Nikolaus Schmidt, and Markus Balser

Abstract

(a) **Situation faced**: INSUR is one of the top fifteen insurance companies in Germany. Between 2000 and 2015, the organization focused on (1) external growth through several acquisitions as well as (2) the integration of these acquisitions including the corresponding IT landscape into the overarching organization. From 2016 onwards, INSUR's strategic focus shifted to actively shaping its group's digital journey, including the build-up of new digital capabilities to fulfill the agility and innovation requirements of the business units. INSUR's strategy focused on growth and efficiency gains through digitalization as well as on fostering innovation in developed digital solutions and services.

(b) **Action taken**: At the end of 2015, INSUR's top management started a strategic digital transformation initiative to define the cornerstones of the groups' innovation and digital agenda. This agenda followed six strategic imperatives: (1) creating digital awareness throughout the organization; (2) developing a group-wide common understanding of digitalization and establishing the first digital and innovation strategy; (3) selecting and

J. Weingarth (✉)
University of Cologne, Cologne, Germany
e-mail: weingarth@wiso.uni-koeln.de

J. Hagenschulte
CBRE GmbH, Stuttgart, Germany
e-mail: julian.hagenschulte@cbre.com

N. Schmidt
Accenture GmbH, Düsseldorf, Germany
e-mail: nikolaus.schmidt@accenture.com

M. Balser
Rhön Klinikum AG, Bad Neustadt an der Saale, Germany
e-mail: markus.balser@ieee.org

© Springer International Publishing AG, part of Springer Nature 2019
N. Urbach, M. Röglinger (eds.), *Digitalization Cases*, Management for Professionals, https://doi.org/10.1007/978-3-319-95273-4_13

validating strategic focus areas for digitalization; (4) enlarging the company's digital ecosystem using collaborations with startup accelerators and universities; (5) setting up a digital lab to develop and prototype digital use cases and (6) enhancing and scaling the digital lab towards a digital factory.

(c) **Results achieved**: INSUR successfully initiated its digitalization journey and developed a high-level, group-wide digital and innovation strategy and selected its digital focus topics. Further, it set up an innovation management process and enlarged its digital ecosystem. The digital lab that INSUR started, however, did not take on as well as expected. Realizing that a small incubator is insufficient, INSUR is currently upscaling and transitioning the lab towards an integrated end-to-end digital factory.

(d) **Lessons learned**: While all changes might require some management support, the nature of digitalization requires top management support across all business and functional areas right from the beginning. Even if there are still legacy systems that need to be shut down or renewed, digitalization should be addressed early on while continuing to renovate the IT. Furthermore, fostering cultural change to be an attractive employer for new digital talents, which are required on all levels to make the digital transformation a success, is a key success factor. Finally, handling and actively managing concerns and required cultural change within the organization are paramount.

1 Introduction

Digital technologies have been changing the rules of the game for most industries. For the insurance industry, those changes are particularly challenging because the industry is historically conservative and cautious regarding change. Coming from a business model where risk needs to be hedged and stability over decades is the key to success, moving into the fast-paced, risk-taking world of digitalization is daunting.

However, in competitive markets where new digital business models from InsurTechs and the consumer sector with its built-to-order approaches threaten the traditional insurance market, change cannot be delayed any longer. This is aptly portrayed by the case of INSUR, which we will present in the following.

INSUR is one of the top fifteen insurance companies in Germany. It offers personal, commercial, and industrial insurance as well as re-insurance and is structured as a multinational group with several subsidiaries and business areas. It has grown significantly not only organically but also through consolidations and acquisitions.

At the beginning of 2016, INSUR took the first step towards digitalization and away from primarily consolidating its past. Section 2 starts with an outline of the situation that INSUR faced when it started the first digitalization initiatives. To fully grasp the starting situation, the section describes the years of transformation that the IT function experienced in particular. Several acquisitions left the company with a diverse, decentralized and largely redundant legacy IT. Some of the business units were already running individual digitalization activities; however, none of them were aligned or synchronized. Digitalization efforts thus faced a post-consolidation landscape with a number of siloed digitalization activities requiring alignment, strategic cornerstones and innovation aspirations in order to yield long-term results.

Section 3 shows the actions that INSUR took to start preparing itself for a digital future. With an organization still fatigued from the years of transformation, INSUR did not opt for a large-scale digital transformation but rather for a small "speedboat" approach. Accentuated, top-management-guided actions marked the start of the initiative, for example executing a "Future Day" to spark the spirit of digital innovation or the setup of a digital lab. This and the further results achieved are detailed in Sect. 4. Section 5 draws a conclusion and summarizes INSUR's lessons learned.

2 Situation Faced

To fully understand the starting situation when INSUR embarked on its digitalization journey, we first outline the key elements of the prior IT transformation before summarizing the situation at the beginning of 2016, when the digitalization initiative was started.

INSUR's first decade of the century was marked by growth through acquisitions, requiring intensive integration and transformation efforts. From 2010 onwards, INSUR focused on the integration of subsidiaries and further profitability improvements at the group level. Because heterogeneous, decentralized and legacy IT structures hampered integration efforts, INSUR started IT programs with a focus on the reduction of complexity, consolidation and the modernization of the IT landscape. One of the largest changes was the foundation of an internal IT-service provider and the centralization of most of the group's IT.

The transformation focused on the restructuring and consolidation of the IT landscape and thus provided the technical, structural and financial foundation for the digitalization initiative. It had two focus areas: (1) *infrastructure and IT operations* and (2) and *IT-architecture and IT systems landscape* (see Fig. 1 for an overview). The program followed strict, tightly managed transformation approaches that turned many historically grown structures upside-down.

(1) *Infrastructure and IT operations*:

The IT operations were professionalized (>90% standardization), for example, by the introduction and consistent use of Information Technology Infrastructure Library (ITIL) processes. Furthermore, a well-defined IT location concept was established with different focus areas and clear responsibilities, and a prior redundant service delivery was centralized. Workplace virtualization and automated client systems, including the integration of over 400 applications

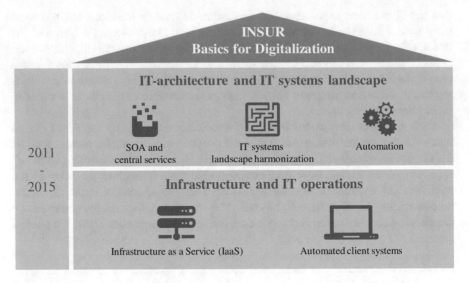

Fig. 1 Overview pre-digitalization transformation

into virtualized Windows 7 and the introduction of follow-me printing, were introduced to offer an accelerated implementation of new solutions. Mobile, decentralized work was enabled through the flexible and secure use of renewed mobile networks. Finally, an infrastructure as a service (IaaS) model was adopted.

(2) *IT-architecture and IT systems landscape*

Most importantly, the fragmented, partially redundant IT system landscape was harmonized. A major first step of the harmonization was the shutdown of over 15% of legacy systems and the introduction of modern standard software including the outsourcing of commodity system elements such as SAP basis. Figure 2 provides an overview of the application clusters and exemplary application sub-clusters, including the percentage expressing the reduction of legacy systems.

Furthermore, essential architectural elements such as service-oriented architecture (SOA) and central services were established. The implementation of a central workflow and process management engine enabled digital business processing, such as the handling of customer documentation with little to no manual intervention. First steps towards a multi-speed IT approach were taken which should enable the combination of fast, digital developments with stable, strictly managed core systems.

In summary, the IT landscape was modernized and largely centralized with some legacy systems and further optimization potential remaining. Central elements of a service-oriented architecture approach existed, however, consistent, group-wide implementation was still ongoing. The former redundant, instable legacy structure

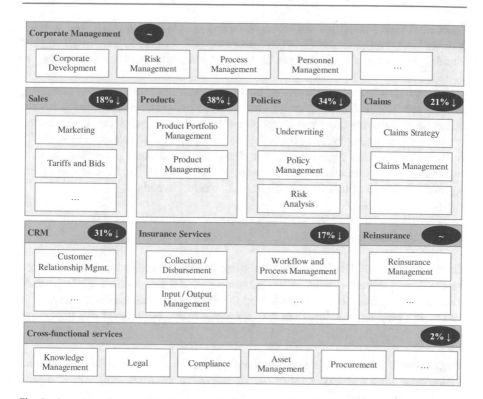

Fig. 2 Overview of application clusters (% indicates reduction of legacy systems)

had been transformed into an organized, lean and stable landscape. However, these optimizations led to a lack in speed and agility, among others due to more standardized, centralized processes and structures. Digitalization now required concerted breakthroughs that allow for fast and flexible implementations.

The organization was also still fatigued from the many years of transformation. While technologies and structures might have been overhauled, a traditional mindset and resistance to change was still prevalent throughout the organization. The digitalization journey had to be about not only technologies and processes but also people and culture.

Until the end of 2015, a structured digitalization approach was not part of the management agenda. However, the first thoughts about digitalization were already prevalent throughout the organization, and several (not or only partly aligned) digital activities had already been started. For example, the enhancement of online sales channels (e.g., price optimization, listing at aggregators such as Check24 etc.) was planned, and the underwriting team was provided with a real-time analytics solution supporting the assessment of risks. Additionally, a digital ecosystem was set up, allowing insurance companies, employers and employees to manage insurance contracts online. Last but not least, several apps were released as part of the individual digital activities, for example an app to submit claims. INSUR was not alone: at that time, almost 50% of Germany's top 500 companies were at the stage of running individual digital projects as shown by a study from Accenture (Meyer 2015).

These individual activities alone, however, could not live up to the increasing market pressure and ever-changing customer needs. Furthermore, they were not adequate to fully leverage the large efficiency and sales gains that digitalization provides the insurance industry according to a study from Bain (Naujoks et al. 2017). Still, no group-wide digital strategy existed, and no central governance unit or unified approach was available. Therefore, at the end of 2015, INSUR's top management decided to explicitly put digitalization on its agenda.

3   Action Taken

By the end of 2015, INSUR's CEO mandated its CIO as well as the COO of its key business units to start a digitalization initiative. Rather than establishing a large-scale project, only a small team was mandated to initiate the digitalization journey.

For this purpose, the digitalization "speedboat" team established five imperative actions:

Imperative 1 *Creation of awareness for digitalization throughout the organization including a powerful kick-start of the digital transformation initiative as a joint business and IT effort.*

To manage a group-wide digitalization initiative, not only did the executive board members need to be aligned, but additionally, the leaders across the organization had to be engaged for the digitalization spirit to trickle down and spread as far as possible. To that end, a "Future Day" was planned with the goal of making digitalization exciting and tangible as well as offering a platform for inspiring interaction among colleagues. More than 20 board members and executives, including the CEO, spent an entire day on digitalization, which clearly prioritized the topic on the management agenda and was a first step on the road towards digitalization.

The day was spent at several stations, where participants could gather hands-on experience and test digital solutions that were either already rolled-out or currently being implemented. The focus was placed on innovative, customer-oriented and efficiency-enhancing solutions. For example, a real-time analysis of user data and digital pricing for motor insurance and the networked geo-data for industrial insurance were shown. For many participants, this was the first time seeing and experiencing digital activities across all business units combined and comprehending the digital potential that already existed.

To include external stimuli as well, several external showcases were shown. These showcases included, for example, the application of drones in industrial insurance and a telematics app. Additionally, internal and external impulse speeches were given.

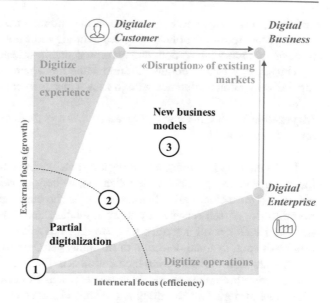

Fig. 3 Digitalization framework, adapted from Accenture Strategy (2015)

Imperative 2 *Development of a group-wide common understanding of digitalization and creation of first digital and innovation strategy.*

In the beginning of 2016, no common understanding of what the "buzzword" digitalization actually meant for INSUR was prevalent. To structure the discussion and the intense stakeholder alignment efforts, the framework depicted in Fig. 3 was used.

The framework distinguishes between digitalization activities that focus on growth, the customer experience (y-axis) and activities that focus on efficiency and the enterprise operations (x-axis) or both (digital business). Activities that fully aim at both, the digital customer and the digital enterprise, result in new digital business models (3) that disrupt existing markets. Activities that focus on either the external or the internal perspective can lead to partial digitalization of a company (2).

While these distinctions might seem trivial, they provided for the first time a common ground to discuss future digitalization initiatives. For example, it was quickly decided that INSUR would not focus on new business models right away but mostly pursue initiatives and projects that focus on digitizing the customer experience or its internal operations.

Based on the framework, a first high-level digitalization and innovation strategy was agreed upon. Taking into account market research, specific levers for digitalization along the value chain, such as call center virtualization and big data fraud management, were identified. These levers were estimated with respect to their EBIT effect and communicated to the business areas as a guideline for their digitalization efforts. Aligned with the overall focus, most levers aimed at the digitalization of the customer interface and internal operations. INSUR planned to take first steps toward identifying new digital business models in cooperation with startup accelerators, which support companies to get access to the international start-up market. Furthermore, human resources policies targeted at hiring more digital natives and at starting to develop a more innovation- and entrepreneurship-oriented working culture.

The strategy further defined an innovation management process that includes a regular innovation conference with top-level management ownership.

Imperative 3 *Selection and validation of strategic focus areas for digitalization via an as-is assessment.*

In the course of defining a new digital strategy, INSUR's management selected three strategic focus areas for digitalization, namely, *portal*, *analytics* and *collaboration*. *Portal* includes all activities regarding the customer interface via an online portal, such as self-services or a web solution for online contract conclusion. *Analytics* includes all activities that use data analytics to improve either internal efficiency such as fraud detection or customer service offerings such as automated claims valuation. *Collaboration* includes all activities that digitally support collaboration between employees and/or customers such as customer consultations via a video tool or digital underwriting and claims management.

As mentioned, dispersed individual digitalization activities were already ongoing throughout the organization. To get an overview of the status-quo and to validate the extent to which the ongoing activities already matched the focus areas, an as-is assessment was conducted. In an executive workshop series across all business units, the current digital activities were compiled and classified according to the digitalization framework and clustered regarding their focus.

Figure 4 shows the results of the digital as-is assessment. 70 digital activities were documented, all of which were classified as a partial digitalization activity. Activities regarding the digital customer experience had a slight majority with approximately 40% of all activities. There were no activities classified as a new digital business model. Approximately 75% of all activities already concerned one of the three focus areas. The rest of the largely dispersed activities were clustered as *other*.

Overall, the assessment provided an overview of INSUR's digital baseline and identified redundancies. The three platforms, portal, analytics and collaboration,

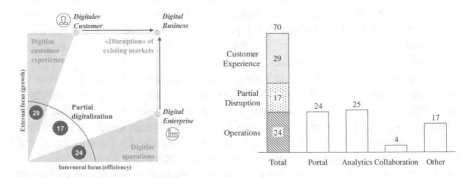

Fig. 4 Overview results of digital as-is assessment

were confirmed as focus topics and were thus used as an input for the following imperatives. However, the fact that 25% of all activities were dispersed and did not have a specific focus underlined the need for an overarching structure, particularly an institutionalized innovation management process to guide further digitalization activities.

Overall, the results of the assessment were used as an input for the next two imperatives: the creation of a digital strategy and the design of a digital lab.

Imperative 4 *Foster own innovation management and enlarge the company's digital ecosystem using collaborations with startup accelerators.*

The as-is assessment had shown that a purely siloed innovation management process can lead to redundancies and a loss of focus. Thus, INSUR decided to set up an overarching innovation management process to structure the steps from idea generation, via evaluation and prioritization of innovations, to selection, implementation and monitoring of innovation measures.

A central innovation management council, led by the group head of strategy, was created. This council was mandated to discuss and evaluate current trends relevant for INSUR and to continuously monitor innovation ideas and measures across all business units. Its initial task was the development of an overarching innovation strategy including the definition of interfaces with the group's digital strategy as well as the development of an innovation award for INSUR. Furthermore, the council was responsible for the consolidated reporting of all innovation topics to INSUR's board of directors.

Regarding innovation, INSUR realized that its own workforce would not be sufficient to generate cutting-edge digitalization innovations. Therefore, the innovation council was also tasked with establishing a structured approach to cooperate with startups and InsurTechs. Specifically, startup accelerators offer a solid digital network, including access to the start-up scene, i.e., young startups or InsurTechs that develop innovative ideas for the insurance and financial services industry. INSUR therefore opted to initiate joint ventures with a selection of startup accelerators and creative agencies. The goal of these joint ventures was to identify disruptive technologies along the insurance value chain to further align the company towards new customer needs (e.g., new channels, automated processes).

Another benefit was the chance to network with young talents from the startup sector or from universities. Furthermore, the joint venture partners helped to gain access to these talent markets with marketing activities such as hackathons. This creates opportunities to recruit the right people for a digital journey, which had so far been an immense challenge for INSUR.

Imperative 5 *Setting up a digital lab to develop and prototype digital use cases in the areas of portal, analytics and collaboration.*

Business and IT agreed on the need for a multi-speed IT operating model. With the traditional IT already in a mature state, INSUR's main concern was the introduction of a "fast lane IT." Considering the multitude of past transformation efforts and the still-high resistance to change, INSUR tried to tackle the fast lane approach with a digital lab as an incubator and accelerator instead of another large reorganization.

The lab was set up as part of a new digitalization group within the IT department. The group's main responsibilities were the development of capabilities that drive digital transformation. For example, it should establish methodological competencies such as design thinking and prototyping, as well as competencies regarding technologies such as the Internet of Things (IoT) and cloud services. Last but not least it should foster interdisciplinary cooperation between the different business areas and IT.

These new capabilities should then be concentrated in the digital lab as the core incubator and multiplier of the digital transformation. The goal was to advance the digitalization of both the customer interface and internal operations and to enable innovations from the initial idea up to a first prototype/minimal viable product. It was also intended to be the starting point and accelerator for agile development practices.

The digital lab started with approximately ten employees, all of whom were knowledgeable in agile and innovation methodologies. INSUR staffed the lab with some of its best IT employees and hired some new employees to ensure a high-quality skillset.

Imperative 6 *Enhancing and scaling the digital lab towards a digital factory.*

The sixth imperative was not developed from the onset of the digital transformation initiative but rather several months down the road, when INSUR realized that the lab did not achieve the results it had hoped for. The lab was intended to be the proof of concept for a new way of working, but it resulted in being the proof of concept that small changes do not always create big waves (for details, see Result 5 in Sect. 4). INSUR thus decided to upscale the digital lab towards a digital factory.

The digital factory should take the first steps of the digital lab to the next level and provide a stronger lever to promote the digital transformation throughout the organization. Due to personnel availability and start-up proximity, Berlin was chosen as the target location for the digital factory assuming that the pilot phase with the new location would be successfully concluded. The declared goal was to create a place of innovation and entrepreneurship with a start-up culture rather than a historically cautious insurance culture.

Also, the factory should not only be a place where methodologies such as design thinking are used and developed, but also a place from which the first agile development projects beyond prototyping would be started. This should lead to much faster times to market with minimum viable products for instant customer feedback.

Because a quick scaling with only internal resources would not have been possible, external partners were chosen to complement the team from the digital lab, which served as a starting point for the digital factory.

At the time of writing, the digital factory was still in the initiation phase and not yet fully operational.

4   Results Achieved

Now, 2 years after INSUR kicked off its digitalization initiative, several results have been achieved, which are presented in the following.

Result 1 *"Future Day" was a successful event, radiating across the entire organization and kicking off the digitalization journey.*

The "Future Day" transpired in the beginning of 2016. Compared with the market, this is a late start into the digitalization journey. The event itself was successful, with positive reactions across all participants. As the top-level management does not have day-to-day contact with the different digital solutions, the tangibility of the activities presented made a big difference compared with a regular strategy workshop. The participants experienced the benefits of the solutions first hand and were positively surprised by the multitude of activities already ongoing throughout the organization.

After the "Future Day," the CEO, CIO and COOs gave their combined sponsorship for the upcoming digital transformation and put digitalization on top of their own, as well as their executives', agenda. The day offered a powerful kick-start to the digital transformation and sparked a group-wide digital spirit.

In the following, two representative feedback examples are given (translated from German):

> Congratulations to the different speakers; they were clearly whole-heartedly engaged. It was a great opportunity to network with my colleagues and agree upon follow-ons for specific digitalization topics.

> The Future Day exceeded my expectations by far and clearly improved my opinion regarding the progressiveness of our IT. We should use the momentum of the Future Day and use disruptive technologies to catch up to the market. However, this includes doing our homework regarding our policy management systems.

Although the event itself was successful, the momentum it created was not fully used. For example, no central budget for a larger digital transformation program was provided and the digitalization transformation continued to be driven by the small "speedboat" team.

Result 2 *INSUR developed a high-level, group-wide digital and innovation strategy.*

The digital and innovation strategy is based on a clear definition of "digital" that has been accepted across the organization. While this might seem like a small achievement, the common terms and understanding were crucial for all following discussions and for the remaining content of the digital strategy. A recent Gartner study confirms that the industry still struggles to establish a common understanding of "digital insurance" and recommends a company-specific definition of the term with IT and all business stakeholders (Weiss and Harris-Ferrante 2017). Based on the common understanding and the as-is assessment, INSUR confirmed its digital focus topics for the near-/mid-term future, namely, portal, analytics, and collaboration.

Further, the strategy clearly defines EBIT targets for high-level digital levers in each business area. The levers have been created based on market research as well as already ongoing digital activities and are therefore well targeted to the individual business situations. On the one hand, this quantifies the outcomes expected from digitalization and thus sets goals for the different business areas while on the other hand, it leaves enough room regarding the specific digital content.

A digital strategy with both business and IT ownership is an achievement. However, the strategy remains at a very high level and does not set many specific goals except for the EBIT targets. The fact that the individual business areas are solely responsible for implementing the digital levers and that there is no overarching governance could lead to diverging outcomes. Some of the diverging tendencies might be caught by a solid innovation management process, but only time can tell whether the strategy sets sufficient impulses as well as boundaries to successfully guide the digitalization journey.

Result 3 *INSUR obtained an overview of all its digital activities with the help of an as-is assessment.*

The as-is assessment resulted in an overview and a baseline of the current state of digitalization of INSUR. It documented, classified and characterized all digital activities and thereby confirmed the digital focus topics of portal, analytics and collaboration. Most importantly, it became apparent that INSUR was already pursuing digitalization initiatives, albeit in an unstructured way, partially redundant and without an overarching governance. This finding strongly supported the need for a group-wide innovation process, which had already been documented in the digital and innovation strategy.

Apart from these general findings, the results from the as-is assessment were not put to any specific use. For example, the maturity of the digital activities was estimated; however, this information has not been analyzed in detail or used in any of the following activities.

Result 4 *INSUR established an innovation management process and enlarged its digital ecosystem.*

An important result of INSUR's digital journey is the establishment of an innovation management (IM) process and governance. A central element of the IM governance is the innovation council that meets every three months. Every business unit has selected one innovation spokesperson to represent the interests of the business unit in the innovation management council. The main task of the innovation council is the pre-analysis and selection of innovation topics with an overarching relevance to business units. All identified topics are documented in innovation reports and regularly presented to INSUR's management board. The board then selects topics for a detailed analysis including a high-level technical concept and business case. As soon as these inputs are developed by the council, they are again presented to the board for a final selection and prioritization of ideas. Next, all selected ideas are handed over to the portfolio management, which is tasked with the preparation of the selected ideas for development and implementation (e.g., using the digital lab). During and after implementation, innovation control tracks to what extent the expected benefits have been achieved.

The IM process itself is designed in a way that has the potential to integrate activities from all business units and that consistently keeps innovation on the top management agenda. However, the process by itself does not create or implement innovations. Regardless of how good the process itself might be, without relevant innovations or without the capabilities to implement these innovations, the process will yield no value. As the process has just recently been set up, the results cannot yet be judged.

To foster innovations from outside its own workforce, INSUR has been cooperating with two leading international startup accelerators since 2016, thereby obtaining access to a worldwide network of startups and other leading digital players in the insurance industry. Both partners are continuously screening startups worldwide. INSUR is part of the process to select promising startups for the mentoring programs of the accelerators.

Using these mentoring programs, the selected startups receive the chance to obtain professional support and guidance to further develop their business model. In addition to joint projects, INSUR and the startups will identify potential joint ventures or joint investments.

Result 5 *A digital lab was established to promote collaborative ideation and prototyping of digital use cases.*

The digital lab was introduced as a dedicated, institutionalized way to foster digitalization and innovation across the entire organization. Furthermore, it is intended to serve as the owner for the advancement of the three digital focus topics: portal, analytics and collaboration. As one of the specific results, the lab helped to quickly develop a reusable IT platform for customer portals, which was already tested by customers and released in one business unit. Moreover, it introduced new methodologies such as design thinking and rapid prototyping to foster collaboration between business and IT within the digital projects.

However, the lab did not establish itself as well as INSUR's management had hoped for because reaching the defined goals of the digital lab posed several challenges. For one, the ways of working in an innovative setting (design thinking, customer centricity, interdisciplinary collaboration etc.) differ immensely from

INSUR's standard way of working and not many employees were able to adjust as quickly as expected. Furthermore, the original innovation focus was somewhat undermined by the specific, pre-defined focus of many of the lab's projects. The overarching importance and high integration requirements of some of the projects caused significant friction due to the limited scale and equipment of the lab. Additionally, there were only limited possibilities for scaling because projects of the lab consistently faced internal resistance, which could only be resolved with substantial management support.

Overall, it became apparent that a small lab with only approximately ten employees and without strong connections within the organization does not provide the desired results. This was partially caused by the fact that the lab was part of the IT department and not a truly shared business-IT unit; thus, it was not always seen to be at eye level with the business department. Rather, the lab was treated as a high-quality IT service provider but not a common innovation incubator. Additionally, the exclusive consideration of front-end or user experience issues proved to be inadequate. The missing end-to-end responsibility was heavily reducing development speed, productivity and thus, the time to market of new ideas. All of these learnings have been integrated into the design of the digital factory, which is outlined in the following section.

Result 6 *The transition from a digital lab to a digital factory was started.*

In light of the experiences with the digital lab, INSUR decided to update the lab towards a large-scale, end-to-end integrated digital factory, a transformation that is still ongoing. Figure 5 provides an overview of the vertical integration of the factory compared with the lab. The vertical integration of the digital factory spans from user experience design down to application-operations. Only backend capabilities remain in the line organization. This is substantially different the prior digital lab, which only addressed front-end development.

The organizational structure of the digital factory is shown in Fig. 6. The matrix organization is a combination of functions (horizontal columns) and undertakings (vertical columns). The functions comprise what was previously the digital lab, front-end and sales, platforms and operations. The digital lab is responsible for topics such as digital initiatives, tech-stack definitions, and innovation methodologies. Front-end and sales is responsible for topics such as maintenance and change-management of existing systems as well as the implementation of new systems. The platform function is responsible for topics such as the management of standard software and the operations function is responsible for topics such as bundling the running of existing and new applications, container orchestration etc.

The undertakings are subdivided into the categories "innovate the business" and "run the business". The main advantage of this structure is the possibility to scale the factory over time. With the shutdown of more legacy systems and the introduction of DevOps, INSUR expects that many of the resources currently focused on legacy-related topics can be transferred to new innovative topics. This shift will entail extensive training of existing employees or the hiring of new employees.

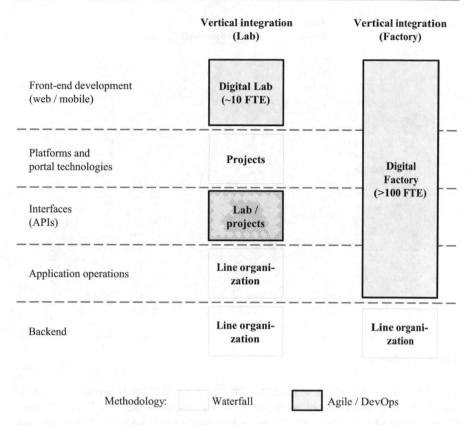

Fig. 5 Enhancement of digital lab towards digital factory

Furthermore, the factory includes an agile academy where the resources from other departments will be continuously trained regarding agile technologies and methods to foster change within the whole organization.

To ensure that the digital factory integrates the learnings from the digital lab and becomes a successful cornerstone of INSUR's digitalization, a set of premises has been defined. For one, dependencies are to be reduced by the bundling of required functions in one agile unit. This goes hand in hand with an end-to-end delivery responsibility created by integrating application development and application operations into one single unit. Furthermore, focus has been placed on a lean organization and the support of agile, lean development concepts within the unit.

Instead of small, mostly internal teams, intensified external support was chosen to create a stronger multiplier effect and push the establishment of the digital factory. The setup was designed to achieve projects with high speed and deliver usable results within shorter timeframes.

At the point of writing, the setup of the digital factory was validated with a first platform and a CDO role has been established to increase Business-IT alignment.

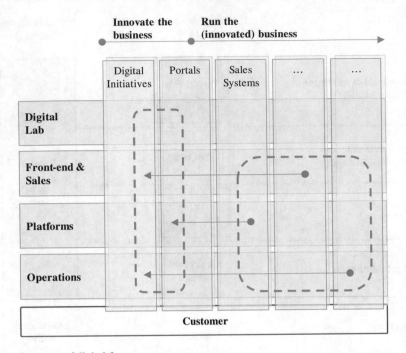

Fig. 6 Structure of digital factory

However, this is not adequate to anchor the digital lab within the organization and to substantially increase the momentum of the digitalization for a digital transformation, particularly, because INSUR still significantly relies on external support. The factory must be consistently used and scaled up significantly with internal resources to stabilize the "fast lane." Last but not least, INSUR must become accustomed to not assigning resources to projects one hundred percent of the time but rather also dedicate time and resources to innovation activities.

5   Lessons Learned

The insurance industry has traditionally been conservative and digital advances have been slow. INSUR does not stand out as an industry laggard but rather aptly reflects the issues that many other industry players face. INSUR is at the beginning of its digital transformation journey as along with several of its competitors. After the first 2 years into the process, several lessons have been learned that can help INSUR with its next steps as well as other companies who face a comparable situation.

Ensure management buy-in for the digital journey right from the beginning
Management buy-in might be an obvious success factor for any change initiative, but it is nevertheless also true for a digital transformation. While some changes might

only require management support for their specific line of business, digitalization spans across all departments and functions. Therefore, not only the CIO but also the CDO, CEO, and COO need to be fully committed to a digital transformation and agree on the most important aspects as it will require company-wide budgeting, personnel and determination. Furthermore, the roles of top management within a new digital organization should be transparent from the beginning. In particular, the role of the CIO is important and needs to develop from a pure IT/technical leadership perspective towards a shared business perspective. Management support is not a one-shot game; it should be kept up throughout the entire transformation.

Regarding its role as the head of IT, the CIO should define and promote a clear vision for the IT organization. For example, if a multi-speed approach is chosen, the CIO should draft a compelling journey for building a "fast-lane" capability while updating the IT core where necessary to enable long-term digitalization goals. Concerning the role as a business leader, the CIO should develop a strategic vision of how digital technologies will transform the business and create a plan for how the business can utilize those technologies (Harris-Ferrante 2017). Right from the beginning, momentum should be created with a kick-off that includes all relevant stakeholders and sparks excitement for digitalization throughout the organization.

Do not fixate on fixing the past but rather start digitalization early on while continuing to renovate and clean up your IT
A truly digital company cannot exclusively be based on a legacy IT. However, if consolidation efforts take too long, important first steps toward digitalization might be missed. The current speed of change and technological disruption are faster than any consolidation project could ever be. It is thus advisable to start digitalization efforts early on, for example, with a multi-speed approach, where small digital advances can first be made in a lab environment while at the same time the renovation of the legacy IT is continued. To successfully move on from the early lab stages, important factors are scaling resources, suitable platforms such as cloud technologies, DevOps processes and creating a digital culture.

Regarding IT consolidation, the focus should be placed on an infrastructure and architecture that creates room for digitalization. The consolidation should increase IT efficiency to free funds for reinvestment into digitalization activities ("New IT"). After the consolidation, the IT landscape should be modular and largely decoupled with clear interfaces for flexible integration of data and functionalities, using standards such as microservices. The renewed infrastructure should be scalable and based on service cloud technologies to foster speed and agility. Finally, to prepare for digitalization, the IT department needs to build up core capabilities such as a central database and analytics management.

When heading down the road of digitalization, clearly define areas within business and IT where stability is king and failure is not an option ("slow lane"). On the other hand, be clear where "new" ways of working are paramount and trial-and-error in small, iterative steps are explicitly mandated. This "fast lane" should be based on human-centered design and prototype-based development with early and continuous involvement of the customer as well as IT operations. To this end, siloes need to be broken down, enabling DevOps approaches for fast development cycles. This should be fostered by a high degree of automation with continuous integration and end-to-end tool support.

Introduce and promote the new digitalization role of IT
It is crucial that the CIO (organization) understands new technologies and acts as a driver towards the business units. Disruptive technologies should be identified and evaluated via standard processes and then fed into the innovation cycle. The CIO should proactively support all successful business and IT innovations to foster an innovation-focused culture. A digital lab can serve as an incubator for digitalization, focusing on generating innovative ideas in collaboration with the business units and developing minimum viable products (products with enough features to satisfy early customers and to provide feedback for potential future features). Emphasis should be placed on quick results and clear value for the business, for example, via reusable platforms. Depending on the company's structure and culture, an incubator might not be adequate to initiate change, and a larger-scaled approach may be required to progress from experimentation to market-ready products.

Educating IT employees in business processes and customer journeys is essential to enable smooth cooperation and value-add driven by the IT department. The business-IT interface should be optimized by introducing truly mixed teams along agile development models. Furthermore, IT should not only "be reorganized" but also reorganize itself, and IT needs to be knowledgeable in new approaches such as DevOps, Scrum, or design thinking.

A digitalization journey is a long-term challenge and quick, tangible results especially in the initiation phase are crucial to create long-term stamina. The IT needs to be one of the drivers of quick results and move away from its former role as a pure service provider that is always a little too slow and a little too expensive. IT architecture and IT operating models need to be advanced to meet ever-increasing implementation speed requirements. Speedboats from a digital factory can serve as lighthouse projects and thereby create momentum throughout the organization.

Foster cultural change to be an attractive employer for new digital talents, who are required on all levels to make the digital transformation a success
No matter how hard cultural change is and no matter how little attention "soft" factors have received so far—a digital transformation without cultural change and digitally skilled employees will inevitably fail. This is particularly important for insurance companies, who are not always attractive enough for the digital talents that bring in the new required skills around agile methods etc. INSUR might have realized the importance of people and culture, but it has not reacted quickly enough. The current focus has now been shifted towards the re-skilling and empowerment of employees, for example, via the agile academy.

The enablement of innovations, an error-accepting culture and values such as result orientation, continuous learning, and entrepreneurial thinking, must be on top of the priority list. A few brochures and posters are not sufficient; a mindset and "DNA" change is necessary to break up siloed structures and enable seamless integration of business and IT in all digital endeavors. All actions should be directed toward the customer and proactivity, responsibility, and customer relevance need to be values lived by all employees.

Knowledge is power; not only should IT employees be knowledgeable in business processes but also business needs to understand the basics about relevant technologies. "TechXperts", technology-savvy business employees, can serve as multipliers.

The top management must have a clear vision of where it wants its culture and organizational structure to go. The future lies in liquid, self-organizing structures with distributed power, with only some hierarchical structures left for stability and efficiency. Each company should decide how far down this road it wants to go and which hard changes it needs to face to get there.

Only a few large, well-established companies have sufficient digital potential among their own employees and the infusion of new talent is indispensable. Unfortunately, hiring new, digital talent can be a "chicken-and-egg problem." Few digital talents want to work for a company with outdated structures and a rigid culture, but cultural change is hard without new talent from the market. Companies should try to hire "digital heroes" first who are willing to break down cultural walls in exchange for a fast, flexible and custom-fit career. Most managers will have to step far out of their own comfort zone to manage the balancing act between what is customary and where the company wants to go.

Cope with and actively manage concerns and required cultural change within your organization

The cultural change will be harder than any other part of the transformation. Resistance and fear will be widespread among those recognizing that they do not naturally fit into the new world. Executives across all levels of hierarchy should be aware and trained to address those left behind. Not everyone will be able to partake in the digital journey, and a concept for those employees should be available. Not all employees need to change completely, and a coexistence of old and new culture is possible; however, it needs to be managed wisely. Executives should lead open and honest conversations and try to resolve conflict head-on rather than letting it simmer. If the majority of employees do not want to go along with the digital change, the resistance can be hard to overcome.

Leadership needs to come out of its comfort zone (i.e., both hard and soft skills such as negotiation, influence, collaboration, and change management skills are needed) as they are required to lead, promote and support the creation of new digital capabilities (e.g., digital lab), resulting in new value for the enterprise stakeholders.

In particular, managing the fears and concerns, e.g., from the "slow lane organization", of becoming obsolete are very important because this part of the organization is often driving the reaction of rejection of the newly developed digital capabilities (e.g., digital lab).

References

Accenture Strategy A (2015) Digitalization framework – three lenses model. Accenture internal

Harris-Ferrante K (2017) The top 10 digital insurance IT imperatives for ensuring IT agility and flexibility. https://www.gartner.com/document/3672921. Accessed 29 Sept 2017

Meyer T (2015) Digitizing insurance: recognizing the roadblocks. http://insuranceblog.accenture.com/digitizing-insurance-recognizing-the-roadblocks. Accessed 15 Sept 2017

Naujoks H, Mueller F, Kotalakidis N (2017) Digitalization in insurance: the multibillion dollar opportunity. http://www.bain.com/publications/articles/digitalization-in-insurance.aspx. Accessed 11 Sept 2017

Weiss J, Harris-Ferrante K (2017) Defining 'digital insurance' beyond the buzzword. https://www.gartner.com/document/2973118. Accessed 23 Sept 2017

Janina Weingarth is a Manager at Accenture Strategy and has over 7 years of experience in advising c-level clients regarding their IT operating model and digital transformation. Her area of expertise are strategies for the agile enterprise, about which she is currently also doing her PhD at the University of Cologne. Further, she is in training to become an Integral Business Coach at the Coaching Center Berlin to advise clients on agile enterprise transformation from a consulting, academic and individual point of view.

Julian Hagenschulte is Director at CBRE, leading the Digital Advisory business line. He gained over 8 years of experience in strategy consulting at Accenture, advising clients on the c-level about Digital Business Models, Digital Strategy and Digital Transformation. Julian's track record includes projects in the Financial Services and Corporate Real Estate industry. Julian is especially passionate about disruptive technologies and how they influence companies' organizations. He enabled the enterprise digitalization of leading global companies e.g. by shaping digital strategies, managing digital transformation journeys and providing organizations with industry trend know-how.

Nikolaus Schmidt is a Senior Manager in the Financial Services practice group within Accenture. He leads the Financial Services Cloud Enablement offering group for Germany, Austria and Switzerland. In addition, he owns lectureships in information systems at the University of Cologne and the Frankfurt University of Applied Science. Nikolaus holds a PhD in information system from the University of Cologne. His academic and personal interests evolve around the topics digital transformation through emerging technologies, cloud implementation in financial services and IT sourcing strategy.

Markus Balser was a Managing Director in Accenture's Technology Strategy practice and is now CIO of a German hospital chain. During his time with Accenture he led the Enterprise Architecture and Application Strategy capability domain for the German speaking countries. During his career, Markus has advised clients from various industries along the whole IT value chain—from IT-Strategy to large-scale IT transformation efforts. For the past decade Markus has almost exclusively focused on Financial Services—Insurance where he advised clients how to re-align, modernize and transform their application landscapes, and hence overcome legacy and enable their transformation towards digital capabilities.

Part III

Digital Transformation

Digital Transformation of ABB Through Platforms: The Emergence of Hybrid Architecture in Process Automation

Johan Sandberg, Jonny Holmström, and Kalle Lyytinen

Abstract

(a) **Situation faced**: ABB faced four decades of successive digitization of core technology in the process automation business, i.e., platform technology for process control. The infusion of digital technology into the physical production environment generated recurrent disruptions of the business model calling for drastic adjustments that lead to an emergent transformation process. Digitization of ABB's business scaled and traversed multiple social and technical settings whereby the platform evolved from product-focused into sustaining a digital ecosystem comprising a complex system of actors and value generation processes.

(b) **Action taken**: Successive digitization with four distinct strategic foci; (1) replacement of analogue equipment for digitally enabled efficiency in restricted and well defined products and processes, (2) internal integration of information systems for efficiency in maintenance and engineering, (3) open and semi-open boundary resources for improved data integration and information services with critical partners, and (4) orchestration and adaptation of externally induced technical innovation on the platform to enable data-driven operations.

(c) **Results achieved**: ABB transformed their operations and successfully adapted to digital disruption by adopting new business models. The company managed the threat of digital disruption by newcomers and incumbents in the software industry, despite the constant dissolution of product

J. Sandberg (✉) · J. Holmström
Umeå University, Umeå, Sweden
e-mail: johan.sandberg@umu.se; jonny.holmstrom@umu.se

K. Lyytinen
Case Western Reserve University, Cleveland, OH, USA
e-mail: kalle@case.edu

© Springer International Publishing AG, part of Springer Nature 2019
N. Urbach, M. Röglinger (eds.), *Digitalization Cases*, Management for Professionals, https://doi.org/10.1007/978-3-319-95273-4_14

boundaries and the risk of unbundling of value creation. ABB is now a global leader in the process automation industry, and the digital agenda and capabilities have been integrated into the mission and business model.

(d) **Lessons learned**: (1) Physical and digital architecture enables different dynamics (episodic change vs. emergence), hybrid architecture is subject to clashes between these logics. (2) Digitalization is cumulative and emergent. In this case, it happened across four phases categorized by shifts in functional levels, decision rights, combinatorial options, boundary configurations and value propositions. (3) Since digitalization inverts the organization's strategic emphasis, collaboration across boundaries becomes a pivotal capability to succeed. (4) Through new functionality and more sophisticated responses, digitalization increases organizational capacity to deal with complexity, but also triggers new types of stimuli. (5) When faced with significant tensions, signals from management generate amplifying deviation loops with unexpected consequences (butterfly effect).

1   Introduction

The compound effects of digital technologies are fundamentally reforming organizations across many industries, a process often referred to as digital transformation (e.g., Agarwal et al. 2010). Digital transformation describes the realization of new business models, caused by technology-induced change, that substantially deviate from the established organizational logic. It embraces the necessary goal-oriented organizational, processual, and technological transformation for organizations to succeed in the digital age. Such change is radical by nature and contests an organization's vision, mission, strategy, and operating philosophy (Seo et al. 2004). These fundamental shifts are spurred by the technical process of digitization, defined as "the encoding of analog information into digital format" (Yoo et al. 2010, p. 725), and the exponential improvements of capacity in digital technologies.[1] Over time, the new set of available technologies and resultant options for action generate new business logic regarding the speed of decision making, scale and scope of strategy, and sources of value creation that organizations need to adapt to (Bharadwaj et al. 2013). Thus, effects of digitization become established through digitalization, "a sociotechnical process of applying digitizing techniques to broader social and institutional contexts" (Tilson et al. 2010, p. 749).

---

[1]In the semiconductor industry, this process is often referred to as Moore's law. Similar developments can be seen across other computer components such as storage and transmission capacity.

During the last decades, a new set of industrial products has emerged in which physical and digital components (and associated functionalities) are increasingly integrated. Such platforms can be described as a hybrid as their defining characteristic is the intermingling of modular physical components with digital functionality to increase their variability and evolvability. Examples include power transmission and exhaust systems for engines (Lee and Berente 2012), process automation systems, and smart cities (Desouza and Bhagwatwar 2012). In these platforms, states of the physical world are continually mapped to digital representations (using sensors embedded in physical components) then the world is operated and controlled through a set of actuators (digital to analog converters). This combination necessitates the integration of design and governance principles associated with both physical and digital platforms, which generates tensions when the two architectures need to be combined.

We examine successive digitization over four decades of automation platforms for industrial processes and the resultant organizational transformation of the provider ABB. We study the evolution of the process control system offerings from ABB, extending from the 1980s to the current version of their digital platform. We mainly analyze how the functionality of the control system, firmly grounded in the physical production process, gradually expanded and simultaneously embraced architectural principles that followed digital system design such as loose coupling, fluid boundaries, and adaptability. While the system was initially designed exclusively to control physical production equipment with long life cycles, its later evolution and incarnations have added novel digital functionality to the platform and radically increased its complexity. As the platform grew in scale and evolved in type, it came to play a significant role in ABB's transformation during the years around the millennium shift as it dissolved product boundaries and enabled a new organizing logic for value creation.

This process occurred across four phases distinguished by increasing digital capacity in the platform versions. While the first two versions induced continuous change patterns and incremental efficiency improvements in ABB's practices, the third version instigated radical change by largely dissolving existing technical product boundaries and thus, challenging organizational boundaries as well as the identity of the firm. After some years of exploring the available strategic options (Sandberg et al. 2014), ABB consolidated their core business and focused their efforts on building capacity to translate the digital innovation logic into industrial contexts. In the following, we first describe the initiating conditions concerning the first two digitization phases (the Master and the Advant platform) that lead up the situation faced. We then outline the actions taken as the company explored the new platform boundaries, enabled by distinct architectural principles in phase three (the AIP platform). Finally, we analyze the results achieved in phase four (800xA) and identify lessons learned.

PLATFORM EVOLUTION

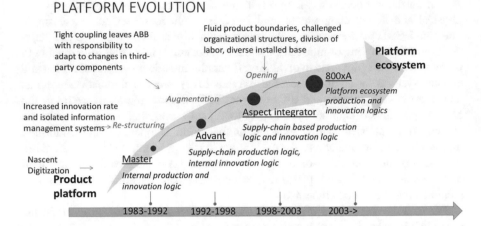

Fig. 1 The digitalization process

2   Situation Faced

By the end of the millennium, the increasing digitalization of organizational practices gained momentum in the process automation industry. Consequently, ABB faced the challenge to make the transition into a digital innovation logic involving distinct capabilities, focus, collaborations and governance measures (Svahn et al. 2017). The increased digitalization was made possible by the emergence of the Industrial Internet of Things that drove the next generation of process automation. Underlying the transition in focal concerns was an ongoing successive digitization process with four distinct strategic foci; (1) replacement of analogue equipment for digitally enabled efficiency in restricted and well-defined products and processes, (2) internal integration of information systems for efficiency in maintenance and engineering, (3) open and semi-open boundary resources for improved data integration and information services, and (4) orchestration and adaptation of externally induced technical innovation to enable data-driven operations. This process is illustrated in Fig. 1.

In the following, we first briefly describe the context and characteristics of distributed control systems for process automation and then provide an overview of the initiating conditions, and the evolution of the process control system offerings from ABB.

The Context: Distributed Control Systems for Process Automation

Distributed control systems are used to automate complex industrial processes within industries, such as mining, pulp, oil, and nuclear energy. These use contexts are characterized by the use of heavy machinery and extreme production environments regarding, for instance, intense noise, heat, dirt, vibrations. Consequently, high reliability in platform performance is critical. While industrial processes are managed through extensive digital capabilities, the actual processes remain very much dependent on physical equipment.

Contemporary distributed control systems are built up of interconnected digital processing units that steer a dynamic manufacturing process (as compared to a discrete one) based on events. These systems can be represented in layers, and they are distributed in the sense that the controller elements are not centralized. Instead, they are located in the production environment and steers a restricted part of the process. Communication networks connect these controller elements for monitoring and coordination purposes. Data is integrated into the distributed control systems that both controls production according to programmed logic and offers monitoring services for operators. At the lowest level of the system, the process level, sensors and actuators record signals and transmit them to controllers in real time. Based on these signals, controllers respond according to the preprogrammed logic and instruct actuators to execute commands that change the process. All of this happens in milliseconds, as the system must respond to process changes swiftly. Modern control systems also communicate with enterprise applications on issues, such as inventory, produced volumes, maintenance orders, etc. To provide such integration without compromising security, systems are often designed with a demilitarized zone (DMZ) where data and services can be exchanged. Table 1 provides an overview of the functional hierarchy of these systems.

Early analog control systems were relay-based and steered manually by switching currents, for example pushing buttons on large instrument panels that cut or activated electrical currents to production equipment. System and process states were represented by light bulbs on large instrument panels, which in some cases covered all of a massive wall. Relay-based control systems had limited adaptability since their logics were hard-wired into the physical designs. Large systems required a lot of space and cabling, and they could only be changed by physically re-wiring connections. Therefore, physical restrictions such as availability of space and information on the system's structure substantially limited the scope for change and modification. Also, documentation processes were costly and often inadequate, leading to high maintenance costs. A shift towards more sophisticated functional demands in the late 1970s and early 1980s also amplified the systems' complexity, increasing costs of their adaptation and maintenance. During this period, digital technology started to have a significant impact on automation control system design. As digital technology became cheaper and more advanced, it developed into a viable alternative to relay-based systems for processes with non-trivial functional requirements.

Table 1 Functional model of process production systems: Purdue reference model as applied in ISA-99

Zone	Layer	Description
Enterprise zone	Level 5: Enterprise network	Centralized IT systems and functions, enterprise resource management, business-to-business and business-to-customer services
	Level 4: Site business planning	Extension of the enterprise network, basic business administration performed through standard IT services. Access to internet, e-mail and enterprise applications such as SAP. Non-critical plant systems such as manufacturing execution systems and plant reporting such as inventory
Demilitarized zone: Provides a buffer zone where services and data can be shared between manufacturing and enterprise zones		
Manufacturing zone	Level 3: Site manufacturing operations and control	The highest level of the distributed control system, manages plant-wide automation functions. Reporting such as cycle times and predictive maintenance, detailed production scheduling, asset and material management, control room workstations, patch launch server, file server. Domain services such as Active Directory, DHCP, DNS, WINS, NTP. The staging area for changes in the manufacturing zone and share data and applications through the DMZ. These applications are primarily based on standard computing equipment and operating systems, hence they tend to be implemented and supported by personnel with IT skill set
	Level 2: Area supervisory control	Applications and functions associated with supervision and operation of each area such s operator interfaces, alarms, control room workstation. Communicates with controller in level 1 and share data with level 3 and/or level 4 and 5 through the DMZ
	Level 1: Basic process control	Controllers that steer automation of process based on input from level 0
	Level 0: Process	Input and output units such as sensors, actuators that measures and perform the functions of the manufacturing system. Control engineers typically design and implement solutions that often remain unaltered for an extended period

Phase 1: The Master Platform 1983–1992

In 1983, Asea,[2] released the Master product platform with a modular architecture and digital components in the process (basic process control, and area supervisory

---

[2]A Swedish electrical engineering company that came to merge with the Swiss Brown Boveri to form ABB.

control levels). The Master product family, which was released in 1983, was ABB's first step towards a unified platform for process automation. The Master system was centered on digital PLC systems and microcomputers. Digitizing the control layer de-coupled control of physical machinery from the actual wiring, as a result, the design of the logic for process automation systems was done by adapting the software. The primary drivers for introducing digital technology were increased standardization and re-use of physical modules and interfaces.

The Master product family digitized steering of physical production equipment and provided significant advantages by reducing technological complexity, hence simplifying maintenance, adaptations, and capacity extension. By replacing physical hard-wiring of logic with programmable software, the physical design was increasingly standardized. Standardization of components and modularization, enabled by replacing analog capabilities with digital ones, allowed both ABB and customers to streamline current operations without severely affecting existing social structures and organizations. Large portions of the system were custom built by ABB. For example, they developed the operating system, database, hardware, and software for the graphical interface internally. The in-house production allowed ABB to take a user-oriented approach to product design. Architectural changes were aimed at using existing physical production equipment more efficiently.

Phase 2: Base Service Digitization and Integration 1992–1998
As ABB and customers started to appreciate potential benefits from sharing information throughout processes and organizations, openness became a factor. To leverage substantially improved computing capabilities in the IT industry, and to increase re-use of components in layer two and three, ABB released the object-oriented Advant platform in 1992. While the Master product family allowed re-use of engineering solutions for physical coupling, and digitized level 1 basic process control, all commissioning of automation systems regarding representations and logical design was done from scratch. When adding layers, and hence expanding the platform upwards in the process automation hierarchy, ABB faced crucial decisions concerning sourcing strategies (i.e., what to produce in-house and what to procure from suppliers).

While ABB developed most of the components in-house for the Master product family, it became increasingly clear this was not a sustainable strategy. The IT industry was evolving rapidly in the late eighties and early nineties both regarding business models and technological performance and to remain competitive, ABB needed to tap into this innovation. ABB's solution was to use Unix as operating system and hardware from Hewlett Packard in their workstations. More importantly, ABB decided to increase the use of open standards widely applied in the IT industry and develop an object-oriented architecture that integrated data into a common database. Compared to the Master product family that mainly standardized the lower levels of process automation systems, ABB now sought to re-use both externally developed technology and in-house developed engineering solutions, such as libraries. Consequentially, the technology became more intimately connected with the development of the general-purpose IT industry.

Advant became a success; from 1992 to 1994 ABB doubled their market share. Integration was a crucial concept in developing Advant, and it was implemented through standardization of system design and physical and logical interfaces. The technological structure was designed with a set of stable modules necessary for all installations that could be integrated with a large number of add-on modules. Regarding functionality, the platform promised increased integration both for physical interfaces but also in regards to information sharing across boundaries at the production plant.

The most significant new functional feature implemented in the Advant platform was arguably simplified engineering. The object-oriented architecture increased integration and re-use of data, and modules with function blocks and process graphics reduced the need for programming logic. The system was also capable of self-configuration by recognizing newly added stations without input from engineers. The object-oriented architecture, automatic adoption of new units, and, separation of services from devices enabled systems to be extended and reconfigured without having to hard-code the configuration from scratch. Through these functions, the Advant platform introduced the idea of re-using digital resources in the engineering of production automation. More importantly, it exposed ABB to a new digital innovation logic.

3   Action Taken

Phase 3: Decoupling Service and Content 1998–2003
In the years following the release of the Advant platform, ABB initiated a learning process focused on the effects of both technology and strategy. During the late 1990s and beginning of the new millennium, digitalization started to affect ABB's overall strategy in unforeseen ways. As the platform gained substantial digital capabilities, product boundaries were no longer defined by physical types of automation and restrictions associated with tight couplings between product layers. Instead, increasingly blurred technological boundaries challenged ABB's strategy and current organizational configurations.

> A couple of years after we released the Advant we ran into trouble. The system integrated information, data, but we could not get other actors to change their data format, which meant that we had to assume responsibility for data storage for a lot of external systems. [...] We realized pretty soon that it was not sustainable. So we decided to integrate applications instead [...]. So we developed APIs for our system and an adaptation module that could hook into APIs in other systems. Then we didn't have to care, applications could store data wherever they wanted, we just made sure we could access the data they produced through the API they published. At about this time we started thinking that this idea of holding information together was interesting for a lot of actors, not only engineers. It's interesting for operators, maintenance staff, production managers, etc. [...] at first, we thought we were developing an integration platform for engineering tools, then for connecting all the different parts of the control system, then to integrate different products and units in ABB, and eventually to integrate the whole world. (R&D Manager, ABB)

The new capacity to integrate information from a wide range of sources suggested that the utility of the platform technology was not confined to industrial settings but could be applied to a multitude of use-contexts. Strategic discussions were based on the general sense of the upcoming transformative impact of IT on the business landscape and the perception of integration as a core aspect of this change. The construction and surveillance industries were, for example, seen as two possible targets and talks were initiated with potential partners. ABB expected the competition in new use contexts to be a game changer and allied with partners such as Microsoft, Intel, and Accenture to realize the potential benefits of an integration platform across industries. The solution to a bounded technical problem was thus starting to challenge foundational assumptions within the organization.

In the early years before and after the millennium, considerable enthusiasm for the transformative impact of digital technology grew. ABB responded to the perceived opportunities using an exploratory approach by investing in proprietary web-based sales channels and community building efforts. ABB also made significant investments as a minority owner in a venture capital company for "business-to-business e-commerce" to gain access to new technology and formed alliances to develop a web-based platform for the pulp and paper industry.

To address the growing sense of urgency to leverage digital technologies for new business models, ABB introduced the Aspect Integrator Platform (AIP) and Industrial IT, a concept of a shared architectural standard. The strategic intention was to leverage the integrative capacity of AIP and provide certified solutions from both ABB and external actors for a wide range of automation contexts that customers could trust would be compatible. While still an emerging concept under development, contextual conditions and amplifying actions rapidly propelled Industrial IT's strategic position in the organization. In a meeting of ABB's top management in the spring of 2000, the manager of the automation division declared that *"Industrial IT is the future. Within a year, all products from my division must be Industrial IT-certified"*. While many of the participants were enthusiastic about these changes, one of the R&D managers for the Industrial IT concept noted that nobody really knew what this certification meant. The automation unit manager contacted the control system R&D group to discuss the certification concept and asked them to develop an appropriate strategy. The result was a four-level integration certification scheme in which higher levels represented tighter degrees of integration. Level zero was established because the IT manager of the power division wanted to participate in Industrial IT, although this division had no software. It came to mean that all of the relevant information about a product (i.e., service manuals, maintenance information, user manuals, calibration information, etc.) was available in a digital format.

> . . .it turned into some kind of competition in ABB about who had most certified products, this is where it got out of hand. Then the division manager became the CEO of ABB. Everybody who wanted to be something had to talk about Industrial IT and AIP, whether they knew what it was or not [. . .] in one of the annual reports, ABB was a huge company then with about 200,000 employees, the only product mentioned was the Aspect Integrator platform. (R&D Manager, ABB)

The Industrial IT certification program snowballed, 1100 products were certified in 2002, and a year later 35,000. During this time, the officially communicated organizational identity changed and both process automation and Industrial IT became central elements of the strategy. In the annual report for 2000 the company mission is described as follows, under the heading "Who we are":

> We are a leading global provider of products and systems incorporating advanced technologies and innovative applications of those products and systems, specializing in automation and process technologies for a broad range of industrial and commercial customers. [...] We are transforming our business portfolio, focusing on high value-added, high return businesses that capitalize on our market and technical expertise and offer innovative products incorporating sophisticated software applications. We apply our expertise to develop creative ways to integrate our products and systems with our customers' business processes to enhance their productivity and efficiency. We refer to this integration as 'Industrial IT.' Our increased commitment to Industrial IT has been supported by our recent strategic initiatives and our research and development efforts. Collaboration with our customers and our commitment to Industrial IT will be further enhanced by the realignment of our business operations along customer lines. (Annual report 2000, p. 5)

During this period, ABB increasingly explored options for expanding product boundaries for AIP and Industrial IT. For example, in 2000 the company acquired a majority stake in Skyva, a company developing software for integrating business processes. The ambition was to expand the integration offering from process automation to related business processes, as described by the automation division manager:

> Through its Industrial IT commitment, ABB aims to do for industry what Microsoft has done for the office environment—'bundle' productivity tools all the way from process automation to business automation. Our partnership with SKYVA will further expand the Industrial IT arena—all the way from the web store to the plant floor. (Automation Division manager in ABB Review 2/2001)

However, these ambitious expansion strategies came to an abrupt halt in 2002, when the company ran into severe financial problems. The problems mainly related to overly ambitious acquisition strategies, economic recession, and asbestos claims against the acquired company (i.e., Combustion Engineering). The financial situation forced ABB to focus its efforts on core businesses and divest a significant share of the company.

4 Results Achieved

Phase 4: Towards a Platform Ecosystem 2003
During these years, the Advant platform migrated across multiple operating systems and the technical debt incurred became significant. In addition to co-evolving with the Unix HP-UX (from 8.x to 9.x and 10.x), there were versions for Open VMS and the Windows NT family. Maintaining these versions and ensuring compatibility between

components and system versions became increasingly complex and costly. ABB's response was to abandon the multi-homing strategy and standardize the platform on the Windows OS. In 2003, the 800xA platform was released. The 800xA based on AIP architecture and the released version referred to as version 3 (AIP versions being 1 and 2). With this release, ABB changed its product strategy, streamlined system evolution and simplified maintenance by standardizing the functionality to one OS (Windows) and packaging incremental innovation from previous years into one integrated platform.

The 800xA platform was well received by the market. Systems were sold to 2500 customers in 2006, 6000 in 2010, and approximately 10,000 in 2017. Following its release, the system came to challenge the organizing logic, for both ABB and customers. The 800xA architecture considerably increased the inflow of variety from the technological environment by extending openness in the design. The open architecture provided significant extensions of functionality but also amplified tensions arising from differences in the evolutionary rates of digital and physical components, and connectivity. ABB successfully transformed their operations and adapted to the wake of digitalization by developing new business models. The company has successfully managed the threat of digital disruption by newcomers and incumbents in the software industry, despite the dissolution of product boundaries and potential unbundling of value creation. ABB is now a global leader in the process automation industry, and the digital agenda and capabilities are integrated into the mission and business model.

The 800xA platform built on openness in three dimensions towards the techno-logical environment: horizontally, vertically and laterally. This openness increased both connectivity and the inflow of externally developed functionality. Compared to Advant, the 800xA expanded horizontal openness by enabling plant-wide data integration, vertical openness through enterprise system level connectivity, and lateral openness towards the IT industry through the increased use of COTS and standards.

Horizontal reach was expanded in various ways, for example through extended functionality for system-wide operations, engineering, safety, analysis, and compat-ibility with the seven control systems in ABB's product portfolio (the Advant and Master systems developed in-house, and five acquired systems). It was enabled by an openness towards the installed base in the production environment and implemented through providing diverse kinds of support, such as for various communication standards (fieldbuses, communication protocols), I/O units, and data types.

Vertical reach was provided through functionality for remote clients and integra-tion with enterprise systems (e.g., maintenance management, production-planning systems, and supplier websites). It was enabled by an openness towards the enter-prise environment and implemented through integration functionality stemming from the AIP architecture.

Lateral coupling, referring here to architectural linkages between the platform and external modules, was reinforced as ABB further increased use of commercial-off-the-shelf (COTS) components and standards (most saliently choosing Microsoft COM technology as the foundation for software component communication). As the IT industry matured, competition hardened, and customer demands for functionality became more heterogeneous, decomposing the system and reusing available components instead of developing proprietary solutions was deemed appropriate.

With the 800xA, the platform's evolutionary rate became tightly linked to that of the IT industry in general and Microsoft in particular. The software in the automation environment became much more dynamic and subject to frequent patches, and ABB's version management dependent on Microsoft. For example, version 6.0 was released the same day as extended support expired on Windows XP that some customers continued to use. ABB released a new system version or service pack every year up until 2014, except 2009, which was a radical shift compared to previous practices. Due to the increased use of third-party products and open standards, and a high level of integration, 800xA is profoundly affected by changes in the ambient IT environment and requires continuous maintenance. Rapid and continual innovation results in a steady stream of new technological solutions with better performance, making existing solutions obsolete and incompatible:

> When shifting from making all products and systems ourselves to using Windows, both ABB and our customers have ended up in a situation where we do not control the development of IT products. We are purchasing hardware from third-party suppliers, and these products have their own life cycles. [...] Furthermore, updates and patches are frequent for Windows systems in home PCs, and the situation is the same with our systems. (Project manager, ABB)

This shift confronted ABB with new challenges regarding maintenance and software compatibility because top priorities of production sites are ensuring safety, meeting environmental concerns and minimizing costs associated with standstills. Digitization provides new functionality for process automation, but risk avoidance is critical for ABB's customers due to the extreme implications of system failure:

> You don't want to install updates that is a disturbance. There are always risks involved with installing updates. We minimize updates and only make changes in the software when there are obvious problems, or the version of Windows is so old that it is not supported anymore. That is the only circumstances we do it, I cannot recall us updating because we needed new functionality. (IT Manager MineCo)

From a customer perspective, incentives for increasing digital functionality are also limited as production environments remain anchored in a physical realm where the mechanical systems confine efficiency improvements. The physical production equipment is both expensive and long-lived (often 30–40 years in many contexts). Replacing machinery requires substantial investments and many plants operate continuously, except for a brief annual maintenance stop when equipment can be replaced. This further limit the evolutionary rate of the physical production technology. For example, during our study, ABB was engaged in a project with a 5-year schedule to modernize electrical equipment at a mining site. In summary, many customers consider making changes in digital systems once installed as a risk factor with limited rewards.

As horizontal and vertical connectivity increased, so did dependencies and vulnerabilities, because digitizing and connecting the large numbers of artifacts in production environments at multiple levels dramatically increases system complexity. For example, in 2012, PulpCo had about 25,000 I/O signals, 5342 I/O cards, 544 I/O integration modules, 235 nodes including various stations and controllers, 14 different control systems at multiple levels, and 56 software systems. Dependencies may only become apparent (potentially disastrously) when compatibility issues between upgrades or patches and the firmware in the equipment arise. Tracking firmware versions in all the I/O cards is daunting due to the large numbers of units and actors that might replace them (contractors, ABB, or in-house maintenance personnel), and time constraints in times of break-downs when re-starting the systems is the main priority. ABB explored options for extracting the required information automatically but has not found a viable solution due to lack of communication capabilities in much of the older technology.

When extending the vertical reach towards enterprise systems and remote clients, security issues also become increasingly important: measures such as firewalls between the enterprise and production environment are standard, but keeping the software updated becomes essential. Threats posed by security breaches caused increasing concern during the later years of the 800xA's lifetime, due to both increased awareness and reports of growing vulnerability. Symantec reported that vulnerabilities in control systems increased eightfold between 2011 and 2012. Steps taken by ABB to counter these threats include partnership and certification of third-party security solution such as "Industrial Defender" in late 2012.

Openness along the three dimensions also affected competency requirements, maintenance processes and business models for both ABB and customers. Requirements for general computer engineering competency have significantly increased, and as system complexity has grown, so have needs for specialist skill. Due to rapid changes in software and associated reductions in hardware lifetimes, maintenance of digital components has become highly prioritized and resource-consuming. Partly for these reasons, ABB's automation business is increasingly reliant on services, such as the software subscription package Sentinel, launched in 2007, which provides access to all 800xA upgrades, plus system maintenance and check-up services.

Based on increased competition and lower margins on products, services are an increasingly important income for ABB. Such service delivery is often dependent on information on both operational technology and ABB customized and certified solutions. An example of such services is software subscription ensuring customers access to the latest certified solutions and information on compatibility problems. ABB also sells regular maintenance of IT systems. For example, twice a year they inspect the state of all hard drives in the production site. They also try to increase the amount of service sold such as engine maintenance and pre-paid consultant hours. Further, they work to ensure a satisfying level of spare parts available in site stock. In all these activities, 800xA is the fundamental block that ABB uses to position themselves to create an attractive ecosystem for process automation. Although 800xA itself might stand for only 5% of total revenue from projects, the brand on the control system often decides which company that gets to deliver other products and services to the customer. With 800xA, ABB has implemented a digital architecture concerning controlling processes. Nevertheless, these processes remain anchored in the physical world, and they are performed by expensive, high-reliability equipment. This hybrid logic implies that ABB needs to manage both the logic of a physical, modular platform and a digital layered one.

5   Lessons Learned

Through a cumulative learning process, ABB has made the transition in focal concern from the optimization of separate sub-tasks to digitally enabled system automation and analytics. This learning process involved a digital transformation of three fundamental elements of ABB's operations: core technology, business models, and organizing logic. While only partially planned and foreseen, the hybrid platform was the shared vehicle that coordinated the transformation of these elements. ABB succeeded well in orchestrating their platform evolution process. Consequentially, at least five lessons can be learned from the case:

1. Physical and digital architecture enables different dynamics;
2. Digitalization is cumulative and emergent;
3. Digitalization blurs organizational boundaries and inverts the organization's strategic emphasis from bounded optimization to interaction configuration;
4. Digitalization is both a response to and a trigger for complexity;
5. When organizational members perceive an imminent change of significant scale managerial actions amplify and generate unforeseen consequences.

1. *Physical and digital architecture enables different dynamics (episodic change vs. emergence), and the tensions between them require careful consideration.* The infusion of digital technology into physical equipment challenges the dominant approaches to deal with change on the side of providers as well as user organizations. The tension in dynamics arises from differences in digital and physical architectures' propensities for emergent and episodic change. It is grounded partly in differences in openness to stimuli (as noted below) and partly in differences in costs, risks, and rewards associated with change. Information-based couplings (e.g., links in social relationships, software interfaces) promise far greater combinatorial power than energy-based couplings (e.g., in natural or mechanical systems) (Boisot and Child 1999). The feasibility and costs of combining and re-combining digital and analog resources are dramatically different. Thus, digital technologies increase the potential for recombinant innovation and emergent change. In a digital context, continuous inflow of innovation is often required to maintain competitiveness: if the functionality of a digital platform is not regularly extended, it will soon be outmoded. For physical machines and devices, replacement is often more economically efficient than upgrading functionality. Hence, "death" is the most important agent of change in

their life cycles (Van Alstyne 2013). For substantial investments, longevity is required to gain a return on investments. The innovation logics are very different. Furthermore, process automation is a risk-aversive context due to both high economic consequences of malfunction and the risk of physical injuries. So, for ABB's customers, the physical machinery imposes high costs for change, restricts rewards that can be gained from increasing digital functionality and raises risks for extremely costly breakdowns.

2. *Digitalization is cumulative and emergent.* In the process we studied at ABB, digitalization happened across four phases categorized by shifts in functional levels, decision rights, combinatorial options, boundary configurations, and value propositions (see Table 2 for a summary). This process was one of gradual digitization that scaled upwards in the process automation hierarchy. Main aims in the first two phases were to improve control and engineering in the process control environment by enhancing the efficiency of current practices. Crucial objectives in phases three and four leveraged digital technology for process innovation. Regarding organizational impact, operational technology was digitalized in the first phase, internal routines in the second, boundaries blurred in the third, and the fourth resulted in a new overarching digital-physical hybrid conciliation logic. At ABB, these phases where cumulative in the sense that the introduced digital components in one layer enabled the introduction of new digital components at a higher functional level. Thus, the introduction of technical elements in one layer resulted in capabilities that technical elements could draw on in the next wave of digitalization of a higher layer. The phases were also cumulative in a social sense as they instigated emergent use and design patterns that revealed new architectural options. For example, digital components in the physical process constitute a required but not sufficient condition for later service integration. This, in turn, revealed new insights on how to design APIs and other couplings.

3. *Digitalization blurs organizational boundaries and inverts the organization's strategic emphasis.* This re-orientation involves a shift from internal optimization to dynamic reconfiguration, that is, an increased focus on the orchestration of interactions and adaptation to the external ecosystems. Collaboration across both internal and external boundaries becomes a pivotal capability to succeed in such an environment due to connectivity related tension. Increased connectivity generates gains from connections between elements as well as complexity due to the increased number of elements and types of interactions. The combinatorial power of digital couplings increases the potential for recombinant innovation in both the core components and among peripheral ones that interact through the platform. The dynamics that platform providers and users need devoting resources to is also amplified with connectivity. In the case of ABB, the blurring effects on boundaries scaled from mainly affecting the internal organization in the first phase (e.g., collaboration across functional boundaries since a broader set of competencies was needed) into challenging strategic configurations in the third phase (e.g., organizational identity or target markets). As the platform evolved from a closed system built on proprietary technology into an open system including general purpose IT, adapting to changes implemented by other actors

Table 2. Cross-phase analysis

Characteristic	Phase 1 Master 1983–1992	Phase 2 Advant 1992–1998	Phase 3 AIP 1998–2003	Phase 4 800xA 2003–
Salient tension (s)	Nascent digitization in the technology environment	– Accelerated evolutionary rate in digital technology – Isolated information management systems	– Use-boundaries blurred – Organizational boundaries challenged – System maintenance complex and demanding	– Different change patterns in digital and physical machinery – Risk versus reward: Machinery provides a limit for functional improvements from new software
Levels	Process control	Process control and engineering	Oscillating, potentially unbounded	Process control, enterprise systems, and trusted remote clients
Control over design	Retained, closed systems	Mostly retained. Exceptions include Unix, hardware, and content in the engineering environment	Distributed in technology environment as ABB must react to changes in standards and Windows OS	Distributed in technology environment as ABB must react to changes in standards and Windows OS
Combinatorial options	Digital technology first implemented, recombination and integration of limited sections of process	First external components, integration of both certain plant-wide information and engineering systems	Radically increased options for service integration with third-party applications	Continuous inflow of design options from Windows updates and other standard compliant components
Boundary configurations	Relatively closed systems. Division of labor in engineering and reuse enable more complex solutions. R&D and users connected to the IT market	Inflow and stimuli from the IT industry through (1) interfaces towards external systems and (2) external components and standards in the platform	Product boundaries dissolved. Exploration of radical expansion in scale and scope	Openness results in loss of control over the rate of change, a substantial inflow of stimuli from the IT industry

(continued)

Table 2. (continued)

Characteristic	Phase 1 Master 1983–1992	Phase 2 Advant 1992–1998	Phase 3 AIP 1998–2003	Phase 4 800xA 2003–
Value proposition	*Product platform* Modularity, re-use, and adaptability in process control domain	*Product platform with digital services* Modularity, re-use, and adaptability in process control domain, and digital services for control and engineering	*Software platform* Integrate process control systems, software applications and value chains for business automation	*Hybrid platform* Integrate relevant information from any source for optimizing physical operations in the process

became increasingly important. This continuous flow of change also meant that orchestrating interactions with technology suppliers and customers required careful consideration and significant resources to ensure system reliability.

To remain competitive over time innovation must be turned into platform functionality. The use contexts of hybrid platforms are often relatively stable compared to the general IT industry, and in the short run, increased dynamics might decrease the efficiency of platforms in use. Openness towards the technological environment enables access to larger pools of resources for the platform provider to draw on. However, openness also decreases control over technological trajectories and rates of change (Lyytinen et al. 2016). With the high speed of innovation in the IT industry, it is challenging for any organization to efficiently maintain sufficient proprietary development. Furthermore, communication capacity enables benefits from integration with other devices and systems, but also creates risks for attacks and malfunctions through dependencies.

4. *Digitalization is both a response to and a trigger for complexity.* Through new functionality and more sophisticated responses, digitalization results in an increased ability to deal with complexity. However, it also triggers generation and inflow of new types of complex stimuli. The organizational response is often a self-reinforcing cycle of further digitization that scales across hierarchies and boundaries.

Drawing on Ashby's (1965) law on requisite variety, we argue that this process of ongoing and expanding digitization was driven by self-reinforcing cycles of complexity in response and stimuli. In this mechanism, that we refer to as "The Digitization Mechanism", digital technology is introduced to increase the variety of system functionality in response to adaptive tension. Such tension may either arise from perceived beneficial variation, that is, functionality raising the system's performance, or from an inability to manage the inflow of stimuli. In the context of platforms, the first can be understood as a move to increase the option value and the latter as a move to address technological debt (Woodard et al. 2013). The new digital technology creates novel interactions among agents. These interactions increase the range of stimuli the system must respond to again calling for further digitization. As the mechanism progresses upward in platform and organization hierarchies, the tensions described below also scale.

5. *When the organization faces significant tensions, uncertainty or perceives an ongoing transformation of the environment, signals from management generates amplifying deviation loops with unexpected consequences (butterfly effect).* In the years around the millennium shift, there was a hype around the expected transformative impact of digitalization on industries. Combined with the potential value of the integrative capacity of the AIP, managers and organizational members sensed that early adoption of digital technology and incorporation into products and processes was highly relevant. As described previously, managerial support for the Industrial IT concept, which still was still not very developed, lead to an internal hype. This hype meant that the R&D team had to devote substantial resources and develop solutions to satisfy internal actors rather than entirely focus on improving the business solution. This example suggests that management needs to carefully consider the messages they communicate through words and actions during such times, and explore options diligently before acting on them.

References

Agarwal R, Gao G, DesRoches C, Jha AK (2010) Research commentary—the digital transformation of healthcare: current status and the road ahead. Inf Syst Res 21(4):796–809

Ashby WR (1965) An introduction to cybernetics. Methuen and Co Ltd, London

Bharadwaj A, El Sawy OA, Pavlou PA, Venkatraman N (2013) Digital business strategy: toward a next generation of insights. MIS Q 37(2):471–482

Boisot M, Child J (1999) Organizations as adaptive systems in complex environments: the case of China. Organ Sci 10(3):237–252

Desouza KC, Bhagwatwar A (2012) Citizen apps to solve complex urban problems. J Urban Technol 19(3):107–136

Lee J, Berente N (2012) The division of innovative labor: digital controls in the automotive industry. Organ Sci 23(5):1428–1447

Lyytinen K, Yoo Y, Boland RJ Jr (2016) Digital product innovation within four classes of innovation networks. Inf Syst J 26(1):47–75

Sandberg J, Mathiassen L, Napier N (2014) Digital options theory for IT capability investment. J Assoc Inf Syst 15(7):422–453

Seo M, Putnam LL, Bartunek JM (2004) Dualities and tensions of planned organizational change. Marshall Scott Poole, Andrew H. Van de Ven. Handbook of organizational change and innovation. Oxford: Oxford University Press:73-107

Svahn F, Mathiassen L, Lindgren R (2017) Embracing digital innovation in incumbent firms: how Volvo cars managed competing concerns. MIS Q 41(1):239–254

Tilson D, Lyytinen K, Sørensen C (2010) Research commentary—digital infrastructures: the missing IS research agenda. Inf Syst Res 21(4):748–759

Van Alstyne M (2013) Why not immortality? Commun ACM 56(11):29–31

Woodard CJ, Ramasubbu N, Tschang FT, Sambamurthy V (2013) Design capital and design moves: the logic of digital business strategy. MIS Q 37(2):537–564

Yoo Y, Henfridsson O, Lyytinen K (2010) Research commentary—the new organizing logic of digital innovation: an agenda for information systems research. Inf Syst Res 21(4):724–735

Johan Sandberg is an associate professor at the Swedish Center for Digital Innovation at the Department of Informatics, Umeå University. His overall research interest lies within the area of digitalization and organizational transformation. In particular, he explores how rapidly changing governance and technology configurations in digital ecosystems affect organizing logics. He explores these issues in studies of (1) orchestration of innovation networks, (2) organizational strategy in uncertain and adaptive business environments and (3) digitization of product platforms and physical operational technology. Sandberg has received the Börje Langefors award for the best doctoral dissertation in Sweden within Information Systems, and, the Swedish Association for Information Systems' award for outstanding pedagogical achievements. He has been a visiting scholar at the Center for Process Innovation, Georgia State University. Sandberg has published his work in European Journal of Innovation Management, Information Polity, the Journal of the Association for Information Systems, and, proceedings of international conferences.

Jonny Holmström is a professor of Informatics at Umeå University and director and co-founder of Swedish Center for Digital Innovation. He writes, consults and speaks on topics such as IT management, digital innovation, digital strategy, digital entrepreneurship, and strategies for leveraging value from digitalization. His work has appeared in journals such as Communications of the AIS, Convergence, Design Issues, European Journal of Information Systems, Information and Organization, Information Systems Journal, Information Technology and People, Journal of the AIS, Journal of Strategic Information Systems, Research Policy, and The Information Society. He currently serves as senior editor for Information and Organization.

Kalle Lyytinen (PhD, Computer Science, University of Jyväskylä; Dr. h.c. Umeå University, Copenhagen Business school, Lappeenranta University of Technology) is Distinguished University Professor and Iris S. Wolstein professor of Management Design at Case Western Reserve University, and a visiting professor at Aalto University, Finland. Between 1992 and 2012 he was the 3rd most productive scholar in the IS field when measured by the AIS basket of 8 journals; he is among the top five IS scholars in terms of his h-index (79); he is the LEO Award recipient (2013), AIS fellow (2004), and the former chair of IFIP WG 8.2 "Information systems and organizations". He has published over 300 refereed articles and edited or written over 30 books or special issues. He conducts research that explores digital innovation especially in relation to nature and organization of digital innovation, design work, requirements in large scale systems, diffusion and assimilation of innovations, and emergence digital infrastructures.

Digitalization of Information-Intensive Logistics Processes to Reduce Production Lead Times at ENGEL Austria GmbH: Extending Value Stream Mapping with Subject-Oriented Business Process Management

Christoph Moser and Karel Říha

Abstract

(a) **Situation faced**: ENGEL is a strongly customer-oriented company with a focus on flexibility and innovations. These priorities are projected into a constant effort to offer customer-oriented solutions with short delivery times and the highest possible quality. Driven by this strategy, one of the company's goals was to further decrease the lead time of one of the main components for the injection molding machines by at least 30%. We were facing a cross-company process spanning over several different departments (logistics, production, IT, etc.), dozens of involved process actors, and no available process documentation.

(b) **Action taken**: The first step was to use Value Stream Mapping (VSM) to document the production process and to identify weak points and potential improvements. However, the defined lead time reduction could only be achieved by considering the production process in conjunction with accompanying administrative processes. Both areas are information-intensive as they are largely based on the processing and transfer of data. This required a combination of VSM with subject-oriented Business Process Management (S-BPM) as basis for specifying new and improved processes which were then implemented in an SAP ERP System environment.

C. Moser (✉)
ENGEL Austria GmbH, Schwertberg, Austria
e-mail: Christoph.Moser@engel.at

K. Říha
ENGEL Strojírenská spol. s.r.o., Kaplice, Czech Republic
e-mail: Karel.Riha@engel.at

© Springer International Publishing AG, part of Springer Nature 2019
N. Urbach, M. Röglinger (eds.), *Digitalization Cases*, Management for Professionals, https://doi.org/10.1007/978-3-319-95273-4_15

(c) **Results achieved**: The main achievement was the optimization of cross-company processes and the digitalization and automation of formerly manual processes. This resulted in greatly reduced process costs, reduced work in process, a reduced production lead time for individual components, and a reduced overall lead time by approx. 45%.

(d) **Lessons learned**: By using the VSM method we produced a detailed description of our production processes. The S-BPM method provides a modeling language that is easy to learn and can document complex processes at a high level of detail. It can provide a process description that complements the VSM with the required description of the information flows. The focus on the information flow of a process allows for process improvements and the digitalization of processes to be implemented in existing software environments with relatively little effort and still achieve significant results. A detailed and concrete process description can support the IT department to directly digitalize and automate process steps, reducing the time needed for additional verification steps and test runs.

1 Introduction

ENGEL is a traditional manufacturer of injection molding machines from Austria which was founded in 1945 by Ludwig Engel. After the introduction of the first injection molding machine in 1952, ENGEL became a market leader with 1.36 billion euros consolidated turnover worldwide in 2016. The completely family owned company employs approx. 5900 employees in nine production plants and over 85 branch offices (Engel 2018).

ENGEL is a strongly customer-oriented company with a focus on flexibility and innovations. These priorities are projected into a constant effort to improve the companies processes to offer customer specified solutions with short delivery times and the highest possible quality. Driven by this strategy and the development of the market, the management board defined the goal to decrease the lead time of one of the main components for the injection molding machines by at least 30% without increasing the production costs, while maintaining or even increasing process stability and quality. This goal is part of a bigger project to decrease overall delivery times for our standard injection molding machines by improving processes in general and specifically utilize existing digital solutions more efficient. The production process for the main component is a cross-company process that spans over two production plants, several different departments (disposition, production planning, production, etc.), several dozens of involved process actors, and a corresponding IT environment.

To reach the defined goal, our first task was to get an overview of the process and to create a proper process model, as there was no documentation available at the time. For this, we began with the standard approach for production processes, Value Stream Mapping. The following analysis revealed several weaknesses and possible improvements in the process, like warehousing strategy, handling, transportation, and of course in the production steps. While these improvements had an impact on the overall process quality and stability, it was only possible to reduce the overall lead time by approx. 6%—by far not close to the desired 30%. We concluded that the main potential must lie in the administrative parts of the process and now were facing the situation that the Value Stream Map focuses on the material flow of processes and offers only a rudimentary view of the information flow. From our perspective, this focus on the material flow did not offer a transparent way to describe the information flow between the involved process actors in detail or how the information is transported (e.g. by mail, telephone, paper, speech, ERP system, etc.).

To solve this problem and to get a detailed view of the information flow and the corresponding process steps we switched from VSM to an approach involving subject-oriented Business Process Management (S-BPM) (Fleischmann et al. 2012). Using the VSM as a starting point we created a more refined and detailed process model with S-BPM. Through the combined use of VSM and S-BPM we gained a holistic view of the overall process, considering both the material flow of the production and the information flow between productive and administrative process steps. We identified process steps in which employees had to manually add information to properly carry out the production order. The subject-oriented process model was our basis to define an underlying set of rules for these steps, which were then implemented in our SAP system using automatically executed transactions. The major challenge during the project was not the actual implementation but to figure out in detail what steps to digitalize. We could show that with a thorough process documentation and analysis it is possible to describe even very abstract and information-intensive processes, allowing digitalizing these processes using existing system platforms without too much effort. In our case this resulted in new and more efficient processes, with reduced work-in-process, fewer process interfaces, a reduction of manual process steps and corresponding workload for employees reduced production lead times for component parts required for the main component and a reduced overall lead time for the main component by 45%—significantly exceeding the initial 30% target.

Our work is consistent with recent insights and emerging methodologies regarding the digital transformation of organizations including the production industry. Most of these approaches regard digitalization not simply as the implementation and execution of (previously manually executed) processes in software. They emphasize the importance of embedding the IT implementation in a systematic procedure that starts with a thorough analysis and optimization of the processes to be digitalized (Otto et al. 2015; Schoenthaler et al. 2015; Parviainen et al. 2017). Yet, in many information-intensive processes such as those resulting from the use of modern digital technologies (Janiesch et al. 2017) traditional methods for process modelling are inadequate as they emphasize control flow at the expense of information flow. The subject-oriented approach to process modelling, with its focus on information flow and executability, has been shown to provide a solid basis for the analysis and design of digitalized processes (Walke et al. 2013; Kannengiesser et al. 2015).

2   Situation Faced

The strong focus on customer needs and the ongoing development towards shorter delivery times led to the definition of a company-wide objective: the reduction of the overall process lead time through digitalization of logistics processes for all variations of a standard main component by 30%. The digitalization strategy was to utilize existing (software) solutions as efficiently as possible and keep changes within the possibilities of the organizational structure and the intended timeframe. A project team was created to survey and analyze the existing processes and to implement required improvements.

The first step of any optimization process is the mapping of the status to get more detailed knowledge about the flows of material and information, and all factors that can have an impact on the process. At the time of project launch, there was almost no explicit information regarding the overall process, the detailed process steps or the involved process actors available.

All we knew was, that the process spans two production plants located in different countries (let us call these Factory A and Factory B) and that it consists of three relevant product groups:

- Product 1:
  - The finished frame for the injection molding machine which is assembled in Factory A.
  - It is mechanically treated and assembled using Product 2 and other components.
  - The overall lead time for Product 1 includes the order processing, production and delivery of components (Product 2) and subcomponents (Product 3).
- Product 2:
  - The untreated frame and its oil tank which are produced in Factory B.
  - Product 3 is welded to Product 2.
  - Even though it is a standard component, there are several dozen variations of Product 2 depending on the customer's requirements.
- Product 3:
  - A set of bars, profiles and pre-cut material produced on demand in Factory A.
  - There are several variants for Product 3 depending on the ordered frame.

Figure 1 shows a rough schema of the supply chain between the factories. The breaking point is the customer order of the injection molding machine in Factory A. The finished Product 1 is delivered to the assembly line, which we regard as the customer for the project.

This process is controlled through orders that are sent between the factories. When an order arrives at a factory it is registered and through the resulting demand for the product a production order with a corresponding delivery date is created. In case that the registration process takes longer than 2 working days, the production order will not arrive in production on time. In the initial situation approx. 95% of all orders between the factories were registered too late. These orders then had to be

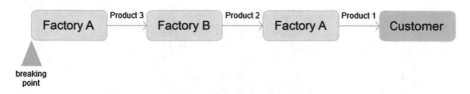

Fig. 1 Schema of the supply chain between factories

processed manually with a lot of troubleshooting, resulting in an internal delivery reliability for Product 2 of only 39%. This in turn caused additional problems for the production planning in Factory A and delays in the production of Product 1.

The timeframe of only 10 weeks to achieve the defined goal, the two factories being in different countries with different languages, and the little information available about the process were major challenges for the project. The narrow timeframe available resulted in further restrictions for the project: It would not have been possible to introduce new software or technical solutions. The introduction of such far-reaching changes is a strategic decision and requires a lot of manpower, money, risk management and time, and a corresponding level of maturity of the organizational structure. This meant that changes to the existing processes had to be implemented in the existing organization and IT environment. More disruptive measures necessary for further improvements can only be introduced after the initial project goal has been achieved.

3   Action Taken

Except for a superficial description of the material flow between the factories there was no explicit process information available. As a proper process documentation is fundamental to understand the overall process and to identify optimization potential, our next step was to document and analyze the production process through Value Stream Mapping (Rother and Shook 2004; Erlach 2010), an already established tool for production process documentation in our company.

For a first mapping of the process it was necessary to select a proper representative product, which involves most of the production steps and covers most of the material flow. We decided to use a variant of Product 2 for the mapping. This selection was based on an ABC analysis of all product variants and the corresponding working plans. The selected variant of Product 2 accounted for 30% of the overall production volume, had the most complex working plans, and the highest overall lead time of the three considered product groups.

By following the material flow on the shop floor level across both factories, surveying relevant KPIs (stock, production lead times, customer cycle, etc.), and interviewing the responsible employees we could create a Value Stream Map for Product 2. Figure 2 shows the VSM of the production process and its hierarchical

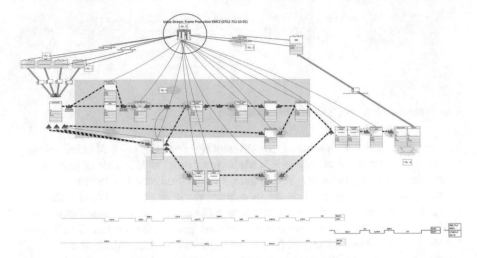

Fig. 2 Value Stream Mapping of the production of "Product 2"

structure to give the reader a general understanding of the process. The results of the Value Stream Analysis (VSA) were as following:

- The production process of the Product 2 consists of two parts: production of the frame and production of the oil tank. The frame and the oil tank are then put together to form Product 2
- The oil tank and the frame are produced independently without any production synchronization beyond the initial production order.
- Due to missing production planning, work-in-process stock comes along with long waiting times. Only approx. 10% of overall production lead time is operating time.
- There is optimization potential in the production process to reduce the lead time through production planning etc., yet the potential reductions are not enough to reach the desired goal.

In addition, by following the existing information flow we gained more concrete information about the ordering process between the factories and enhanced our process description accordingly:

- The demand for Product 1 originates in Factory A from where an order for the required variant of Product 2 is sent to Factory B.
- The order for Product 2 is processed and the acquisition of required components, among them Product 3, begins.
- Factory B now orders Product 3 from Factory A.
- The order for Product 3 is processed in Factory A and the production begins.

- As soon as Product 3 arrives in Factory B the production of Product 2 starts and the finished Product 2 is then sent back to Factory A.
- When Product 2 arrives in Factory A the assembly of Product 1 starts.
- This process is always the same for each machine, independent of the variant of Product 1.
- Most of the information necessary for production planning and production is controlled manually, slowing down the order processing. This means there is a big potential in the order processing part of the information flow to reduce the time for production orders to arrive on the shop floor.

Through the VSM method we identified two main weak points in the overall process: the lack of production synchronization and the non-optimized, mainly manual, order processing. However, the production synchronization is directly linked to the respective production planning process. During a brief analysis of the planning process we concluded that long-lasting improvements are only possible by completely reorganizing and restructuring the operations of the process planning department and changing the overall way of thinking. While this would have been a necessary change, we could not implement it in the timeframe of the project. We therefore concentrated our effort on the ordering process and its optimization potential as we identified it as a possible "quick-win" for our project.

This provided us with an entry point to start a comprehensive process survey especially regarding the possibility to improve the existing information flow by decreasing manual input and increasing the degree of digitalization. However, the VSM was still missing relevant process information to describe the overall process and the corresponding information flow in detail, e.g.:

- limited knowledge of the overall process
- no detailed information about the interactions between the involved parties
- no information about which steps in the process are automated and which steps are manual
- no concrete information about the transactions used in the ERP System (SAP/R3)
- no information about the timelines of the information flow
- no verification of the provided information

Since the VSM method focuses on production processes and mainly describes the material flow between process steps, we soon realized that we needed a different approach. We had to use a supplementary method to gather the missing information to be able to describe the information flow at the required level of detail to be able to thoroughly analyze it regarding possible optimization potential.

The next step was to create a process model that documents and describes the information flow between all involved parties (people, systems, etc.) in the process. To complement our existing Value Stream Map, we introduced subject-oriented Business Process Management (S-BPM) (see Fleischmann et al. 2012). We chose S-BPM as a new approach because of our past experiences and the problems we encountered with the modelling methods most often used at our company, namely flowchart models with swimlanes. In past utilizations of these swimlanes, the process models either provided an overview of the process but were not detailed enough for a thorough process analysis, or the processes models were so detailed that it became very difficult to maintain an overview. In addition, in our experience the swimlane model is not suited to visualize the individuals involved and their dependency on each other in a transparent form, especially in more complex processes, which often led to an incomprehensible description of the information flow of the process. The lack of transparent process descriptions has led to tedious implementations of IT solutions in the past, preceded by week long development and testing phases.

Experience has shown that the people involved in the processes, their individual approaches, knowledge, and experiences are a critical driving force behind a company's processes and mandatory for successful processes (Liappas 2006; Riempp 2004). The ways in which the information flow between these process actors is organized seems to have a major effect on business process performance (Kock et al. 2009). S-BPM specifically focuses on the depiction of processes from the point of view of the involved process actors, so-called "subjects", and their interactions in the process environment.

A subject may be a machine, an IT system or a person. The S-BPM modelling method employs two layers to describe a process, the Subject Interaction Diagram (SID) and the Subject Behavior Diagram (SBD). The interaction between the subjects is visualized in the SID, which describes the information and communication flow between the parties involved. The SID can provide a process overview and helps to identify each subject's role in the overall process. The SBD describes the individual process steps of an involved subject from the subject's point of view. The subject behavior is described through three different tasks (called "states" in S-BPM) that the subject performs: "sending", "receiving", and immediate accomplishment of a task called "function". As the part of a process relevant for a process actor is encapsulated within the respective subject, each SBD represents a self-contained sub-part of the process. It is not necessary to describe the whole process at once or in a strict sequence, e.g. if information is missing or not available, a part of the process is not relevant, etc.

The S-BPM notation consist of five symbols that are defined by their meaning and not directly by shape, although recommendations exist. Two symbols are used for the SID to represent the subject (e.g. rectangular shape) and the interaction (e.g. an arrow), and three symbols for the SBD to represent each individual state (most often rectangular shapes in different colors). A benefit of such a simple modelling notation is the possibility to model processes simultaneously in a top-down and bottom-up approach, bringing together the traditionally separate fields of business process management and lean production (Kannengiesser 2014) depending on the required and available level of detail of the information. Although there exist dedicated software solutions for modelling S-BPM, we utilized the simple and customizable notation to create our own MS Visio Template. This enabled us to immediately focus on the modelling and analysis of the processes without investing resources and time into the application of an external technical solution—a common pitfall in many

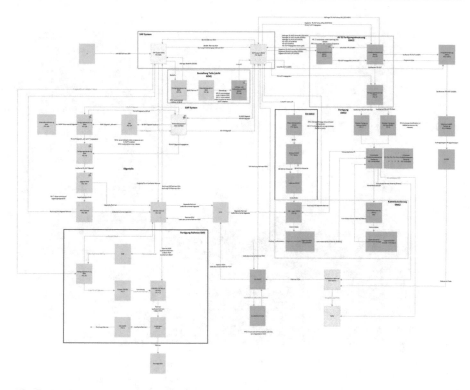

Fig. 3 Subject Interaction Diagram (SID) of the production and ordering process

companies when process modelling is implemented (Schmelzer and Sesselmann 2013). In addition, even if the introduction of new software solutions was not an option at the time of the project, the S-BPM method offered new possibilities for future applications, especially for reducing the effort needed for the digitalization and implementation of processes. By utilizing the S-BPM method it is possible to directly transfer process models into running processes and integrate these into existing software environments (Fleischmann et al. 2012).

Through more refined personal interviews, we created a model of the first layer of the process, the SID. The resulting process model of the as-is situation revealed that the logistics and production process is very complex, with approx. 40 involved subjects spread over the production of all three products. The final version of the resulting SID and the used notation can be seen in Fig. 3. The figure depicts the general communication structure of the process and how the various subjects interact with each other. The concrete names of the subjects or the content of the exchanged messages is not relevant for the further understanding of the actions taken. The rectangular shapes represent the various subjects involved in the process and the lines represent the information flow between the subjects. To distinguish between the two factories, we color-coded the corresponding subjects in green for Factory A

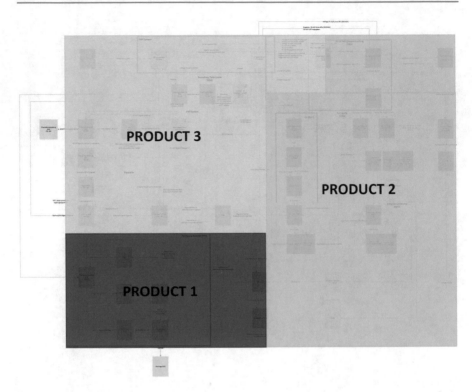

Fig. 4 SID and the corresponding products

and orange for Factory B. Further, we marked those subjects representing SAP systems using shading, to highlight the already digital parts of the existing process.

Although there is just one ERP system shared by both plants, for a more structured visualization we split the system in accordance with the respective departments (SAP system A, SAP system B, and SAP system A Disposition). Because of the number of involved subjects and the overall complexity of the process it wouldn't have been beneficial to survey and model all subject behaviors without a defined frame for our next steps.

To define such a framework, we used the SID to identify and analyze the main nodes and bottlenecks in the process of the corresponding product (Fig. 4). The most noticeable part of the process was the order processing itself. The order of Product 1 through Factory A, the order processing and the acquisition of Product 2 through Factory B, and the production of Product 3 in Factory A involved up to 12 subjects (3 SAP Systems and 9 people) and took up to 15 working days (lead time). Also, only 65% of Product 2 were finished on time because the order processing took too long and the orders arrived too late at the production center (approx. 95% of all orders). This had a direct impact on the production of Product 1 and on process stability. The delivery times could only be achieved with lots of extra effort and troubleshooting in the production department.

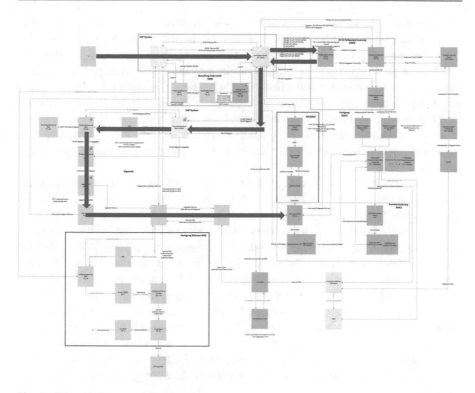

Fig. 5 SID with the process path for Product 3 (arrows)

We decided to focus on this material acquisition process, because relative to the complexity of the provided components (standard Product 3), the process itself is very complex and time-consuming. We defined the scope for our process survey as follows:

The focus will be on the logistics departments in Factory A and Factory B. This includes the production of Product 3 in Factory A, as it is directly organized under the logistics department and thus part of the process, and production of Product 2 in Factory B. The raw material acquisition in Factory A and the actual assembly of Product 1 in Factory A will not be part of the survey. See Fig. 4 for a visualization of the process and the corresponding products.

We surveyed the relevant process steps by further interviewing the involved employees in one-on-one interviews, accompanying the employees during the process, and simultaneously modelling the subject behavior diagrams. This allowed us to clearly highlight the process path for Product 3 (see Fig. 5), document detailed information about the SAP ERP system and the transactions used, and allowed the interviewees to follow the process modelling procedure live.

With the SAP transactions clearly described in the SID and SBD, and by following a dummy order through the system, we recreated the various steps of the SAP system. This also allowed us to distinguish between digital and manual steps, to verify the surveyed process model, and to document the actual process lead times. Figures 6 visualizes the subject behavior of one of the employees who handles the processing of production orders in factory B. This employee verifies if there are production plans available for planned production orders. Then all planned production orders with available production plans are summarized using a defined, but not explicitly documented, set of rules and are released for production. Several employees do this manually for every production order, with several thousand orders a day. For each production order such a manual input is required during four different process steps. This accumulated to a workload of approx. 7 h per day in total for Product 3 alone.

For the SBD, we used rectangular shapes and different colors to represent the three states; red for the "sending" state, green for the "receive" state, and yellow for the "function" state (see Fig. 6).

The overall workload for the whole survey, all interviews, and the time needed to complete and verify the process models accumulates to approx. 200 performed person hours. This is a relatively small effort compared to other process optimization projects, given the complexity of the process models, and the level of detail. With more detailed knowledge about the involved subjects available we created a timetable for the process based on the collected data and the data documented in the SAP system (ordering times, lead times, etc.). This timetable includes all organization and production steps and their respective lead times. For instance, the lead time for one of the Product 1 variants, from order acceptance in Factory B to the delivery of the finished Product 1 to the assembly line in Factory A, was approx. 30 working days (Table 1).

In collaboration with the employees the existing working plans were reworked, updated and improved. This led to updated and reduced lead times for the working steps, as well as a reduced number of working steps by merging existing ones. In this case a reduced number of working steps means fewer subjects as well as fewer behavioral states. During the analysis, we identified several similar process steps that were carried out differently in Factory A and Factory B. In Factory A, some necessary process steps had to be executed manually, but were done automatically by the SAP system in Factory B, and vice versa. Additionally, existing automated SAP batch jobs were disrupted because required manual input was missing between steps. These jobs were scheduled at two defined times during the working day and if at these times the manual input was missing the whole order had to wait up to one whole working day. These circumstances could occur several times for each order, which in the end could result in a delay of several working days.

The documented process models describe concretely defined processes, including all the relevant process steps in the SAP system, all the required SAP transactions, which use these transactions, and the interaction between the system and employees. Because of the detailed process documentation, our IT department was able to directly implement the relevant subject behaviors to create new standardized and automated processes, rework existing ones and streamline the processing schedule of existing batch jobs for both factories. This included steps like order acceptance, order opening, order release in both plants and delivery of the order papers to

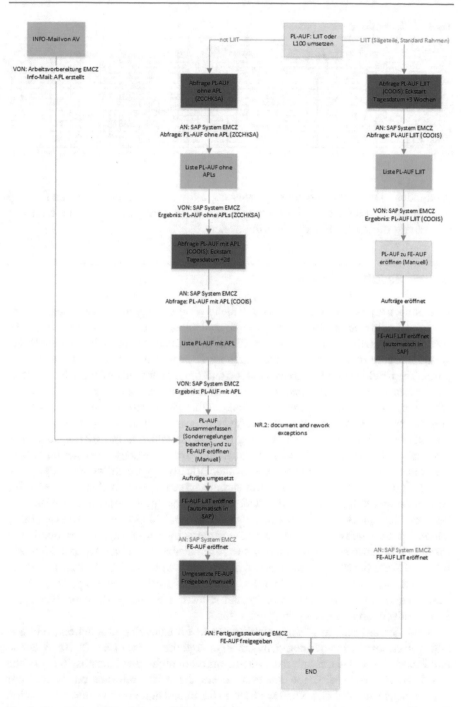

Fig. 6 Exemplary subject behavior diagram of an employee

Table 1 Time table for as-is process

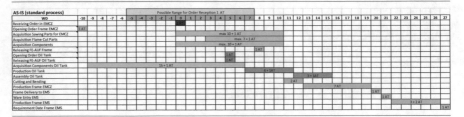

production. The automatic order processing allowed for order-related and timely processing of Product 3 in Factory A, which in turn enabled us to realize a completely digital KANBAN ordering system.

4 Results Achieved

One of the achieved results was a new warehousing strategy and reassessment of the stock that allowed us to rework the overall stock and to implement a digital KANBAN system for critical parts required to produce Product 3 in Factory B and simultaneously freeing space in the warehouse by reducing the stock of non-critical parts. The newly created KANBAN stock and the higher value of the affected parts resulted in an overall increase of the component stock value by approx. 209%. However, this only had a minimal impact on the overall stock level with a total of approx. 10,000 €. We realized this KANBAN system by replacing the traditional Kanban cards through a digital ordering process integrated in our ERP-system. The system uses production and order information to track the active production orders, the demand, and the available stock and automatically triggers follow-up orders. The new link between our system and the supplier systems ensures that the respective supplier receives the order as intended. The required components are then directly delivered into production by the respective supplier. This increased the availability and reduced the delivery times for all bought parts. Interruptions of the production of Product 2, because bought components were not available, could take up to 15 working days. After the changes, all required components were available within 1 working day either by direct delivery or through a safety stock at the supplier. A huge improvement of the process stability and reduction of the work in process for a comparatively small increase in stock value.

Value Stream Mapping is an established tool for analyzing production processes and well established in our company. Even though literature (Erlach 2010; Wiegand and Franck 2004) and our external consultants often highlighted the possibility of the VSM to not only describe material flows but also information flows, our expectations were not met when we tried to document and visualize the information flow. If most of the relevant information is available, it is possible to describe the

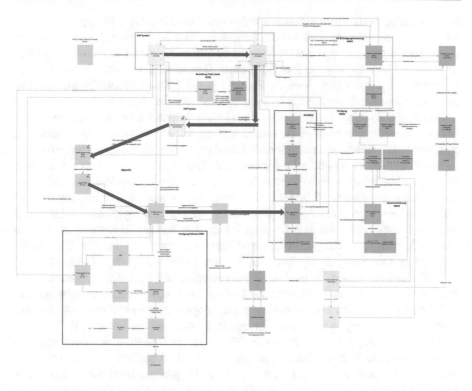

Fig. 7 SID with new process for Product 3 (arrows)

administrative processes and the information flow with a Value Stream Map. However, based on our experiences the VSM is not suitable for a process survey of information flow with partially abstract information. The application of S-BPM allowed us to use an easy to learn modeling notation which can nonetheless provide very accurate and detailed process models. The involved employees could understand, read and correctly interpret the S-BPM notation by themselves and began verifying their own process models (the subject behavior) without the input of the method specialists. This resulted in a high acceptance of the process survey and the following changes in the process as the employees were directly involved in the documentation and the identification of optimization potential in the processes.

The implemented rescheduling and digitalization of previously manual process steps led to a more standardized process and a reduction of the involved subjects from 12 to 8 (see Fig. 7). Fewer subjects means fewer interfaces in the process which in turn reduces process complexity and increases process stability. In addition, this relieved the employees of time-consuming and repetitive tasks—time which could then be used in more effective ways. The increased degree of digitalization and the resulting automation as well as the new planned schedule resulted in a new process lead time of 2 days (down from 5–10) for the order processing. Due to the detailed and clearly defined process our IT department could implement the process changes in the existing system environment within only 3 working days. The production and shipping process for Product 3 could be reduced to 3 days, down from approx. 5–6 days. This means that we could reduce the overall lead time of 11–15 working days of Product 3 by 87% down to 2 working days. These changes resulted in an increased adherence of the delivery dates for Product 3: the delivery reliability increased to 89% after four weeks of the implementation and to 97% after 1 year.

In the initial situation, the relatively long time needed for the order processing of Product 3 resulted in most of the orders arriving too late or on very short notice in Factory A. The newly created automated SAP processes led to a faster processing of orders from Factory A within the departments of Factory B. This in turn resulted in a shorter ordering time for Product 3 and an earlier production start of other components required for Product 2. The result was a reduction of initially 95% of orders registered too late down to only 12%, highly increasing process stability and process quality, and reducing the need for troubleshooting in both factories. The overall lead time of the production and ordering process of Product 2 could be reduced by 7 working days (approx. 38%), down from 19–23 days to 12–14 days.

The transformation of manual work into reworked and digitalized processes in the SAP system resulted in a reduced workload for the involved employees by approx. 5–6 hours per day to 1 hour per day. The employees now had to manually process orders only for very specific components that could not be covered by the SAP system and the implemented set of rules. The impact of these changes accumulates to a calculated process cost reduction of approx. 65,000 € per year. The implemented improvements and corresponding changes on the process level reduced the lead times for Product 2 and 3, and resulted in a reduced overall lead time for Product 1: from 26–33 working days, down to 18–20 working days. This is an overall reduction of approx. 45% for the whole ordering and production process (compare Tables 2 and 3). If Product 1 is not delivered within a narrow timeframe due to delays, it might jeopardize the actual delivery date for the end customer. To compensate for such delays a high investment of resources and man power is necessary and the strict delivery schedule is strained further. The implemented changes resulted in a higher delivery reliability towards the customer (the assembly line in Factory A) and a lower planning risk for the assembly line.

We were not only able to reach the defined goal of 30% lead time reduction, we surpassed this reduction by digitalizing and automating process steps and the

Table 2 Time table for as-is process

AS-IS (standard process)	Possible Range for Order Reception 1 AT	Duration
Receiving Order in EMCZ		
Opening Order Frame EMCZ		1AT
Acquisition Sawing Parts for EMCZ		max 10 + 1AT
Acquisition Flame Cut Parts		max. 7 + 1AT
Acquisition Components		max. 10 + 1AT
Releasing FE-AUF Frame		1AT
Opening Order Oil Tank		1AT
Releasing FE-AUF Oil Tank		1AT
Acquisition Components Oil Tank		15 + 1AT
Production Oil Tank		4 + 1AT
Assembly Oil Tank		3 + 1AT
Cutting and Bending		2AT
Production Frame EMCZ		7AT
Frame Delivery to EMS		1AT
Ware Entry EMS		1AT
Production Frame EMS		1 + 2AT
Requirement Date Frame EMS		1AT

Working days (WD): -10, -9, -8, -7, -6, -5, -4, -3, -2, -1, 0, 1, 2, 3, 4, 5, 6, 7, 8, 9, 10, 11, 12, 13, 14, 15, 16, 17, 18, 19, 20, 21, 22, 23, 24, 25, 26, 27

Table 3 Time table after process changes

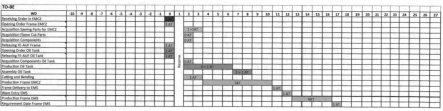

corresponding information flow. This further led to a reduced work in process with an overall value of several hundred thousand euros over the whole process.

Our results show that it is possible to realize significant reductions in lead time and manual work load by optimizing and digitalizing the information flow. The increased level of digitalization and the related process transparency can help to achieve further improvements and to better understand the processes in future analyses (cf. Parviainen et al. 2017). Although, as mentioned previously, the implementation of specialized S-BPM tools was deliberately avoided, the introduction of the S-BPM methodology might offer a foundation for an even more comprehensive digitalization of the existing processes. The S-BPM method and supporting modelling tools allow for a direct transformation of process models into running processes (Fleischmann et al. 2012) which can significantly reduce the effort required for the future digitalization of processes of all kind.

5 Lessons Learned

The most time-consuming and important phase of the project was the survey of the process and the resulting process model. A proper process model helps to understand the process, recreate process steps, and fill in missing relevant information, which is mandatory for an analysis of the process and the identification of weak spots and optimization potential. This phase may appear unproductive at first, because the project team cannot offer concrete process improvements and the responsible managers may get impatient, especially if the defined goal and expectations are very ambitious. After the initial survey phase, the close cooperation between the project team, the process actors, and the IT department allowed for an implementation of the defined improvements and measurable results in a short timeframe; in our case two weeks.

Value Stream Mapping is a valuable tool to describe and analyze production processes. Especially in a production oriented company the first focus regarding process improvements tends to be on the production process on the shop floor. The VSM method further supports this behavior as it offers a structured procedure for a detailed survey and analysis of production steps and concrete material flows. However, the VSM has its drawbacks if it is necessary to model administrative processes with abstract information flow as it might not be possible to describe the process in concrete process steps. The description of the value stream solely through process steps neglects the involvement of actual people and their communication in the process. Employees involved in such information-intensive processes also have difficulties to recreate their own process steps as the chronological order of the steps disregards who is executing the process step. Depending on the level of detail of the VSM, it gets very difficult for third parties to read or understand the whole process or get an overview of their overall role in the process. Nonetheless, especially in a production-oriented company the production processes are the most clearly defined and structured part of the organization and a VSM may offer a concrete basis for process analysis to begin with, even if there is very little process information available.

Subject-oriented Business Process Management offers a method of process modelling that can be used to expand on the knowledge gained through VSM and to create a broader process model. The base notation only uses five different symbols to describe even complex processes, which keeps the learning curve flat. The five-symbol notation can be further customized to add additional information or structure. In our case, different colors and filling patterns were introduced to distinguish subjects of the different factories or automated subjects. Even participants without prior training in the method could read and interpret the notation after a brief introduction (10 min). The distinction between two process layers, the Subject Interaction Diagram and the Subject Behavior Diagram, enables the modelling expert to model a process with a top-down and bottom-up approach simultaneously. This approach worked very well in our case: during the modelling of subject behaviors we gained additional information of the overall process and could immediately update the Subject Interaction Diagram, and vice versa. The interviewees were able to locate themselves and their respective role in the overall process in the SID. The SBD helped them to understand and verify their concrete process tasks and the chronological order of these tasks.

However, the distinction between SID and SBD has its drawbacks too. Because of the two layers and the encapsulated Subject Behaviors it might become very difficult to follow the chronological order of the process steps across different subjects. One might have to jump between several SBDs to follow the overall process, and it becomes increasingly difficult not to lose the process overview. To keep track of the lead time we had to create an additional timetable. In addition, without a proper framework to limit the initial survey the resulting SID may become overly complex as more and more subjects are added to the process model. It is mandatory to define a clear scope to reduce effort due to modeling unnecessary parts of the process. In our experience, the combination of Value Stream Mapping and subject-oriented Business Process Management can help to create synergy effects and to mitigate each other's drawbacks.

All changes in a system must be thoroughly tested in a simulated environment, and normally several test runs are necessary before the IT department can implement the desired changes into the running system. This becomes even more challenging if the intended changes are restricted to, and by, the existing software environment (in our case SAP ERP). Such systems provide a benefit only if it is possible to integrate your processes into them. Processes can be digitalized without big changes in the existing IT system if you know and master your processes. Providing a clearly defined process model that shows detailed and concrete information—i.e., the process steps executed in the system, the transactions the employees need, the systems using these transactions, and the interactions between the parties involved—greatly reduces the effort needed for digitalizing, testing, and implementing new or changed processes. Digitalizing even small parts of a manual process can provide significant and long-lasting process improvements, without introducing totally new technical solutions. In our case, the digitalization and subsequent automation of manual process steps directly affected only 12 of the 42 people involved in the process and yet we achieved a lead time reduction of approx. 45%. The digital transformation does not end with the completion of the project. It is an ongoing, companywide change process with the absolute precondition that the organization is ready for the intended changes.

References

ENGEL AUSTRIA GmbH: Facts & figures. Retrieved February 20, 2018.: http://www.engelglobal.com/en/uk/company/facts-figures.html

Erlach K (2010) Wertstromdesign. Der schlanke Weg zur Fabrik. (2. bearb. und erw. Aufl.). Springer, Berlin

Fleischmann A, Schmidt W, Stary C, Obermeier S, Börger E (2012) Subject-oriented business process management. Springer, Heidelberg

Janiesch C et al (2017) The internet-of-things meets business process management: mutual benefits and challenges. arXiv:1709.03628

Kannengiesser U (2014) Supporting value stream design using S-BPM. In: Proceedings of the 6th international conference on subject-oriented business process management (S-BPM ONE 2014), Eichstätt, Germany, April 22–23

Kannengiesser U, Neubauer M, Heininger R (2015) Subject-oriented BPM as the glue for integrating enterprise processes in smart factories. In: Ciuciu I, Panetto H, Debruyne C, Aubry A, Bollen P, Valencia-García R, Mishra A, Fensel A, Ferri F (eds) OTM 2015 workshops, LNCS, vol 9416. Springer, Cham, pp 77–86

Kock N, Verville J, Danesh-Pajou A, DeLuca D (2009) Communication flow orientation in business process modeling and its effect on redesign success: results from a field study. Decis Support Syst 46:562–575

Liappas I (2006) Vom Business zu den Prozessen. In: Scheer A-W, Kruppke H, Jost W, Kindermann H (eds) AGILITÄT durch ARIS Geschäftsprozessmanagement: Jahrbuch Business Process Excellence 2006/2007. Springer, Berlin, pp 43–56

Otto B, Bärenfänger R, Steinbuß S (2015) Digital business engineering: methodological foundations and first experiences from the field. In: BLED 2015 Proceedings, Bled, Slovenia: 58–76

Parviainen P, Kääriäinen J, Tihinen M, Teppola S (2017) Tackling the digitalization challenge: how to benefit from digitalization in practice. Int J Inf Syst Proj Manag 5(1):63–77

Riempp G (2004) Integrierte Wissensmanagement-Systeme, Architektur und praktische Anwendung. Springer, Berlin

Rother M, Shook J (2004) Learning to see – value-stream mapping to create value and eliminate muda. Lean Enterprise Institute, Cambridge, MA

Schmelzer H, Sesselmann W (2013) Geschäftsprozessmanagement in der Praxis – Kunden zufriedenstellen, Produktivität steigern, Wert erhöhen. Carl Hanser Verlag, München

Schoenthaler F, Augenstein D, Karle T (2015) Design and governance of collaborative business processes in Industry 4.0. In: Proceedings of the workshop on cross-organizational and cross-company BPM (XOC-BPM) co-located with the 17th IEEE conference on business informatics (CBI 2015), Lisbon, Portugal, July 2015

Walke T, Witschi M, Reiner M (2013) Case study @ Swisscom (Schweiz) AG: iPhone 5 self-service order app and process-workflows. In: Fischer H, Schneeberger J (eds) S-BPM ONE – running processes, CCIS, vol 360. Springer, Berlin, pp 264–273

Wiegand B, Franck P (2004) Lean Administration I – So werden Geschäftsprozesse transparent. Lean Management Institute, Aachen

Christoph Moser is manager of Warehouse and Intralogistics at ENGEL Austria GmbH at ENGEL's head office in Schwertberg, Austria, since 2014. He studied industrial engineering at the Technical University in Vienna with the study focus on quality and process management. During his studies he gathered practical experience as Process Manager with Taraneon Consulting Group and as Factory Planer with Fraunhofer Austria.

Karel Říha is employed at ENGEL Machinery in the Kaplice manufacturing plant, Czech Republic, and is responsible for the development and implementation of general logistic concept. His specialization is warehousing and internal transportation design and automation in internal logistics. He started his career as a logistic specialist in the team responsible for the implementation of lean manufacturing and warehousing principles by Schneider Electric in the manufacturing plant in Pisek, Czech Republic. He graduated at master level on the Faculty of Economics at the South Bohemian University at České Budějovice, Czech Republic. Karel Riha stayed on the Department of Management at the Faculty of Economics during his doctor studies where he focused his work on the social costs in the transportation as a part of the total logistic costs within the Supply Chain.

Digitalization in Public Services: Process Automation and Workforce Management at BruderhausDiakonie, a Social Services Organization

Ulrich Müller and Thomas Deelmann

Abstract

(a) **Situation faced**: In Germany's public sector, one of the main challenges is the demographic change and the resulting lack of skilled human resources. At the same time, digital solutions for e.g. citizens, businesses or other stakeholders move from "nice to have" towards "must have". The automation of services seems to be a promising approach to combine these two developments. This paper features BruderhausDiakonie, a social services organization which is growing horizontally at many new locations in order to ensure closeness to its clients. This process leads to an increase in complexity for its daily business and necessitates a change in thinking regarding the organization's IT towards increased digitalization.

(b) **Action taken**: In 2016, BruderhausDiakonie initiated a change process. The central message, which guided the project team from the beginning, gets to the root of the problem regarding digital transformation: Standardization before digitalization. The first step of a thorough analysis is the identification of routine tasks. Additionally, the vision of no more "Turnschuh-IT-Administration" (eng: "IT department in sneakers") was developed and communicated. An easy to use technology platform was implemented, mobile devices were integrated—and data security was given number one priority.

(c) **Results achieved**: The digitalization process of BruderhausDiakonie is not yet finished. However, first results are already visible. In August 2017, five

U. Müller
Operational Services GmbH & Co. KG, Frankfurt am Main, Germany
e-mail: ulrich.mueller01@t-systems.com

T. Deelmann (✉)
FHöV NRW, Cologne, Germany
e-mail: thomas.deelmann@fhoev.nrw.de

© Springer International Publishing AG, part of Springer Nature 2019
N. Urbach, M. Röglinger (eds.), *Digitalization Cases*, Management for
Professionals, https://doi.org/10.1007/978-3-319-95273-4_16

pilot offices were reorganized towards the new model. Until 2020, the process is to be finished for all offices. The first effects are already observable, along with the feedback of the involved employees. After all, the tangible benefits of digital transformation take a certain amount of time to become clear to employees. The IT department can help to start a new process, but everyone can and should be actively involved. The employees working in care or other departments feel the change happening, which is indicative of how their daily work is going to be in the future. Their work becomes more convenient, more comfortable and less time-consuming in regard to purely administrative tasks. Additionally, BruderhausDiakonie is also taking a pioneering position in how they will implement the benefits of the Internet of Things (IoT) as quickly as possible in their offices. In the future, employees should not only be provided with mobile devices, but also intelligent working materials, which not only make their work with clients easier, but diagnosis and care as well.

(d) **Lessons learned**: Digital transformation is a challenge, but it is feasible. It is important to choose an IT which allows for a gradual development towards the digital age. Knee-jerk solutions seem to be counterproductive. More promising is a step-by-step change process in regard to digital transformation, because it allows all involved parties a smooth adjustment to the digital requirements of the future. Three lessons learned stand out: (i) digital transformation is more complex than expected; (ii) all employees need to be involved and creating acceptance is a continuous task; (iii) one has to carry on and not to stop after the first successes.

1   Introduction

Public services are mainly local, regional or national services. Only in cases of deregulation and privatization do competitive forces enter the industry. In Germany's public sector, one of the main challenges is the demographic change and the resulting lack of skilled resources. At the same time, digital solutions for e.g. citizens, businesses or other stakeholders move from "nice to have" towards "must have". The demographic change seems to be of very high importance in the sub-sector of social services for at least two reasons: Besides the difficulties to find skilled and motivated employees, the number of people who ask for care, e.g. the elderly, is expected to increase significantly over the next years.

The automation of services seems to be a promising approach to combine these two developments: A traditional business situation in public services can be transformed with the help of digital technologies and become a less personnel-intensive digital public business.

Based on practical experience, three key levers, which are crucial for the digitalization (digital transformation) of public service organizations, can be identified: (i) connecting separate units or departments for a better flow of information, (ii) the introduction of self-services and the automation of routine tasks in order to free up resources, which can be used on more specialized and high-value tasks, and (iii) closing data security loopholes with the use of cloud services based in Germany (Reimann 2017).

The goal of this paper is to present a case in which information and communication technology (ICT) is used to redesign work in a social services organization based on process automation and workforce management. The case takes place at BruderhausDiakonie and reflects the situation as of mid-2017.

BruderhausDiakonie is a Christian social work and charity foundation. It was founded by theologian, social and charity work pioneer, and industrial entrepreneur Gustav Werner (1809–1887) in Reutlingen, Germany. BruderhausDiakonie helps older people, disadvantaged young people, and people with disabilities or mental illnesses partake in society. In currently 15 administrative and municipal districts of the German state of Baden-Württemberg, BruderhausDiakonie offers a wide range of support and assistance services, along with housing, professional training, job opportunities, counsel, inpatient and outpatient care, youth social work, career advice, reintegration programs for people with disabilities or mental illnesses, sheltered workshops, refugee relief, pastoral care, and other social and welfare services. It has partnerships with various municipalities and local communities and enjoys active exchange of ideas and experiences with many religious communities, associations, and other members of society. To facilitate social inclusion, different institutions of BruderhausDiakonie along with its partners and affiliates allow disadvantaged people to partake in the regular job market. Its roughly 4200 employees guide and support approximately 10,000 people (BruderhausDiakonie 2017a, b).

The guiding principle of social inclusion and the "Bundesteilhabegesetz"[1] accelerate the decentralization and regionalization of its offices in more and more districts and municipalities. This process presents BruderhausDiakonie with difficult challenges along the way. Unlike companies, which are often trending towards increased centralization, BruderhausDiakonie is growing horizontally at many new locations in Baden-Württemberg in order to ensure closeness to the people. Frequently, this leads to one office developing into several new, smaller institutions. This also raises the importance of outpatient care; after all, every person should be able to optimally partake in society, make decisions for him- or herself, and receive personalized support. This process also leads to an increase in complexity for

---

[1]The "Bundesteilhabegesetz" (short version) or "Gesetz zur Stärkung der Teilhabe und Selbstbestimmung von Menschen mit Behinderungen" (long version) is a German anti-discrimination law. It focuses on the participation of persons with disabilities in society.

BruderhausDiakonie's daily business; new administrative and management procedures are needed as well as another way of providing the institution's services. Consequently, this necessitates a change in thinking regarding the organization's IT towards increased digitalization.

After this introductory section, Sect. 2 first outlines the situation the public sector in Germany faces in general. In a second step, the specific challenges of BruderhausDiakonie are presented. These are mainly challenges of flexibility and responsiveness. Section 3 covers the actions taken by BruderhausDiakonie and their ICT service provider to overcome the challenges. During the transformation, it became clear that digitalization must go hand in hand with automation, that the "Turnschuh-IT-Administration" (eng: "IT department in sneakers") cannot remain, that a platform-based solution is necessary, and that using the platform should be as easy as using Google. Section 4 presents preliminary results of the transformation process and Sect. 5 summarizes the results for both BruderhausDiakonie on a case-level and for public services on a broader level.

2   Situation Faced

The public sector in Germany can generally be described having several distinctive characteristics, which will be shortly described below: it mainly delivers services, human resources are the key production factors, the main goal is public welfare, and many of its problems have the characteristics of political issues:

- *Services*: In contrast to products, are intangible goods (Meffert et al. 2015, 33). Only after the service delivery, the client is able to evaluate the services (and sometimes not even then). Services are goods which rely on trust and experience (Nelson 1970, 312; Darby and Karni 1973, 69). The so called signaling & screening approach aims to mediate this situation (Greschuchna 2006, 54 ff). Additionally, services cannot be produced in advance and stored for use at a later point in time. They are performed directly for the client (or the client's goods) and therefore need the client's cooperation (Meffert et al. 2015, 31 ff).
- *Personnel*: Can be seen as the main resource or production factor of service delivery. This means, public services scale more or less linear, i.e. input and output develop in the same way (as opposed to e.g. the network effects of social networks) (West 2017; Bettencourt et al. 2007). In addition to this, people affect public services in at least two more ways: First, the demographic change sometimes makes it difficult to recruit the right quantity and quality of human resources ("War for Talent"). Second, there is a shift in the client structure of public services. In many Western countries the average age of the population is increasing significantly.
- *Welfare*: To provide services to the public is the main driver for public service organizations. Typically, they focus more on public welfare than private organizations do. Regardless of their legal structures, public service organizations are mostly nonprofit organizations. This does not imply that they do not work in a

cost-efficient manner or that they do not create profits—but the increase in profitability is seldom a long-term goal.

- *Political issues*: Despite their goal of supporting and increasing public welfare, public services face many political challenges. While this might not be that important for their day-to-day operations, the strategic management of public service organizations faces strategic issues, which in turn have essential characteristics of political issues: conflicts, certain methods of conflict handling, negotiations, application of micro-political tactics, forming of coalitions, seeking consensus and support, and winning and utilizing power (Bamberger and Wrona 2012, 5–6).

Over the past decades, the spectrum of tasks covered by the public sector increased. However, its decision-making and management freedom decreased with respect to financial resources and legal guidelines. Additionally, one can observe that there are only limited personnel resources available for service delivery (i.e. due to demographic change). These developments lead towards a gap between given input and requested output, the so-called modernization- and performance-gap (Reichwein 2014; Budäus and Schwiering 1999, 145–146).

The specific situation at BruderhausDiakonie mirrors this overall description and makes it more precise and tangible. BruderhausDiakonie is part of the sub-sector of social services, which is traditionally driven by the desire to help and care.

Speed and flexibility are hardly seen as core competencies of social service organizations. The culture of these organizations is more often associated with long-term orientation, security, reliability and sustainability. Due to a strong organizational culture, "new" requirements are often met with a certain time delay. BruderhausDiakonie "realized only in 2014/2015, that they not only have to build up the right technology to face the challenges in sight, but to create an attitude of change in the organization as well. It is important to start sooner rather than later with a process re-design in order to work effectively and efficiently in newly created, smaller units" (Joos-Braun 2017[2]).

The Digital Economy and Society Index (DESI) 2017 shows that Germany's greatest challenge in digitalization is to improve the Digital Public Services. Among 28 EU member states, Germany ranks 23rd (European Commission 2017).

BruderhausDiakonie was one of the very first organizations in the public services sector which read the signs of the times and started—to borrow the term—a "digital therapy" for the whole organization in order to make it fit for the digital future.

In a first step, BruderhausDiakonie had to lay the foundation for its transformation. One key element was to transform the existing information technology architecture and its building blocks. The overall goal was to make the existing business

---

[2]This and the following statements and information were taken from an interview with Gerburg Joos-Braun, CIO of BruderhausDiakonie, and one of the authors; translation by the authors.

and change processes as easy and simple as possible. Three considerations had to be taken into account:

- There was an increasing number of offices and agencies within the organization, where an IT roll-out had to be carried out and which had to be connected.
- Employees who work out of office, and close to their clients, needed to get equipped with the right technology.
- Information and data, e.g. on clients, technology, medicine, etc. had to be accessible from any place at any time—always with respect to data privacy regulations.

In 2017, many processes at BruderhausDiakonie are still paper-based. Information is gathered in single departments but not shared organization-wide. These shortcomings should be resolved (Joos-Braun 2017).

3   Action Taken

Starting Point: Digitalization Means Automation
In 2016, BruderhausDiakonie initiated a change process in their organization, which has been advanced continuously and consequently since then. The primary goal is to put their clients at the center, in order to provide services tailored to the specific needs of the individual client. To ensure that this is the case, employees need to be able to focus on their actual social core tasks, and implement workflows quicker and more easily. It is vital that the employee is provided with the right piece of information at the right place and at the right time through the means of digitalization. The following report shows, which challenges came with that process. The overarching goal was the transformation of a rather traditional, social work institution into "BruderhausDiakonie 4.0". They aimed to become a service organization with a client-centric view on all processes. This way, the institution wanted to ensure closeness to their clients and fulfill their need for digital and fast services. Furthermore, their employees should also benefit from the new developments through convenient and less time-consuming administrative tasks as well as mobile devices and intelligent working materials. This is important, because employees are more and more requesting new working models: IDG shows, that 60.5% see clear benefits in innovative and mobile workplace concepts. They are looking forward to flexible working hours (63.7%) and locations (63.5%), easier access to information (61.5%), better work-life-balance (59.5%) and many more chances (IDG 2017).

Key success factors for achieving this goal are a strategic and integrated vision and a systematic approach; the digitalization of an organization is a many-layered process and consists of much more than just providing employees with mobile devices. Additionally, it is a change that impacts front- and back office processes at the same time.

The central message, which guided the project team from the beginning, gets to the root of the problem regarding digital transformation: "Nothing can be digitalized if it is not standardized first. If processes are to be supported via new technologies, at least 80% of them should be standardized, otherwise you are reinventing the wheel for each one of them again and again." (Joos-Braun 2017) In the end, the goal is being able to provide the client with social services, which are perfectly tailored to each client's demands. This goal necessitates a thorough analysis of the processes and requirements of the organization's different business units to find out, how processes can be streamlined and supported via new technologies.

The first step of the analysis is the identification of routine tasks, which might hinder the digitalization process. According to a survey, managers spend two working days each week carrying out administrative tasks, like writing e-mails or filling out forms. The workload in this area will continue to increase, since internal interactions between employees will do so too; on average, a typical employee is in contact with four different business units while carrying out his tasks (ServiceNow 2015). Connecting all participants through technology is a challenge, which requires a new information and communication architecture that should aim to emulate the consumer. Modern consumers are able to utilize a far wider range of digital solutions than many companies. For example, from the comfort of their own home, consumers can book a journey or register their car for a service check. They are able to do this by utilizing user-friendly tools which have been available to them for a long time.

Challenge and Motto: No More "Turnschuh-IT-Administration"
To foster a new digital identity in an organization like BruderhausDiakonie, a change in thinking in the IT department is necessary. It requires the IT to get more familiar and involved with the work of the other departments in the organization. Only through thorough engagement with the other departments' work will the IT department be able to understand their demands and be able to create structures which are flexible, scalable, and able to keep up with the constantly changing requirements of the digital age.

"Weg mit der Turnschuh-IT-Administration!" (eng: "No more IT department in sneakers"; Joos-Braun 2017). This motto should make it clear to the employees of BruderhausDiakonie's IT department, which challenges they will face in the future. The job profile of the IT department will shift from providing single services or devices towards a strategically and conceptually challenging area of work. The work itself will not lose its "sportiness", agility, and dynamic, quite the opposite in fact: It will demand a new, challenging mindset. The IT department will become an "interpreter", who receives input from all departments, transfers it—both internally towards the department and externally towards supporting service providers—and finds the best solution. The smoother this process can be realized, the more conclusive the end result will be. The goal is, to transform BruderhausDiakonie into a service organization for internal and external stakeholders.

Experiences from the industry validate this approach: The "IT department 4.0" has to evolve from a purely delivery-focused organization towards becoming an active service department, which fulfills the demands of the other departments and provides them with the appropriate solutions if necessary—or makes it possible for them to find the solutions themselves, when they need them. Studies show that the cooperation between IT and other departments improved in the last years. Communication became more common and both sides try to understand each other's needs better (e.g. Capgemini 2017).

This is important: It will no longer be the IT specialist who has to be contacted via phone or e-mail to fix something or provide a new device when something does not work as it should. Rather, processes have to develop in a way, which makes it possible for employees to order and receive the services they might need during work "automatically" at the press of a button. This reduces additional expenditure, which would further limit the already finite time of employees, to a minimum. Ordering services or support needs to become easier. This does not only hold true for IT support, but also for tasks like booking a business trip or registering for training courses; employees should be able to realize these processes easily via technology. The same goes for access to knowledge, which is an essential aspect of the work of BruderhausDiakonie. The know-how accumulated in a company—from legal requirements to forms to expertise gained in training courses—should be available to all employees intuitively and in real time, and should always be kept up to date. To ensure this, most companies need to improve their knowledge management. Only 25% offer an attractive knowledge database which is actively used by the employees (Wissensmanagement 2015).

Vision: An Integrated Platform Becomes the Foundation of Change

BruderhausDiakonie chose ServiceNow as their technical solution. This IT automation platform allows users to order services, such as the requisition of a PC by themselves in a matter of seconds. As convenient as ordering something online, the employee is able to review the status of his internal order at any time. That way, he always knows when his new device will arrive.

However, the platform offers more than just easier IT support. It also aids companies by helping to provide employees of all departments with the services they need—no matter if it is HR, marketing, accounting or procurement. Deloitte's Tech Trends 2017 states that "Everything-as-a-Service" is a strategic and operational blueprint that will likely begin upending business and operational models, and redefining the fundamental goals of core modernization (Deloitte 2017).

For BruderhausDiakonie, "Everything-as-a-Service" is based on an integrated foundation of data along with an IT-supported solution, which centralizes all information and tools and keeps them updated at any time. Through a service catalogue, which can be preconfigured for the needs of different users, these users can choose the service they need via a graphical user interface. Working behind the service catalogue are consistent service chains, which interface with all departments in a company, and the actual provision of applications or data is carried out via inter- or intranet. Additionally, third-party applications can be installed on the platform to make additional offers available for users. The selected technical solution is based on the general idea of "requesters" and "providers" of services, no matter if the services consist of systems or persons. Different management features are also installed, through which decision-makers can control the company based on workflow information; the service model makes all of this possible through a single integrated platform. This way, a digital transformation of the organization as a whole becomes easier to achieve.

Goal: Ensuring the Best Service Possible
A SPOC (single point of contact) for all offices: Through an integrated platform, establishing a network between IT and other departments, which allows for "Everything-as-a-Service", becomes possible. This also fulfills BruderhausDiakonie's requirement of a shared "knowledge pool". Depending on the individual system privileges of each employee, information can be retrieved in real time and without differences in currency between employee and system. Additionally, employees can interact, store data, reorganize tasks into structured processes and consequently improve the quality of their work, all through a centralized platform. Sending e-mails with attached documents or manually distributing forms becomes a thing of the past, and gives important impulses for the future, since not only mutual exchange of information, but also demand-based access to information will be crucial to success in the working world of tomorrow. Connecting service automation and platform solutions increases productivity and raises employee satisfaction, while simultaneously reducing costs. With these measures, BruderhausDiakonie becomes a service organization which uses digitalization to achieve benefits for employees and clients.

Approach: As Easy as Googling
Everything is supposed to become easier—but then employees receive a new, complex IT tool, which they first need to get familiar with? ServiceNow works like Google—this was one of the main reasons why BruderhausDiakonie chose it. In most cases, employees need to train themselves to use a new IT tool, but they prefer to use self-explaining tools which do not require extensive training. "We were looking for a user-oriented tool. Our employees come from the social sector, they are not technology experts, and we would also never expect them to be, which means that it was important to us that our new service portal was very easy to use. Our employees need to visit enough training courses in their specialized fields; a supporting technology on the other hand should be usable without a long learning phase. That is the case with our approach. We do not need workshops; its functions are instantly obvious and not just in the front end. In the back end, our IT department has a system, which is easily customizable. We are able to adjust the system by ourselves, which allows us to develop flexibly and autonomously" (Joos-Braun 2017).

Example: Higher Efficiency and Quality Through Mobile Devices
One practical example which shows how work processes at BruderhausDiakonie are being changed: Until now, employees working in geriatric care used paper records for their clients' files. They manually took notes for each client and transferred the notes to the digital records at the end of the day—at the risk of missing details and with the additional effort of having to record everything twice. A trend shows that social institutions start to consider the use of mobile communication solutions (FGW 2017).

Thus, BruderhausDiakonie decided to equip their employees with mobile devices as to ensure their access to necessary information at any time. This means that employees can access existing data, enter new data, complete the work process, and visit the next client, all while in the field. Not only does this save time, but does also ensure a higher quality of service.

Important Framework Conditions: Safety for Client Data
Organizations like BruderhausDiakonie store a large amount of sensitive private and patient data, which means that there is still a reluctance towards storing data digitally and even more towards storing it in the cloud in many organizations in the social sector. This reluctance is unnecessary; in Germany, data can be safely stored in highly secure data centers. Almost three quarters of the participants of a digitalization study see IT security as the basis for successful digitalization (Bundesdruckerei 2017). Also, for BruderhausDiakonie, data security was an issue which was central to the choice of their ICT service provider, who would support BruderhausDiakonie in IT matters and provide the required solution. The selected ICT service provider managed to convince BruderhausDiakonie with its security measures. It is the only company providing the ServiceNow platform solution from a dedicated German cloud. Data storage and process execution is conducted in highly secure data centers in Germany. Separate communication systems are in place for each individual client to encrypt data securely, which ensures compliance with German data protection regulations. Other reasons, why migrating to a cloud-based environment is the right choice for organizations in the social sector are reduced costs and increased efficiency; no unnecessary, additional expenditures, like investment costs for personnel, hardware and software, and data centers.

Key Success Factor - The People: Live and Inspire Change and Involve All Employees
Employees have to be convinced of a large-scale change process towards a digital transformation, have to be motivated to take the—admittedly ambitious—steps, and have to help in actively designing the change process. After all, practical experience shows that every change process causes unease for most people, which can grow into anxiety and even rejection of the process. This behavior can cause many transformation processes to fail. The reason for that is not due to choosing the wrong technology, but rather due to inconsistent communication. In many cases the problem is that employees are not sufficiently involved in the process, which can cause them to feel like foreign elements inside the process and to reject it. Effective change management and supporting employees by conveying the individual steps of the process are crucial to success. However, the problem is that few companies possess the necessary empathy to recognize this. Project communication does not include sufficient, dedicated resources when it comes to personnel, time, and budget (GPM[3] 2017).

BruderhausDiakonie prevented this from happening from the very beginning. Primarily, this is due to the positive attitude of the executives towards the change process, since digital transformation "travels downwards" from the management level in every organization. This is crucial for involving all employees on all levels

---

[3]GPM; Deutsche Gesellschaft für Projektmanagement e.V.; a German society for project management.

of hierarchy actively and believably in the change process. At BruderhausDiakonie, the change process of the IT was not just "commanded" from the top, but has been shaped by all involved parties from the beginning, to achieve a high level of acceptance from everyone involved. Usability has been determined to be the most important aspect in this case and has been evaluated by the users during the process, which ensured that future users will also be involved in the development of solutions from the beginning. Through articles in the company newsletter or internal mailings, employees are always kept up to date about the status of the process, experience any progress in real time, are informed about advantages and requirements, and are thus able to identify with the development.

However, the challenge remains: 40% of the employees of BruderhausDiakonie are over 50 years old and are consequently no "digital natives", who would be more able to intuitively deal with such change processes. Still, with these steps BruderhausDiakonie ensures that all of their employees are future-proof: digitalization will become a staple of the working world—no matter, if one accepts this fact or not. Those who do not deal with it now, will be left behind. Due to this fact, BruderhausDiakonie not only invests into digital development, but also into the training of its IT department and the support of the next generation of employees. Also, BruderhausDiakonie's internal training programs are already paying off. "Because we train them internally, our IT staff now consists of 50% employees who have adopted the behavior and act like the members of the Generation Y. They see valuable prospects for them with us, and they can identify themselves with our goal of putting IT proficiency in an ethical context. And who like to be here. That makes us proud, especially considering how competitive the market is for a company looking for IT talent" (Joos-Braun 2017). BruderhausDiakonie has also managed to become an attractive prospective employer for both young people and experienced employees. This is essential, because the war for talents gets harder every year. In Germany, there are 55,000 vacancies for IT professionals (Bitkom 2017).

Transparency and generous involvement of their employees was an important aspect for BruderhausDiakonie in regard to the development process of their IT technology. "This process of automation and standardization, which we are currently going through, requires close cooperation between our IT department and all other departments, which can only be achieved through shared practice and teamwork. This is why we formed work groups, which consist of employees from different departments and levels of hierarchy; IT experts and end users. That way, we are able to bring people with different needs and perspectives together. Only through this comprehensive exchange of ideas are we able to develop the best solution for our future" (Joos-Braun 2017).

4   Results Achieved

Even if the digitalization process of BruderhausDiakonie is not yet finished, first results are already visible. In August 2017, five pilot offices were reorganized towards the new model, more are to follow in time. Until 2020, the process is to be completed for all offices.

The first effects are already observable, along with the feedback of the involved employees. "We have been waiting for this: finally streamlined workflows and easy, mobile access to documents and data", reported one of the employees of the pilot offices to one of the authors of this paper. However, not every employee welcomes change with open arms. As experience from other change processes shows, reservations are a natural part of such processes (Doppler and Lauterburg 2014). After all, the tangible benefits of digital transformation take a certain amount of time to become visible to employees. The reduced workload for example, is hardly noticed in the beginning of such complex transformation processes. Employees first have to get used to the new processes and teams first need to understand that the change process is an investment into the future for all involved parties. As soon as the first period of adjustment is over, the improvements become tangible for everyone involved during their daily work. At BruderhausDiakonie, there were already many advocates of the new model—even at early stages—who recognized the benefits quickly and communicated these positive experiences to their colleagues.

Getting ready for the future—this guiding principle reinforces the identification of employees with their employer. The new job description of the IT employees makes BruderhausDiakonie an attractive employer for potential colleagues: Instead of routine tasks, the ability to design and strategize becomes more and more important. The IT department can help start a new process, but everyone can and should be actively involved. Analysis, design and professional execution through new technology and agile methods are crucial. These are the challenges, which future IT experts are looking for and which they can find at BruderhausDiakonie.

The employees working in care or other departments also feel the change happening, which is indicative of how their daily work is going to be in the future. They are prepared today for the digital challenges of tomorrow, instead of being overwhelmed by them at some point. Their work becomes more convenient, more comfortable and less time-consuming in regard to purely administrative tasks. Additionally, BruderhausDiakonie is also taking a pioneering position in how they will implement the benefits of the Internet of Things as quickly as possible in their offices. In the future, employees should not only be provided with mobile devices, but also intelligent working materials, which not only make their work with clients easier, but diagnosis and care as well.

It will take some more time, before the definite increase in efficiency, which the selected automation platform provides, can be gauged in numbers, but one aspect is already obvious: Since the platform can be autonomously and flexibly adjusted to meet different requirements, IT teams can use it internally too—without contacting and contracting external specialists first. In addition, it allows BruderhausDiakonie to digitalize and automate processes step-by-step.

5   Lessons Learned

Overview The much-vaunted digital transformation is a challenge, but it is feasible for all sectors, including the municipal and social sectors, which are often still relying on traditional, paper-based processes, and which are infamous for being slow to change. That makes it all the more important to choose an IT technology, which allows for a gradual development towards the digital age. Knee-jerk solutions are counterproductive—in every department and industry. More promising is a step-by-step change process in regard to digital transformation, because it is not a sudden upheaval for IT experts and employees, but rather allows all involved parties a smooth adjustment to the digital requirements of the future. The advantage of the selected software solution at BruderhausDiakonie lies in its ability to allow gradual change; processes which are to be automated can be digitalized gradually and fine-tuned at a later stage. This allows every department to face the challenges of digitalization flexibly and at its own pace.

Lesson Number 1 One lesson all involved parties learned during the process: Digital transformation is more complex than expected, especially considering their currently decentralized organizational structure. The experiences from one pilot project in one office are not easily transferred to other locations. And most importantly, the process proved to be time-consuming—more time-consuming than expected—due to its complexity. However, the organization developed new, agile methods to add more flexibility to the innovation process, which is a step many organizations take, when they are confronted with a large variety of data and are forced to adjust their IT structures accordingly. Agile software development methods like Scrum or process optimization through DevOps become increasingly important, because they are often the only solutions, which are able to meet new requirements quickly and satisfactorily. However, this gap between "as is" and "can be" is wide. According to the 2016 Bitkom and Detecon survey, 80% of all businesses consider agile structures to be important, but only 25% are actively developing them (Bitkom and Detecon 2016).

Lesson Number 2 Another lesson learned is that all employees need to be involved. Creating a general acceptance for the transformation within all employees is a continuous task, which has to accompany the process. "The change process is highly dependent on the enthusiasm of the individuals and multipliers involved, and also on the commitment of the management team, which should motivate employees for the cause, so the task is stemmed by everyone together." (Joos-Braun 2017) With its innovation initiative, the challenges were faced and—as the results show so far—the organization positioned itself strategically for the future.

Lesson Number 3 Carry on! One has to stand behind the digitalization initiative and develop plans for additional service platforms, new Internet-based devices for employees, and other innovations.

Generalization of Lessons Learned These lessons can easily be abstracted from the specific situation towards the overall situation of public services: (i) Digitalization seems to be helpful to close the modernization- and performance-gap. Technology itself seems to be one key element—but not the only one. (ii) People matter—and they have to be involved. (iii) Quick successes are necessary—but the solution has to be sustainable. (iv) The solution for the problem seems to be easy—but very often it is not.

Political and public organizations in general need to face the challenge of digital transformation. No matter if universities, schools, town halls, civil service, police or any other public institution: They are all forced to change and adapt innovative opportunities for their daily business. Because their customers—businesses, citizens and other stakeholders—expect digital solutions and efficient processes to receive their services fast and easy. This is what they are used to from their private and working life, and they do not want to abstain from these services when it comes to interactions with public bodies. To be able to offer what is required, public institutions need to optimize and automate their services, because the demographic change causes a lack of skilled employees. Service automation is an efficient way to benefit from the digital solutions available today, and to gain agility and speed—especially for political and public organizations which are known for slow changes.

References

Bamberger I, Wrona T (2012) Konzeptionen der strategischen Unternehmensberatung. In: Bamberger I, Wrona T (eds) Strategische Unternehmensberatung. Springer Gabler, Wiesbaden, pp 1–44

Bettencourt LMA, Lobo J, Helbing D, Kühnert C, West GB (2007) Growth, innovation, scaling, and the pace of life in cities. Proc Natl Acad Sci USA 104:7301–7306

Bitkom (2017) Der Arbeitsmarkt für IT-Fachkräfte. https://www.bitkom.org/Presse/Anhaenge-an-PIs/2017/11-November/Bitkom-Charts-IT-Fachkraefte-07-11-2017-final.pdf. Accessed 13 Dec 2017

Bitkom and Detecon (2016) Digitalisierung und Internet of Things (IoT) – Anforderungen an agile Organisationen. Cologne

BruderhausDiakonie (2017a) Geschichte. https://www.bruderhausdia konie.de/wir-ueber-uns/geschichte/. Accessed 23 Sept 2017

BruderhausDiakonie (2017b) Das Leitbild der BruderhausDiakonie. Reutlingen

Budäus D, Schwiering K (1999) Die Rolle der Informations- und Kommunikationstechnologien im Modernisierungsprozeß öffentlicher Verwaltungen. In: Scheer A-W (ed) Electronic business and knowledge management. Springer, Berlin, pp 143–166

Bundesdruckerei (2017) Digitalisierung und IT-Sicherheit 2017. https://www.bundesdruckerei.de/de/Newsroom/Pressemitteilungen/Bundesdruckerei-Studie-zu-Digitalisierung-und-IT-Sicherheit-2017. Accessed 13 Dec 2017

Capgemini (2017) Studie IT-trends 2017. https://www.capgemini.com/de-de/wp-content/uploads/sites/5/2017/02/it-trends-studie-2017.pdf. Accessed 13 Dec 2017

Darby MR, Karni E (1973) Free competition and the optimal amount of fraud. J Law Econ 16:67–88

Deloitte (2017) Tech trends 2017. https://www2.deloitte.com/au/en/pages/technology/articles/every thing-as-a-service.html. Accessed 13 Dec 2017

Doppler K, Lauterburg C (2014) Change Management – Den Unternehmenswandel gestalten. Campus, Frankfurt am Main

European Commission (2017) Digital economy and society index. https://ec.europa.eu/digital-single-market/en/scoreboard/germany. Accessed 13 Dec 2017

FGW (2017) Digitalisierung in der sozialen Dienstleistungsarbeit. http://www.fgw-nrw.de/fileadmin/user_upload/FGW-Studie-I40-05-Hilbert-komplett-web.pdf. Accessed 13 Dec 2017

GPM (2017) IPMA 4-Level-Zertifizierungen, Nuremberg

Greschuchna L (2006) Vertrauen in der Unternehmensberatung. Deutscher Universitätsverlag, Wiesbaden

IDG (2017) Arbeitsplatz der Zukunft. http://up-download.de/up/docs/studie/de/IDG-Research-Studie_Arbeitsplatz-der-Zukunft-2017.pdf. Accessed 13 Dec 2017

Joos-Braun G (2017) Interview. 07.08.2017

Meffert H, Bruhn M, Hadwich K (2015) Dienstleistungsmarketing. Springer Gabler, Wiesbaden

Nelson P (1970) Information and consumer behavior. J Pol Econ 78:311–329

Reichwein A (2014) Moderne Verwaltung. In: Paulic R (ed) Verwaltungsmanagement und Organisation. VfW, Frankfurt am Main, pp 23–65

Reimann O (2017) Bröckelt die digitale Fassade in der Verwaltung? Frankfurt am Main

ServiceNow (2015) Today's state of work – the productivity drain. Research Report, 04/2015, http://www.servicenow.com/content/dam/servicenow/ documents/whitepapers/sn-state-of-work-report.pdf. Accessed 23 Aug 2017

West GB (2017) Scale – the universal laws of life and death in organisms, cities and companies. Weidenfeld & Nicolson, London

Wissensmanagement (2015) Wissensmanagement Umfrage 2015. http://www.wissensmanagement.net/services/news/einzelansicht/studie_wissensmanagement_unternehmen_haben_erheblichen_nachholbedarf.html. Accessed 13 Dec 2017

Ulrich Müller is Spokesman of the Board of Directors of the ICT service provider operational services GmbH & Co. KG, a joint venture of Fraport AG and T-Systems International GmbH, since 2010. Prior to that he spent eight years with T-Systems International in various management positions, including T-Systems North America in New York. He reported to the CEO of T-Systems International since 2008 as Senior Vice President Corporate Strategy. Before his career at T-Systems, Dr. Müller had worked in the fields of management consultancy since 1993. He is the author of numerous publications ranging from ICT services to digitization, is a member of the Münchner Kreis and the supervisory board of BENOCS GmbH.

Thomas Deelmann is Professor for Public Management at the University of Applied Sciences for Public Administration and Management of North Rhine-Westphalia (FHöV) in Cologne, Germany. Until 2016, he was Professor for Corporate Consulting and Management at BiTS Iserlohn as well as the head of the strategy development department for a leading global ICT service provider. Currently, he serves as the editor for a consulting handbook and as a jury member of the WirtschaftsWoche's "Best of Consulting" award.

Digital Health Innovation Engineering: Enabling Digital Transformation in Healthcare: Introduction of an Overall Tracking and Tracing at the Super Hospital Aarhus Denmark

Sven Meister, Anja Burmann, and Wolfgang Deiters

Abstract

(a) **Situation faced**: Digitalization is changing healthcare. Especially hospitals are under tremendous pressure and there is a recognizable difference of digital maturity compared along the European states. Besides German hospitals, Fraunhofer ISST is supporting the Danish Government as they are in an outstanding restructuring process with the aim of building five super hospitals in different regions. The vision, fixed by the Danish DNU Hospital in Aarhus, was to allow the overall vertical and horizontal digitalization of processes by having one common information architecture. Fraunhofer ISST was contracted by DNU to support the definition and valuation of a reference architecture.

(b) **Action taken**: We started with a very lean approach and identified three key requirements: (1) support of operative processes, (2) analysis and optimization, and (3) automation and planning. A first idea was to implement an "Automated Transport Service" in a logistical scenario by combining the "trolley service" with the "task management service". The whole vision could be reduced to one aim: Optimization by automation. To reach this aim we identified the need for a structured process for digital transformation that will pay attention to the demand and needs as well as the competences of the employees. Therefore, Fraunhofer ISST started to develop the approach called "Digital Health Innovation Engineering" (DHIE).

S. Meister (✉) · A. Burmann
Fraunhofer ISST, Dortmund, Germany
e-mail: sven.meister@isst.fraunhofer.de; anja.burmann@isst.fraunhofer.de

W. Deiters
Hochschule für Gesundheit, Bochum, Germany
e-mail: Wolfgang.deiters@hs-gesundheit.de

© Springer International Publishing AG, part of Springer Nature 2019
N. Urbach, M. Röglinger (eds.), *Digitalization Cases*, Management for Professionals, https://doi.org/10.1007/978-3-319-95273-4_17

(c) **Results achieved**: Making use of digitalization in healthcare requires a structured process called digital transformation to enable health companies, hospitals and other facilities to do so. The preliminary results deduced from the learnings at the DNU hospital were used to define the basic framework of DHIE. Furthermore, we detailed the method called "maturity index for hospital 4.0" to measure the digital maturity of hospitals paying attention to technical as well as human factors.

(d) **Lessons learned**: We identified, that the introduction of digital solutions and processes requires a structured process. Digitalization is more than technology; it is a process of transformation. Especially in healthcare, the human-to-human interaction like patient to physician plays an important role. Thus, digitalization has to define solutions how processes can change with respects to its human actors.

1   Introduction

There is a recognizable change in healthcare driven by several factors and the need for new concepts to cope with the demographic change. An increased share of elderly citizens and chronically ill patients as well as more expensive forms of treatment challenges healthcare systems around the world (Gløersen et al. 2016). Off the beaten track of healthcare, two terms are driving development and investigations in several industries: Industry 4.0 and digitalization. Both of them address the lack of skilled workers at the one hand and the need for increased productivity at the other hand. Industry 4.0 is described by two mayor paradigms—decentralization and automation (Kagermann 2015). Decentralization enables the distribution of service provision along different sites and service providers to ensure high flexibility and productivity. Digitalization is supporting the industry 4.0 metaphor by allowing new ways of communication and interchange between service providers (Vogelsang 2010; Legner et al. 2017). Furthermore, digitalization fosters the thinking of new business models, driven by data (Legner et al. 2017). In terms of data-driven value chains, data is the new oil. The fusion of data through heterogeneous and highly distributed data lakes combined with state of the art data processing technology, e.g., artificial intelligence, is making the production of demand-fulfilling information the gold nugget of the twenty-first century (Morabito 2015).

With respect to healthcare, the questions are: What can the healthcare sector learn from the other industries and what are the chances and risks of transferring the basic concepts of industry 4.0 and digitalization (Thuemmler 2017)? It is obvious, that the healthcare sector has to cope with several similar problems compared to other industries. Today, there is a recognizable lack of skilled workers, e.g., for elderly care or nursing in hospitals. Service provisioning in healthcare is highly distributed—one is talking about 'intersectoral healthcare' and the demand for concepts enabling a better collaboration between primary and secondary healthcare providers. Besides these challenges, large internet companies show how personal or health related data, e.g., gathered by smart devices, could be used within apps or web-services to strengthen health and fitness.

Making use of digitalization in healthcare requires a structured process called digital transformation to enable health companies, hospitals and other facilities to do so (Meister et al. 2017). Therefore, Fraunhofer ISST started to investigate the approach called "Digital Health Innovation Engineering" (DHIE). Starting from a vision for healthcare 4.0, the three-step approach helps to describe users' needs and demands, regulatory and legal requirements, market, and competitors in the first step. The second step focusses more on the company itself measuring digital competency and digital health maturity. Only now, within the last step, technology will be introduced, surrounded by concepts to ensure the competence of the users.

In the following, we will describe a digital transformation process at the Aarhus University Hospital "Det Nye Universitetshospital (DNU)" to enable an overall tracking and tracing information architecture. Parts of the Digital Health Innovation Engineering methods were designed upon the experiences made at DNU.

2   Situation Faced

For more than a decade, Danish hospitals and companies have worked together on improving logistics in hospitals. The overall aim has been the creation of just-in-time solutions in order to optimize coordination and efficiency and reduce the patients' length of stay. According to a central Danish strategy for renovating the Danish healthcare system, several super hospitals are being built in the different Danish regions, one of which is DNU in Aarhus. Innovations in that hospital building project are massively built on logistics and information and communication systems (IcT). Therefore, DNU has among others placed an order for the development of a system ("det generelle system/det initiale system") supporting service logistics basing on a general tracking and tracing infrastructure. One requirement for the order was that the developed system is open with respect to extensibility and interoperability.

In Denmark, the focus on hospital logistics has played an important role in achieving a 30% increase in hospital productivity since 2003. When the New Aarhus University Hospital is completed in 2019, it will be the largest hospital in Northern Europe, spanning approx. 500,000 m^2 and employing around 10,000 people. To achieve the productivity targets set for a hospital of this size, a Real Time Location System (RTLS) is necessary to support the logistics processes.

Optimal coordination and utilization of resources require careful planning. However, the constantly changing activities in the hospital make this sort of planning difficult. To overcome this challenge, a full real-time overview of the location of colleagues, patients, and equipment in the hospital enables the hospital personnel to locate their colleagues and needed equipment. At the New Aarhus University

Fig. 1 Overall architecture integrating horizontal and vertical information streams

Hospital, an IT system should enable real-time localization of people and equipment right down to room level.

A "paper based" evaluation that uses documentation and interface specifications provided by the vendors of the tracking and tracing system can only answer this question on a conceptual level. Therefore, DNU decided to let Fraunhofer ISST develop a "new service" to make real world experiences with the tracking and tracing infrastructure—this service should direct into the issue of process automatization.

3   Action Taken

When Fraunhofer ISST was contracted by DNU, there was a lack of methods supporting the process of digital transformation. Thus, we accompany DNU in several parts especially in the conceptualization and implementation. Figure 1 shows the vision of DNU by having an all-encompassing interconnection of IcT. Thus, one can locate medical devices or staff. Furthermore, processes can be monitored in real-time and rules can be defined to automatically detect deviations during process execution.

Fraunhofer ISST participated at workshops to identify the key goals and requirements for this horizontal and vertical integration: Support of operative processes, analysis and optimization, and automation and planning.

3.1 Support of Operative Processes

The introduced infrastructure e.g. aims at supporting the logistics process for different object flows (beds, food, linen, sterile goods etc.). Taking food delivery as an example, food arrives at the central goods reception to be transported to the various handover places, which is documented by the transporters in the IcT. The system will generate tasks for people from different wards to fetch the food and to bring it into the patient rooms. The same holds for the delivery of beds etc. Outbound delivery works the same way: People at the wards bring the objects to the pickup places, a transportation task is delivered and a transporter is notified that there is some container to be brought back to the central goods reception area. The different people are synchronized with the task management system, always being noticed "just in time", if there is a certain task for them to do. The task management system does the optimization in work assignment, informing the people at the destination place, informing people who are closest by the place of work, informing people who have the least workload or applying any other selection strategy. In many cases, the algorithm does some kind of preselection, determining a small set of people who reasonably could do the task. The people can then decide among themselves who is taking over the job. By that, people are capable to organize their work environment; the task management application does the global process coordination and synchronization.

The fact that all objects are tagged and are tracked in the system gives an effective access to these objects. If a nurse needs certain objects, e.g., a fresh bed for a new patient or a mobile X-ray device for a certain medical treatment, he/she easily can look up in his/her smartphone where the nearest object is, book it, immediately go, and fetch it. Time-consuming searches are avoided and the booking mechanism (that is possible for "now" but also for time slots "in the future") reduces concurrent access of resources by different people.

3.2 Analysis and Optimization

Tracing and tracking does not only give the current localization of objects (by that avoids searching), but also supports a deeper analysis of the objects usage, movements, and so on. Taking the example of bed management, the system does not only give information where a certain bed is, but it can also return information of the bed's status. By that it becomes possible to determine time periods a bed is occupied with patients, times beds were out for maintenance or cleaning, and times in which beds have been ready for use but unoccupied. It becomes possible to analyze how many unused beds are in different wards, floors, and buildings. The IcT will be able to optimize processes like reducing the amount of unused objects, moving and storing them close to the places where they are needed.

3.3 Automation and Planning

Having knowledge about the hospital's status (e.g., where which objects are) also enables the IcT for automation. Taking up the example of food delivery mentioned above, it becomes possible to produce tasks for pick up if a transporter leaves a certain container at a handover place automatically. The idea behind "automation" is to use the information that is provided by the comprehensive tracking and tracing infrastructure to trigger events. Those events may then initiate tasks (e.g., transport task, cleaning bed order, etc.) or notifications of clinical and non-clinical staff or issue calls to external IT-systems (ordering new clothes, etc.). Automation is not only an additional service that bases on the tracking and tracing system installed in the DNU. Automation adds a horizontal and process oriented view by combining the tracking and tracing system with inter services communication. For achieving this in a flexible way "det generelle system" would have to offer resp. system functionality (e.g., a rule engine).

Therefore, process automation has to be developed further up to the level of process planning. The rule engine used for triggering the tasks can reflect various other parameters considering the avoidance of bottlenecks of problems. If, for example, in the case of empty food containers (the same idea holds for every other object flow) a task for outbound transportation is automatically delivered as soon as a trolley is put into the handover area, this might lead to a jam of containers in the central good reception. If lorries from the central kitchen will only arrive in a couple of hours for the transport out of hospital, there would be a resp. accumulation of containers there. The algorithm in the rule engine triggering the different tasks can put this information into account. Based on a time table when which lorry will be arriving at the goods reception, it can compute the hospital internal transportation time and trigger tasks for optimizing internal transportation (i.e., avoiding container jams in the reception). Various optimization parameters can be thought of, e.g., optimizing the load capacity of elevators, ensuring that sterile good is at surgery at the time when it is needed there, etc. Process planning can contribute to optimization and a "just in time" logistics in the hospital. Based on estimated data we could show that this kind of optimization is possible and has a reasonable effect.

3.4 Conceptualization and Implementation of a Prototype

Having defined the key requirements mentioned before, a first idea was to implement an "Automated Transport Service" in a logistical scenario by combining the "trolley service" with the "task management service". The "Automated Transport Service" generates a transport task in the "task management service", if a trolley (e.g., containing goods for department X) arrives in a predefined area (for department X) at the logistics traceé. The transport task notifies the responsible personnel to pick up and to transport trolleys containing the resp. goods to the appropriate place in department X, then. Doing so, a twofold result has been developed:

- The developed functionality enables DNU to step into process automation, i.e., the system is extended by a prototype giving new useful functionality.
- Adding a new component into the system gives direct feedback on "det generelle system" and allows evaluating that system w.r.t. openness and extensibility.

The localization of equipment and beds is possible because everything is equipped with different intelligent tags such as radio frequency identification (RFID) and plastic embedded tags. The advantage of using RFID tags is that it is a low-cost solution for tagging equipment, which does not require batteries. Other tags with batteries are used for bed status management. Additional functions can be connected to the system, e.g., Wi-Fi technology for alerts or temperature monitoring.

We have implemented a small prototype demonstrating this feature. By defining a rule engine that accesses the tracing database (by that recognizing that a certain container has been deposited at the handover place) it becomes possible without any manual intervention to automatically generate new tasks into the task management system triggering the retrieving of the container from that place to its next destination. Processes are carried out by manual tasks of employees combined with an automated triggering of follow on manual or automatic tasks by a process engine. This approach adopts and turns the industry 4.0 idea into a more service-oriented way of work.

4   Results Achieved

After the implementation and evaluation of the prototype interacting with the IcT, we recognized several pits and falls. The drawbacks were not technical ones (e.g., bugs) but rather more questions arising from a strategic point of view:

- What is the strategic outcome of the digital solution?
- Which companies can supply additional modules to develop further and prepare for upcoming requirements?
- How does the given solution pay attention to changing regulatory affairs (e.g., medical device regulation) or new statutes?
- What is the common information model that should be shared among all IcT modules?

We identified a missing thread running from the CEO perspective through the CIO, CTO and/or CDO level. Thus, we deduced the need for a structured process and started to define the DHIE method upon the experiences received out of the DNU project. The DHIE method is shown in Fig. 2.

The starting point for DHIE is a vision, often defined by the CEO level in cooperation with the underlying levels. In hospitals, you will find the management

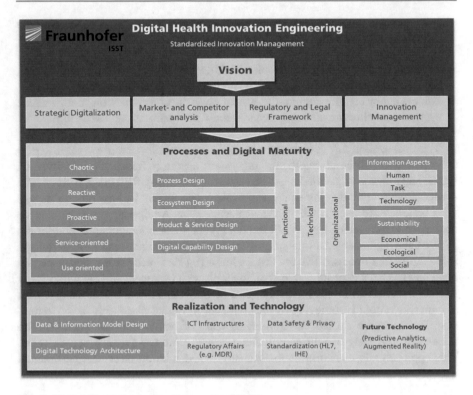

Fig. 2 Digital Health Innovation Engineering (DHIE)

directors accompanied by the nursing management, the IT management as well as the clinical directors. After defining the vision, one has to deduce and document the basic requirements in a requirements specification (RS). The RS would be the starting point for a structured market and competitor analysis and the identification of relevant regulatory and legal frameworks. With respect to the latter, the processing of data has to comply with the national data privacy and security requirements. The flow of information could also consider personal data, e.g., to track the location enabling a more efficient routing of resources. The aim of the market analysis would be the identification of possible suppliers and solution experts to make them part of the next steps. Together with the Danish hospital and the solution supplier, Fraunhofer ISST would organize the next steps:

- Elicitation of the existing processes and definition of required new process fragments.
- Elicitation of the digital maturity of the processes and surround ecosystems.

The process of elicitation and definition would pay attention to human factors like human computer interfaces and the ability or competence of employees to cope with a process of higher degree of maturity, talking about digital competence and digital sovereignty of employees. Both affect the factor of success when it comes to transform an existing process and making it digital. Only now, the process of conceptualization and implementation would start.

One of the key questions, coming from a defined vision down through the aspects of strategic digitalization, innovation managements and so on, is the predominant digital maturity of a hospital, of thinking and behavior. Thus, there is a need to quantify the digital maturity in terms of an index. As an outcome of the DNU activities and part of DHIE we developed a maturity index for hospitals.

Developing a methodology to enable a structured organizational digital transformation raised the need to assess, qualify and quantify the degree of digitization of a hospital. Measuring digital maturity is a matter the industrial sector is dealing with in several approaches for a couple of years. Examples to be named are Gottschalk's domain-specific analysis of interoperability of administrative software (Gottschalk 2009), the more general approach of a strategic imperative from Fitzgerald et al. (2014) or the suggestion of the Industry 4.0 Maturity Index (Schuh 2017). As already pointed out in Sect. 3, an adaption of a digital transformation methodology with respect to the specific ecosystem is required, especially since healthcare markets comprise legal and economical frameworks substantially different from the industrial sector. The same applies regarding the derivation of a structured methodology to elicitate digital maturity in healthcare. One finding of the collaboration with DNU was, that digital maturity, according to the definition of Humphrey's maturity levels (Humphrey 1988), comprises an operational as well as a strategic dimension. Evershorter development cycles imply that the digital transformation of a hospital does end neither with the implementation of singular or even integrated software solutions, nor with a high penetration rate concerning the use of these applications. In fact, a high digital maturity inherits the ability to constantly adapt to changing ambient conditions, both on the operational as well as on the personal level (Fig. 3).

In order to qualify and quantify the operational components of digital maturity, we identified four main dimensions, each comprising several subcategories. Namely, these dimensions are Medical Care, Logistics/Procurement, Management/ Controlling, and Human. Exemplary subcategories of the dimension Medical Care are external and internal communication or documentation. The elicitation of each of these subcategories encompasses a survey on how digital the certain process is

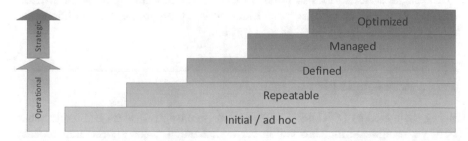

Fig. 3 Operational and strategic dimension of digital maturity, according to Humphrey's maturity levels in software development (Humphrey 1988)

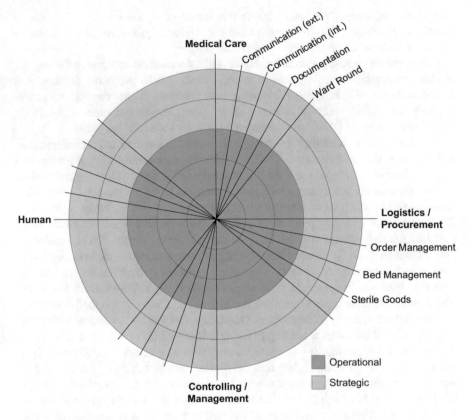

Fig. 4 Digitization dimensions and exemplary subcategories

executed and managed. The derived levels of digitization, starting with a paper-based and ending with a fully integrated digitally mapped process, can then be pictured in a kiviat diagram, as depicted in Fig. 4. In order to address the mentioned strategic level, additional strategic components are basing on the qualifiable operational characteristics. In a next step, the developed evaluation matrix should be validated and revised in a wider context. Furthermore, a standardizing and weighting of the single subcategories in order to achieve a comparability between different assessed hospitals as well as to consider different environmental conditions and target definitions should be taken into account.

5   Lessons Learned

Being contracted by DNU during the process of conceptualization and implementation, we recognized that innovation for digitalization needs a structured process. Like constructing a new building, a construction plan is needed, whereas the areas defined within the plan should fulfill user's demands. The difficulty is to pay attention to possible things coming up in the future like new large medical devices in hospitals. Digitalization in healthcare is more than talking about medical apps, Wi-Fi availability, and so on. For achieving digitalization, there is much beyond technology: A clearly defined vision, independent from a technological point of view, has to be defined to understand the overall process of transformation. Every process needs one or a set of process owners in terms of a responsibility assignment matrix (RACI). The process needs to be management and directed by humans and the efforts are time consuming. Therefore, we recommend the installation of a strategic innovation management as one or a set of full time equivalent, depending on the size of the hospital and the RACI matrix.

From our experiences, digitalization will only be successful if three levels will be addressed within the strategic innovation management:

- Change management level: Digitalization is not a one-time project with a defined starting and endpoint. It is more a continuous process and it will rather be a challenge for the next decade. Thus, one has to implement mechanisms to achieve a constant change process in terms of chain management with a defined process owner who is part of the innovation management team. The owner has to pay attention to upcoming innovations, monitor the existing process and define CAPA (corrective and preventive actions) to ensure the handling of misleading threads. New innovations, regardless of whether they are technology-driven or human-centered, they have to be documented and positioned on an innovation roadmap. A structured valuation process will help to deduce the next milestones for the whole innovation process.
- Technology level: Early reviewing and valuation of upcoming technology is an important part within the change level. One has to do intensive market surveillance and has to have profound knowledge to deduce strengths and weaknesses of new approaches. Especially standardization namely IHE and HL7 is an important requirement for sustainable IcT infrastructures lasting over decades and enabled to cope with the next evolutionary steps. Contracts and orders for innovations have to follow by a clearly defined specification of requirements. Innovation has to fit with the defined vision and not vice versa. This is a new way of thinking, as hospitals tend to accept the rules defined by the industry today. The technology level is directly related to the human-centered level as technology affect the manner how humans interacted within processes and with the process itself.
- Human-centered level: Digitalization will only be successful if it fits to the end users' needs and their way of working. People are differently affine to digitalization: you will find those that are keen on almost every new technology (by that taking profit for business from gadgets and services that they are already using at home), others are more reluctant. In order to cope with that, there has to be a strong participation of people in the design of digital supported processes. Besides those involved in early phase of implementation of these processes, there has to be a set of procedures to allow education as well as training of all employees. Those procedures will contribute to a constantly improving health literacy of the different user groups and the whole organization. It is not only the

responsibility of the government but also of the hospital to ensure the improvement of digital skills. We can show that digital competence as well as digital sovereignty foster the acceptance of new technology within handed down, paper-based process.

Digital Health Innovation Engineering is supporting the implementation of the above-mentioned levels for the digitalization in hospitals. One key methodology is the digital maturity index for hospitals. Every method within DHIE relates to one responsible within the RACI matrix. With Digital Health Innovation Engineering, we developed a framework to structure digital transformation within hospitals. The results we derived from our work at DNU has to be declared as preliminary results. Thus, there will be a set of steps following to advance the DHIE framework:

- We are already onboarding more hospitals to evaluate the existing methods, especially the measurement of digital maturity.
- The measurement of health literacy, digital competence and sovereignty within the digital maturity index has to be refined.
- Together with the Hochschule für Gesundheit (University of Applied Science), we will work on a method to structure education and trainings for health professionals. The technology level will be the key input parameter to deduce relevant competences.

References

Fitzgerald M, Kruschwitz N, Bonnet D, Welch M (2014) Embracing digital technology: a new strategic imperative. MIT Sloan Manag Rev 55:1

Gløersen E, Drăgulin M, Hans S et al (2016) The impact of demographic change on European regions. European Union, Brussels

Gottschalk P (2009) Maturity levels for interoperability in digital government. Gov Inf Q 26:75–81. https://doi.org/10.1016/j.giq.2008.03.003

Humphrey WS (1988) Characterizing the software process: a maturity framework. IEEE Softw 5:73–79. https://doi.org/10.1109/52.2014

Kagermann H (2015) Change through digitization—value creation in the age of industry 4.0. In: Albach H, Meffert H, Pinkwart A, Reichwald R (eds) Management of permanent change. Springer Fachmedien Wiesbaden, Wiesbaden, pp 23–45

Legner C, Eymann T, Hess T et al (2017) Digitalization: opportunity and challenge for the business and information systems engineering community. Bus Inf Syst Eng 59:301–308. https://doi.org/10.1007/s12599-017-0484-2

Meister S, Becker S, Leppert F, Drop L (2017) Digital Health, Mobile Health und Co. – Wertschöpfung durch Digitalisierung und Datenverarbeitung. In: Pfannstiel MA, Da-Cruz P, Mehlich H (eds) Digitale Transformation von Dienstleistungen im Gesundheitswesen I. Springer Fachmedien Wiesbaden, Wiesbaden, pp 185–212

Morabito V (2015) Big data driven business models. In: Morabito V (ed) Big data and analytics. Springer, Cham, pp 65–80

Schuh G (2017) Industrie 4.0 maturity index: managing the digital transformation of companies (acatech STUDIE). Herbert Utz, München

Thuemmler C (2017) The case for health 4.0. In: Thuemmler C, Bai C (eds) Health 4.0: how virtualization and big data are revolutionizing healthcare. Springer, Cham, pp 1–22

Vogelsang M (2010) Digitalization in open economies. Physica-Verlag HD, Heidelberg

Sven Meister is heading the department "Digitization in Healthcare" at the Fraunhofer Institute for Software and Systems Engineering in Dortmund. He holds a diploma degree and doctorate in computer science, focused on the procession of bio-medical data. Since 10 years, Sven Meister is driving the research on disruptive digital innovation in healthcare at Fraunhofer ISST forward. As data has become more and more important, actual projects are asking for data-driven solution as well as strategies for real-world implementation of them. Sven Meister is (co-)author of over 40 publications.

Anja Burmann is Scientist in the Department "Digitization in Healthcare" at the Fraunhofer ISST. During her academic career, she gathered practical experience at Dräger Medical, Siemens Healthcare and the Medical Technology Department at the Research Organization SINTEF. At Fraunhofer she is working on research topics gathering around digitizing hospital processes, both operationally and strategically, and assessing Digital Maturity.

Wolfgang Deiters is a professor for Healthcare Technologies in the Department of Community Health at the Hochschule für Gesundheit (University of Applied Science). In this position he mainly views healthcare innovation from the end user's perspective for obtaining a user oriented health technology and process development. His re-search topics are digitalization strategies in healthcare, hospital engineering, user oriented healthcare services for prevention, therapy and care, mobile health and especially health literacy.

Digital Transformation in Healthcare: How the Potential of Digital Health Is Tackled to Transform the Care Process of Intensive Care Patients Across All Healthcare Sectors

Charlotte Vogt, Martin Gersch, Claudia Spies, and Konrad Bengler

Abstract

(a) **Situation faced**: The digitalization case reports from the care process of the fictitious mechanically ventilated patient, Mr. Müller. After inpatient treatment in the ICU of the Charité, Mr. Müller is awaiting his discharge to the outpatient nursing care facility of LRD that is an outpatient care provider for long-term mechanically ventilated patients. The current care process of long-term mechanically ventilated patients is determined by insufficiently coordinated care processes between the inpatient and outpatient care providers and missing standards and tools for information exchange and communication between the care providers, as well as between the care providers and the patients. Motivated by the unsatisfactory patient data management across all healthcare sectors, Mr. Müllers takes part in the feasibility study of the scientifically supported innovation project Bea@Home. The aim of the project is to develop, test, and evaluate an innovative, integrated, and digitally supported care model for mechanically ventilated patients.

(b) **Action taken**: This section focuses on the digital transformation of the care process introduced by the innovation project Bea@Home and describes the implemented inter-organizational, technological, and organizational changes in detail. As digital innovations in German healthcare typically face the

C. Vogt (✉) · M. Gersch
Freie Universität Berlin, Berlin, Germany
e-mail: charlotte.vogt@fu-berlin.de; martin.gersch@fu-berlin.de

C. Spies
Charité Berlin, Berlin, Germany
e-mail: claudia.spies@charite.de

K. Bengler
Linde Remeo Deutschland GmbH, Munich, Germany

© Springer International Publishing AG, part of Springer Nature 2019
N. Urbach, M. Röglinger (eds.), *Digitalization Cases*, Management for Professionals, https://doi.org/10.1007/978-3-319-95273-4_18

challenges of idiosyncratic and often non-interoperable IT infrastructures and applications as well as non-coordinated processes, the development and implementation of coordinated organizational processes across the relevant healthcare sectors is an essential basis for any intersectoral change process before technological aspects, such as the implementation of digital health solutions, can be addressed. The inter-organizational changes refer to collaboratively developed process and quality standards that integrate the relevant healthcare sectors. The technological changes refer to the digital solutions implemented in the feasibility study, including an inter-sectoral EHR, a video conference tool, and AAL services. The organizational changes refer to the change processes within each organization that are triggered by the aforementioned inter-organizational and technological changes. These are the adjustment of firm internal process standards and their documentation, HR training on the use of the digital solutions, the creation of new organizational positions, as well as the specific customization of the digital solutions.

(c) **Results achieved**: The qualitative evaluation of the feasibility study from the perspectives of the care providers and the patients shows a distinct amelioration of the quality of life for the mechanically ventilated patient, Mr. Müller. Furthermore, an increase in the quality of care, especially in outpatient care, as well as during the discharge and re-admission process, is indicated. The quantitative evaluation of the new care model from an economic perspective, being a process cost analysis of digitally supported care processes, shows an unbalanced allocation of benefits and costs between the inpatient and outpatient healthcare sector. Due to the higher commitment of the hospitals' physicians during the outpatient care process, the new care model causes a distinct increase of the personnel related process costs for the hospital. At the same time, the personnel related process costs decrease for the outpatient care providers due to the reduction of patients' re-hospitalization.

(d) **Lessons learned**: This digitalization case highlights five key lessons learned: (1) the necessity of changing governance structures for successful digital transformation processes, (2) the necessity of adequate business models for the different actors involved, (3) the meaning of a strategic fit between digital solutions, and market regulations and standards, (4) for the special case of German healthcare—the necessity of changing reimbursement models for innovative digital care models, and (5) the reciprocal relation between digitalization and inter-organizational collaboration.

1   Introduction

The digitalization case sheds light on the digital transformation in German healthcare. Specifically, the case reports from the digital transformation of the care process of mechanically ventilated patients across all healthcare sectors as part of a scientifically supported innovation project. The focus lies on the inter-organizational, technological, and organizational aspects of digital transformation processes. They have effects on the focal actors including the inpatient and outpatient care providers and the patients. In detail, the digitalization case portrays the situation currently faced, as well as the actions taken in the innovation project Bea@Home, the achieved results and the lessons learned. Bea@Home, funded by the German Federal Ministry of Education and Research, has been conducted from 2013 to 2016 as a collaboration of the Charité—Universitätsmedizin Berlin (Charité), the provider of outpatient nursing care facilities for mechanical ventilated patients, Linde Remeo Deutschland GmbH (LRD), several providers of information technology, telecommunication systems and digital health solutions, as well as academic institutions. The aim of Bea@Home was to develop, test, and evaluate an innovative integrated care model for mechanically ventilated patients under the premises of digital supported process and quality standards, as well as economic efficiency across all healthcare sectors. Looking at digital transformation, a special focus of this digitalization case lies on the digital solutions supporting the integrated care process, including an electronic patient record (EHR), a video conference tool, and ambient assisted living (AAL) services accessible via a tablet PC. Further, the aligned process and quality standards. The effects they have on the focal actors were also examined. Thereby, the quality of patients' care throughout the care path ought to be improved and the costs of care—for each care provider, as they are in the best case, the total costs for the health insurances—ought to be reduced.

As the organizations and the research project described in the case are real, the mentioned persons, the patient Mr. Müller in particular, are fictitious. However, all characters are representative for persons as they actually occur in the innovation project, Bea@Home and in the organizations.

2   Situation Faced

The core of this digitalization case is the care process of the fictitious mechanically ventilated patient, Mr. Hans Müller. Mr. Müller, 78 years old, suffers from a very severe form of chronic obstructive pulmonary disease (COPD GOLD grade 4) after 50 years of intensive tobacco smoking. After a severe aggravation of his medical condition, Mr. Müller was admitted to the Charité and was treated there in the ICU for 10 weeks.

The Charité is a maximum care hospital with over 3000 beds in Berlin and is Europe's largest university clinic. The ICU, being the biggest clinical unit of the Charité, is responsible for 26% of the revenues and 24% of the costs (data from 2016). Thus, besides a strong focus on the quality of intensive care, the physicians of the ICU also operate under a high cost pressure. They must constantly rationalize the relationship between the reimbursement they receive from the health insurances based on the diagnosis related groups (DRG) and the actual treatment costs. This leads to economic incentives for early discharges of patients from the ICU to another clinical unit or outpatient care facilities. In consequence, the patients' need for further non-acute intensive care might be less considered and assessed. This effect is reinforced by the lack of adequate outpatient care solutions for intensive care patients currently existing in German healthcare. In particular, long-term mechanically ventilated patients often still have a need for non-acute intensive care after their discharge from the ICU that is still crucial for preventing later re-admissions to the hospital. Frequent re-admissions (so-called 'revolving door-effect') pose a very costly und unsatisfying challenge for both the hospitals and health insurance because mechanically ventilated patients often arrive at the hospital in a much deteriorated health status with a high need for new, cost intensive care. Furthermore, re-admissions often represent a clear decrease of the health-related quality of life for the patients, as they need to be hospitalized again. Balancing this trade-off between providing and assuring a high quality intensive care, not only within the ICU but also, in the subsequent care process, and rationalizing costs and revenues determines the daily work of the physicians and nurses in the Charité's ICU.

At this point, Mr. Müller is mechanically ventilated via a tracheostoma, conscious and responsive, but immobile. After a recent medical examination, his treating physician at the Charité assigns a further palliative medical treatment, as the cure from COPD is not possible anymore and he currently does not show potential to be weaned from the invasive mechanical ventilation (so-called 'weaning potential'). However, since his mechanical ventilation is stable and well adjusted, the treating physician advises to proceed with the palliative care in the outpatient care sector. He recommends the discharge to the local outpatient nursing care facility of LRD that is specialized in the intensive long-term care of mechanically ventilated patients.

LRD is a German subsidiary of Linde AG, a global provider of medical gases. The company entered the market in 2005 and currently operates 7 outpatient nursing care facilities with 160 beds in total in Germany. These facilities specialize in the intensive long-term care of mechanically ventilated patients. Like every outpatient nursing care facility, LRD's facilities must be (re-) accredited by the federal state nursing care insurance fund. Since the (re-) accreditation process does not acknowledge the special structural, personal, and financial conditions, requirements and care services of specialized nursing care facilities, LRD's nursing care facilities and their care services are reimbursed at the same rate as non-specialized care facilities. This results in financial distress for LRD and the need for selective contracting with health insurances in order to balance the costs of the specialized care provided and the reimbursements received. The selective contracts LRD settles with health insurances are based on high quality standards, such as special training of the nursing staff, a high staffing ratio, special technical equipment, nursing care practices, and collaboration with local care and service providers (e.g. physicians, therapists, hairdresser, catering, and entertainment). Thus, in its competition with non-specialized nursing care providers, LRD puts a strong emphasis on the quality of their nursing care services. However, LRD's nursing care, information, communication processes, and quality standards, are not yet aligned with those of preceding care providers such as hospitals and results in a strong competition for target patient groups.

As Mr. Müller wishes to not spend his time left in a clinical setting, he appreciates the advice of the physician and asks him for the exact procedure of the discharge. The physician tells him that with the situation faced by Charité and LRD, the current care and discharge process of a mechanically ventilated patient presents as follows: Mr. Müller's discharge from the Charité to LRD will most likely be realized without a proper information exchange between the care providers in a joint discharge conference. Even though joint discharge conferences of the inpatient and outpatient care providers are strongly recommended by the relevant medical guidelines (Randerath et al. 2011; Schönhofer et al. 2014), they are not realized in most cases as time capacities are rare for Charité and LRD staff. Instead, Mr. Müller's arrival at LRD will be requested and organized by phone. His physician letter with the key patient data and information on his inpatient treatment will be sent to LRD via fax—in the best case, on the discharge day but in most cases, within the first days of outpatient care. In the event that the physician finds time, additional information on Mr. Müller's inpatient treatment can be collected and handed over to the LRD's case manager on the discharge day as an extra paper-copy or sent to LRD via fax upon request later on in the outpatient care process.

Once Mr. Müller has arrived at LRD, the nursing staff has to create a new paper-based patient file for Mr. Müller, representing LRD's firm internal patient data management system and then manually transferring the patient data provided in the physician letter and any potential additional documents. As the physician letter does not contain a proper nursing anamnesis of the patient, LRD's nursing staff then has to sit down with the patient and fill out the new paper-based file word by word.

As frequent re-admissions of Mr. Müller to the Charité will be necessary for, firstly, regular medical examinations and technical check-ups, and, secondly, cases of emergency, the challenge of exchanging patient data and insufficient coordinated care and communication processes regularly occurs during the outpatient care process as well. For elective re-admission to the Charité, LRD, firstly, needs to request an appointment by phone with an average waiting time of 2–4 weeks. During this time, the patient remains in LRD's facility. On the day of re-admission, LRD, secondly, needs to collect all the relevant patient data in the paper-based patient file and create paper-copies for the Charité. Once the patient is in inpatient treatment again, LRD is obliged to keep the bed for the patient without receiving the full reimbursement rate from the health insurances. When the patient returns to LRD, the information exchange process via paper-copies, fax, and phone calls repeats itself. For emergency re-admissions, the process is slightly different, as the patient has to be transported to the nearest hospital by an ambulance, without any documented patient data in most cases. According to a Charité's physician, the care process of long-term mechanically ventilated patients like Mr. Müller is currently determined by, firstly, insufficiently coordinated care processes between the Charité and LRD, enforced by a missing consensus of the key actors on process and quality standards, especially in outpatient nursing care. Secondly, it is determined by missing standards and tools for information exchange and communication between the care providers, as well as between the care providers and the patients. In consequence, the process of gathering, documenting, and exchanging patient information and data across all healthcare sectors is very time consuming, tiring, and unsatisfactory for the Charité and LRD, as well as for the patient. Furthermore, the process results in frequent re-admissions of mechanically ventilated patients to the Charité, representing a critical cost factor for the hospital, LRD, the health insurances and the healthcare system.

Considering the unsatisfactory information and patient data management during the discharge and care process across all healthcare sectors and motivated by the possibility to reduce the number of elective re-admissions to clinical care, Mr. Müller is very interested in taking part of the feasibility study of the innovation project Bea@Home as a test patient.

3   Action Taken

The aim of the innovation project Bea@Home is to develop, test, and evaluate an innovative, digitally supported integrated care model for long-term mechanically ventilated patients that bridges the currently existing gap between the inpatient care in a hospital and the subsequent outpatient care in nursing care facilities. A special focus of Bea@Home lies in the stronger integration of the different inpatient and outpatient care providers along the care path, and the support of this integration by adequate digital solutions, such as an EHR, a video conference tool and conceivable AAL services. The latter are accessible by means of a tablet PC the patient receives as part of the feasibility study. The objective of the digital transformation of the care process across all healthcare sectors is first, to improve the quality of patients' care and second, to reduce the costs of care—for each care provider, as well as, in the best case, the total costs of care for the health insurances.

The Charité's motivation to participate originates predominantly from the insufficient coordination of the inpatient and outpatient process and quality standards, as well as from the high cost pressure due to the frequent re-admissions of long-term mechanically ventilated patients to the ICU. Conversely, LRD sees the innovation project mainly as an enabler for the company's IT strategy to replace the currently used paper-based patient data management system (PDMS) with an EHR. In the following, it is seen innovative to exchange patient data with previous and subsequent care providers of the care path, such as ICUs and local physicians, therapists and home care providers. LRD's objectives are, firstly, to promote the standardization of their care and business processes and thus, to promote the establishment of their current business model in German healthcare. Second, LRD's objective is to integrate their processes with those of previous and subsequent care providers, which marks an important part of their future planned business model. Thirdly, the patients' tablet PC provides a chance to test various digital health solutions for information and knowledge management, such as an e-learning service customized to train mechanically ventilated patients and their families to enjoy a more self-determined life. The patient's motivation to take part in the innovation project originates predominantly from Mr. Müller's fear of the frequent regular re-admissions to clinical settings for medical and equipment check-ups and the necessary inpatient treatment accompanied with it.

The outlined case is characterized by the typical challenges of digital-based, inter-sectoral innovations in German healthcare: idiosyncratic IT infrastructures and applications with a lack of interoperability, as well as process and incentive systems that are not coordinated between the relevant healthcare sectors. Therefore, the development and implementation of coordinated governance architectures and inter-organizationally coordinated processes represents an essential basis for any intersectoral change process before technological aspects can be addressed. Thus, the action taken at the inter-organizational level, followed by the technological and the organizational level of each organization, will be discussed successively in the following.

Inter-organizational Changes The basis of the inter-organizational changes made in the innovation project are, in the first step, the collaborative modeling and analysis of the current care process across all healthcare sectors using BPMN and EPC,[1] as well as an extensive requirement analysis considering the different target patient groups and their special needs of care and digital support. The results are a process model displaying the current care, business, and information processes and a set of personas representing the different target patient groups and their specific needs of medical treatment, nursing care and digital support. In the second step, the project partners develop a target process displaying the entire care process from inpatient care in Charité's ICU over outpatient care in LRD's nursing care facility to outpatient care in the patient's home setting. Besides the actual care processes of the inpatient and outpatient care providers along the care path, the target process model also shows the business, documentation and information processes of the focal actors, as well as the used documents and information systems (Kastrup et al. 2017) (Fig. 1).

The most relevant inter-organizational changes apply to the following sub-processes of Mr. Müller's care process: the discharge process from the Charité's ICU to LRD, the outpatient care process at LRD and the re-admission process to the Charité and back to LRD.

The inter-organizational changes in the first sub-process schedule that a first video conference with the support of the EHR takes place 1 h before Mr. Müller's actual discharge to LRD. Therewith, the new care model accommodates the recommendations of the relevant medical guidelines and supports the inter-sectoral integration in the discharge process via digitally supported joint discharge conferences. Besides the Charité's staff in charge (treating physician and clinical

---

[1]These abbreviations refer to the two widespread modeling notations in business process management: Business Process Model and Notation (BPMN) and Event-driven Process Chain (EPC) (Laudon et al. 2015).

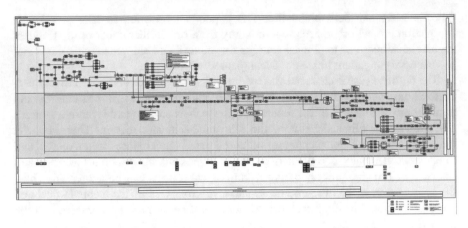

Fig. 1 Target process model of Bea@Home (Kastrup et al. 2017) (CC by 4.0: https://creativecommons.org/licenses/by/4.0/)

case manager), Mr. Müller's local general practitioner (GP) and LRD's staff in charge, a case manager and the future main contact nurse, take part in the video conference. Mr. Müller's stationary treatment in the ICU during the past 10 weeks, the current status of his mechanical ventilation and weaning potential, and his overall health status are discussed. Thereafter, the documentation of this information in the EHR is checked. Furthermore, the care providers already arrange the date for the next video conference that is taking place within the first 5 days of outpatient care. As a result, Mr. Müller is digitally transferred in the EHR from the responsibility of the Charité to LRD's responsibility and after that, physically transported to LRD with a patient transport ambulance (PTA). As scheduled, the next video conference takes place within the first 5 days of Mr. Müller's outpatient care at LRD. There, the Charité's physician and the LRD's case manager and nurse discuss the start of the nursing anamnesis and care process at LRD. The Charité's physician and Mr. Müller's GP also discuss his current medical condition, the current status of his mechanical ventilation, possible development scenarios of his medical condition and weaning potential. They conclude that all settings can be maintained for the moment. At the end of the video conference, the results are documented in the EHR and the last video conference of the discharge process is scheduled for in 5 weeks. Five weeks later, the key actors of the care process meet again digitally in order to check and discuss Mr. Müller's medical condition and mechanical ventilation status. The Charité's physician assigns a conscious wound care by LRD's nursing staff and treatment with antibiotics by the local GP, as Mr. Müller's tracheostoma looks slightly infected. Furthermore, the Charité's physician and the local GP agree to conduct video conferences every 3 months during the outpatient care process for regular check-ups. Thereby, the inter-sectoral discharge process in the new care model is completed.

In the second sub-process, the inter-organizational changes become especially apparent in the regular video conferences between the Charité's physician, LRD's nursing staff and case manager, and Mr. Müller's local GP. Mr. Müller's overall health status is examined, the status of his mechanical ventilation are regularly checked, and his weaning potential is analyzed. Sometimes, Mr. Müller actively participates in the conference while other times, just an exchange of know-how between the care providers is necessary. Additionally, the care providers conduct video conferences on demand, either to clarify relevant questions and discuss current concerns or to check on observed indicators for an increasing weaning potential of Mr. Müller.

The inter-organizational changes in the third sub-process, the re-admission process of Mr. Müller from LRD to the Charité and back again, refer again to video conferences taking place to prepare the elective re-admissions of Mr. Müller. Here, the care providers inform each other about Mr. Müller's current medical condition, the planned examinations and the results. Additionally, an appointment for elective re-admissions can be made using the email and calendar service operating on Mr. Müller's tablet PC and via the EHR.

Besides the development of the new inter-organizational and inter-sectoral target process, the collaborative development of quality standards and quality indicators across all healthcare sectors represents another important inter-organizational change. Here, the Charité and LRD agree on a set of quality indicators for the inpatient and outpatient care of mechanical ventilated patients. They regulate, for instance, that a patient's local GP has to be determined and contacted before the patient's discharge from the hospital and that an EHR has to be used that is accessible to all care providers along the care path. Furthermore, the quality indicators require that the next control examinations and video conferences have to be scheduled before the patient's discharge and the outpatient care process has to be accompanied by a standardized contact possibility to the Charité, such as a video conference tool.

Technological Changes The technological changes introduced by the innovation project Bea@Home refer to the digital solutions implemented in the care process and the necessary regulatory and technological changes made in the information exchange processes within and between the focal actors. In detail, an EHR is used that is accessible for all care providers along the care path, a video conference tool is used for the real-time visual communication between the inpatient and outpatient care providers, as well as between the care providers and Mr. Müller. Additionally, several AAL services are used that are accessible via the tablet PC provided to Mr. Müller. Focusing on these digital health solutions, Bea@Home stresses three of the central digital health solutions currently discussed, developed and used in German healthcare and in international healthcare systems (Gersch and Wessel 2018). In the following, they are described in more detail.

The EHR is used for the documentation of Mr. Müller's personal, medical, and nursing care data and is accessible by all care providers along the care path. Such inter-sectorally integrated EHR are currently not yet widespread in German healthcare and are only used as prototypes in innovation projects in most cases (Amelung et al. 2017). One main reason for this is the still not established telematics infrastructure, as well as the incomplete observance and implementation of international standards (on a syntactic, semantic, and pragmatic level). Passed by the SHI modernization act in 2004 and further concretized by the act on secure digital communication and applications in the health care system (E-Health Act) in 2016, the German Bundestag enacted to develop and establish a telematics infrastructure that works as the basis for the usage of various digital health solutions, such as an EHR, an electronic medication plan and an electronic physician letter. Although, researchers and industry experts generally assess the telematics infrastructure as a promising and important step towards a better integration of healthcare sectors, organizations, actors, and data, it is not yet established in German healthcare. As a consequence, the sector wide establishment of innovative digital health solutions and their interoperable integration with other existing information systems, such as hospital information systems (HIS) and medical practice management software (PMS), still suffer from the lack of a safe and secure infrastructure (Wessel et al. 2017). Thus, already existing EHR in German healthcare do not yet span the borders of the healthcare sectors and inter-organizationally integrate actors and data in most cases.

Considering LRD's motivation to take part in the innovation project—the replacement of the current paper-based PDMS by an EHR and the data exchange with key actors—LRD is willing to invest in an EHR. After consulting with the Charité's physicians on the minimal medical requirements of an inter-sectoral EHR, LRD buys the standard version of an EHR from a middle-sized IT provider. The EHR supports internationally established IT interfaces, such as IHE and HL7 (Gersch and Wessel 2018), and internationally established IT and nursing care standards. However, being an EHR standard version for nursing care in a clinical context, LRD needs to customize the EHR to their special needs. These are, firstly, their internal process and quality standards, as well as those required from the medical experts in the innovation project; secondly, the outpatient nursing care processes for mechanically ventilated patients with special equipment lists, nursing care, and quality indicators as well as thirdly, the data exchange with the Charité as an external partner. Here, the innovation project represents itself as an arena of high value for LRD since the company can profit directly from the collaboration and exchange of information and know-how with the Charité's medical experts. Even though the initial acquisition of the EHR and its customization process represent high investments for LRD, the value of an EHR customized to its special needs and the subsequent possibility to scale the EHR to other nursing care facilities is foreground for the company. For the innovation project, however, a full integration of the EHR and the HIS of the Charité is not possible due to the Charité's strict data security policy and the time restriction of the project. Nevertheless, the possible integration of the EHR with HIS and PMS of local physicians in the future, based in the interoperability due to emerging integration standards (Federal Ministry of Education and Research 2017), is one main argument for LRD to invest in the EHR.

The other digital health solutions are the video conference tool used for real-time visual communication between the care providers, and between the care providers and Mr. Müller, and the AAL services that are accessible via Mr. Müller's tablet PC. Therewith, Mr. Müller can communicate with his family via a private video communication tool, and an email and text messaging service. Further, he can arrange and organize medical appointments and video conferences via a calendar service. Additionally, the AAL services encompass an e-learning service to support a more self-determined life, providing teaching videos related to mechanical ventilation care in a home setting and the technical details of mechanical home ventilators.

Organizational Changes The organizational changes introduced by the innovation project Bea@Home refer to the processual, technological, and personal changes within each organization, triggered by the inter-organizational and technological changes made during the digital transformation of the care process. The inter-organizational changes introduced by Bea@Home, namely the target process model, require processual changes within the organizations of the inpatient and outpatient care providers. In detail, Charité and LRD need to modify their internal care, business and information process, such as documenting the patient's data in the EHR and scheduling time and human resources for the video conferences. LRD, in particular, also needs to change their internal care process so they fit to the standards of structural, processual, and outcome quality required by the Charité.

These processual changes also come along with the necessity of personal changes within the organizations. In detail, LRD decides to include the new organizational position of a respiratory therapist in their nursing care facilities. Respiratory therapists are fully trained nurses or physiotherapists with a special further education that allows them to provide special care for patients with respiratory and pulmonary diseases in close collaboration with physicians and nurses.

Second, technological changes introduced by Bea@Home, namely the implementation of an inter-sectorally integrated EHR, a video conference tool, and AAL services, require technological changes within the organizations of the care providers. In detail, the implementation of the EHR requires LRD's investment in the acquisition and customization of an EHR. Secondly, this decision involves the replacement of the firm internal paper-based PDMS by the EHR, accompanied by a comprehensive modification of the firm's internal process guidelines. In a third step, the implementation of the EHR requires an intensive customization process of the EHR to the special needs of LRD as a specialized outpatient care provider for long-term mechanically ventilated patients. Therefore, LRD commissions the IT-provider to map the firm internal processes as well as the collaboratively developed processes in the EHR, and to include the relevant LRD and Charité staff with the corresponding system rights in the EHR. Fourthly, the implementation of the EHR, as well as the video conference tool and the AAL services, requires intensive HR trainings of LRD's and Charité's staff. Therefore, the company holds several firm internal IT workshops to train its nursing staff and to support the digital change process triggered by the Bea@Home.

4   Results Achieved

After the feasibility study of Bea@Home is completed, the evaluation phase of the scientifically supported innovation project begins. Different researcher teams evaluate Bea@Home, shedding light on the user perspective, being the care providers and patients, the medical and nursing care effects, and the economic effects of the innovation project on the different actors. In order to analyze qualitative and quantitative results, the researcher teams conduct interviews with patients and key actors, undertake participatory observations in care settings and project meetings, analyze several documents, and conduct an economic analysis of the digital transformation process implemented in Bea@Home.

The interviews with Mr. Müller revealed that at the run-up of the feasibility study, he had some concerns regarding the use of the video conference tool because he fears his lack in technical skills when using digital products. Furthermore, he is afraid that the fewer direct contacts to the Charité's physicians in the feasibility study might lead to more and stronger aggravations of his medical condition and hence, more frequent re-admissions to the Charité. Instead, he reports that he constantly felt very well taken care of and supported, not only by LRD's nursing staff and his local GP, but especially, by the Charité's physicians and medical experts. In his experience, all care providers constantly had a high level of information about his medical condition and his personal wishes and goals for the care process. He received good support and training on using the video conference tool and the AAL services via the tablet PC; furthermore, he could always ask for help. Good support on the one hand and the close connection and integration of the care providers, as well as of the care providers and him as a patient on the other hand, made him feel safe and secure. Thus, he felt more relaxed in his aggravated health status.

The Charité's and LRD's assessment of Mr. Müller's medical and nursing care condition confirm Mr. Müller's positive experiences made in the feasibility study of Bea@Home. In particular, the relevance of the EHR-supported video conferences clearly revealed to the Charité's physicians and to LRD's staff. First, the intersectorally accessible EHR enabled the electronic documentation and organization of patient data and allowed the digital exchange of patient data between the inpatient and outpatient care providers. Therewith, the care providers constantly had a good overview of Mr. Müller's current health status and weaning potential. They were able to react in a well-informed manner to questions and concerns that arose during the care process. Second, the video conference tool enabled a real-time digital communication based on collaboratively agreed process standards. Thus, frequent re-admissions of Mr. Müller to the Charité that were necessary for medical examinations and technical check-ups in the current care process, could have been avoided. Instead, re-admission resources were saved for cases of emergency and other clearly clinical scenarios. As described below, this had a clear effect on the cost structure of both the Charité and LRD, as well as the health insurances. Third, the usage of the EHR and especially the video conference tool proved to be trust building in the doctor-patient-relationship. In the end, the use of the EHR-supported video conferences on a regular basis, as well as on demand, enabled a closer relation between Mr. Müller, the LRD's staff, the Charité's physicians and the local GP.

Regarding the economic evaluation of the digital transformation process introduced by and implemented in Bea@Home, a team of management and information systems researchers conducts a comparative process cost analysis. The analysis focuses on the costs related to personnel deployment and compares the process costs between the current and the target care situation (Häkkinen et al. 2013; Dyas et al. 2015). The aim is to analyze the economic effects the new care model has for the main care providers, Charité and LRD. In detail, the process cost analysis is performed as a static analysis, shedding light on the processes in one single point in time. Likewise, the dynamic analysis sheds light on the processes over a time span of 12 months. Four sub-processes are chosen that show the highest digital support by the EHR and the video conference tool, with the aim to overcome the current prevalent sectoral borders between inpatient and outpatient care. These four sub-processes are: (1) the patient's discharge from the Charité to LRD, (2) the nursing care process at LRD, (3) the re-admission of a patient to the Charité, and (4) the new patient transfer from the Charité to LRD after a re-admission (Gersch et al. 2017). As expected, the results of the process cost analysis show an unbalanced allocation of benefits and costs between the main care providers: as the process costs related to personnel deployment in the sub-processes increase for the Charité, they decrease for LRD.

Regarding the Charité, the static process cost analysis shows that the process costs related to personnel deployment in the target care process increase by 28% over all sub-processes, compared to the current care situation. This result represents the higher personnel deployment necessary to conduct the video conferences throughout the care path and to document all the relevant patient data in the EHR. This result is put into perspective by the dynamic process cost analysis for the Charité. The dynamic analysis still shows an increase of the process costs related to personnel deployment for the Charité. However, at 3% it is much lower than in the static analysis. Concerning the process costs due to the extra documentation in the EHR, these process costs result from the missing integration of the EHR and the Charité's HIS. In case of a full integration of the information systems in the future, the process costs due to personnel deployment for the extra documentation of the patients' data in the EHR would disappear. As a consequence, the observed high process costs of the new care model for the Charité would decrease and the allocation of benefits and costs between the Charité and LRD would be more balanced.

However, the results of the static and dynamic analysis show that the objective of a closer integration of the Charité with subsequent care solutions (e.g., LRD's facilities) is associated with higher personnel deployment to conduct video conferences in the discharge process on a regular basis. Furthermore, the demand during the process of outpatient care and in the case of necessary re-admissions of a patient to the Charité rises. However, in light of the increased quality of care and quality of life of the patients, as the medical evaluation indicates, the small increase of the process costs of 3% compared to the current care situation seems to be justifiable and acceptable for the Charité (Gersch et al. 2017). Besides, these effects illustrate the necessity of innovative contract and finance models that acknowledge the positive effects of increasing quality of care and quality of life, as well as decreasing the revolving door effect for health insurance funds (Gersch et al. 2011; Vogt et al. 2017a). In detail, adequate contract and finance models should accommodate the additional personnel and technical efforts of hospitals related to innovative care models, such as regular video conferences. A conceivable legal basis for such contract and finance models are special care models, referred to in § 140a SGB V. According to this article, a management company can make an agreement with a health insurance fund for the full-service solutions of an integrated care model and allocate the returns to the actors involved in the integrated care model.

Regarding LRD, the process cost analysis shows that the new care model leads to a cost reduction for LRD. This result is in line with the aforementioned unbalanced allocation of benefits and costs between the two main care providers. In detail, the dynamic process cost analysis shows a decrease of costs related to personnel deployment over all four sub-processes in the target care process of 68%. This result represents the much smaller personnel deployment necessary in the discharge process of the patient from the Charité to LRD, during the care process at LRD, as well as in the re-admission process. Here, the digital support of the sub-processes by the EHR and the video conference tool shows the highest impact. For LRD, patients' re-admissions to a hospital require the attendance of LRD's nursing staff during the patient transport. During the hours-long absence of the nursing staff, the nurse is missing as working staff at LRD and at the same time, the hours of absence are not reimbursed by the health insurance funds. Thus, the frequent re-admissions and patient transports in the current care process, both for regular check-ups and in the case of emergency, represent a severe cost factor for LRD. In the feasibility study, many of these re-admissions could be realized as digital meet-ups via EHR-supported video conferences, saving costs for LRD (Gersch et al. 2017). Thereby, the workload for the nursing staff to organize complex and cost-intensive patient transports to the hospital, which are mandatory based upon the relevant medical guidelines (Windisch et al. 2010), could be reduced.

However, these results have to be interpreted in relation to the high investment necessary to buy and customize the EHR, the subsequently necessary reengineering of the internal care processes and process guidelines, the special IT-training of the nursing staff and the costs accompanied with the new certification and accreditation of the nursing care facilities. These investments only prove reasonable if (1) LRD succeeds in scaling the EHR to their national and international nursing care facilities, (2) the process and quality standards inscribed in the EHR are aligned with medical practice guidelines being currently and in the future in force, and (3) a sustainable reimbursement solution can be settled with the health insurance funds that acknowledges the high investment made into the digital support of the new care model.

5   Lessons Learned

Digital Transformation and Changing Governance Structures As a first lesson learned, this digitalization case sheds light on the relation between the digital transformation in healthcare and governance structures of integrated care models. In the current situation, the care process of mechanically ventilated patients in German healthcare is determined by insufficient care, business, and information processes. Legally and economically independent actors interact with each other along the care process on the basis of single transactions, representing a rather market-like governance structure. Conversely, in the new integrated care model developed in the innovation project Bea@Home, legally independent but economically integrated and thus, dependent actors, particularly the inpatient and outpatient care providers, realize the integrated care model together as a full-service-solution for the patient. Interpreted from a governance perspective, the new care model rather represents a network-like governance structure (Vogt et al. 2017b). Accordingly, formal governance mechanisms, such as collaboratively developed inter-sectoral process and quality standards, and the integrated EHR, as well as informal governance mechanisms, such as consensus about process and quality standards and information exchange via video conferences, are applied and determine the configuration of contract, collaboration and finance models (Vogt et al. 2017b). In conclusion, this digitalization case reveals the need for change of governance structures and mechanisms in healthcare as the digital transformation of healthcare services, business models, and actors' communication increases.

Digital Transformation and Adequate Business Models As a second lesson learned, this digitalization case highlights the need for adequate business models for a successful digital transformation in the healthcare sector (Vogt et al. 2017a). This applies for inpatient and outpatient care providers, health insurance funds and providers of information systems and digital solutions. For the realization of innovative integrated and digitally supported care models that put the patient and his care path center stage, the actors involved need to clearly understand themselves as service providers that collaboratively offer a full-service solution to the patient. In addition, this digitalization case reveals the need for the courage to invest in innovative care solutions before the market and the contract situation of the future are clarified. However, as long-term and high-risk approval procedures are common for innovative care solutions in the primary healthcare market in Germany, the courage to invest can hardly be realized by start-ups and established market players operating under severe financial distress (Rogowski 2016).

Digital Transformation and the Fit with Market Regulations and Standards As a third lesson learned, this digitalization case sheds light on the relationship between the digital transformation in German healthcare and the fit of digital solutions with current market regulations and standards. On the one hand, current market regulations and standards (e.g., laws), medical practice guidelines and standard procedures (e.g., IHE and HL7), function as a point of reference. Thus, they represent drivers of the specific and risky investments care providers need to make in the acquisition, customization, and implementation of digital solutions. If current market regulations and standards promote the usage of digital solutions, the necessary specific investments are less risky for the investing care provider (Vogt

2017). In this digitalization case, this aspect is especially revealed in the case of the EHR. As the EHR is not fully integrated with the currently existing information systems (HIS, PMS) and is not yet based on a nation-wide established telematics infrastructure, the specific investments made by LRD in the acquisition, customization and implementation of the EHR (including staff training and process adaption) pose a high financial risk for the company. If the aspired future integration of the EHR with HIS of other hospitals and PMS of local physicians cannot be realized, the investments made will become, at least in part, sunk costs for LRD (Vogt 2017). Here, the paradox of specific investments, as analyzed for various other empirical fields (Gersch et al. 2013; Afflerbach 2015), also proves relevant for the empirical field of (German) healthcare (Gersch and Kops 2012; Vogt 2017). This paradox may also motivate actors to try to collaboratively influence current market regulations and standards so that they promote and secure the usage of digital solutions the actors have invested in (Vogt 2017). On the other hand, current market regulations and standards may also function as security for already established market players in German healthcare. As they promote the usage of digital solutions, the specific investments already made by actors are secured for their first-best use (Vogt 2017). Another aspect is the attempt of actors to collaboratively shape existing or develop new market regulations and standards by various activities. This may encompass the active integration of institutional actors, such as medical expert associations and politicians, in the collaborative development process of new regulations and standards in innovation projects. Co-creation processes of new regulations and standards, as well as collaborative activities to legitimate regulations and standards at the institutional level, are other observable strategic activities of actors in German healthcare (Adler 2015; Vogt 2017).

Digital Transformation and the Reimbursement by Health Insurance Funds The fourth lesson learned from this digitalization case sheds light on a more industry-specific aspect of German healthcare: the reimbursement of healthcare services by health insurance funds. This digitalization case stresses the relevance of adequate contract and finance models that account, first, for the positive quality effect integrated and digitally supported care models often have, and second, for the additional effort of and costs for the care providers necessary to realize such innovative care models. Only if highly committed and innovative care providers receive a financial compensation for their additional effort and costs, integrated and digitally supported care models will successfully and sustainably work and establish. Here, an inter-sectorally integrated quality assurance is of high relevance, too. A board of experts mandated to monitor the quality of care of all care providers along the care path and to regularly report on it to the health insurance fund is just one conceivable formal governance mechanism to realize a reimbursement for innovative digital solutions and rationalize the balance between the quality and the costs of care at the same time (Vogt et al. 2017b).

Digital Transformation and Inter-organizational Collaboration: A Reciprocal Relationship Finally, yet importantly, this digitalization case sheds light on the reciprocal relationship between the digital transformation in German healthcare and the inter-organizational collaboration of actors. On the one hand, digital solutions, such as the EHR and the video conference tool aim to further integrate the processes and information of inter-organizational actor. Thus, function as enablers of inter-organizational collaboration. On the other hand, the collaboration of actors from different healthcare sectors, organizations, professions, and scientific disciplines is a prerequisite to successfully implement and establish digital solutions that encompass actors from different organizations. Consensus about process and quality standards, responsibilities and technical terms needs to be achieved among the collaborating actors before an innovative digital solution that breaks with long-term established and rigid process habits can be successively implemented and established in the market (Wessel 2014; Vogt 2017).

References

Adler H (2015) Balanceakt Innovation: Das Management unternehmungsexterner und -interner Entwicklungsverläufe über Proto-Institutionen. Dissertation, Freie Universität Berlin

Afflerbach P (2015) The business value of IT in light of prospect theory. Bus Inf Syst Eng 57:299–310. https://doi.org/10.1007/s12599-015-0400-6

Amelung VE, Eble S, Hildebrandt H, Knieps F, Lägel R, Ozegowski S, Schlenker R-U, Sjuts R (eds) (2017) Innovationsfonds: Impulse für das deutsche Gesundheitssystem. Medizinisch Wissenschaftliche Verlagsgesellschaft, Berlin

Dyas SR, Greenfield E, Messimer S, Thotakura S, Gholston S, Doughty T, Hays M, Ivey R, Spalding J, Phillips R (2015) Process-improvement cost model for the emergency department. J Healthc Manage 60:442–458

Federal Ministry of Education and Research (2017) Medical informatics funding scheme: networking data – improving health care

Gersch M, Kops C (2012) Das Paradoxon spezifischer (E-Health-) Investitionen: Diffusionshemmnis oder Innovationsmotor? In: Deutsche Gesellschaft für Gesundheitsökonomie (ed) Jahrestagung der Deutschen Gesellschaft für Gesundheitsökonomie (DGGÖ) 2012

Gersch M, Wessel L (2018) E-Health und Health-IT. In: Gronau N, Becker J, Kliewer N, Leimeister JM, Overhage S (eds) Enzyklopädie der Wirtschaftsinformatik: Online-Lexikon, 10. Auflage. GITO, Berlin

Gersch M, Schröder S, Hewing M (2011) Erlös- und Finanzierungsmöglichkeiten innovativer Versorgungs- und Geschäftssysteme im Gesundheitswesen – Systematischer Überblcik und exemplarische Analyse ausgewählter Geschäftssysteme. E-Health@Home-Projektbericht

Gersch M, Rüsike T, Reichle F (2013) Competence building in electric mobility – solving the paradox of specific investments in nascent industries. Int J Automot Technol Manag 13:273–288

Gersch M, Vogt C, Gertz C (2017) Ökonomische Evaluation eines integrierten, IT-unterstützten Versorgungskonzepts im Gesundheitswesen: Eine ökonomische Analyse von E-Health-unterstützten Versorgungsprozessen aus betriebswirtschaftlicher Perspektive. Freie Universität, Berlin

Häkkinen U, Iversen T, Peltola M, Seppälä TT, Malmivaara A, Belicza É, Fattore G, Numerato D, Heijink R, Medin E, Rehnberg C (2013) Health care performance comparison using a disease-based approach: the EuroHOPE project. Health Policy 112:100–109

Kastrup M, Tittmann B, Sawatzki T, Gersch M, Vogt C, Rosenthal M, Rosseau S, Spies C (2017) Transition from in-hospital ventilation to home ventilation: process description and quality indicators. Ger Med Sci 15. https://doi.org/10.3205/000259

Laudon KC, Laudon JP, Schoder D (2015) Wirtschaftsinformatik: Eine Einführung, 3., vollständig überarbeitete Auflage. Pearson Studium, Munich

Randerath WJ, Kamps N, Brambring J, Gerhard F, lorenz J, Rudolf F, Rosseau S, Scheumann A, Vollmer V, Windisch W (2011) Durchführungsempefhlung zur invasiven außerklinischen Beatmung. Pneumologie 65:72–88

Rogowski W (ed) (2016) Business Planning im Gesundheitswesen: Die Bewertung neuer Gesundheitsleistungen aus unternehmerischer Perspektive. Springer Gabler, Wiesbaden

Schönhofer B, Geiseler J, Dellweg D, Moerer O, Barchfeld T, Fuchs H, Karg O, Rosseau S, Sitter H, Weber-Carstens S (2014) Prolongiertes weaning. Pneumologie 68:19–75

Vogt C (2017) Spezifische Investitionen in Innovationsvorhaben: Kooperative Managementstrategien zur Steuerung von spezifitätsbedingtem Commitment. Freie Universität, Berlin

Vogt C, Gersch M, Koch H (2017a) Geschäftsmodelle und Wertschöpfungsarchitekturen integrierter, IT-unterstützter Versorgungskonzepte im Gesundheitswesen. Diskussionsbeitrag, Wirtschaftsinformatik, Freie Universität Berlin

Vogt C, Gersch M, Gertz C (2017b) Governance in integrierten, IT-unterstützten Versorgungskonzepten: Eine Analyse aktueller sowie zukünftig möglicher Governancestrukturen und -mechanismen. Diskussionsbeitrag, Wirtschaftsinformatik, Freie Universität Berlin

Wessel L (2014) Inscribing as institutional work: a case study of the implementation of an inter-organizational information system in a German integrated care network. Dissertation, Freie Universität Berlin

Wessel L, Gersch M, Harloff E (2017) Talking past each other. Bus Inf Syst Eng 59:23–40. https://doi.org/10.1007/s12599-016-0462-0

Windisch W, Brambring J, Budweiser S, Dellweg D, Geiseler J, Gerhard F, Köhnlein T, Mellies U, Schönhofer B, Schucher B, Siemon K, Walterspacher S, Winterholler M, Sitter H (2010) Nichtinvasive und invasive Beatmung als Therapie der chronischen respiratorischen Insuffizienz.: S2-Leitlinie herausgegeben von der Deutschen Gesellschaft für Pneumologie und Beatmungsmedizin e. V (Non-invasive and invasive mechanical ventilation for treatment of chronic respiratory failure. S2-Guidelines published by the German Medical Association of Pneumology and Ventilatory Support). Pneumologie 64:207–240

Charlotte Vogt is a postdoctoral research associate at the Department of Information Systems at the School of Business & Economics of the Freie Universität Berlin. Charlotte Vogt has been working in the research areas of technology-driven change and transformation processes in the field of healthcare. As the sub-project coordinator in the interdisciplinary research project "Beatmungspflege@Zuhause (Bea@Home)" (BMBF funding 2013–2016) and as the research coordinator of an interdisciplinary research funding initiative to the German Research Foundation (DFG) on the topic of transformation in healthcare, Charlotte Vogt has gained special expertise in various healthcare related research areas (e.g., governance and collaboration structures in integrated care models, process analysis of integrated and IT supported care processes, business model innovation) as well as in coordinating and moderating interdisciplinary group processes at the intersection of economics, information systems/digitalization and healthcare. Charlotte Vogt received her PhD on the topic "Specific Investments in Innovations: Cooperative Strategies to Manage specificity-related Commitment" in 2017 at the Freie Universität Berlin.

Martin Gersch is full professor at the School of Business & Economics at the Freie Universität Berlin and there a founding member of the Department Information Systems. He is also the head of the Entrepreneurship Education at FU Berlin ("Digital Entrepreneurship Hub (DEH)") and served as a responsible researcher at the DFG Pfadkolleg Research Center on "Organizational Paths" at the Dahlem Research School of Freie Universität Berlin as well as at the Focus Area "DynAge" (Excellence Initiative of the German Research Foundation DFG). Since 2017 he is Principal Investigator ("Digital Transformation") at the Einstein Center Digital Future (ECDF). Martin Gersch has been working in the fields of technology-driven change and transformation processes, e-business/e-health, entrepreneur-ship, service engineering, business model analysis, management and economic theory, innovative teaching and learning concepts (e-/blended learning arrangements). He published more than 140 papers and serves as a reviewer for, amongst others, the DFG, WI/BISE, OSS, ICIS, ECIS, AMCIS, EGOS, SMS, AoM, MF.

Claudia D. Spies, born 1961, studied medicine in Erlangen-Nuremberg, and at Harvard University. She graduated, passed her ECFMG exam and received her doctorate in 1987. From 1987 to 1993 she was trained in Anesthesiology and Intensive Care in Nuremberg and at the "Freie Universität Berlin". Since 2005 she is Head of the Department of Anaesthesiology and Intensive Care Medicine at Charité Campus Mitte and Campus Virchow-Klinikum, being responsible for >50,000 anaesthetics a year, 93 ICU beds, and 2 pain clinics. From 2011 to 2014 she was Vice Dean for Educational Affairs at the Charité. She is a member of the executive committee of the "AWMF", the National Academy of Science "Leopoldina", and the "Apparateausschuss" (DFG).Her scientific interest focusses on risk prevention in anaesthesiology and intensive care, postoperative delirium, neuro monitoring and patient-centered long-term outcomes such as cognitive dysfunctions. Scientific indices: h-index 55, scientific papers 699, total citations 14,527 (Scopus searched Oct 20th, 2017), impact factors 1,425,921. Grants: public and non-public >20 Mio €.

Konrad Bengler is working since 2007 in several roles at the Linde group, since 2012 as Managing Director for the German Remeo country organization with seven locations in Germany. He was co-founder of the BMBF founded research project Bea@Home. Within this project he was responsible for the project lead. Konrad Bengler is a trained ICU Nurse and Nurse Manager and holds a MBA in Management and Communications from the FH Vienna, University Applied Sciences of WKW. He has been invited as speaker in national and international congresses.

Data Innovation @ AXA Germany: Journey Towards a Data-Driven Insurer

Alexa Scheffler and Christian Paul Wirths

Abstract

(a) **Situation faced**: AXA is transforming towards a data-driven insurance company to fully unlock the potential of its data. However, the transformation faces several challenges: Firstly, implementing a living data-driven decision-making system, demands a cultural change in the business lines. Secondly, the heterogeneous infrastructure complicates the deployment of advanced technologies. Data harmonization techniques are outdated, causing low computing performance, and high maintenance costs. Thirdly, insurers have to fulfill new legal regulations ensuring strict data protection. Since the functional roles to address the aforementioned challenges are not clearly assigned, a new organizational entity within AXA Germany was required.

(b) **Action taken**: The Data Innovation Lab was founded to focus on these tasks. It is a cooperation of the units Data Analytics, Data Management Office, and Data Engineering under one transversal roof. Data Analytics drives innovative data analytic projects and designs new solutions for complex business challenges. The Data Management Office is concerned with process efficiency, compliance, stability, and evolution. This includes tasks such as initiating activities for data quality improvements, providing data architecture and prioritizing data protection. Data Engineering builds the technical infrastructure, accelerates the evolution of the IT landscape and implements a data lake.

(c) **Results achieved**: A target operating model shows how AXA Germany operates the tranformation towards a more digital, data-driven, and customer-centric organization. The target operating model (TOM) of Data Analytics states the tasks, role definitions and a cooperation model of how to

A. Scheffler (✉) · C. P. Wirths
AXA Konzern AG, Paris, France
e-mail: alexa.scheffler@axa.de; christianpaul.wirths@axa.de

© Springer International Publishing AG, part of Springer Nature 2019
N. Urbach, M. Röglinger (eds.), *Digitalization Cases*, Management for
Professionals, https://doi.org/10.1007/978-3-319-95273-4_19

operate innovative data analytic projects. The TOM of Data Management Office states the tasks, role definitions and disciplines of how to provide an efficient and compliant data organization. The TOM of Data Engineering states the tasks, role definitions, and a cooperation model of how to develop and operate the data lake.

(d) **Lessons learned**: It is essential to build up an interdisciplinary work environment as Data Analytics and the Data Management Office operate at different speeds. A bottom-up transformation, which actively involves every member of the enterprise, is required to establish a cross-sectional data culture. The funding is allocated depending on several factors: Data initiatives have financial incentives but also an experimental orientation. Most of the data management activities are necessary due to future regulatory requirements. Furthermore, a major success factor on the data-driven journey is the support and the commitment of the top-management.

1   Introduction

AXA is a worldwide leader in insurance and asset management, serving 107 million clients, operating in 64 countries and employing 165,000 people in 2016. AXA Germany serves 8 million clients and employs 9217 staff. AXA Germany is yielding a yearly revenue of 10.7 billion Euros, which is around 10.7% of the AXA Group. The revenue comes from 26.8% Protection & Health, 35.4% Savings & Asset Management and 37.8% Property & Casualty (P&C). AXA is constantly seeking future improvement to "empower people to live a better life" (AXA 2017a, b). To meet the fast evolving customer needs and to grow in the challenging economic environment, "transform" is one of the two pillars of AXA's strategic plan called Ambition 2020 (AXA 2016a, b). In this plan, data plays a key role for digitalization. Today, the traditional business model of the insurance industry is faced by environmental drivers like *technology, market conditions, customer behavior*, and *regulations*, which, in turn, force the industry to rapidly develop digital capabilities. These drivers are illustrated in the following.

Major progress in *technology* allows us to handle the tremendous increase in data volume and formats—IDC expects 163 zettabytes in 2025 (IDC 2017). Technological innovations such as machine learning, artificial intelligence, robotic process automation, and on-demand computing power via cloud solutions enable the insurance industry to improve their business in two major aspects, to offer highly customer-oriented products and to increase operational efficiency. First, the technological innovations open a new dimension to design insurance products that satisfy customer needs. Pricing techniques are becoming more tailored to the actual profile of the insured person. To illustrate the impact for a specific product, in car insurance the geographic, driving behavior, and vehicle data predict whether a driver will claim his/her car insurance, allowing fairer premiums. Quantitative marketing strategies are providing more detailed customer segmentation. Thereby, products for high-risk cases can be designed which were previously not available. Furthermore, insurers are discussing methods to forecast chronic diseases based on patient data in order to optimize prevention methods in the health insurance sector. Additionally, AXA is accessing new use case scenarios. For example, AXA supported modeling the flood risk of the Seine via geographical and water data to ensure early evacuation actions (AXA 2016a, b). Summarizing, AXA is moving from a service provider that is focused on quantifying risks to a partner who proactively contributes to risk reduction and who uses the technological innovations to enhance operational efficiency. As an example, claims processing could be automated and simplified, leading to a notable increase in throughput.

The transformation is correlated with challenging *market conditions*. Low interest rates are reducing investment returns and contractual payouts of products such as life insurances. Thus, AXA is exploring alternative ways of revenue generation by designing new products. As the first insurance, AXA launched "fizzy", a blockchain platform for parametric insurance against flight delay (AXA 2017a, b). AXA's ridesharing insurance in cooperation with BlaBlaCar reflects another new innovative product (AXA 2015a, b).

This movement is a response to changes in *customer behavior*. Direct medial distribution channels make information and services more accessible than ever. The P&C branch is redefining itself, since a growing number of online intermediary services allow the customer constant price comparisons. AXA enters these distribution channels to offer the best market price to both current and future customers.

New *regulations* are constantly emerging: Phenomena such as constant data tracking raise customer's concerns about data protection. The European Union addresses this issue by the General Data Protection Regulation (GDPR 2016). The insurance sector is adapting to the new regulations by reviewing their data compliance standards. AXA is firmly committed to the ethical use of its data (AXA 2015a, b). One of AXA's main objectives is to build trust and a reliable relationship with its customers, by ensuring data transparency and protection.

All these drivers send a clear message: To stay competitive within the fast-changing insurance sector, it is essential to fully unlock the potential of the owned data. However, the transformation goes beyond launching some new technology. It requires an infrastructure that provides the right data in the right format and with the right quality at the right time, combined with appropriate analytical tools and operated at an efficient cost level. Becoming a data-driven organization means to cover both back and forward looking functions and to answer precisely the "w" questions: who, what, when, why and where (Anderson 2015). Therefore, data must be managed efficiently and professionally through a partnership of business leadership and technical expertise. The long-term goal of AXA is to create a cross-divisional culture that turns challenges into opportunities, all of these facilitated by data-driven decision making. The following case describes how AXA Germany is driving the organizational change by founding the Data Innovation Lab.

2   Situation Faced

In this section, we describe the situation we faced and which led to the foundation of the local Data Innovation Lab.

- *Organization*
    The organization of insurance business is highly complex and various. Every business line relies on its own specialized knowledge and has established its proven workflows. For instance, business units in operations such as the customer contact center, have developed profound know how in their field of expertise and a specific data processing logic. However, these workflows have not been fully adapted to the complete chain from producer to consumer. To create a data-driven culture we have to reduce "knowledge monopolies" and make the shift towards a holistic view. We need the capability to combine the specific know how with the available enterprise data assets to maximize the synergy effects. As an example, valuable insights about the customer could be obtained if structured data can be extracted straight from the incoming calls of the call center. This data can be used for cross-selling opportunities and for improving the customer retention rate.
- *Infrastructure*
    The technical infrastructure is highly heterogeneous: Every business line has individual procedures of storing and accessing data. Data is stored in separate silos, by several legacy systems, each using its own structures and access technologies. Hence, modernization of the IT system landscape is required. As there is no enterprise-wide data repository, business lines are forced to implement individual solutions (e.g. excel macros) to harmonize data according to their needs. However, only the authors of these solutions might understand the logic behind those scripts and a sufficient level of quality for the application in other domains is not always guaranteed. Several functions may be performing comparable tasks with different logics, leading to inconsistent key performance indicators (KPIs), creating execution errors, and inacceptable run-time performance. These individual computing solutions should be reviewed and replaced by professional reporting solutions across the entire enterprise.
- *Governance*
    Many legal regulations such as the General Data Protection Regulation (GDPR 2016) greatly influence the data governance. For instance, customers can demand the personal information and its usage. Furthermore, access to such data is only permitted to employees who need to process it for business purposes like claims handling. If data is no longer required for business purposes, then it has to be deleted. Consequently, insurers have to comply with the GDPR requirements by precisely tracking customer data and by implementing data purging mechanisms. Besides the legal regulations, new innovations also raise ethical questions. In the beginning, we briefly mentioned the potential to predict chronic diseases based on patient data. In times of big data, what are ethical principles to be followed besides installing the "hard" regulatory requirements? An example is the breakthrough in

Table 1 Organizational structure of the Data Innovation Lab at AXA Germany

Unit (lead)	Division	Objectives	Tasks
Data Analytics (Chief Data Scientist)	Strategy (CSO)	Innovation, impact, revolution	• Initiate and operate innovative data analytic projects • Experimental work
Data Management Office (Chief Data Officer)	Finance (CFO)	Process efficiency, compliance, stability, evolution	• Ensure communication lines and decision committees • Initiate activities for data quality improvement • Provide data architecture • Safeguard data compliance • Serve as single point of contact for business lines
Data Engineering (Head of Development)	Information Technology (CIO)	Infrastructure ("enable")	• Implement data lake • IT landscape evolution

human genome sequencing that has massively extended the amount of available genomic data. To what extent is it ethical or justifiable to analyze this data?

Summarizing, the challenges in *organization*, *infrastructure* and *governance* demonstrate that we have to address topics such as data access, data architecture, data quality, data protection, information security and data analytics. So far, these functions have been spread across many business units. Seeing the big picture to run data-driven innovations on an enterprise-wide scope is difficult, given the current status quo. A central instance is required to coordinate data-related issues and projects.

3 Action Taken

To address the challenges stated in the previous section, AXA Germany founded the new units, *Data Analytics* and *Data Management Office*. Together with *Data Engineering*, these units now form the *Data Innovation Lab* as a virtual, cross-divisional team under one transversal roof. The mission of the Data Innovation Lab is to drive innovations, to increase operational efficiency, to foster technological advances and to ensure data protection. The objectives and tasks of the Data Innovation Lab units are summarized in Table 1.

4   Results Achieved

The results of this paper are target operating models of the Data Innovation Lab units. These target operating models contribute to embed digitalization into the daily business and transform AXA Germany towards a more digital, data-driven and customer-centric organization. In our sense, a target operating model consists of he required processes, tasks and role definitions.

4.1   Target Operating Model for Data Analytics

The objective of Data Analytics is to drive innovative analytic projects such as advanced statistical modeling in the claims process or the use of artificial intelligence in customer service. For example, a prototypical dialog system for customer service has been developed that has been currently extended into an independent project. The dialog system analyzes unstructured data like insurance contracts and thus, answers questions about contract terms or coverage. In the claims process for car insurances, a geospatial model is already in use to navigate customers to the next partner garage of AXA Germany.

Data Analytics is led by the *Chief Data Scientist*. His[1] main mission is to act as the local change agent in order to move AXA Germany towards a data excellent insurer and to define and drive the data strategic vision aligned with the enterprise strategy.

Core Activities of the Chief Data Scientist
- Gather business requirements for data analytics and drive innovative use cases and technology trends
- Scope and funnel the smart data initiatives portfolio, i.e. the objectives, deliverables, timeline, success criteria etc.
- Guide pilot testings of smart data solutions, lead the teams handover of successful solutions to both deployment and operation
- Educate and evangelize agile methodologies, tools and best practices

A *data scientist* systematically analyzes data to obtain new knowledge. He applies statistical methods via analytical applications to compute predictive or prescriptive models.

---

[1]The role description presented in this paper applies for female and male persons. To increase readability we used the male form throughout the text.

Core Activities of a Data Scientist
- Work closely with business experts to understand the operation needs and translate business needs into mathematical problems
- Collect, understand, analyze, integrate, and explore internal and external, structured and unstructured data, partly provided by data engineers
- Develop predictive and prescriptive models as well as simulation and optimization procedures and successively ensure the relevance, performance and robustness of the developed models

At AXA Germany, data analytic projects are called *smart data initiatives*. Smart data initiatives result in predictive and prescriptive models to generate insights for the business. Typical applications are fraud detection or pricing. Smart data initiatives also provide solutions for more unspecific questions like "What can we make better in the claims process?" without knowing what results to expect. Hence, we prefer the term "initiative" rather than "project" (a project has to have a defined result right from the start). Furthermore, we use the term "smart data" instead of the term "big data", because smart data initiatives are not only focused on big data but also use "traditional" structured data. To deliver business value, smart data initiatives focus on fast customer-facing and performance-oriented products. Agile approaches like design thinking and rapid prototyping are common methods used. Following a test-and-learn approach, ideas are tested in an early stage to see if they are working and if not the idea is quickly discarded and a new idea is tried. The team of a smart data initiative is working in a self-organizing, agile and cross-divisional way (Fig. 1). The core team consists of members from Data Analytics (data scientists), Information Technology (data engineers) and business line experts. Data architects and data stewards from the Data Management Office are guiding the smart data initiatives. These roles are described in detail in the following section about the target operating model of the Data Management Office. The steering committee is represented by members from the business lines, from data analytics and optional from IT. In cooperation with the business lines, the Chief Data Scientist prioritizes and manages the portfolio of smart data initiatives.

4.2   Target Operating Model for Data Management

The main mission of the *Chief Data Officer* is to ensure data is handled as an enterprise asset. He aligns business and IT roadmaps and defines guidelines and standards regarding data handling across the enterprise and coordinates data compliance activities. Furthermore, he acts as the change agent to promote a data culture throughout the enterprise.

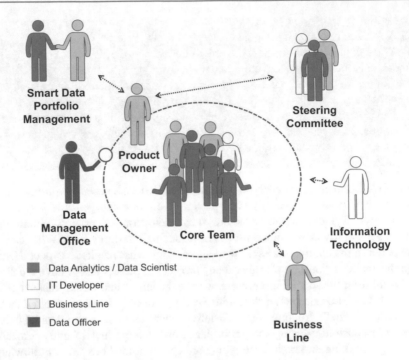

Fig. 1 Organization of a smart data initiative

Core Activities of the Chief Data Officer
- Initiate and develop the data management discipline
- Drive development of the smart data platform
- Propose investment prioritization with regard to business data strategy and support implementation of data-intense projects
- Trace risks in data handling by rating the criticality of processes, applications and service providers and arrange decisions for risks treatment (transfer, cure, accept or avoid)
- Install and run a board structure for data compliance

The primary mission of a *data architect* is to manage complex data and information delivery throughout the enterprise. He identifies new strategic data architecture topics and defines the data architecture vision to implement the business strategy in constant exchange with other architecture domains (business, application, IT infrastructure).

Core Activities of a Data Architect
- Review solution architecture and align it to enterprise data architecture
- Define data architecture guidelines and principles
- Design and maintain data architecture artifacts
- Identify data stakeholder groups, their information requirements and shared data elements
- Define data governance processes
- Guide and implement a common vocabulary and understanding of business data
- Monitor and enforce compliance of data standards
- Hold product ownership of metadata infrastructure, assist data stewards in creating business content and facilitate publication of meta data content within business and technical communities

A *Data Steward* is responsible for a specific data domain. He monitors the consistent use of data in IT applications in cooperation with data stewards of other data domains as well as with other data architects. He also ensures an appropriate data quality level and the compliance with enterprise guidelines. As a member of the internal control system he supports the data owner to comply with the guidelines. To fulfill these objectives, a data steward has a profound knowledge of the data repository and its business use.

Core Activities of a Data Steward
- Consult data base developers and review conceptual data models
- Gather data quality requirements and monitor data quality KPIs
- Identify and initiate measures for substantial data quality improvement
- Ensure clear storage of data elements (review duplicates and ambiguities)
- Review and validate meta data documentation

The core activities of the Data Management Office are to standardize data lifecycle management, to provide an efficient data service portfolio to the business lines, to facilitate data protection, information security and compliance, to uphold ethical principles and to spread data and meta data quality requirements across the enterprise. The activities are allocated to the data management disciplines data governance, data compliance, data architecture, data quality (The Data Management Association 2017). The product ownership of the smart data platforms reflects the technical infrastructure. The objectives of the data management disciplines are stated in Fig. 2.

Data governance ensures that all data is managed properly, according to principles and best practices about data access, usage, security and documentation.

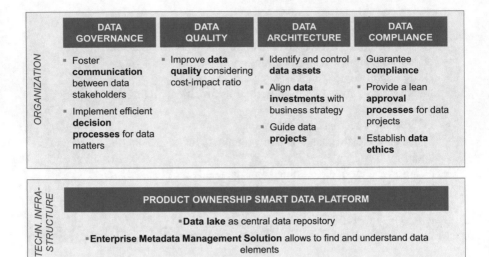

Fig. 2 Objectives of data management disciplines

Data governance is also framing how decisions about data matters are made, how roles are defined and how processes are designed.

The objective of *data quality* is self-explanatory—to improve data quality. Measures for data quality improvement need to be assessed regarding the trade-off between cost and efficiency. A first step towards a value oriented data quality management is the definition of data quality KPIs. These may serve as a guideline for decision making about future data quality measures.

The primary goal of *data architecture* is to identify the relevant data and to design and maintain its documentation. The purpose of the documentation is to guide data integration, to control data assets and to align data investments within the business strategy. Data architecture covers business architecture as well as application and IT infrastructure architecture. To guarantee alignment between these architecture disciplines, a constant exchange between data architecture and business architecture is essential.

The purpose of *data compliance* is to safeguard and audit the consistent creation, storage, and archiving or deletion of data according to business requirements and in accordance with legal and regulatory compliance (data lifecycle management). Furthermore, it drives the anchorage of data ethics within the company. To achieve this, it requires the collaboration of several units. Besides Data Protection, Information Security and Data Management Office, this involves the units Operational Risk Management and Compliance. To underline the close cooperation between these units, we named it "compliance & risk family". The compliance & risk family consists of two entities: The *compliance & risk council* brings together all decision makers and is concerned with strategic, cross-divisional issues. The *compliance & risk working group* is dealing with operational issues and advises projects and business lines on data questions.

The Data Management Office as provider for smart data infrastructure is the product owner of the smart data platform. The *data lake* is a data storage solution based on big data technologies. The *enterprise metadata management solution* assists in finding and understanding particular data elements not only on the data lake, but also throughout the whole enterprise IT landscape. Both, data lake and enterprise metadata management are core solutions for our new technical infrastructure for smart decision-making—the smart data platform. As product owner, Data Management Office gathers and prioritizes requirements, drives iteration goals and defines acceptance criteria.

4.3   Target Operating Model for Data Engineering

To deliver insights in a timely manner, AXA Germany introduced the data lake technology—a data storage and data analytics solution that offers more agility and flexibility than a traditional data warehouse. The data lake is an emerging technology that meets these criteria, because it allows us to store all our structured and unstructured data in one central data repository.

The Data Management Office is the product owner and together with *Data Engineering* we will build up the data lake in an agile project setting.

> **Core Activities of a Data Engineer**
> - Collect data, build and operate the data ingestion pipeline
> - Execute data cleansing
> - Logical and physical data modeling, implement data integration and data processing
> - Implement data encryption and decryption, data masking (pseudonymization and anonymization)
> - Provide access mechanisms to stored data
> - Operate housekeeping processes and data deletion on basis of legal requirements

In the initial phase, we are connecting about 20 internal database systems and 25 external data sources to the data lake over a streaming solution platform. Streaming makes data available in real-time which is a mandatory feature for solutions like fraud detection. During the ramp up phase of the data lake the selected data sources are connected. The objective is to industrialize the connection of source systems, so that we can progressively connect more source systems to the data lake in the following phase and thus, progressively enlarge the data repository. The cooperation model for the data lake is shown in Fig. 3.

1. Data Analytics and business lines or other implementation projects place their data requirements at the Data Management Office. The Data Management Office

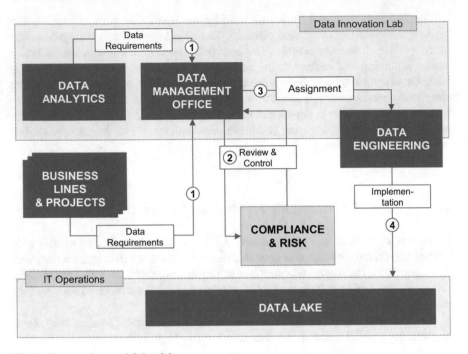

Fig. 3 Cooperation model data lake

validates the requirements and passes them to the compliance & risk working group.

2. The compliance & risk working group reviews the requirements for accessing the data lake regarding regulatory compliance risks and data ethics, and imposes any necessary compliance and risk conditions.

3. The Data Management Office inquires a change request to Data Engineering.

4. The Data Engineering team implements and operates the data lake together with IT operations in order to provide a technical solution for Data Analytics and the business lines.

5   Lessons Learned

Data Analytics and Data Management Office may have opposing positions that may result in conflicting objectives: being innovative versus being compliant, fast development versus stable processes, being efficient versus trial-and-error. While Data Analytics is able to quickly put smart data initiatives in operation, Data Management Offices drives the organizational change and builds the technical infrastructure, which often runs at a much slower pace (Fig. 4).

In daily business the different speeds appear in two issues: (1) the standard approval process slows down smart data initiatives and (2) data scientists spend

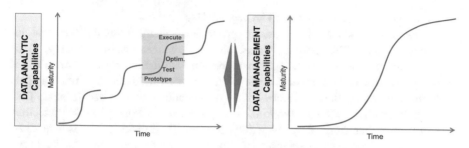

Fig. 4 Different speeds of the Data Innovation Lab units at AXA Germany

most of their time gathering the data rather than working on the data analysis itself. We handled the different speeds by founding the compliance & risk work group and by improving the data provision by a use case oriented prioritization in the data lake project.

First of all, smart data initiatives need a light-weight and agile compliance process that ensures that initiatives follow the strict legal and regulatory standards of the insurance industry throughout the whole lifecycle (prototype, test, optimize, execute) and that approvals are documented. As mentioned earlier, it is crucial for smart data initiatives to be tested as early as possible. To accelerate the existing process for smart data initiatives, the owner of a smart data initiative pitches his story in front of the compliance & risk working group which meets on a weekly basis. By doing so, most of the necessary compliance checks can be completed in a single meeting. The second issue concerns the data access as data scientists demand quick and easy access to data. The existing heterogeneous data landscape does not fit in with this requirement and thus, data scientists have to spend most of their time with collecting, integrating and understanding the data. To allow data scientists to concentrate on their core activity—which is to develop analytical models—a growing number of data sources are connected to the data lake. Following this use case driven approach, we are able to provide a growing data repository on the data lake that satisfies an increasing number of use cases.

Besides these insights on how to handle the two different speeds of Data Analytics and Data Management, we also want to share some further lessons that we learned.

- *Build up an interdisciplinary, agile working environment*

  Together with the Data Analytics team, Data Management Office created a shared office space at the center of the enterprise campus where people from different units can come together to work on smart data initiatives and other data projects. We use agile methods like sprint planning or design thinking to reduce the time to market and promote this way of working in other business areas. This working environment may not sound revolutionary, but is a challenge for an insurance company like AXA that was organized in hierarchical structures in the last decades.

• *Different disciplines—different ways of working*

   The compliance & risk working group is challenged by the fact that its members have different educational and professional origins. Usually, Data Protection members have a legal background, Information Security members a computer science background, Data Management Office and Operational Risk Management members an information systems and economic background. This leads to different ways of working. For instance, the work of Data Protection members is characterized by reviewing activities. Their main activity is to analyze the intended purpose of data usage and to map it to legal requirements. To do so, they demand a fully formed explanation of the project. Typical outcomes are documents such as advisory opinions or official statements. In contrast, Information Security, Data Management Office and Operational Risk/Compliance need less written evidence and receive their input via interviews. Therefore, it is much easier for these members to follow an agile approach.

• *Establish a bottom-up data culture*

   Data culture is the awareness of all staff members about data as an asset. The business lines play a key role in the journey towards a data-driven company. Therefore they have to attend the whole transformation process right from the start. The activities of the Data Innovation Lab are all about supporting the business lines to create value for the customer. A mere top-down approach is not sufficient to convince managers and specialists in the business lines to invest capacity into data activities. For instance, the business lines take the responsibility for the data they produce. Each division has its data owners who take into account the appropriate treatment of data issues. The Data Management Office supports them to establish processes for the appropriate treatment of risks regarding data and information. As we experienced some skepticism in the beginning, we started common activities to build bridges. E.g. a community meeting is held in the Data Innovation Lab office space on a regular basis. It is open to any specialist who wants to engage in the data community. In the community meeting, we present current technological developments and discuss their impact and potential. Our claim is not to sit in an ivory tower, but to actively participate and consult in enterprise initiatives and projects as partner.

• *Funding*

   The portfolio of smart data initiatives is diversified, solid financial initiatives, such as pricing and fraud detection, and highly innovative initiatives with an undetermined outcome. The profitable smart data initiatives provide funding for a kind of "innovation playground" where new ideas can be tested. Furthermore, regulatory induced mandatory projects such as GDPR (GDPR 2016) require mature data management capabilities and therefore, give funding to build up the data management organization.

• *Top management support*

   Top management has to be aware that such a journey is a long term investment. The data driven journey can only be completed with long-lasting and sustainable support from the top management. As the different speeds of the Data Innovation Lab units have shown, data management capabilities cannot be achieved in a short period and need to grow over the years. Adequate KPIs as well as reporting and control systems allows the tracking of progress for data maturity capabilities over time. It is difficult to measure the outcome of data management activities in monetary KPIs. Monetary benefit tracking would not represent the contribution of the data management and the impact of mature data architecture can hardly be described in quantitative terms, rather data management is creating qualitative benefits. For instance, data architecture deliverables improve the understanding of the existing data landscape and help business lines and projects to refine their planning and the architectural design of their solutions. Therefore, non-monetary KPIs are required to establish and control targets for data management resources and to create incentives for the business lines to participate.

References

Anderson C (2015) Creating a data-driven organization. O'Reilly, Sebastopol, CA

AXA (2015a) BlaBlaCar and AXA launch first-of-its-kind ridesharing insurance product. https://www.axa.com/en/newsroom/press-releases/blablacar-insurance-ridesharing. Accessed 14 Oct 2017

AXA (2015b) Has big data become too big? https://www.axa.com/en/spotlight/ story/big-data. Accessed 14 Oct 2017

AXA (2016a) Ambition 2020. https://www.axa.com/en/about-us/ambition-2020. Accessed 8 Jan 2018

AXA (2016b) How scientist and insures can come together to fight flood risk. https://www.axa.com/en/spotlight/story/Paris-flood-research-insurance. Accessed 14 Oct 2017

AXA (2017a) We want to empower people to a better life. https://www.axa.com/en/newsroom/news/we-want-to-em.power-people-to-live-a-better-life. Accessed 14 Oct 2017

AXA (2017b) AXA goes blockchain with fizzy. https://www.axa.com/en/newsroom/news/axa-goes-blockchain-with-fizzy. Accessed 14 Oct 2017

GDPR (2016) General data protection regulation. Regulation (EU) 2016/679 of the European Parliament. http://ec.europa.eu/justice/data-protection/reform/files/regulation_oj_en.pdf. Accessed 14 Oct 2017

IDC (2017) Data age 2025. https://www.seagate.com/files/www-content/our-story/trends/files/Seagate-WP-DataAge2025-March-2017.pdf. Accessed 14 Oct 2017

The Data Management Association (2017) Data management body of knowledge, 2nd edn. Technics Publications, Basking Ridge, NJ

Alexa Scheffler is Head of Data Management Office at AXA Konzern AG Germany. After her master degree in computer science, she worked as research associate at the Fraunhofer Project Group Business & Information Systems. Her Ph.D. is dealing with the economic evaluation of in-memory databases. She worked as consultant for enterprise architecture at Capgemini. In 2016, she joined AXA Konzern AG as Head of Data Management Office and is responsible for the implementation of AXA's data strategy.

Christian Paul Wirths is a Junior Data Strategist at AXA Germany. He has studied B.Sc. Econometrics & Operations Research at Maastricht University, including a 6 months exchange program at the Chinese University of Hong Kong. During his studies he gathered practical experience as an intern in Consulting and Investment Banking. As Data Strategist at AXA Germany, he consults the business lines focusing on data visualization and dashboard design by applying modern data exploration tool techniques. As part of the Data Management Office, he is supporting the setup of a data-driven working environment.

Volkswagen Education Lab: Accelerating the Digital Transformation of Corporate Learning

Mathias Wildgrube, Nils Schaupensteiner, and Jan Wehinger

Abstract

(a) **Situation faced**: As a car manufacturer, the Volkswagen Group faces a challenging business environment due to digitalization and new requirements regarding mobility. Those trends force automotive companies to review their portfolio. The development of new products and services results in a changing competence need within the (existing) workforce. To achieve the required skill transformation, new corporate education and training solutions based on innovative concept development is rapidly gaining importance.

(b) **Action taken**: The Volkswagen Group Academy is responsible for the training and development of the entire organization's workforce. To get an understanding of new technologies and trends in corporate education, the organization initiates the Education Lab as an independent unit. The lab's core idea is target group centered problem-solving. The development of new solutions starts with user problems regarding corporate learning at Volkswagen, which are examined by quantitative and qualitative methods. The lab therefrom uses an iterative, experimental method to validate the potential of the derived solutions to meet the identified user problems.

(c) **Results achieved**: When implementing the Education Lab's methodological approach, a key result is the development of prototype solutions that meet the target group needs. The accuracy with which the prototypes meet the needs of the target group validates the methodology of the Education Lab. In

M. Wildgrube (✉)
Volkswagen AG, Wolfsburg, Germany
e-mail: mathias.wildgrube@volkswagen.de

N. Schaupensteiner · J. Wehinger
MHP GmbH, Ludwigsburg, Germany
e-mail: nils.schaupensteiner@mhp.com; jan.wehinger@mhp.com

© Springer International Publishing AG, part of Springer Nature 2019
N. Urbach, M. Röglinger (eds.), *Digitalization Cases*, Management for
Professionals, https://doi.org/10.1007/978-3-319-95273-4_20

addition, the entire organization benefits from the lab's incubator-like approach, which helps to build technological expertise based on research and scouting. Herein, the lab empowers employees to participate in developing new ideas outside their day-to-day business and departmental structures.

(d) **Lessons learned**: Implementing an innovative approach such as the Education Lab within a traditional corporation results in a variety of challenges. The existing structures grew over a long time—and they work well in serving the current purpose. Hence, projected changes are often associated with uncertainty. The learnings gained out of the implementation of the Education Lab provide the opportunity to derive concepts and ideas about how to overcome innovation barriers within traditional organizations.

1   Introduction

Within every transformation process, the human is a central factor. The ongoing disruptive change transforms processes and products into fully connected and "always online" objects. Herein, the Education Lab puts its focus on people, not on technologies. To take affected people along during this transformation, it is important to provide them with state-of-the-art knowledge and therefrom, to create an understanding of the driving technologies and the overall change process. Profound knowledge about why respective changes proceed increases both, acceptance rate and probability of success. The Education Lab promotes this competence development. Its methodological approach and the learnings out of different implementation phases provide relevant insights for companies and organizations that face digitalization challenges especially within the transformation of the workforce skill set.

One of the key questions is how corporates such as Volkswagen can manage this proclaimed skill set transformation. Although there are many ideas evolving rapidly within the education technology sector, today's overall corporate adaption ratio is quite low due to regulation, fragmentation, and low investment volumes in educational research activities (Chatterji 2017). Looking beyond corporate structures, there are fields where adapting to innovative educational concepts is possible—and a proceeding agenda. For example, if we look at the academic sector, then it has become usual for top universities to offer their high-quality education in the form of MOOCs publicly and mostly free of charge (e.g. Stanford University and the University of Edinburgh or via platforms such as edx.org and coursera.org). The digitalization fosters the widespread distribution of training and education in a scalable, cost efficient manner. The World Wide Web and the connected objects and services based on it allow a new way of exchanging ideas, establishing collaboration, foster competence development, and further mutual learning activities. It reorders traditional hierarchical structures and enforces the worldwide distribution of knowledge (Davidson and Goldberg 2009).

Therefore, today's companies are driven by the necessity for a rapid adaption to this more than ever changing technological and economic environment. Education and training play an important role within this transformation. By utilizing new technologies and digital solutions, the corporate learning sector can contribute its share to the transformation of workforce and competence development structures. By using suchlike innovation-driven opportunities, corporate education offerings can overcome the former limitations of high cost and low individualization (Vernau and Hauptmann 2014; Wildi-Yune and Cordero 2015).

Traditional corporate education takes place at a predefined location, where a limited number of teachers teach a selected number of learners regarding the same content at one speed for all. In contrast, digitized education solutions deliver fully customized and learner-centred content. Herein, the learner is able to choose, which content at which place at what time he or she wants to study. By combining technology and education, new learning approaches can overcome the historical restrictions of being a one-way process. In the future, learning can be mutual and interconnected, where teachers and learners give and receive immediate feedback on their practice and progress. The variety of opportunities enabled by the digitalization and the utilization of new technologies and methodologies for education and training will be a game changer for the transformation of traditional organizations (Wildi-Yune and Cordero 2015).

Today, the Volkswagen Group is undergoing a massive change process. As a traditional car manufacturer and a global player with more than 600,000 employees, Volkswagen aims to transform itself from a car manufacturer towards a sustainable mobility provider in the near future. Therefore, a significant percentage of its workforce needs training and development in competence fields, which are not yet part of the traditional car manufacturer skill set. The digitalization is therefrom the core trigger for such competence needs, but it also provides a variety of solutions to meet this demand.

To explore the new competence fields and to understand the specific skill sets needed for future tasks within the disruptively changing mobility sector, Volkswagen searches for a new approach in corporate learning. The Volkswagen Group Academy is herein responsible for vocational and employee training, management development as well as academic-oriented education for employees at Volkswagen. To provide an outlook on the future of learning as well as to create an understanding of the necessary changes in corporate training, innovative approaches and ideas have to be considered and accelerated. Hence, the Volkswagen Group Academy founded the Education Lab as an independent part of the organization. To achieve the stated goals, the lab team develops and adapts methods of future thinking. With a consistent focus on the target groups of teachers and learners, the methodology of the Lab establishes iterative, experimental approaches in order to explore both, needs and potentials of corporate learning within the workforce.

2   Situation Faced

The transformation within the mobility sector has major effects on the direct workforce in production and assembly lines of traditional car manufacturers. Therefrom, new requirements for competence development and skill training arise. Whereas the complexity of the production process is reduced, the skills needed by the direct workforce within car factories are changing. In addition, the development of new energy vehicles and autonomous driving results in significant changes within the indirect labour. As of today, automotive design, powertrain and electronics development require traditional, mainly mechanical engineering design skills. In contrast, new energy vehicle powertrain and car concepts need significant lower number of components and a higher number of electronic and software solutions (Winterhagen 2016). Therefore, in the era of fully connected and autonomous mobility, a development team needs enhanced IT skills in programming, IT infrastructure, platform and cloud technology, machine learning and data science. In consequence, a significantly different skill set is required to manage future tasks and to remain competitively viable within the automotive sector. Hence, traditional car manufacturers are not only competing with their own kind, but with completely new competitors. Since the needed skill sets are the core competences of software companies, heavy weight global players such as Apple and Google stir up the mobility sector (European Sector Skills Council 2016; Balser and Fromm 2016; Fowler 2017).

In order to survive within this new economic setting, car manufacturers such as Volkswagen need to adapt quickly to the changing skill requirements. They have to reskill and upskill their existing, experienced workforce and make it ready for future tasks. In a state-of-the-art working environment with digital communication and collaboration focusing on problem-solving, companies have to equip their employees with all the required competencies and tools they need (World Economic Forum 2016).

The former concept of learning and studying for one particular job is obsolete. Personnel development and lifelong learning become even more important, since the speed of development and change regarding digital technologies and required skills accelerate exponentially. In addition, the demographic change exacerbates the demand to constantly extend and enhance the workforce's skill set. In addition, corporate education is a key factor for sustainable change, since developing competencies in new technologies is a prerequisite for a successful transformation towards new business solutions and models (Vernau and Hauptmann 2014; Bersin et al. 2016).

New educational solutions and technologies offer the chance to train a scalable number of people within a short period with lower costs at scale than traditional learning approaches. Even though the adoption rate of digital technologies in the corporate education sector is not as advanced as in other industries, both use cases and utilization of respective technologies are rapidly growing (Chatterji 2017). A key enabling factor is the pervasion of digital technologies within the workforce. As more employees have access to connected mobile devices, acceptance and potential of digital technologies for education and training purpose increase likewise (Davidson and Goldberg 2009). Even though the discussed opportunities seem to be obvious, companies need to put effort in evaluating the actual benefit of using digital education technologies, since traditional learners are not necessarily convinced about the advantages or just not used to apply the needed tools (Howard et al. 2016).

3   Action Taken

To accelerate and broaden digital learning, the responsible department for education and training within the Volkswagen Group—the Volkswagen Group Academy—initiates the Education Lab as an independent environment for iteratively testing new learning methods and technologies. The Education Lab should enable the organization to get an overall understanding of current and future developments in the corporate education sector. For testing its assumptions, the Education Lab creates its own methodology and finally specific corporate education solutions to foster the transformation of the entire Volkswagen Group workforce.

Therefore, the core approach of the Education Lab is a target group centred method. Each approach or product idea starts with the focus on users (learners or teachers). Using qualitative and quantitative methods, employees are directly involved during the entire concept and product development phase. By collecting the needs of the target groups through interviews, surveys, and observations, the lab's research team develops a comprehensive understanding of the actual pain points regarding corporate learning within the organization. Therefrom, the development of prototype products fully bases on real learner, teacher, and organizational needs.

In order to solve these pain points, the Education Lab analyses trends, technologies and scientific work within the educational sector, which derive from learning sciences, neuro sciences, learning theories and outlooks about the future of learning. Consequently, the lab's team starts with a problem-oriented ideation phase, which considers all collected information. A validation method based on Blank's Customer Development Model is adapted to the specific enterprise environment and utilized to develop solutions based on real user pain points (Blank 2006) (see Fig. 1).

In the ideation phase (phase 0), the identified trends and concepts in corporate learning are combined with actual user problems. Thus, many conceptual ideas are created in short time and subsequently evaluated. By using this target group oriented, iterative experimental approach, the Education Lab collects a significant number of innovative corporate learning ideas in a so-called prototype funnel.

In the validation phase, the solution concepts collected in the prototype funnel are examined. In phase 1, the definition for a "minimum demand" regarding the specific concept is set based on research assumptions and organizational goals. Thereupon, the actual demand for the respective solution concept is evaluated using an initial offer (prototype), which is presented to the target group (e.g. a landing page that simulates a new learning offering, but without any actual features). The response rate

VALIDATION   IMPLEMENTATION

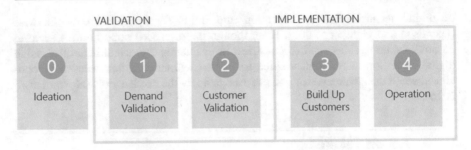

Fig. 1 Iteration method of the Education Lab based on Blank (2006)

to this initial offer is compared with the stated "minimum demand". If a sufficient demand is detected, the solution concept is selected for extended customer validation.

In phase 2, the development and utilization of a realistic prototype enables the lab's team to collect user experience at first hand in a fast and cost-efficient manner. The Education Lab therefore uses a lean startup based approach. The main goal is to gain knowledge regarding a new solution (the product) and the target customer in an iterative process (Ries 2011). Implicit ideas about how both product and market might work result in explicit assumptions. The goal is to consider assumptions for the current working environment in order to proceed continuous validation (Ries 2011; Harms 2015). Continual learning and iteration shapes this experimental method and hence enables an innovative product development phase. The Education Lab's goal using this lean startup approach is to solve problems that the target groups face within the corporate learning environment at Volkswagen and identify fitting solutions, e.g. by using new technologies. In addition, the validation results enable the lab's team to validate the Education Lab's methodological approach and to foster a continuous improvement process.

If the validation phase is successful, the next step is the first-time implementation of the product. In phase 3, an extended number of target users is contacted to scale up the solution. This phase is still part of the experimental process. Only if the user base grows significantly based on predefined goals, the product is pushed to the next level: the operations phase (4). The validated solution product is delivered to a target department, which takes care of the actual product rollout. The Education Lab thereafter restarts the whole ideation and validation process regarding a new target group pain point.

To establish a suchlike innovation process within the respective departments, an open mindset and widespread collaboration is needed. The Education Lab strives to forward this change process for the corporate learning division at Volkswagen. In addition, the lab acts as a hub to connect both, organization and startups. Those connections are not limited to education startups only, since exchanging with innovators and learning about new technologies encourages the internal Volkswagen innovation potential likewise. Finally, this continuous learning process enables the lab's team to derive specific solutions for the target group problems.

4   Results Achieved

Within the ideation phase of the Education Lab's approach, over 150 first conceptual solution sketches were created based on several user-centered workshops. The ideas within this prototype funnel were ranked and prioritized regarding their user acceptance, usability, and sustainability. Consequently, the following three concepts were selected:

1. A platform to rethink and reorganize competence development within the entire company.
2. A virtual robot training for the factory's workforce.
3. A concept to enable employees to train artificial intelligence in a scalable manner.

The respective product ideas and the Education Lab's methodological approach for product development are presented in the following:

As a first result, the so-called **Competence Development Platform** is designed based on the needs of the learners, which frame the specific challenges with current learning solutions and corporate education processes. Where the learners are missing the relevance of their personal learning activities, the company has extensive need for new competencies. As a multi-sided hub, the Competence Development Platform connects three parties that benefit from this new approach of interaction, communication, and collaboration regarding a transparent corporate skill enlargement. On the platform, departments that search for employees especially in new competence fields are connected with motivated employees, which are interested in personnel and professional development. Such potential learners are connected to internal and external providers of digital learning content, which offer a competence development path targeting the fitting skill set for the advertised job. Therefore, the Competence Development Platform achieved a new way of thinking about decentralized, democratised reskilling and upskilling of the existing workforce. The feedback collected of test learners during interviews is consistently positive. Respective employees are eager to provide ideas to enhance the entire concept. The possibility to learn future-oriented skills in a self-paced environment is identified as the key factor of success. In addition, the Education Lab's team continuously stays in contact with the learners through regular learner meetings and occasional calls. Moreover, it fosters the launch of an online learner community in order to guarantee support and guidance during the entire learning path.

However, the platform concept faces major challenges, especially regarding the integration of external learning providers. Overall, the effort needed to overcome such barriers in fields that are as promising to support the necessary competence development of the workforce is still immense.

The second result is the so-called **Holographic Robot Training**, which offers an innovative way of learning about industrial robot controls. Where as of today, physical robots are set up in a training area; this augmented reality (AR) based training enables instant and flexible learning about controlling different types of robots. Learners get the possibility to train whenever and wherever an AR head mounted device (HMD) is available and connected to the software. The HMD therefrom projects the virtual robot and its training setup onto a predefined, reality training area. This innovative solution is designed not to substitute but to expand the robot training possibilities. In the future vision, the Holographic Robot Training connects learners, independent from their location for collaborative trainings. As a result, it allows to:

- Learn about and simulate dangerous situations in training context, such as damage or miss functional behaviour of robots or connected applications.
- Virtually install any desired number of robots of any type and brand within the training area and therefore, create a learning environment that extends the working environment in reality.
- Reduce cost for hardware robot cells that are especially set up and only used for training purposes.
- Enable remote learning and guidance, which saves travel expenses.
- Support collaboration between learners from different regions, countries, and company brands.
- Record training sessions for later review and sharing.

This AR based concept consequently results in cost and time reduction as well as in a comprehensive, learner-centred training approach that motivates employees to enlarge and improve their robot control skills. The Holographic Robot Training is developed jointly in cooperation with an innovative startup named Viscopic GmbH. Once the first step of building a stand-alone version is finished, a detailed evaluation phase with teachers and students will take place (Fig. 2).

As the third result, the disruptive concept of **Teach a BOT** focusses the growing market and use case variety of artificial intelligence (AI). The concept targets the exploration of a new business area for the educational sector. Education professionalized the transition of knowledge from human to human. The ongoing automation, which complements human workforce with machines, will also affect the indirect labour (office based knowledge work), since the growing utilization of software and algorithms increases the number of available intelligent systems and applications. Machine learning and AI enable and accelerate this process. In traditional computer science, programs have to be hard coded. With machine learning and AI, the software is taught to master new tasks as an opposite to predefined rules that define how tasks are executed. The core idea of Teach a BOT is that machines (bots, digital assistants, algorithms, etc.), which support humans in knowledge work, have to be trained. In contrast to the teaching of subjects that might be substituted by automated technologies in the near future, the concept target is to prepare the human workforce for future AI training tasks.

Since its core idea is to ease the teaching of AI software, the concept needs acceptance within the organization and departments, which utilize AI. However, Teach a BOT faces two major challenges: Implementing an approach, where a scalable number of employees trains algorithms, results in significant resistance based on doubt and concerns regarding AI. Secondly, transferring the necessary

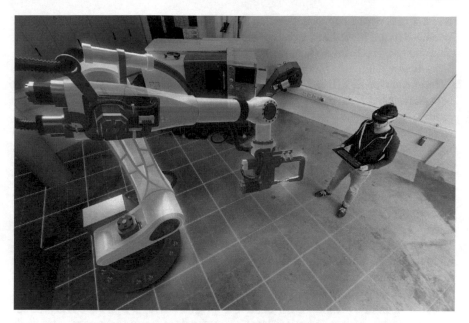

Fig. 2 Prototype of the Holographic Robot Training (Viscopic GmbH)

expert knowledge to AI teaching employees (even in small parts) results in a completely new challenge regarding didactics. Herein, a special trainer is needed that transfers this knowledge piece by piece while motivating the employees for training the algorithms over a long time. It is therefrom valid to state, that scalable AI training as a part of the educational process of a large company such as Volkswagen is still at its very beginning. Even with a thought through concept and first experience from the proceeded pilot, the historically grown structures of a large company need time to understand the necessity of hosting AI training competence inside the organization to avoid dependencies from external providers.

Finally, when reflecting the **overall results** gained out of the implemented methodology, several profiteers are identified within the organization. The improvements affect the company's learners in the first place. In addition, organizational structures and the strategic scope of the Volkswagen Group Academy benefit from those effects as well as the entire organization. The results achieved can be summarized in three main aspects as follows.

1. The organization benefits from the Education Lab's **technology expertise** gained during research and scouting in the fields of the future of learning.

At first, the research approach of the Volkswagen Education Lab offers the department's employees a very new thinking about the future of corporate learning and linked technologies. This mindset and the research based approach enables the Volkswagen Group Academy to orientate within new competence and technology fields. It therefrom supports decision making towards the departments' strategic focus and future investments. Hence, the Education Lab serves as a qualified mentor when it comes to learning technologies, methodologies, and learner needs.

2. The incubator-like Education Lab serves as a **fast track for ideas**, which accelerates innovative concepts for corporate training.

   The second achievement is the implementation of a product validation and implementation method within the Volkswagen Group Academy, which expands the department's scope towards startup-like process and business models. The employees therefrom learn about respective methodologies in order to utilize them for the "reinvention of corporate learning". The incubator-like approach empowers the employees to develop and share new ideas as well as to further particular solution concepts on a prototype level. This approach proves to be effective, because it starts from the users' point of view and existing problems, ineffectiveness, and pain points. As the main result, it creates and enhances relevance for learning activities. In other words, the willingness to invest in such activities increases on both sides: management and workforce.

   On the learner side, the learner-centred approach provides a positive and productive learner experience. The employees get a comprehensive idea of why their learning investment is relevant to themselves but also to both department and company. Since the developed education solutions target individual learner needs, participating employees perceive that their success is the Education Lab's core target.

   On the management side, the acceptance for necessary investment in resources and educational technology raises because of the positive employee experience. It lies within the management scope, that employee satisfaction and employer attractiveness have a significant positive impact on productivity and cost efficiency. Therefore, investments in new ways of learning through the Education Lab pay off in the long run.

3. Eventually, the **experiences** gathered during the Education Lab's set up (e.g. the overcome of historical grown organizational boundaries or limitations for startup onboarding) are of significant value for similar approaches in the company's future.

   In the end, the Education Lab invents and implements new education solutions, products, and business models with an adequate method. As a result, innovative ideas are actually pushed forward even in a traditional and complex corporation such as Volkswagen. As an accelerator for innovative ideas, the Education Lab gains experience and expertise regarding the overcome of barriers and limitations, which are of high value for future projects within the organization. The Education Lab therefore serves as a mentor for new trends and technologies in the corporate education sector and is eager to spread experience and expertise within and beyond the organization. The lab's team consequently connects people and departments within online platforms as well as on (hosted) internal and external education technology conferences.

5   Lessons learned

The Education Lab is a wholly new institution within Volkswagen. It therefore has a young history and strives for continuous learning and improvement. The provided lessons learned shall inspire others to initiate similar projects accordingly and to get in exchange about new ideas and approaches. The learnings gained out of the first ideation, validation, and implementation iteration are presented in the following.

1. Building a lab space within established structures is a challenging task. Processes and target systems that are not always conducive for creating new solutions or business models control the existing organization. The Education Lab's method of developing concepts together with users, the validation and experimentation before deciding whether an idea will be implemented or not is in contrast to what the majority of traditional organizations work like.
   - For Example: Using a lean-oriented and empathy focused method leads to start with the profound examination of existing problems. If the management is not familiar with this method, starting by presenting problems as a first, interim result can immediately lead to rejection.
   - Crucial for the Lab's success is the strong commitment of the management regarding the problem-oriented methodology. In addition, it is essential to communicate with all levels of the existing organization throughout all project phases. People that feel left out might be the first detractors of the entire proposal. People, who get the feeling of being left behind, may be the first to negatively influence the project.
2. When implementing the Education Lab's concept, the cooperation with start-ups turned out to be a key factor in order to accelerate innovation and decrease cost. Establishing such cooperation between a large company and a (young) startup is a complex process, from which further lessons learned could be derived: Establishing a "corporate-startup-cooperation" takes time, as it requires a legal and (IT) infrastructural framework. In addition, the established rules and processes of the corporation can slow down the innovation process of the startup. The requirements for technological solutions stated by the corporation (e.g. IT and data security, purchasing process, liability) can make it even more difficult to cooperate. Bureaucracy can simply obstruct innovation and creativity.
   - For Example: Establishing the "corporate-startup-cooperation" for realizing the Education Lab's holographic robot approach took over half a year until the contract was concluded. However, overcoming these barriers is worth the effort, since a successful "corporate-startup-cooperation" has enormous potential for both partners.
   - In addition, communicating "at eye level" is a decisive success factor for establishing a beneficial and sustainable cooperation with startups. Both the

startup and the corporate partner must have a real added value and a common goal. Traditional companies are mistaken in believing that all startups are just waiting to finally work with the old industry. The examination of the way of thinking and working of startups by the lab team has shown that the truly innovative founders want to create real added value instead of just PR. The *really* innovative startups can choose their industrial partners.

3. To transform traditional into digital organizations, intensive examination of new technologies is essential. The department, which wants to benefit from digitalization, must therefore build up new expertise and competencies.
   - For Example: During the construction and implementation of the sub-project Teach a BOT, profound knowledge in the field of artificial intelligence and the teaching of algorithms was needed—and therefore built up in the Education Lab. This knowledge has direct benefits for future projects such as learning analytics or customized learning paths that base on the same technology. If Teach a BOT had been commissioned externally, future projects would have to start again from scratch.
   - By initiating a lab approach that has the goal of building new solutions and that is responsible for the technical implementation, the required competence regarding new technologies is developed *almost* automatically. Therefore, the activities of the lab immediately increase the sustainability of the entire business. The newly gained knowledge flows continuously back into the organization.
4. When innovative technologies come into the market, diverse businesses try to exploit them in order to benefit from the innovation. Nonetheless, a significant number of solely technology-driven use cases provide only little real value.
   - For Example: Virtual and Augmented Reality has been spreading to the education sector for some time. However, many applications seem to be technology-driven and without a proper business case. Therefore, respective solutions do not last long and create no real added value. Due to the close contact with learners and their specific problems, the identified use cases within the Education Lab justify the need for such new technologies. The use of these new technologies is not an end in itself, but enables solutions to the problems found.
   - Applying a user-centered approach that starts with user problems and needs instead of technology, significantly reduces the risk of creating a solution that uses new technologies but does not generate significant value.

The initiation of the Education Lab as well as creating structures and collaboration was and still is an exciting and challenging task. The first iteration process of ideation, validation, and prototype implementation provided every person involved with a completely new perspective on the known organization, established processes, as well as on improvement potentials. The next steps are to pass the prototype solutions to the responsible departments, enable the respective employees for further development, examine the lessons learned, derive improvement ideas, and finally, to start the next iteration phase. After focusing on learner problems in the first iteration in 2017, the second run-through in 2018 with a 6-week problem-finding phase followed by a 4-week ideation phase will be concerned with the teachers' point of view and their problems and ideas regarding corporate learning at Volkswagen.

References

Balser M, Fromm T (2016) Die Angst der Autobauer vor dem Google-Ei. Süddeutsche Zeitung
Bersin J, Pelster B, Schwartz J (2016) Global human capital trends 2016 – the new organization: different by design. Deloitte University Press, London
Blank SG (2006) The four steps to the epiphany – successful strategies for products that win. Lulu. com
Chatterji A (2017) Innovation and American K-12 education. Paper presented at the NBER innovation policy and the economy forum
Davidson CN, Goldberg DT (2009) The future of learning – institutions in a digital age. Massachusetts Institute of Technology. John D. and Catherine T. MacArthur Foundation Reports on Digital Media and Learning.
European Sector Skills Council (2016) Report: European Sector Skills Council – automotive industry. http://www.etrma.org/uploads/Modules/Documentsmanager/skill-council-automotive-report-2016---stampa4.pdf. Accessed 31 Jan 2018
Fowler D (2017) EVs and autonomy drive new skills requirements in the automotive industry. https://www.theengineer.co.uk/skill-requirements-in-the-automotive-industry/. Accessed 31 Jan 2018
Harms R (2015) Self-regulated learning, team learning and project performance in entrepreneurship education: learning in a lean startup environment. Technol Forecast Soc Change 100:21–28
Howard SK, Ma J, Yang J (2016) Student rules: exploring patterns of students' computer-efficacy and engagement with digital technologies in learning. Comput Educ 101:29–42
Ries E (2011) The lean startup – how constant innovation creates radically successful businesses. Penguin Books, London
Vernau K, Hauptmann M (2014) Corporate learning goes digital. How companies can benefit from online education. Roland Berger Strategy Consults, München. https://www.rolandberger.com/publications/publication_pdf/roland_berger_tab_corporate_learning_e_20140602.pdf. Accessed 31 Jan 2018
Wildi-Yune J, Cordero C (2015) Corporate digital learning – how to get it "right". KPMG AG Wirtschaftsprüfungsgesellschaft. https://assets.kpmg.com/content/dam/kpmg/pdf/2015/09/corporate-digital-learning-2015-KPMG.pdf. Accessed 31 Jan 2018
Winterhagen J (2016) Weniger Teile, weniger Arbeit, weniger Jobs? Frankfurter Allgemeine
World Economic Forum (2016) New vision for education: fostering social and emotional learning through technology. World Economic Forum. http://www3.weforum.org/docs/WEF_New_Vision_for_Education.pdf. Accessed 31 Jan 2018

Mathias Wildgrube is the founder of the Volkswagen Education Lab, an environment for putting new learning technologies to the test. He studied economic sciences at the Leibnitz University Hannover and wrote his dissertation at the University of Stuttgart about competence management in procurement. He gained experience in the field of personnel development by first working in the Volkswagen Procurement Academy and was then tasked with assisting the Volkswagen Group Academy's senior management as well as leading the project "Knowledge Campaign on Digitalization".

Nils Schaupensteiner is part of the digital innovation team at MHP, a leading management and IT consulting that enables its clients to manage the digital transformation. His consulting focus is on the development, implementation and management of digitalization projects in the automotive industry. He studied industrial engineering and management at the Technical University of Berlin and is writing his doctoral thesis at the Technical University of Braunschweig in the fields of intercultural qualification in China. He gained his practical experience during national and international projects at a tier-one automotive supplier as well as at one of the world's largest carmakers.

Jan Wehinger is Head of the digital innovation team at MHP, a leading management and IT consulting that enables its clients to manage the digital transformation. His consulting focus is on the development, implementation and management of digitalization projects in the automotive industry. He studied industrial engineering and management at the Technical University of Braunschweig and wrote his doctoral thesis at the Technical University of Braunschweig in the field of innovation management.

Navigating Through Digital Transformation Using Bimodal IT: How Changing IT Organizations Facilitates the Digital Transformation Journey at Deutsche Bahn Vertrieb GmbH

Lea Fortmann, Ingmar Haffke, and Alexander Benlian

Abstract

(a) **Situation faced**: Deutsche Bahn Vertrieb GmbH (DB Vertrieb) is a sales company, operating as part of the DB Group in the passenger transportation industry. Around the millennium, the firm introduced digital sales channels in addition to its traditional ones. The inherent increasing visibility of DB Vertrieb's IT systems for the customer required a flexible and fast IT function. Fifteen years later, the importance and pervasiveness of IT accounted for the need to integrate all parts—traditional and digital—of DB Vertrieb's channel strategy to allow for a smooth omni-channel customer experience.

(b) **Action taken**: The company reorganized its IT division twice. First, it established a second IT function within its online and mobile channel division. The new IT unit was small and flexible, incorporating a start-up culture. The divisionally separated bimodal IT approach lasted for about 15 years before both functions were reintegrated within the firm's new digital division. DB Vertrieb also introduced a framework for scaling the agile approach of the former online IT to the corporate level.

(c) **Results achieved**: The bimodal IT design enabled the company to implement changes quickly with regard to the online and mobile channels. However, the setup also led to cultural differences between the two IT units impeding desirable collaboration. After the restructuring into a single digital division IT unit, channel-spanning strategies were possible and DB Vertrieb experienced a boost in motivation and employee engagement. Nevertheless,

L. Fortmann (✉) · A. Benlian
Technische Universität Darmstadt, Darmstadt, Germany
e-mail: fortmann@ise.tu-darmstadt.de; benlian@ise.tu-darmstadt.de

I. Haffke
Detecon Consulting, Cologne, Germany
e-mail: ingmar.haffke@detecon.com

© Springer International Publishing AG, part of Springer Nature 2019   393
N. Urbach, M. Röglinger (eds.), *Digitalization Cases*, Management for
Professionals, https://doi.org/10.1007/978-3-319-95273-4_21

bringing the modes of operation together takes more time than expected, so the new setup still lacked the desired success in terms of tangible results.

(d) **Lessons learned**: The case demonstrates how bimodal IT as a tool can facilitate the IT transformation necessary to accomplish a company's digital transformation. A continuous reassessment of the bimodal IT type is vital. It enables the IT unit to support the business in satisfying changing customer needs in the best way possible. In addition, certain strategic components, such as omni-channel strategy, seem to be in need of a specific type of bimodal IT. Furthermore, the case indicates which leadership roles, training styles, and measures are pivotal for successful transformation through bimodal IT and how adaption of a different type of bimodal IT helps to push core IT topics.

1   Introduction

In the era of digital business transformation, flexibility and speed of IT delivery play a crucial role. Facing disruptive business models, shorter innovation cycles, and real-time responses to customer requirements, companies are forced to rethink the mode and purpose of their IT unit. How to integrate the novel requirements stemming from digitalization into operations? How to become a driver of digital innovation? How to support business best when satisfying the rapidly changing customer needs?—Digital transformation challenges the IT function in many ways.

In order to cope with these challenges, many firms introduce two modes of IT delivery (thereby creating a bimodal IT setup; Gartner 2017), one agile enough to react quickly to market and technological changes and another stable enough to operate large IT systems and offer traditional IT services. With the aim of enabling the right balance between IT exploration and exploitation, companies establish different forms of bimodal IT. The types reach from singe agile development projects within the IT function to a second IT unit outside of the traditional IT (Haffke et al. 2017; Horlach et al. 2017) (see Fig. 1). In addition, according to Haffke et al. (2017), these separated bimodal IT types are often not the end in itself. Rather, they are steps towards an overall more agile reintegrated IT function able to deliver all, stability, quality, and flexibility at a reasonable speed, thus, paving the way for a successful digital transformation (see Figs. 1 and 2).

This study sheds light on the stages of IT transformation. We examine the IT transformation journey of DB Vertrieb alongside the red pathway drawn in Fig. 2 from a traditional to a reintegrated bimodal IT setup. Through interviews with the Chief Information Officer (CIO), Chief Digital Officer (CDO), as well as the Head of Sales Processes in 2016 and 2017, we gained deep insights into the situations and

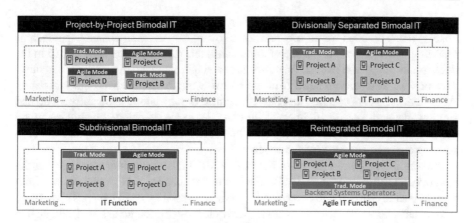

Fig. 1 Types of bimodal IT. Adapted from Haffke et al. (2017)

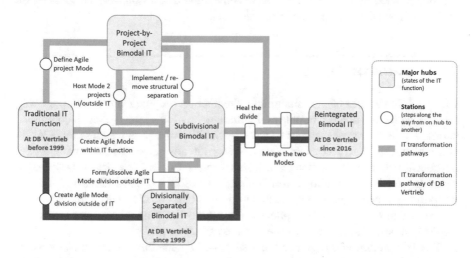

Fig. 2 IT transformation pathways. Adapted from Haffke et al. (2017)

motives that drove DB Vertrieb to adopt different bimodal IT settings and the actions taken to enable and facilitate their implementation.

The company is a subsidiary of the DB Group, operating mainly in Germany. Its headquarters office is located in Frankfurt, Germany. The approximately 5800 employees are responsible for the various sales channels through which the group is selling its mobility services. Due to the rapid pace of changing customer requirements in the late 1990s, the company established in 1999 an IT function responsible only for supplying the digital sales channels, such as its website and mobile app (Online IT function). It was placed outside of the existing IT unit, which maintained the large systems and processes needed for traditional sales channels including travel centers and ticket vending machines (Traditional IT function). The Online IT function was small and agile, able to respond quickly to the always-changing digital environment.

In comparison, the Traditional IT function was managed more conventionally and cost-driven. The need for an organization allowing for an omni-channel approach as well as the increasing importance of digital channels resulted at the end of 2015 in the decision to merge the two IT functions into a single one (Reintegrated IT function). The new IT unit was embedded in the likewise newly established digital division. After almost 2 years of transition, the reintegrated organization is now fully set up and frameworks and roles are defined. With first release cycles planned within the novel setup, DB Vertrieb is now ready to proof the effectiveness of the changes on the way to provide an excellent customer experience.

Taking the pathways from Haffke et al. (2017) as a guideline, we start with the description of the situation that led to the two major changes in IT organization—from a traditional to a divisionally separated bimodal to a reintegrated IT type. Then, we go into detail about the specific actions performed by the company to facilitate the transformation steps, followed by highlighting what the bimodal IT transformation journey resulted in. In the end, we derive some important lessons learned for decision makers to consider during their IT transformation.

2 Situation Faced

Right before the turn of the millennium, the internet became mainstream, preparing the ground for the dotcom bubble and initiating the ages of stand-alone e-commerce shops. Large enterprises started to test the viability of online business models. As were others at that time, DB Vertrieb was already experimenting with digital approaches to sell its passenger transportation services. The firm established a separate division for online sales besides its traditional sales channels, thereby applying a multi-channel approach (Verhoef et al. 2015). This unit examined different ways to use mobile phones and online ticketing platforms in order to implement new digital sales channels to the end customer.

The IT function was organized in a separate IT department under the control of the CIO (see Fig. 3). Being a pure systems provider to the channel functions (Guillemette and Paré 2012), the company's extensive backend systems and their

Fig. 3 Traditional IT setup at DB Vertrieb

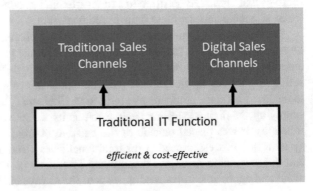

reliable, scalable, and secure provisioning were the core of its responsibility. The metrics used to measure the performance of the IT function mainly included how well it met service level agreements and stayed within allocated budgets. In line with these metrics, the management focus of the IT function strongly geared towards cost efficiency. In particular, this resulted in the decision to provide only two releases per year, thus, inhibiting the IT function's flexibility and speed and making it prone to conflicts about the prioritization of requests.

For the online and mobile sales channels, with their IT systems' direct contact to the end customer, the cost-centric management of the IT unit was an unfeasible approach. "The end customer does not understand if a bug fix is not implemented until 6 months later," stated the CIO. In addition, rapid technological advancements increased (and still increase) the pace of changes of customer requirements. In order to lift responsiveness concerning bugs and new requirements to an adequate level, the online division defined its needs with regard to the IT function at a minimum of least six releases per year and almost weekly patch days. The existing IT department was neither designed nor managed to deliver this speed. Therefore, management decided to establish a second IT unit within the online division in 1999.

In recent years, new competitors popped up in the passenger transportation industry in Germany. They are not only providing competitive services to DB, such as car sharing or long-distance coaches, but also trying to occupy the customer interface by offering digital mobility platforms. Digital channels integrating all forms of passenger transportation services give customers an easy to use single point of contact during their journey. Accordingly, also at DB Vertrieb, the online and mobile sales channels became more than just the "tail of the dog", as the CIO described the proportion of traditional to online channels. The latter, and its IT function in particular, became increasingly visible and important to the core business of the entire company. However, when it came to planning company-wide programs, the online part of it remained a subproject of the overall program. Neither the corporate nor the project structure reflected the new business-critical role of the digital channels leading to a mismatch of resources and requirements allocation.

In addition, the pervasiveness of IT in people's everyday digital life nowadays gives rise to the need of seamless omni-channel journeys. The management of customer journeys across all channels is vital as customers expect the interfaces between the medium used to sell a product or service to be nearly invisible. Achieving smooth crossovers between sales channels requires a central strategy alignment. At DB Vertrieb, the organizational setup restricted the company to distinct strategies for online and traditional sales channels and made incorporating a company-wide omni-channel approach not viable. "So far we had IT silos. They belonged to different channels, providing different systems. That is why we did not have [an] omni-channel [strategy]," the CDO explained. The separation of the division for e-commerce including its IT function on the one side and the CIO division responsible for providing IT services to the traditional sales channels on the other side was defined right below the executive board. "This strict separation", the Head of Sales Processes said, "has already impeded close functional alignment". In addition, traditional and online channel divisions were located in different buildings, raising an additional hurdle for effective collaboration and coordination. Both settings made an aligned omni-channel strategy across the divisions unattainable.

The organizational setup and management focus before 2016 constrained DB Vertrieb to take full advantage of the opportunities of digitization. Both the importance of digital sales channels as well as the relevance of an overarching integration of all sales channels forced the company to take a big step. Setting the goal to deliver the best customer experience in the passenger transportation industry, the firm decided to transform its organization including a reintegration of the two divisionally separated IT functions.

3   Action Taken

DB Vertrieb took several actions in the course of its IT transformations (see Table 1). In order to be able to react appropriately to customer requirements and market changes, the company created a second IT unit outside of the Traditional IT function in 1999, therefore, applying the setup of divisionally separated bimodal IT (see Fig. 4). For sufficient alignment an overarching requirements management was installed inside the Traditional IT function. The overall idea was to structure and manage the Online IT subdivision like a start-up. The firm allocated it in the department for the online and mobile sales channels. This setting allowed for tight collaboration between business and IT employees (depicted by the two-sided arrows in Fig. 4). Thus, IT demand and supply were very well aligned and the Online IT function was perceived rather as an active partner for the business instead of a systems provider. The entire team was collocated and counted around 20 people in the beginning. In addition, functional roles were not entirely separated within the unit. With the aim to work in a flexible and uncomplicated manner, able to react quickly to any necessary changes, the Online IT unit applied its own rules and developed its own culture. IT managers did not see their task in supporting and supplying the business but rather in generating the biggest impact for the customer.

Table 1 Actions taken during IT transformations at DB Vertrieb

Divisionally separated bimodal IT setup (1999–2015)	Reintegrated bimodal IT setup (2016—today)
• Installed small and collocated Online IT unit in the digital sales channel department • Established overarching requirements management unit • Worked with standing teams and product owners (Scrum techniques) in the Online IT function • Enlarged Online IT unit gradually and introduced subunits	• Merged Online and Traditional IT unit in the digital division • Included IT strategy in corporate digitization strategy • Installed innovation labs and omni-channel management function • Introduced the Scaled Agile Framework (SAFe), Scrum and DevOps methods • Trained employees concerning methods and models intensely • Hired transformation coordinator • Established governance board

Fig. 4 Divisionally separated bimodal IT setup at DB Vertrieb

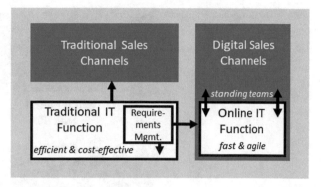

Even though Beck and colleagues wrote the agile manifesto—the central building block of today's agile methodologies—only in 2001 (Beck et al. 2001), "the mindset [within the Online IT] was at that time already very close to what you call an agile mindset nowadays," stated the Head of Sales Processes.

The Online IT division worked with a Scrum-like organization of standing teams—i.e., permanently installed teams for every topic. A team consisted of members from the IT and the business side. Furthermore, the Online IT function had implemented a quite autonomous product owner role. According to Schwaber and Beedle (2002), the product owner is responsible for the management of customer requirements and the communication with the team. At DB Vertrieb, "we had the role of a quite powerful product owner wearing two hats," the CIO mentioned. His responsibility was defined beyond managing requirements and communication within the Online IT division's standing teams. Additionally, a product owner was responsible for the alignment of projects that involved traditional sales channels, hence, also the Traditional IT function. As a subproject manager within channel-spanning projects, he or she had the "very challenging job," the CIO stated, of coordinating an agile team in a traditional company-wide organizational setup and working mode.

Because of the increasing relevance of digitalization for selling passenger transportation services throughout the last 15 years, business functions at DB Vertrieb increasingly demanded services from the Online IT function, shifting their focus away from the Traditional IT function. The growing attention from the business divisions led to an increase in requirements directed at the Online IT function. In order to be able to meet the demand, DB Vertrieb gradually enlarged and reorganized the Online IT division. Counting only 20 people in its early years, the Online IT function grew to 150 employees by the end of 2015. In addition, the firm introduced subunits inside the Online IT function in order to manage the larger workforce as well as the increasing demand.

In the beginning of 2016, DB Vertrieb merged its Online and Traditional IT functions into one unit (reintegrated bimodal IT; see Fig. 5). The company decided to transform its business and IT organization in such a fundamental way in order to pursue the overall goal of delivering an excellent customer experience throughout all

Fig. 5 Reintegrated bimodal
IT setup at DB Vertrieb

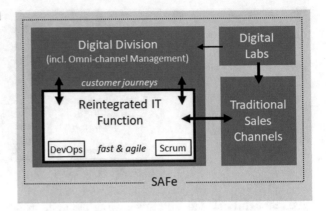

sales channels. In particular, DB Vertrieb aimed at applying an omni-channel strategy, getting more innovative with regard to the traditional sales channels and bringing these innovations to the market faster. With the existing corporate organization including a divisionally separated bimodal IT setup in place, these goals were not achievable.

The Reintegrated IT function led by the CIO is located within the firm's digital division. The digital division is another outcome of the reorganization. It was established in order to account for the importance of digitalization for DB Vertrieb's business of selling transportation tickets and supporting the customer throughout the journey. A newly announced CDO is heading the digital division. He is also part of the executive committee of the company with the purpose to enhance the level of IT understanding within the management team. In line with the focus on an encompassing customer experience, the digital division is structured according to customer journey steps and complemented by an overarching omni-channel management unit.

In the same vein as the IT function became part of the digital division, the IT strategy became part of the corporate digitalization strategy of DB Vertrieb. "The [Traditional IT] unit shaped the digitalization strategy in many ways. Especially, the enterprise architecture management as well as the portfolio management were heavily involved. We say it only makes sense to consider both topics together," explained the CIO. Traditional IT topics, such as replacement of host systems and mainframe computers, therefore, are now embedded in the digitalization strategy.

Around the same time when DB Vertrieb decided to merge its IT functions, the company also installed innovation laboratories. These labs are defined as a competence center, an innovation scout, and creative space. In a separate location, the labs host design thinking and ideation workshops in order to advocate innovation and entrepreneurship throughout the company. Special focus lies on fostering and enhancing exploration within traditional channels. The labs' biggest impact is to work together with very traditional product development units and sales channels and promote innovation methodologies as well as discuss new strategies to approach the market. When this collaboration leads to a prototype or mockup accepted by the business, the IT function conducts feasibility tests and checks for rapid implementation opportunities. Apart from the business units, the Reintegrated IT function itself also uses the possibilities, premises, and expertise of the labs. "They have a pretty nice UX-laboratory, which we use quite often," the Head of Sales Processes named as one example. The two units work closely together to enhance innovativeness in business and IT. The continuous knowledge exchange necessary for the tight collaboration is facilitated by the fact that, due to the IT merger, some former Online IT employees accepted new positions within the labs, strengthening the links.

Besides the reallocation of the Reintegrated IT division within the broader organizational setup, DB Vertrieb also started to gradually transform the IT function itself. The firm's aim is to modify the entire IT function in a way that it resembles the former Online IT unit in being a fast, flexible, and agile partner to business while still providing stable and secure systems and services. The CIO specified the expectations in the following way: "In terms of time-to-market, we want to work on being five times faster end-to-end. That means, when the idea of a pricing campaign comes up, [...] we want to bring that five times faster into production than today." Furthermore, he is targeting release cycles for the Reintegrated IT function on a monthly basis for highly interdependent functionalities and on a weekly basis for independent features. To be able to reach these goals step-by-step, the company heavily invests in the new organizational setup since the reorganization in 2016. It provided a framework to scale the Online IT division's agility. In addition, trainings regarding agile methods and tools are offered to the employees previously working in the Traditional IT function on a regular basis.

To make the agile approach scalable on the corporate level, DB Vertrieb decided to implement the Scaled Agile Framework (SAFe). SAFe is an operational model which specifies rules and procedures to apply in agile organizational setups at a larger scale (Laanti 2014). It is a best practices approach, which provides DB Vertrieb with useful measures to address the biggest pain points when trying to scale agile methods. It supports the company in channeling IT requirements and assists in "how [DB Vertrieb] can reach strategic consensus across business units and bring about a joint prioritization that everybody feels comfortable with and that gives everybody the feeling that an overall optimum was achieved on the group level," emphasized the Head of Sales Processes. In addition to scalability, SAFe allows for a stringent derivation of strategies at the group level. DB Vertrieb has to coordinate its business actions with other group units and SAFe guides the firm in optimizing this alignment. However, the debate regarding the specific design and degree of adoption of SAFe for DB Vertrieb is still ongoing.

As part of SAFe, DB Vertrieb also introduced formal Scrum teams (in contrast to the Scrum-like structure in the former Online IT function) and DevOps methodologies to enhance integration and prevent silo thinking within its Reintegrated IT function as well as between central parts in the IT value chain. During the initial phase of the reorganization, the question arose if an agile approach requires all participating teams to be from inside the company, especially with regard to IT operations. DB Vertrieb's management decided to keep the model, which had been in place, with technical IT operations management provided by the group's IT service provider. For the purpose of facilitating collaboration and achieving greater efficiencies between the two functions, the company initiated a DevOps approach. In particular, the development unit at DB Vertrieb now integrates the operations unit at the service provider earlier in the development process with the aim to enhance collaboration efficacy.

In order to preserve and enhance the agile spirit and the innovation culture, the firm made large investments in the organization to reduce the differences between the Online and Traditional IT units. Besides giving the former Online IT employees a framework to scale the function's agility, DB Vertrieb continuously provides courses regarding agile methodologies and business analysis. Special trainings are offered to those who bring along the right way of thinking and necessary skills for an agile organization to guide them through the transformation and keep up their spirit. To further close the gap, the company additionally organizes cross-functional camps with the aim to advocate a customer-centric, agile, and innovative mindset across the organization. All of these trainings and courses are mandatory to ensure effectiveness and a common understanding. Furthermore, in order to alleviate the spillover of agile ideas and ways of working within IT teams, DB Vertrieb applies an employee-mix strategy. This means that, where applicable, teams consist of former Online IT as well as Traditional IT unit employees.

One and a half years after the start of the reorganization, the firm recently introduced additional roles in order to support the transformation. Inside the digital division, the role of a "conductor," as the Head of Sales Processes labelled the position, was created and staffed hiring an experienced corporate development expert externally. Her task is to "pick up tendencies and vibrations and guard the transformation backlog to make sure that at least some items are pinned to 'Done'," stated the Head of Sales Processes. Since DB Vertrieb transformed not only its entire organization but also the methods used as well as the architecture in place, it saw the need for an explicit role to assist the management. Moreover, the company recently established a transformation governance board. Its purpose is to have a look at what works well and what does not. In addition, it decides on the appropriate measures to take along the transformation journey. The board allows the management to take time to think about the organizational transformation as well as its IT transformation.

4   Results Achieved

DB Vertrieb achieved its main objectives with both, the implementation of a divisionally separated bimodal IT setup as well as with the reintegration of both IT units. At the same time, though, challenges occurred. Table 2 summarizes the results, explained in detail in the following—first concerning the divisionally separated IT setup, then regarding the Reintegrated IT unit.

The separated bimodal IT setup, implemented in 1999, had the aim to enable flexibility and agility for the new online channels and at the same time uninterrupted secure and stable services for the existing traditional channels and backend systems. Indeed, the Online IT division reached a pace of almost weekly releases. Eight to ten

Table 2 Results of IT transformations at DB Vertrieb

	Divisionally separated bimodal IT setup (1999–2015)	Reintegrated bimodal IT setup (2016—today)
Positive results	• Faster Online IT function • Suitable support for multi-channel strategy • Strong business-IT alignment on online channel division	• Better alignment of and emphasis on IT topics • Omni-channel strategy possible • Boost in team spirit and employee motivation • Spread of agile mindset
Challenges	• Application of explicitly agile methods not feasible • Growing cultural gap • Emergence of IT silos and disappearing agile mindset	• Difficult staffing of new positions/roles • Insecurities and sensitivities among employees regarding new measures • High interconnection hampering implementation of SAFe

of those releases per year contained complex functionalities. Compared with the Traditional IT function that worked with two to four releases per year, the higher speed was a huge advantage. The company could more easily respond to the increasing amount of changes with regard to online sales channels in the passenger transport market. Thus, the bimodal IT setup with two rather independent IT units allowed for a suitable support for each of the channel units within the multi-channel approach.

The organization of an IT function within the online channel division had the additional positive effect that there was strong business-IT alignment. The units cooperated well on an everyday basis. The impact on the customer side was in the focus of all online channel employees. The atmosphere was constructive and business as well as IT functions prioritized projects and functionalities hand in hand. "The mutual trust that existed within the unit, to reach the budgetary optimum by establishing a well-functioning multi-project management, was just fantastic. It was an awesome time there," described the Head of Sales Processes, remembering the good alignment and vibe at the online channel division.

On the other side, working with explicit agile methods in the Online IT function was not feasible. Even though it had standing teams and an agile mindset, additional facets of agile methods could not be implemented. The high interconnectedness of DB Vertrieb's traditional and online service offerings created too many interfaces for the Online IT function to act truly agile. Many changes in one channel invoked changes in other channels that were supported by the Traditional IT unit. An application of all agile methodologies, as they are very explicitly described in the Scrum-approach, for example, was not practicable.

In addition, employees within the Traditional IT unit struggled with the existence of a second, more agile and uncomplicated IT. Unlike the Traditional IT function, the Online IT function got the "sexy topics", as the CIO called them. They were allowed to act differently and adhere to different rules. People working in the Traditional IT function "felt like being stuck with systems, procedures, and processes, which are run-out versions and which are not addressed and approached in the way one would do it today," stated the CIO. The disparate amount of releases per year led to additional incomprehension on both sides. The Traditional IT function did not understand the Online IT unit's unwillingness to integrate releases and the Online IT function did not welcome the delay when cross-channel release alignment was necessary. The experienced loss in appreciation on one side and the lack of understanding on the other side resulted in a growing cultural gap between the two IT functions. Hence, both sides showed little willingness for the necessary cooperation.

With the increasing importance of digital channels and the expansion of the Online IT unit, further challenges arose. People began to identify with their subunits. Correspondingly, IT silos emerged and the agile mindset and culture started to disappear. The existing collaboration models between Online and Traditional IT units became less feasible as online topics were not just a part of overall sales channel projects any more but rather the core. Furthermore, the expectations from the business side remained the same regarding the speed of the Online IT function. So, managing the growing Online IT unit, which operated at the heart of the company's business but was not recognized as doing so, and which was introduced to be small, fast, and agile but now turned out to be a lot larger and less flexible, became increasingly difficult. These challenges, in the end, led to the decision to merge the IT functions.

In 2016, the expectations were high with regard to the new company organization and the new setup of the Reintegrated bimodal IT function. Restructuring the whole organization had the goal to set the focus on digital topics and allow for seamless omni-channel business. With promoting digitalization, formulating a digitalization strategy that embeds central IT issues, and reorganizing the IT function as part of the digital division, the company attained the required alignment of and a bigger emphasis on IT topics in general (Matt et al. 2015). Through the digital division, led by a CDO who is part of the executive committee, the CIO as head of the Reintegrated IT unit now has greater attention within the executive board. Even executives with less affinity for IT topics now show a greater understanding for IT issues that were often ignored before on top management level. The CIO described the novel gain in importance and its impact the following way: "The new focus absolutely helps me to push CIO topics because everybody recognizes that IT is the basis of our future business."

The reorganization with focus on cross-channel customer journeys based on one overarching IT implementation also made the envisaged omni-channel approach possible. The CDO highlighted that "now, we threw [the IT functions] together because we said, there can only be omni-channel." By having only one IT function, all sales channels and journeys—traditional and digital—got access to the same IT expertise, flexibility, and speed. Business requirements are now directed to one large IT function. The priorities between requirements are bundled and managed by the omni-channel management unit. Clear responsibilities and higher transparency allow for a better business-IT alignment and easier implementation of customer requirements at the interface of business and IT.

In order to ease the transformation for the employees, DB Vertrieb provided and still provides trainings on methodologies and collaboration models that every employee has to attend. Making the courses mandatory resulted in a boost in team spirit, motivation, and optimistic mood among those concerned. The Head of Sales Processes stated: "This 'jointly-approaching-a-new-method' of the quite motley group of people from different sales channels who did not always voluntarily participate in the transformation led to great team cohesion. [. . .] People even started to organize field-trips themselves." The understanding for each other as well as for the various users or customers and for the specific needs of every sales channel continuously increased. The novel engagement of the employees helped to assemble well-working cross-divisional teams quickly within the customer journey structure.

Concerning the retention of the agile mindset into the new organization and overcoming the cultural gap between the formerly separated IT functions, "the company did a good job", as the Head of Sales Processes stated. It is difficult to scale an agile way of working and the trust inherent in a small, agile IT division. This is especially true for DB Vertrieb, as the company not only merged its IT functions but also strongly expanded. However, mixing the teams, training employees of both sides, and introducing camps that focus on customer-centricity, agility, and innovation, brought people to work together and saved some parts of the agile spirit that was still present in the Online IT function.

Despite these positive results, the merger is not yet completed and the disruptive effects are still noticeable. During the first year and a half of the new organizational setup, most new roles were staffed. However, the company struggled in finding the right people for the right position in some cases. As the definition of some positions and their role in the new setup was not clear yet, the internal turnover rate was high in the beginning. "We had to experience that colleagues whose role became more generalist said 'I don't want this by no means; I see myself only at online [channels]'. They applied back to their known channels, leaving the new roles vacant, "remembered the Head of Sales Processes. Positions that could not be staffed right away and stayed vacant for some time had to then be filled with external personnel temporarily.

In addition, even though the outcome of the trainings led to an increase in employee engagement, conducting these trainings required more time than expected as well as considerable investments to be taken. "We definitely underestimated how intense such trainings and internalization of new procedures are," stated the Head of Sales Processes. Especially, within the Reintegrated IT function, breaking down the deadlocked different methods of working and collaboration is still ongoing. Almost 2 years later, DB Vertrieb is still not where it expected to be.

The introduction of SAFe—although generally guiding management and strategy—triggered insecurities and sensitivities among the employees in the Reintegrated IT function. Since the restructuring, former Online IT employees are struggling with the new rules in place limiting their autonomy, which they were used to within the old setup. Product owners, in particular, had a high degree of freedom. With the introduction of SAFe, alignment with other units of the organization is required, restricting this absolute autonomy. However, the framework challenges not only the former Online IT employees but also those from the former Traditional IT function. Even though SAFe regulates the agile way of working in a large corporate setting, those used to a more traditional approach in software development are overstrained as, for example, traditional milestone planning erodes.

Besides the challenges concerning the people involved, the firm still works on the realization of SAFe within its highly integrated organization. Employees at DB Vertrieb work together to—in the end—sell tickets through various channels, which leads to many interconnections and a highly interdependent architecture. A separation of new functionalities and changes for the service into certain release parts of a certain size—as SAFe suggests—is very difficult. DB Vertrieb is still in the 'trial and error' phase to identify the best way of dividing the release contents. This also applies for the decision on the adoption of continuous deployment, another aspect of SAFe, which is still ongoing. The firm discusses whether the functional units actually need continuous deployment. In addition, the high and varying levels of interdependencies within releases would impede the implementation. Thus, management is rather reluctant to adopt it.

The CIO expressed his overall assessment of the transformation progress in one statement: "We have to deliver now." DB Vertrieb spent almost 2 years with assigning and allocating functions, people, and processes. Still, it is introducing new management measures. Now the operationalization takes place, pending the company to become more flexible and agile in order to deliver an excellent channel-spanning customer experience. However, time will tell whether the transformation yields the expected outcomes, as measurable results, such as five times faster time-to-market mentioned by the CIO, are not visible yet.

5   Lessons Learned

The story of this case offers several interesting lessons learned for companies confronted with challenges similar to those of DB Vertrieb. Digital transformation continuously forces firms to rethink the role of the corporate IT function. The case of DB Vertrieb as a whole is an illustrative long-term example of how to use a bimodal IT approach as a tool in order to reorganize the IT unit on the its way through digital transformation. DB Vertrieb takes several steps of the bimodal IT transformation journey as presented in Fig. 2. In doing so, the firm shows when and how to change the setup and purpose of the IT function to make digital transformation easier to master. The benefits and challenges of the implementation of a bimodal IT organization described in this case provide helpful guidance. Managers can learn about implementing a bimodal IT setup in a way that best responds to a company's specific needs while undergoing digital transformation.

Continuously Reassess the Eligibility of Your Bimodal IT Setup: The case of DB Vertrieb teaches us to reconsider all aspects of the IT function's bimodal setup on a regular basis. There is more than one way to implement a bimodal IT organization. The case shows that the various types of bimodal IT can be used as a tool to transform the IT function. Therefore, it is not just about implementing the bimodal IT but more about which type of bimodal IT is most suitable. And this can change over time. A divisionally separated bimodal IT setup can work best in supporting the business for a certain period of time. A reintegrated unimodal IT setup might be suitable later. Indicators for necessary changes might come from external market and technology changes as well as internal process or strategy adjustments (e.g., multi- vs. omni-channel). New customer expectations, innovative sales approaches, and shifts in the business focus require DB Vertrieb more than once to act concerning the IT setup in place. Companies should continuously challenge their IT function's bimodal organization with regard to its fit to current developments and strategies. Even though switching between bi-, multi-, and unimodal IT types is challenging, a different setup can potentially overcome constraints provoked by the current (bimodal) IT setup.

Omni-Channel Is in Need of a Single and Agile IT Function: A particularly relevant development in the market for DB Vertrieb is the emergence of omni-channel approaches. This case shows that two divisionally separated IT units responsible for different channels impede the implementation of a company-wide omni-channel strategy. Their independence from each other supports well the multi-channel approach in the years prior with optimal working methods and a good business-IT alignment within each channel. In particular, this structure brings about the speed and agility necessary for digital sales approaches. However, the pervasiveness of technology in customers' lives nowadays requires achieving a seamless customer experience. To get there, a company needs to enable intensive alignment between all departments, a customer journey structure, merged databases, and a good responsiveness to necessary changes (Ovum 2017). DB Vertrieb reorganizes itself according to customer journeys and implements an omni-channel management unit. The unit is responsible for managing customer interactions coherently across channels and facilitating business-IT alignment. Concerning the IT organization, the case shows that one single IT function is important for a harmonization and aggregation of data and methodologies, crucial for a personalized and smooth customer experience. It allows for more consistent within-IT alignment an integration of systems. In addition, the reintegration of the previously separated IT functions leads to not having to build agile capabilities from scratch. Thus, the ability to react quickly, especially to changes in digital channels, can be established more easily. The case, therefore, indicates that a unimodal, agile IT division, viewed as a partner for the business, can ensure an improved and seamless customer experience across all sales channels.

Install Particularly Dedicated Governance and Organizing Roles for Transformation Effectiveness: A third interesting point deals with the transformation of the IT function as part of the digitalization journey in a company. Bimodal IT initiatives must be integrated carefully with all digital transformation activities. At DB Vertrieb, the management at first underestimates this complexity. Reintegrating the IT functions, scaling the agile approach to the entire IT unit, and introducing a digital division embracing this new IT unit are three massive transformational projects. Coordination and supervision of these projects is given to DB Vertrieb's managers in addition to their operative and content-related tasks. In this setup, discussions on topics that span departments in particular are difficult and long-lasting. DB Vertrieb chooses to implement a leadership role dedicated only to coordinate and drive transformation activities that relieves the management of this organizing part. Moreover, the newly established governance board gives managers a clear structure for supervising the reorganization. Companies should implement explicit roles and structures like these to enable and free their management for designing the new organization and supporting and guiding employees through transformation initiatives. Otherwise—as the experience at DB Vertrieb tells us—the time needed to get the transformation off the ground increases significantly.

Make Trainings for Methodologies and Collaboration Models Mandatory: The compulsiveness of the trainings at DB Vertrieb leads to a high level of engagement and initiative. A digital division organized in customer journeys with a Reintegrated IT unit working with agile methods is a new situation for everyone. The mandatory trainings bring all employees together and "force" them to exchange experiences and talk about new processes and structures. No matter if some employees already know certain or all aspects of approaches or methods, such as Scrum or the process of business analysis, the degree to and way in which they are applied in a specific company context after a reorganization is new to everyone. Training every employee who has to work in the novel context on the same topics in the same courses brings about higher levels of understanding and sympathy for each other necessary for good collaboration. Especially at the business-IT interface, knowing customers and requirements is important for both sides. Mandatory trainings are one way to enable common understanding.

Reintegrating a Bimodal IT Function Allows You to Emphasize Necessary Core IT Topics: After the reorganization at DB Vertrieb in the beginning of 2016, the Reintegrated IT function becomes part of the digital division. The new organizational setup gives the CIO the chance to include core IT topics in the overall digitalization strategy of the digital division. Hence, issues such as the replacement of legacy systems are integrated under the umbrella of digitalization. In general, these kinds of topics are hard to enforce. Even though essentially important to build the basis for digitalization, the understanding of core IT matters is very limited within the business functions as well as on the management level. By embedding essential IT topics in strategies for digital transformation, IT executives can bypass miscommunication and incomprehension. In addition, they can increase the topics' priority. One possible way to do so is demonstrated by DB Vertrieb in this case with the integration of both IT functions into a single one, which is assigned to the digital division and its strategy.

Finally, we would like to mention that the case results should always be considered with regard to the specific context of a company. DB Vertrieb is responsible for sales activities as part of a large corporation within the passenger transportation industry. Legal standards and security rules in other industries and for other corporate functions might be different, inhibiting or facilitating an IT transformation pathway like that of DB Vertrieb. In addition, the size of the firm might play a role when assessing the applicability of the results. Smaller companies and their IT functions often already use informal agile practices or are too small to be separated into two IT functions. Concerning larger firms, the topic of outsourcing should be taken into account. Many corporations have outsourced parts or even all of their IT activities. These settings might lead to very different pathways of IT transformation. Nevertheless, we think that our findings can give relevant and detailed guidance to decision makers navigating through digital transformation using a bimodal IT approach.

References

Beck K, Beedle M, van Bennekum A, Cockburn A, Cunningham W, Fowler M, Grenning J, Highsmith J, Hunt A, Jeffries R, Kern J, Marick B, Martin RC, Mellor S, Schwaber K, Sutherland J, Thomas D (2001) Manifesto for agile software development. http://agilemanifesto.org/. Accessed 25 Aug 2017

Gartner (2017) IT glossary: bimodal IT. http://www.gartner.com/it-glossary/?s=bimodal+IT. Accessed 14 Sept 2017

Guillemette MG, Paré G (2012) Toward a new theory of the contribution of the IT function in organizations. MIS Q 36(2):529–551

Haffke I, Kalgovas B, Benlian A (2017) Options for transforming the IT function using bimodal IT. MIS Q Exec 16(2):101–120

Horlach B, Drews P, Schirmer I, Böhmann T (2017) Increasing the agility of IT delivery: five types of bimodal IT organization. Paper presented at the 50th Hawaiian International Conference on Systems Sciences (HICSS-50), Hawaii, USA, 4–7 January

Laanti M (2014) Characteristics and principles of scaled agile. Paper presented at the 15th International Conference on Agile Software Development (XP 2014), Rome, Italy, 26–30 May

Matt C, Hess T, Benlian A (2015) Digital transformation strategies. Bus Inf Syst Eng 57(5):339–343

Ovum (2017) Fast-forward to omni-channel management. Ovum TMT intelligence, Informa PLC, London

Schwaber K, Beedle M (2002) Agile software development with Scrum, vol 1. Prentice Hall, Upper Saddle River, NJ

Verhoef PC, Kannan P, Inman JJ (2015) From multi-channel retailing to omni-channel retailing: introduction to the special issue on multi-channel retailing. J Retail 91(2):174–181. https://doi.org/10.1016/j.jretai.2015.02.005

Lea Fortmann is a research associate at the Institute of Information Systems & E-Services at the Darmstadt University of Technology. Her research focuses in particular on digital transformation, agile software development methods, and the consequences of virtual reality. In addition to her research, Ms. Fortmann also supervises events on enterprise architecture management and seminars on digital business models and analytics. Ms. Fortmann holds a Master of Science degree in Business Administration from the University of Munich (LMU). After finishing her studies, she worked for 3 years as an IT management consultant at Detecon International GmbH in Munich and San Francisco before starting her doctorate at the TU Darmstadt.

Ingmar Haffke is a Management Consultant at Detecon Consulting, advising clients worldwide on digital strategy and innovation. He holds a doctoral degree in Management Information Systems from Darmstadt University of Technology (TU Darmstadt) as well as an M.B.A. degree in Finance from the State University of New York at Buffalo. His research interests include digital leadership roles, digital business models, and the changing role of IT in an era of digital transformation. His work has appeared in international journals such as The Journal of Strategic Information Systems and MIS Quarterly Executive and has been presented at international conferences such as the International Conference on Information Systems and the Hawaii International Conference on System Sciences.

Alexander Benlian is the Director of the Endowed Chair for Information Systems & E-Services at Darmstadt University of Technology (TU Darmstadt) since 2012. His former academic position was University of Munich (Ludwig-Maximilians-Universität München), where he received his PhD and worked as Assistant Professor (Habilitand). Between his PhD and assistant professorship, he worked 2 years as business consultant at McKinsey & Company for clients in the financial, telecommunications and software industry. He is fascinated by paradigm-shifting phenomena emerging in and triggered through digital channels. In his research, he studies how firms can benefit from digital transformation, cloud services and agile product development. Prof. Benlian has cooperated with scholars and companies around the globe in several research and consulting projects. He is also a committed entrepreneurship trainer who regularly gives workshops in developing countries. His research has been published in leading academic and practitioner-oriented journals. According to national and international research rankings, he is regularly among the top 1% of Information Systems scholars worldwide.

How the US Federal Communications Commission Managed the Process of IT Modernization

Kevin C. Desouza, James S. Denford, and Rashmi Krishnamurthy

Abstract

(a) **Situation faced**: This case examines how the U.S. Federal Communications Commission (FCC) executed its information technology (IT) modernization effort. In 2013, the FCC was spending about 80% of its IT budget on maintaining its legacy systems. Further, the FCC had experienced constant changes in top leadership that resulted in several fragmented IT modernization efforts. The outdated IT systems were not only costly to maintain but were prone to cyber-attacks and verge of major failure. And, the employee morale was lower, and they feared IT modernization and transformation. Overall, the FCC faced several technical and human challenges with IT modernization.

(b) **Action taken**: Acknowledging the eight previous years of fragmented implementation, the new CIO conducted inventory of both IT and human infrastructure. The CIO commissioned an IT tech team to conduct an inventory of the existing IT infrastructure in the organization with a focus to understand vulnerabilities and level of exposure to cyber security. Further, the CIO also took steps to understand the sentiments of employees, customers, and top leadership about IT modernization efforts. Public agencies often promote silo functioning and employees are fearful about change. Thus, the CIO designed several initiatives to solicit feedback from diverse stakeholders and regularly engage them in the process of IT modernization.

K. C. Desouza (✉)
Queensland University of Technology, Brisbane, QLD, Australia

J. S. Denford
Royal Military College of Canada, Kingston, ON, Canada

R. Krishnamurthy
Queen's University, Kingston, ON, Canada

© Springer International Publishing AG, part of Springer Nature 2019   411
N. Urbach, M. Röglinger (eds.), *Digitalization Cases*, Management for
Professionals, https://doi.org/10.1007/978-3-319-95273-4_22

(c) **Results achieved**: The FCC moved 207 on premise IT systems to either public cloud environments or with a commercial service provider. In the process of this successful transformation, the Commission reduced the amount spent on operating and maintaining systems from over 85% to less than 50%. The FCC achieved this with a flat budget, thereby increasing the percentage of funds available for new development even. The FCC also reduced the time it took to prototype new systems from approximately 7 months to less than 48 h to produce a prototype.

(d) **Lessons learned**: The FCC's IT modernization efforts offer following lessons to C-suite leaders: (1) develop a IT modernization strategy that includes both IT systems and the people supporting it; (2) plan a phased approach that achieves 'quick wins' in cloud implementation to increases momentum; (3) take time to align both top leadership and employees' expectations with the IT modernization effort during planning; (4) adopt an open innovation approach that encourages and empower 'change agents' within the agency to creatively address in a cloud environment the longstanding challenges associated with the agency's legacy endeavors, IT systems, and roles; and (5) effectively engage and communicate openly with internal and external stakeholders.

1   Introduction

Organizations—public and private—often face the challenge of modernizing their legacy IT systems, a critical step towards IT transformation and cloud computing. Legacy IT systems are computer applications that are costly to maintain and operate because they run on old languages and hardware (Kim 1997).

In 2015, the U.S. federal governments were spending more than 75% (about $62 billions) of their budget on maintaining legacy systems (Gwyn 2015). As Tony Scott, Federal Chief Information Officer (CIO) noted, many of the federal IT systems are outdated, and some of the IT systems date back to 1980 or earlier (Moore 2015). Moreover, these outdated IT systems are not only at the risk of failure but are also prone to cyber-attacks.

Modernization of legacy IT systems offers several benefits such as reduction in hardware costs and improvement in technology reliability and accessibility (Almonaies et al. 2010). However, the process of modernization is complicated. Legacy systems often represent years and sometimes decades of organizational investment that includes software, hardware, and human capital, and they accumulate business knowledge, rules, and policies. However, the advancement in IT often makes these systems obsolete (Kim 1997).

In this paper, we draw on the case of FCC to examine and outline how this agency executed its IT modernization efforts. The FCC is an independent agency under the supervision of the U.S. Congress. It regulates interstate and international communications—radio, wire, television, and cable—across all of the 50 U.S. states and territories, including the District of Columbia. The commission governs communication laws, regulations, and technological innovations (FCC n.d). Our case study is based on interviews with the FCC CIO, two of his senior advisors and one of the senior IT managers. Further, the primary source material is supplemented with other published interviews, FCC website data and media reports and analyses of FCC IT activities reflecting the public discourse on their transformation.

Examining efforts undertaken by the FCC's IT systems modernize is important for several reasons. Often, the discussions and discourses about public agencies effort to implement IT systems modernization focuses on failures and complaints. It is commonly reported that many of the IT modernization projects often run beyond schedule and cost more, and worst they often lack desired functionality. Federal agencies have a track record of investing in inefficient IT systems. For instance, the Department of Defense (DoD) abandoned its Air Force's Expeditionary Combat Support System after investing more one billion dollars. The Government Accountability Office (GAO) submitted several reports outlining several scheduled deployments, which resulted in the creation of duplicate systems (GAO 2013).

The FCC's successful IT modernization efforts highlight that despite challenges, old and big organizations are capable of managing and implementing large-scale IT innovation. The case of FCC outlines that with a right leadership, vision, and phased approach, any organization can effectively and successfully navigate the process of IT transformation. The FCC's experience highlights that development, management, and implementation of IT systems modernization process is technical and human intensive. The FCC's open innovation approach promoted participatory environment spurred bottom-up—empowering its employees to act as 'change agents.' The successful case of FCC shows that C-suite leaders aiming to embark on IT transformation need to look inside their organizations and create a cultural of change that encourages employees to actively participate in modernizing IT systems.

2 Situation Faced

The FCC was established by the Communication Act of 1936 to "make available, so far as possible, to all the people of the United States, without discrimination on the basis of race, color, religion, national origin, or sex, a rapid, efficient, Nation-wide, and world-wide wire and radio communication service with adequate facilities at reasonable charges" (FCC 2015, p. 2). The FCC's headquarters is located in Washington, DC with three regional offices, 16 district offices, and 8 resident offices located across the US, organized into 7 bureaus and 10 offices. Five Commissioners appointed by the US President oversee the functioning of the FCC, where the Chairman is the head of the agency. To fulfill its mission, the FCC has developed eight strategic goals: (1) "connect America, (2) maximize benefits of spectrum, (3) protect and empower consumers, (4) promote innovation, investment, and America's global competitiveness, (5) promote competition, (6) public safety and homeland security, (7) advance key national purposes, and (8) operational excellence" (FCC 2015, p. 16). These eight strategic goals dictate initiatives undertaken by the FCC.

Given the nature and scope of services provided by the FCC, it is important for the agency to constantly update its IT systems to safeguard and protect customers against cyber threats. But, in 2013, the FCC housed 207 different legacy systems where more than half were over 10 years old (Hamilton 2014). This infrastructure consumed more than 85% of the IT budget for the FCC. Further, several paper-based filing systems were still in place, which increased human costs to maintain these systems (Wheeler 2015).

Moreover, the FCC had experienced nine different CIOs in less than 8 years before the arrival of Dr. David Bray, the tenth CIO in August 2013 (Bray 2015a). The continuous tumult caused by a rotating door of CIOs resulted in piecemeal upgrades. The upgrade efforts often focused on individual systems and relied on the existing on-premises infrastructure model. The FCC's IT was application-centric, i.e. focusing on individual platform needs and stove-piped data (Harvard University Leadership for a Networked World 2015). With outdated and costly IT systems, the FCC was unable to sufficiently invest in transformational projects to evolve its IT capabilities effectively. The FCC also experienced extremely high retention, where federal employees have been working there for 15½ years and contractors for 16 years (Hamilton 2014).

In sum, the FCC faced three broad challenges. First, the FCC's IT infrastructure was outdated and fragmented. Second, the lack of continued leadership resulted in fragmented IT modernization. Third, the employees not only lacked a coherent picture about the FCC's IT modernization efforts and but were also quite comfortable performing routinized tasks. However, to accomplish its mission of regulating and governing technological innovations, the FCC needs to be agile and up-to-date to manage the ever-changing landscape of technology, particularly the rise of IT related threats and challenges. The following sections highlight the key measures the FCC undertook to leverage emerging technologies to modernize its IT systems and improve employee capabilities for improving organizational functioning.

3   Action Taken

The FCC focused on four key areas to modernize its IT systems: improving IT infrastructure, empowering employees, aligning top management support, and engaging external stakeholder (Fig. 1).

Leveraging Emerging Technologies to Modernize IT Infrastructure
To overcome the challenge of modernizing legacy systems, the FCC developed a plan to create a cloud-based platform for developing an agile enterprise. As a first step, the FCC's CIO commissioned the IT tech team to conduct an inventory of the existing IT infrastructure in the organization (Konkel 2016). The inventory examination was conducted to understand the level of cyber security and assess the

Fig. 1 FCC's IT
modernization: key areas of
focus

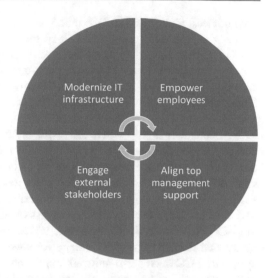

vulnerability of existing IT infrastructure. This process was conducted with the goal of understanding "should we keep this, divest it, modernize it, move to a different version or complete re-engineer it" (Otto 2015). During the initial inventory, it was found that 207 legacy systems were in use at the FCC. Modernizing and transforming these legacy systems would require tremendous capital and human resources. Upon discussions about the needs and priorities of the FCC, the top management, and the CIO decided to streamline 207 legacy IT systems to cloud-based common data platform (Harvard 2015). By 2015, the FCC rationalized and consolidated 207 legacy systems to 102 (Boyd 2015). By 2016, all servers were moved to an off-site managed-services data center run by a contractor as part of the FCC's Operation Server Lift (Rudder 2016). Furthermore, the inventory helped the FCC cancel the requests for new systems to meet the demands of the agency (Otto 2015).

The FCC adopted the following initiatives to retire and shut down its 207 legacy IT systems and migrate them to a cloud-based common data platform. The FCC, in an attempt to improve communications between the agency and its customers, decided to replace its aging Customer Help Center (CHC). The FCC realized that building a new CHC internally would cost $3.2 million and take about 2 years to complete. The FCC CIO brought in an outside change agent to build relationships with key FCC stakeholders and develop an alternative approach that employed a Zendesk cloud-based system to modernize its CHC. The new system cost about $450,000 and was completed in about 6 months (Fretwell 2015).

Moving 32-bit applications to cloud required massive investments that were not feasible with the constrained budget available at the disposal of the organization. To efficiently move these old applications, the FCC adopted a phased approach to lift and shift these servers on-site to an offsite facility by September 2015. As a first step, the FCC moved emails of all employees and contractors to the cloud. Then, the FCC also rolled out virtual desktop to the entire agency, allowed employees to bring their own devices, and moved to Office 365 as a cloud-based office automation solution (Harvard 2015). This quick-win helped the agency to cut the cost of maintaining individual desktops and reduce the risk of disrupting user services when the old servers were moved to an off-site location or retired. The FCC tech team also made a complete copy of 400 terabytes of data on storage network area (SNA). Once the SNA replica was complete, some servers were shipped off-site, and some were retired.

In September 2015, when the FCC attempted to shift its 200 servers and 400 applications to cloud-based services, they faced a major overhaul, which caused delays in customers filing of reports and documents. The IT tech team worked straight for 55 h, and within a few days, the cloud-based system was up and running. And, the CIO communicated to partners and employees about the unintended delay and kept them informed about the progress (Miller 2015). In another instance, when the FCC launched a Speed App test, which allows people to assess and monitor broadband connectivity in the state, efforts were made to educate people about the app. The FCC tech team utilized open code software to develop the app and communicated to the people that the app did not collect IP addresses and their privacy was protected. The app ranked the fourth most downloaded for some time on the iOS App Store, representing a first from any government agency (Hochmuth 2014). Also, the FCC CIO routinely updated his blog with status reports and continually tweeted information relevant to stakeholders (High 2015).

Empowering Employees as 'Change Agents"
In addition to migrating technical infrastructure, the process of modernizing legacy system also involves managing human inertia. The process of implementing IT system modernization through cloud computing may involve navigating much greater levels of employee inertia due to heightened concerns about the loss of their physical infrastructure (Cloud Computing Caucus Advisory Group 2016). Before 2013, several FCC initiatives in the past that created arms-length service-provision relationships necessitated a loss of long-service embedded contractors (Hamilton 2014). The concept of moving to cloud-based platform generated fears in the minds of the employees such as losing their friends and needing to learn new work practices (Jerry 2015).

Further, the constant change in leadership resulted in failed IT modernization program, which created fears in the minds of the employees (Bray 2015a). While the FCC's top management was supportive of IT modernization efforts, the employees were less enthusiastic and resistant to IT modernization. The FCC's CIO focused on empowering IT 'change agents' supporting each bureau and field offices to understand the issues and create a bottom-up innovation approach for addressing IT systems (Dawson and Denford 2015). Thus, the new CIO and his team of 'change agents' spent time listening and understanding the perspectives and concerns of the FCC employees. Then, the CIO framed his narrative about modernization to get these employees excited and mainly, reminding them about their passion for public service and asking, "what brings them joy." For most, it was problem-solving and serving the client (Hamilton 2014).

And, the FCC is organized into 18 bureaus and offices, which has the potential for creating misunderstandings and competition between diverse stakeholders over the form, fit and function of the new cloud-based infrastructure. Upon assuming the role in August 2013, the CIO engaged in collaborative discussion with the "Chairman, Managing Director, the FCC Bureau and Office Chiefs, and all members of the FCC to listen, learn, and identify ways to modernize the Commission's IT enterprise" (Bray 2014). Specifically, the CIO assigned 'intrapreneurs' within each bureau to understand their needs (Harvard 2015).

Towards this end, the CIO collected perspectives of both long-serving and new employees (Harvard 2015). In addition to creating a participatory environment to understand perspectives of employees, the FCC CIO also adopted a bottom-up perspective to modernize agency's legacy system. The CIO encouraged and empowered 'change agents'—creative problem solvers who were able to propose new ideas that were data-driven and cloud-based for modernizing the FCC's legacy systems. The FCC's CIO focused on changing the culture of the organization and promoting risk takers to experiment with new ideas for addressing the FCC's longstanding challenges and issues. In other words, the FCC's CIO took the role of encouraging and empowering employees to take risks for making the agency more effective and efficient. The FCC's CIO also recognized that experimentation can be risky and was willing to adopt the role of 'human flak jacket' (Dawson and Denford 2015).

Assigning a CIO to Align Top Management and Employee Perspective on IT Modernization

The FCC had experienced nine different CIOs in less than 8 years before the arrival of the tenth CIO, Dr. David Bray in August 2013 (Bray 2015a). With the continuous tumult caused by a rotating door of CIOs, Dr. Bray identified that creating trust between the IT leadership both upwards to FCC leaders and downwards to the IT department was critical. Externally, he spent the first 4 months of his tenure meeting with the 18 different bureaus and offices, identifying both their individual needs and what could be considered standard across the FCC (High 2015). Additionally, he encouraged the development of and often implanted intrapreneurs (Desouza 2011) within the FCC bureaus and offices, to serve as a bridge to the IT department (Harvard 2015). Internally, he recognized that the average tenure of IT personnel at the FCC was over 15 years which could have led to investment in the status quo and resistance to change. He addressed this issue in multiple ways, including notice boards for employees to post issues to weekly scrums with staff to track progress (Hamilton 2014), to encouraging 'change agents' within the organization to find better ways of delivering services (Harvard 2015). Both internal and external audiences were also reached through social media, with Dr. Bray being recognized as the most social CIO in the world (High 2015), with a highly active blog and over 110,000 followers on Twitter.

Continuously Engaging and Communicating with Diverse Stakeholders

The FCC also regularly engaged external stakeholders and clients to understand their needs. To modernize FCC's website, The FCC leveraged social media to reach out to citizens and involve them in the design process. The FCC website contains 15 years of materials. Thus, to identify "what content needs to stay, what needs to be retired, what needs to be archived," the FCC engaged internal and external stakeholders and solicited their inputs on needs and requirements (Boyd 2015). The focus of the research was "to identify and understand what different FCC.gov visitors want from our website and how to optimize the way they search, use, and interact with the website." As a first step, the technical team applied web analytics to get "a sense of the web pages with the most traffic and most commonly searched terms by website users." The interactive prototype website was released to solicit feedback from citizens and partners about the new website. They sought public and partners' opinions for 6 months. Then, an FCC tech team analyzed the comments to understand the needs and requirement of the stakeholders. Further, the FCC employees conducted interviews with external stakeholders to understand key concerns and challenges with the website. The FCC team worked about 8 months to research and design a prototype website. The FCC team is continuing to build the new website (Golden 2015). Through this project, the IT team moved from being application-centric and infrastructure-focused to being data-centric and customer-focused, changing the IT role into a business partner and service provider. To improve transparency of FCC's efforts for all stakeholders, the CIO started a blog which explained his vision and strategy and updated all internal and external stakeholders on what could be expected (High 2015).

Further, after several discussions, the members of the FCC identified seven key modernizations tracks to develop a shared understanding (Fig. 2): (1) improve employee telework & mobility, (2) secure internal & external collaborations, (3) strengthen FCC's IT security posture, (4) transform access to FCC enterprise data, (5) modernize legacy systems & tracking, (6) improve FCC.gov & complaint reform, and (7) increase transparency & system usability (Bray 2014).

4 Results Achieved

The several modernization initiatives undertaken by the FCC helped them make their enterprise agile that could react to consumer needs and changes to the environment (Bray 2015a). Figure 3 depicts the key results achieved in four key areas of FCC's IT modernization efforts. The goal of the modernization process was to automate human-intense processes (e.g. move paper filing to an automated electronic system), break silos across the FCC (e.g. each bureau adopted different data collection strategy and operations), and improve efficiencies (e.g. reduce the O&M investments in a legacy system). And, the security posture of existing systems were weak, necessitating a move to the cloud for the safety as well as for efficiency (Hamilton 2014). Given the investment in data centers, moving from the application- to data-centric operations was a significant shift in approach. The FCC developed a pilot

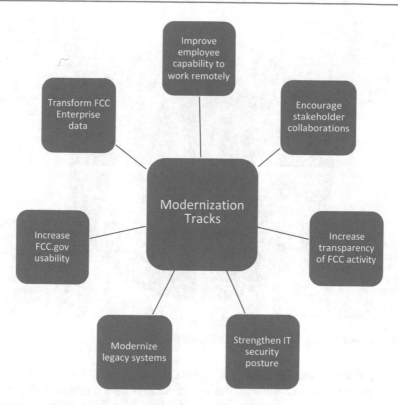

Fig. 2 Modernization tracks: developing a shared understanding

implementation of 60 days for programming at one-sixth the capital cost and one-sixth the ongoing operating cost of a comparable on-premises system. The FCC CIO was able to use the pilot as a 'quick win' demonstrating the potential of the system and was able to move from on-premises to managed services towards the ultimate goal of full cloud implementation (Dawson and Denford 2015).

Further, the new CHC system was built to make FCC more user-friendly, interactive, accessible, efficient, fast, and transparent. The new system streamlined 18 outdated complaint forms to a single web portal. Moreover, the customers can utilize educational materials on the website to decide whether to file a complaint or not. The new system also allows customers to track the status of their grievances (Monteith et al. 2015). Furthermore, the cost of maintaining a cloud-based CHC was about $100,000 compared to $600,000 for the maintenance of an in-house CHC model (Konkel 2016)—an 85% ongoing saving.

While the process of modernizing CHC to a web-based application was straight-forward, some of the legacy systems at the FCC were 32-bit hardwired applications that could not be readily moved to the cloud. However, the process of moving CHC to cloud provided a quick win for the management team, which helped improve agency's morale and overcome resistance (Dawson and Denford 2015). And, the

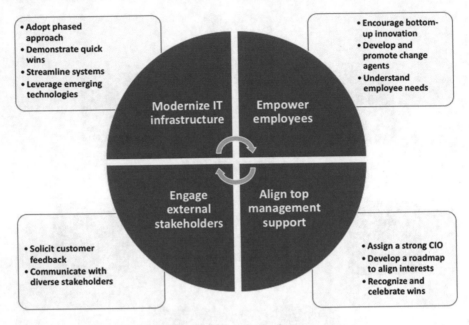

Fig. 3 Results achieved: four key areas of IT modernization

citizens and employees found the new system was easier to use, which further reduced concerns associated with the use of a cloud-based system and provided ground work for modernization of other complicated legacy systems. Moving the servers off-site resulted in reduced cost of maintaining real estate for storing servers in the DC area (which are expensive) (Rudder 2016). In each case, ease of use, rapid delivery and cost savings delivered by cloud implementation generated quick wins that laid the groundwork for future success.

Overall, the FCC CIO was able to move servers from on-premises to off-site, redevelop their help-desk, and bring in cloud-based software such as Office 365 to improve security posture. At the same time, he was able to change the underlying culture of the organization through the inculcation of core values—competence, integrity, and benevolence—within the IT department (Hamilton 2014). These elements are critical antecedents to trust in any professional setting (Mayer et al. 1995). The combination of technical modernization and cultural change enabled the FCC to achieve financial benefits such as reducing IT budget spending on system maintenance from 85% to less than 50%. This evolved the role of IT from custodians of the physical infrastructure to managers of a portfolio of services for the FCC and its customers. Further, the adoption of a cloud-based platform for customer help desk saved more than 60% of taxpayers' money over a 5-year period (Harvard 2015).

Through active, transparent communication, the FCC was able to knit together its diverse stakeholders and manage their expectations. Once the FCC employees realized the commonalities between their public service orientation and the modernization mission, they even volunteered to work during holidays to nail down the specifics of IT systems modernization right for "making the legacy IT at FCC right" (Hamilton 2014). Still, these evolutions of organizational culture take time. The CIO noted that when he met with the IT workforce after 9 months in early 2014 one-third were optimistic, one-third were neutral, and one-third wanted to go back. However, by the time the server move had been completed in September 2015, over 80% expressed enthusiasm for the transformational process (Harvard 2015). Understanding the technical and human needs helped adopt a holistic approach to IT modernization.

This approach helped the FCC to develop a sense of purpose in the agency and empower employees to propose solutions, take actions, and manage innovation for modernizing legacy systems through the cloud implementation. Moreover, the bottom-up approach created a network of these 'change agents' who were able to solicit ideas for spurring innovation. The FCC developed measures to recognize, promote, reward, and celebrate innovation from within the agency.

The efforts undertaken by the FCC's CIO and IT team won them several awards and recognitions as they transformed their agency and evolved their role in it (Bray 2015b). The FCC's IT modernization journey suggest that smart planning coupled with motivated employees can help efficiently navigate and complete IT modernization efforts. While several cases are often cited as an example to emphasize public agencies' incompetence to design, implement, and manage IT systems modernization project, the case of FCC's accomplishment offers an alternative narrative.

5   Lessons Learned

The work undertaken by the FCC to modernize its legacy systems not only has the potential to change the dialogue about the track record of public agencies to implement large-scale IT projects, but also offers critical lessons for public agencies that are planning to embark on the path of modernizing their legacy systems and re-envisioning the role of their agency IT. Table 1 outlines the key lessons. Below,

Table 1 IT modernization: key lessons

	Key lessons
Lesson 1	Develop a IT modernization strategy that includes both IT systems and the people supporting it
Lesson 2	Plan a phased approach that achieves 'quick wins' in cloud implementation that increases momentum and reduces resistance to modernizing IT systems
Lesson 3	Take time to align both top leadership and employees' expectations with a IT modernization effort during planning
Lesson 4	Adopt an open innovation approach that encourages and empower 'change agents' within the agency to creatively address in a cloud environment the longstanding challenges associated with the agency's legacy endeavors, IT systems, and roles
Lesson 5	Effectively engage and communicate openly with internal and external stakeholders during the IT modernization process to gain support for new infrastructure and roles

we discuss the key efforts undertaken by the FCC to manage the technical and social dynamics embedded in their IT modernization.

Lesson 1: *Develop a IT modernization strategy that includes both IT systems and the people supporting it.* A key first step to initiate an IT systems modernization is assessing the operations and performance of the existing IT infrastructure in the organization and creating an inventory with specific attention paid to what systems could be moved to cloud infrastructure. Without a full understanding of the existing as-built IT landscape, modernization efforts are doomed to be patchwork on stovepipes, addressing individual systems and applications. The case of the FCC highlights public agencies need to understand the state of its IT systems and those who manage it before they could design a right strategy to modernize the legacy system and IT role. Indeed, it is best for public agencies to develop a portfolio of existing legacy systems, identify what information is stored within them, and what is the best strategy to transform, replace, or discard these systems without losing critical knowledge and expertise as they evolve the team. By understanding the needs of the organization (e.g. employees, customers), the leaders can develop and articulate a clear IT modernization strategy (Sebastian et al. 2017).

Lesson 2: *Plan a phased approach that achieves 'quick wins' in cloud implementation that increases momentum and reduces resistance to modernizing IT systems.* Moving legacy IT systems to cloud involves considerable planning and managing unanticipated hitches. The larger the project, the more likely it is to fail, and the government is rife with large projects that tend to underperform. While moving some IT systems to cloud-based format is straightforward, other IT systems require planning and implementing several intermediate steps before the full migration is achieved.

As a first step, a public agency planning to migrate to cloud computing needs to develop a strategy. Articulating a strategy for cloud migration helps clarify the big picture and set the stage for migration. According to Orban (2016) there are six main strategies for application migration to the clouds: rehost, replatform, repurchase, re-architect, retire, and retain. An organization can use of one of the migration strategies to develop a detailed plan to implement the process. Defining a migration strategy will help public agencies develop a detailed migration plan and continuously track the progress.

Once an agency has formulated a plan, it should adopt a phased approach that helps achieve 'quick wins' (Dawson and Denford 2015). This involves a combination of change management to overcome internal resistance to adoption and a publicity push to convert external users. The FCC's CHC system modernization effort highlights that by adopting new approach, i.e. leveraging outside vendor to create the system vs. building the system in-house, the agency was able to finish the project within 6 months at a fraction of cost. The approach was highly public from the outset, involving transparency with internal and external stakeholders. This quick win helped the agency not only underscore the importance of modernizing outdated systems, but also achieve a quick win that helped boost the morale of employees and overcome resistance about modernization efforts. Moreover, public managers can use quick wins to report the progress of IT modernization efforts to external stakeholders.

Lesson 3: *Take time to align both top leadership and employees' expectations with a IT modernization effort during planning*. In addition to understanding the 'health of the on-premises operating environment' to define the as-built system, it is important to understand the needs of the organization such as the top management, department heads, and employees to be able to start conceptualizing the to-be system. The successful development of digital transformation strategy depends upon the ability of CIOs to recognize the vision and goals of top management. It is often reported that CIO alone is not capable of implementing an innovation in an organization (Dawson et al. 2016). They often depend upon the guidance of the senior officials to formulate the IT transformation strategy. Further, a better understanding between the CIOs and top management promotes an IT goal alignment and eventually results in the formulation of successful IT strategy. Moreover, if a CIO understands the expectations and goals of top management, he/she can better articulate the plan and get approval of their seniors to implement IT modernization. Dr Bray acknowledged the support he received from the Chairman of the FCC for his various initiatives, but also positioned himself as a 'human flak-jacket' to allow for experimentation should leadership expectations not be immediately met (Dawson and Denford 2015).

To successfully implement IT modernization, the CIOs also need align the expectations of employees. As the case of the FCC highlights, employees may be resistant to adopting and implementing new systems inherent in the IT modernization as their roles change. It is important to engage them in a conversation to understand their issues and concerns and get them excited about the transformation efforts. And, it is important to empower 'change agents' to help them identify and solve problems related to IT modernization. If employees are excited about the project, they are more likely to help CIOs and supervisors complete the project, even if it requires working overtime. The knowledge about the needs and requirements of the key stakeholders not only serves as the foundation for designing a plan towards IT modernization but also aids in navigating resistance and inertia. While developing and implementing the process of IT modernization (or any large-scale IT related project) it is common to focus on technical costs, however ignoring the human time and costs can derail a good initiative. It is that combination of effective management of technical and social change that typifies IT modernization.

Lesson 4: *Adopt an open innovation approach that encourages and empower 'change agents' within the agency to creatively address in a cloud environment the longstanding challenges associated with the agency's legacy endeavors, IT systems, and roles*. Modernizing legacy IT systems often requires a major transformation in organizational functioning and culture as part of a cloud implementation. It is important to adopt an open innovation approach that involves employees from different parts of the organization. To successfully navigate an effective IT modernization, an agency needs to develop a bottom-up approach that leverages internal human capital to drive innovation. Moreover, encouraging a participatory environment that promotes 'change agents' to take risks, propose innovative solutions, and manage the implementation process cannot be ignored. Consider the case of US Census Bureau. The US census Bureau in an effort to increase census response rate leveraged merging digital technologies such as social media. However, the bureau had no prior experience of using emerging technologies. Thus, the agency leaders appointed 14 media expert contractors to teach its employee about using social media tools to disseminate information and engage with citizens about the importance of completing census. These media experts helped the agency not only create better awareness but also reach people across multiple devices and sources (Desouza and Bhagwatwar 2012).

The process of IT transformation is beyond the CIO and top management; it requires the knowledge and efforts of the whole organization, as each component may possess critical information and resources. It is critical for public agencies embarking on IT transformation journey is to empower their human capital to experiment with new tools and processes. Further, empowered employees are more likely to showcase the value of new processes and tools to their counterpart to overcome resistance and fear of change. More importantly, the process of creating change agents delates the burden of leadership from top management to employees and spurs new thinking and innovation.

Lesson 5: Effectively engage and communicate openly with internal and external stakeholders during the IT modernization process to gain support for new infrastructure and roles. Another key aspect of IT modernization is to engage the stakeholders from the initial design through to in-service operations. Involving stakeholders in the designing phase is critical for ensuring the final product (or goal) meets the requirement of its end users. The involvement of diverse stakeholders helps solicit different viewpoints and raise awareness. Moreover, the exchange of ideas among diverse stakeholder improves the quality of conversation and more likely to spur innovation. The US federal government, for instance, create Challenge.gov to crowdsource problems and engage diverse stakeholders to solve untapped problems. Many federal agencies used Challenge.gov to host innovation challenges to engage people within and outside administrative boundaries to solve traditional government problems. The involvement of wide spectrum of people improved the diversity of ideas and helped create innovative solutions to government challenges (Mergel and Desouza 2013).

Further, when stakeholders are part of the process, they are more likely to support during the time of crisis. As the case of FCC's delayed cloud migration attempt highlights, despite best intentions it is impossible to plan for all challenges. While, the FCC encountered unexpected challenges that resulted in delayed customers reports filling, the agency was able to reach out its external stakeholders and explain the situation. The external stakeholders were aware of the IT modernization efforts at the FCC, the CIO was able to effectively manage the delays and stakeholder reactions. Despite best intentions and efforts, public agencies are likely to encounter unintended consequences during the implementation of IT modernization. The regular communication with stakeholders helps to collectively design strategies for resolving issues and challenges as they arise.

To summarize, the efforts undertaken by the FCC highlight that IT modernization involves managing and navigating technical and social dynamics. A key step in initiating an IT systems modernization process is to understand the existing IT infrastructure and human environment in the agency. It is important to have an in-depth knowledge of what exists in the organization, how different systems are connected (or disconnected), and what the key vulnerabilities and threats are. It is important to equally recognize and acknowledge the technical and human dynamics within an organization for ensuring a successful transformation.

Notably, public agencies are buried in rules and regulations that create path dependence. This path dependence has led to the creation of IT legacy systems that are complex and consists of millions of lines of code. Further, the process of IT modernization not only requires massive financial investments and technical infrastructure but also requires human capital to change the business processes of the organization and its structures. And, several institutional and political processes influence the outcome of such projects. Understanding the complexities interwoven in the IT modernization may help CIOs better navigate the process of designing, managing, and implementing large-scale IT projects and organizational change.

The case of FCC outlines that with a right leadership, vision, and approaches, any organization can efficiently and successfully navigate the process of modernization and transformation. Understanding the efforts undertaken by the Commission offers several key lessons to help C-suite leaders in the public sector who wish to develop strategies and plans to modernize their IT systems.

Acknowledgements We thank David Bray and his team at the FCC for providing us material for this case study. All errors and omissions are solely our responsibility.

References

Almonaies AA, Cordy JR, Dean TR (2010) Legacy system evolution towards service-oriented architecture. In: International workshop on SOA migration and evolution, pp 53–62

Boyd DA (2015) FCC CIO leads an IT "intervention." Federal Times. http://www.federaltimes.com/story/government/interview/one-one/2015/05/14/fcc-cio-leads-intervention/27255053/. Accessed 20 May 2016

Bray DA (2014) Modernizing the FCC enterprise. https://www.fcc.gov/news-events/blog/2014/04/28/modernizing-fcc-enterprise. Accessed 20 May 2016

Bray DA (2015a) Case in point: building an agile workforce and enterprise at the FCC. 2015 Public Sect. Future Summit. http://lnwprograms.org/case-point-building-agile-workforce-and-enterprise-fcc. Accessed 2 Feb 2017

Bray DA (2015b) FCC Dr. David A. Bray. Federal Communications Commission. https://www.fcc.gov/general/dr-david-bray. Accessed 21 May 2016

Cloud Computing Caucus Advisory Group (2016) Don't be a box hugger. Cloud Computing Caucus Advisory Group. http://www.cloudcomputingcaucus.org/boxhugger/. Accessed 31 July 2017

Dawson GS, Denford JS (2015) A playbook for CIO-enabled innovation in the federal government. IBM Cent. Bus. Gov. http://www.businessofgovernment.org/report/playbook-cio-enabled-innovation-federal-government. Accessed 2 Feb 2017

Dawson GS, Denford JS, Desouza KC (2016) Governing innovation in US state government: an ecosystem perspective. J Strateg Inf Syst 25:299–318

Desouza KC (2011) Intrapreneurship: managing ideas within your organization. University of Toronto Press, Toronto, ON

Desouza KC, Bhagwatwar A (2012) Leveraging technologies in public agencies: the case of the U.S. Census Bureau and the 2010 census. Public Adm Rev 72:605–614. https://doi.org/10.1111/j.1540-6210.2012.02592.x

FCC (2015) Agency financial report. https://apps.fcc.gov/edocs_public/attachmatch/DOC-336480A1. pd. Accessed 2 Feb 2018

FCC (n.d.) What we do. https://www.fcc.gov/about-fcc/what-we-do. Accessed 20 May 2016

Fretwell L (2015) Inside the new FCC consumer help center. GovFresh. http://www.govfresh.com/2015/01/inside-new-fcc-consumer-help-center/. Accessed 21 May 2017

GAO (2013) Information technology: agencies need to strengthen oversight of multibillion dollar investments in operations and maintenance. http://www.gao.gov/products/GAO-14-66. Accessed 21 May 2017

Golden H (2015) FCC website gets a refresh. Nextgov. http://www.nextgov.com/cio-briefing/2015/04/fcc-unveils-its-new-and-improved-website/110848/. Accessed 21 May 2016

Gwyn BD (2015) The new RFI: request for innovation. FCW. https://fcw.com/articles/2015/08/24/comment-dave-gwyn.aspx. Accessed 20 May 2017

Hamilton G (2014) Major overhaul: how the FCC CIO plans to modernize 207 legacy IT systems. The Enterprisers Project https://enterprisersproject.com/article/2014/11/major-overhaul-how-fcc-cio-plans-modernize-207-legacy-it-systems. Accessed 21 May 2017

Harvard (2015) Leadership from invention to impact: insights from the 2015 public sector for the future summit at Harvard University. http://lnwprogram.org/sites/default/files/2015_Leadership_from_Invention_to_Impact.pdf#12. Accessed 20 May 2017

High P (2015) The secrets of the most social CIO in the world. Forbes. http://www.forbes.com/sites/peterhigh/2015/09/08/the-secrets-of-the-most-social-cio-in-the-world/#1ac1c09a6540. Accessed 2 Feb 2017

Hochmuth C (2014) FCC prioritizes 7 areas for modernization efforts. FedScoop. http://fedscoop.com/fcc-prioritizes-seven-areas-modernization-efforts. Accessed 21 May 2016

Jerry M (2015) David Bray, FCC and Corina DuBois, Office of the Secretary of Defense: change agents in government. CXOTalk. https://www.cxotalk.com/david-bray-fcc-corina-dubois-office-secretary-defense-change-agents-government. Accessed 21 May 2017

Kim YG (1997) Improving legacy systems maintainability. Inf Syst Manag 14:7–11. https://doi.org/10.1080/10580539708907023

Konkel F (2016) Why knowing what you have is key to IT modernization efforts. Nextgov. http://www.nextgov.com/cio-briefing/2016/02/why-knowing-what-you-have-key-modernization-efforts/125852/. Accessed 20 May 2016

Mayer RC, Davis JH, Schoorman FD (1995) An integrative model of organizational trust. Acad Manag Rev 20:709–734

Mergel I, Desouza KC (2013) Implementing open innovation in the public sector: the case of Challenge.gov. Public Adm Rev 73:882–890. https://doi.org/10.1111/puar.12141

Miller J (2015) FCC pulls IT upgrade from jaws of defeat. FederalNewsRadio.com. http://federalnewsradio.com/management/2015/09/fcc-pulls-upgrade-jaws-defeat/. Accessed 21 May 2017

Monteith K, Sohn GB, Cornell D (2015) New consumer help center is designed to empower consumers, streamline complaint system. Federal Communications Commission. https://www.fcc.gov/news-events/blog/2015/01/05/new-consumer-help-center-designed-empower-consumers-streamline-complaint. Accessed 21 May 2017

Moore J (2015) The crisis in federal IT that's scarier than Y2K ever was. Nextgov.com. http://www.nextgov.com/cio-briefing/2015/11/crisis-federal-it-rivals-y2k/123908/?oref=ng-relatedstories. Accessed 20 May 2016

Orban S (2016) 6 Strategies for migrating applications to the cloud. Medium. https://medium.com/aws-enterprise-collection/6-strategies-for-migrating-applications-to-the-cloud-eb4e85c412b4. Accessed 2 Feb 2018

Otto G (2015) Inside the FCC's risky IT overhaul. FedScoop. http://fedscoop.com/david-bray-fcc-it-overhaul. Accessed 20 May 2016

Rudder C (2016) Behind-the-scenes: how the FCC migrated to the cloud (part 1). The Enterprisers Project. https://enterprisersproject.com/article/2016/1/behind-scenes-how-fcc-migrated-cloud. Accessed 21 May 2017

Sebastian IM, Ross JW, Beath C, Mocker M, Moloney KG, Fonstad NO (2017) How big old companies navigate digital transformation. MIS Q Exec:197–213

Wheeler T (2015) Oversight of the Federal Communications Commission. https://apps.fcc.gov/edocs_public/attachmatch/DOC-336448A1.pdf. Accessed 21 May 2016

Kevin C. Desouza is a professor in the School of Management at Queensland University of Technology. He is a Non-resident Senior Fellow in the Governance Studies Program at the Brookings Institution and is a Distinguished Research Fellow at the China Institute for Urban Governance at Shanghai Jiao Tong University. He has held tenured faculty appointments at the University of Washington, Virginia Tech, and Arizona State University. In addition, he has held visiting appointments at the London School of Economics and Political Science, Università Bocconi, University of the Witwatersrand, and the University of Ljubljana. Desouza has authored, co-authored, and/or edited nine books. He has published more than 130 articles in journals across a range of disciplines including information systems, information science, public administration, political science, technology management, and urban affairs. A number of outlets have featured his work including Sloan Management Review, Stanford Social Innovation Research, Harvard Business Review, Forbes, Businessweek, Wired, Governing, Slate.com, Wall Street Journal, USA Today, NPR, PBS, and Computerworld. For more information, please visit http://www.kevindesouza.net.

James S. Denford is an Associate Professor of MIS and the Dean of the Faculty of Arts at the Royal Military College of Canada (RMC). He holds a PhD in Management from Queen's University and both a MBA and a BEng in Engineering Management degrees from RMC. He joined the academic community after a 20-year career as a Canadian Army Signals Officer, with experience in IS training and leadership, simulation systems, network management and IS development. Dr. Denford studies knowledge strategy, dynamic capabilities, strategic alignment, and information systems leadership. He has published his research in leading information systems and knowledge management journals, conferences and books.

Rashmi Krishnamurthy is a Postdoctoral Fellow in the Stephen J. R. Smith School of Business at Queen's University. Krishnamurthy received her Ph.D. from Arizona State University. She is working in the areas of emerging technologies, information technology enabled innovation, and smart cities. She has published articles in Cities, International Journal of Information Management, and Information Polity, among others.

Printed in the United States
By Bookmasters